# HARVARD ECONOMIC STUDIES

## VOLUME XCV

Eli F. Heckscher

(1879–1952)

# AN
# ECONOMIC HISTORY
# OF SWEDEN

*Eli F. Heckscher*

TRANSLATED BY GÖRAN OHLIN

*with a Supplement by Gunnar Heckscher*
*and a Preface by Alexander Gerschenkron*

HARVARD UNIVERSITY PRESS

*Cambridge, Massachusetts*

1 9 6 3

# ACKNOWLEDGMENTS

In the course of preparing *An Economic History of Sweden* for print I have received help from many quarters. The person to whom I am most indebted can no longer receive my expression of gratitude. From the time when first I wrote him, the fall of 1951, suggesting the possibility of an English translation of *Svenskt arbete och liv*, until his death in December 1952, Eli F. Heckscher showed an interest in the project that never relaxed. He immediately accorded translation rights to the Harvard University Press, waived his claims to royalties, and caused his Swedish publishers to do the same. He offered, moreover, to rewrite the portions relating to eighteeenth-century developments in the light of his more recent research; to rewrite and to bring up-to-date the last chapter dealing with the economic evolution in Sweden after 1914; to supply the source references which the Swedish edition lacked; and, finally, to write a special author's preface for the American edition. When in the summer of 1952 I went to Sweden, I carried with me the draft in English of the first four chapters. He read the translation with utmost care, and in long sessions in Uppsala and Stockholm we went over the manuscript paragraph by paragraph, clearing up many difficult technical points, and making innumerable revisions. He was both candid in his strictures and warm in his praise. We agreed that he would similarly review the balance of the translation. Heckscher's death in December 1952 made it impossible to carry out that intention. Nor could he revise the last chapter and prepare his preface. But he had succeeded in revising the eighteenth-century material, in introducing hundreds of minor improvements throughout the book, and in writing a special Postscript to the Introduction. I shall always cherish a deeply grateful memory of his giving so unstintingly from a rapidly dwindling reserve of strength.

I am under great obligation to Eli F. Heckscher's son, Gunnar Heckscher, Professor of Political Science at Stockholm University, who, despite great pressure of other work, has prepared a survey of Swedish economic development since 1914 which appears as a Supplement to this book.

I have received much encouragement from Mrs. Ebba Westberg Heckscher, and I am particularly grateful for her help with illustrations.

Arthur Montgomery, Professor at the Stockholm *Handelshögskolan* and Heckscher's close friend, was never reluctant to give much-needed and much-appreciated advice. The Swedish publishing house, Albert Bonnier, did not hesitate to agree to a gratis transfer of the translation rights. In addition, I must especially thank the firm's Managing Director, Kaj Bonnier, for his help in working out arrangements for supplying the plates from which the illustrations in this book have been reproduced.

I must express my sincere thanks to Dr. Joseph H. Willits and the Rockefeller Foundation for supplying me with a generous grant used to cover the cost of translation and final editing as well as to pay the checking of source references and typing the completed manuscript.

Bengt Svensson, Professor Heckscher's assistant, was faced with the difficult job of supplying and checking the source references after death had left him without Heckscher's guidance and advice in the matter. He acquitted himself of the task in a competent and generous fashion, and also prepared the Chronology of Main Events in Swedish History which is appended to this book.

Göran Ohlin, of Harvard University, a former student of Professor Heckscher and a member of his Seminar, has prepared the present translation. Mr. Ohlin would translate a few pages, whereupon several times each week we would sit down together to scrutinize the manuscript word by word and sentence by sentence. During those two years of close association I have come to admire greatly his resourcefulness, ingenuity, and flexibility of mind. It is not for me to judge the quality of the result, but, I believe, Mr. Ohlin has well understood and lived up to Horace's admonition: *Nec verbum verbo curabis reddere, fidus interpres* . . . He was at all times concerned to render faithfully the spirit rather than the letter of the original.

It was kind of Professor Archibald MacLeish to translate into

English the motto chosen by Heckscher for the Swedish edition of his book.

Upon the completion of the translation, the manuscript was submitted to Mrs. Catherine Galbraith for final editing which she accomplished with great care and competence. Miss Janice Hunter and Miss Mary Raftery, the secretaries in the Department of Economics at Harvard University, typed the manuscript with their customary efficiency and understanding. Robert L. Williams of Yale University drew the maps on pages 2 and 12.

Alexander Gerschenkron

# CONTENTS

# TABLES

# MAPS

# CHARTS

# ILLUSTRATIONS

Eli F. Heckscher                                                   frontispiece

# ELI F. HECKSCHER

Four years ago, the Stockholm Institute for Economic History published a pamphlet entitled: *The Bibliography of Eli F. Heckscher, 1897–1949*.\* This list which contains no less than 1,148 items is incomplete now, because it does not include writings which appeared after 1949. I doubt that Professor Heckscher ever counted the number of words he had written — as Arnold Bennett used to do each New Year's Eve — and his staggering productivity has a meaning other than that of statistical curiosity. It reflects a life which from adolescence to old age was governed by a relentless sense of work to be done. But to work meant to serve and amassing knowledge meant communicating it to others. Heckscher's scholarship was never merely passive, absorptive. He was and remained to the end a scholar in action.

The enormous extent of Heckscher's output makes a comprehensive appraisal of his contribution extremely difficult. A large part of his writings, particularly most of the articles published in the daily press, have remained inaccessible to me. In addition, my grasp of Swedish intellectual life is loose and uncertain, even though I have received enlightenment and guidance from some of the articles on Heckscher which appeared in Sweden after his death, and particularly from the excellent paper by Arthur Montgomery, to which this Preface is much indebted. Accordingly, I can but present here some biographical data and try to stress certain aspects of Heckscher's work, in the hope that the result, though incomplete, will not too badly distort the image of a great economic historian.

## I

Like the annals of peace, a scholar's exterior biography is likely to be short. Eli F. Heckscher was born in Stockholm on November

\* *Eli F. Heckschers bibliografi, 1897–1949*, Utgiven genom Ekonomisk-historiska institutet (Stockholm, 1950).

24, 1879. His father, who had come to Sweden from Denmark, was a lawyer by training and, although a man of affairs, earned a reputation as a student of problems of commercial law. He seems to have had strong economic interests. He translated into Swedish Goschen's classic on the *Theory of Foreign Exchanges* and in his writings he liked to consider the questions of relations between juridical and economic concepts.*

In 1896 after young Heckscher finished secondary school in Stockholm, he went to the University of Uppsala. He remained for seven long years in the little town where the noble towers of the old dome cast their shadows upon streets populated by crowds of white-capped students. There the adolescent came into contact with two men, very unlike each other who lastingly and decisively determined Heckscher's intellectual path: the historian Harald Hjärne and the economist David Davidson. The former had little interest for problems of economic change; the latter was hardly concerned with history in the proper sense of the word. It was left to Heckscher to merge the dual ascendance into a synthesis — economic history — and thus solve what Carlyle regarded as "the first of all problems for a man," namely "to find what kind of work he is going to do in this universe." And implicit in the nature of the synthesis was also the happy Emersonian discovery of a "crowning bias to his main pursuit." For his was to be a novel kind of economic history. Its emphasis was to be drawn away from purely legal and institutional aspects and its subject matter was to coincide more and more with the subject matter of economic theory. Possibly because Hjärne and Davidson were so remote from each other, throwing a bridge between them turned out to be a creative venture of great moment. I do not mean to imply at all that Davidson's influence was comparable to that of Hjärne. Nor do I wish to suggest that at the end of the Uppsala period Heckscher's scholarly course was clearly charted in his mind. This almost surely would be wrong. The road from stimulation to fulfillment was long and winding, and upon it there was light from other beacons. But it was impossible for me to listen to Heckscher's descriptions of his days in Uppsala and to his recurring references to Hjärne and Davidson without forming the impression which I have here tried to render. More will be said later about these and

---

* See, for example, I. Heckscher, *Kreditsalget og Saelgerens Standsningsret, Handelsretslig Studie* (København-Stockholm, 1885), Introduction.

other influences to which Heckscher was exposed. In particular, Hjärne's role deserves much closer attention.

In 1904, Heckscher became *philosophiae licentiatus* and was appointed *amanuensis* (assistant) at the University of Stockholm. Three years later, he received his Ph.D., after having submitted to the "Humanistic Section of the *vidtberömda* [far-famed] Philosophical Faculty at Uppsala" his thesis on *The Significance of Railroads for Sweden's Economic Development*.* It is interesting that Heckscher, at that early point in his career, chose for his dissertation a theme in the field of economic history. It is also noteworthy that the thesis, along with a wealth of statistical material, contains some general methodological references concerning the distribution of emphasis as among several causal factors, a central problem of all interpretative history.

The thesis was publicly defended on May 17, 1907 and immediately thereafter Heckscher became *Privatdozent* at the University of Stockholm. Two years later, at the establishment of the Stockholm Business School Heckscher received the School's first chair of Economics and Statistics, which he occupied for twenty years, until, in 1929, he exchanged it for a Research Professorship in Economic History. This post was combined with the directorship of the Institute of Economic History which formed a link between the Business School and the Stockholm University. The Research Professorship by no means implied withdrawal from teaching. It meant rather the opportunity for confining his instruction to the area in which he was primarily interested. The teaching of economic history had been long neglected in Sweden, but in Stockholm considerable progress was then in the making. Since 1929, the requirements for the degree of a *licentiatus philosophiae* could be actually fulfilled by work in the field of economic history.† In 1936, largely owing to Heckscher's efforts, economic history for the first time became recognized at Stockholm University as a special field for the Ph.D. examination, and Heckscher continued his courses and his seminar in economic history even after his retirement from the Business School in 1944. His final farewell to teaching was not said until 1949 when Heckscher reached the age of seventy.

* *Till belysning af järnvägarnas betydelse för Sveriges ekonomiska utveckling* (Stockholm, 1907).

† Eli F. Heckscher, "The Teaching of Economic History in Universities: Sweden," *Economic History Review*, 3:213 (1931).

*ELI F. HECKSCHER*

Never having been exposed to Heckscher's teaching, I can only say that by all accounts he was a most effective lecturer and a skilful leader of seminar discussions. And in talking to his former students one cannot resist the strong feeling that along with imparting knowledge and exercising thought Heckscher also transmitted something less tangible, but no less important — Seneca's *inaestimabilis res* of intellectual integrity.

The extensive academic teaching, which for decades ranged over the whole field of economics, together with the monumental research effort did not and, in a sense, *could* not confine the sphere of Heckscher's activities. For a keen political interest competed vigorously with his scholarly work. He maintained to the end of his life an intense preoccupation with current problems and a profound concern for the destinies of his country which for him was inseparable from the fate of Western civilization. In the summer of 1952, a few months before his death, I arrived to an appointment with him carrying in my hand a copy of a big Stockholm daily. He upbraided me gently but firmly: that particular paper, he explained, supported the "isolationist" line and he begged me earnestly to change over to another paper to which he had been a contributor for many years and which was in favor of Sweden's espousing much more actively the cause of the Western security system.

It must have been Heckscher's political interest which prompted him, together with Gösta Bagge, to found the *Svensk tidskrift,* of which he remained editor from 1911 to 1918. During that period he contributed to that journal nearly one hundred articles, and he continued to publish there regularly, though much less frequently, for many years thereafter, well into the beginning of the thirties.

One might assume that Heckscher's incessant concern with current affairs had been transmitted to him by Hjärne. In any event, Hjärne's spirit was strong upon the journal; the very name of the publication was chosen to intimate a connection with the old *Svensk tidskrift* which Hjärne used to edit in the mid-seventies, jointly with Sweden's first economic historian, Hans Forssell. Designed to uphold conservative views, during most of the war years (until 1917) the new journal lent strong support to Hammarskjöld's government which, relying on the Conservatives and opposed by the Liberals and the Socialists, steered Sweden along the course of a precarious neutrality. Basically, the journal's conservatism was a combination of strong nationalism and powerful emphasis upon social justice; some affinity to Disraelian philosophy was undeniable. As early as 1890, Hjärne developed his political program which demanded both *försvar och reformer*, that is increased military strength and social reforms, including the extension of suffrage. In 1899, when once more a strike broke out in the turbulent sawmill area of Sundsvall, Hjärne strongly criticized the intransigent attitude of the mill owners. While Hjärne fluctuated in party allegiance until 1902 when he entered Parliament on the Conservative ticket, the general tenor of his political ideas remained undisturbed and he succeeded in permeating with them a group of young academicians, his former students, of whom Heckscher and Bagge seem to have been the outstanding members.

Gösta Bagge had been Heckscher's contemporary in Uppsala. He specialized in labor problems and became, in 1917, professor of Economics and Social Policy at Stockholm University. But at this point the similarity between the two men significantly ceased. Bagge went actively into politics and eventually assumed the leadership of the Conservative Party, which he maintained until 1944. Heckscher succeeded in resisting the temptation, strong as it may have been at times. He remained first and foremost a scholar. Furthermore, Heckscher's political views were developing in a direction different from that of his coeditor on the *Svensk tidskrift*. In the years after World War I a gradual change is discernible leading Heckscher away from Hjärne's conservatism and toward a liberal persuasion (both terms to be taken within their European connotation). The final result was Heckscher's transformation into a staunch supporter of laissez-faire policies. The change did not reduce the intensity of Heckscher's political interests. In this sense he remained faithful to the legacy of his teacher who died in 1922. This was quite compatible with freedom from organizational ties. In fact, Heckscher regarded such freedom as an essential prerequisite for a scholar's contribution to political life. In the very last speech which he delivered before the Swedish Economic Society (*Nationalekonomiska föreningen*) in March 1952, he referred in nostalgic terms to the years after the First World War when "scholars were essentially free of governments, parties, public and private corporations, and other special interests, which made it easy for them to speak their minds without any regard for any mandates, and when they used that freedom to the hilt." * And he noted with regret the changes that have taken place in Sweden in this respect.

Heckscher's own political participation in the political life of his country fully conformed to his idea of independent scholarship. Essentially it was of two types. He continued his journalistic activities, among which his contributions to the big liberal paper *Dagens Nyheter* occupied the first place. Year in, year out, he wrote one, sometimes two articles a month for that paper. In addition, he advised a number of governmental committees, including the Tariff and Treaty Committee and the Experts' Committee on Unemployment. It must suffice here to mention those activities and to stress the strength of his aversion to government intervention in economic affairs. His defense of free trade was quite uncompromising and his suspicion of the effects of the government's unemployment policies went very far. In 1932, at the climax of the Great Depression, he continued to warn that the theory of counter-cyclical policies may be consistent in itself, but that in practice such policies would be adjusted not to the actual course of the cycle, but to the "notoriously wrong" ideas about that course, so that in reality the increased government spending would perpetuate itself.† It is, of course, irrelevant here whether these views were "right" or "wrong." What matters, rather, because it is characteristic of Heckscher's basic attitude, is that, even in these years when unemployment seemed the only economic problem worth thinking about, the danger of power expansion on the part of the government was at least equally important in Heckscher's mind.

It is true that Heckscher was quite aware of the existence of areas where the invisible hand becomes shaky and the price system an inadequate guide of the economy. In a speech before the Association of Swedish Industrialists which he made in 1918 he mentioned several such areas including consumers' ignorance, inadequate time

---

* Eli F. Heckscher, "Den economiska debatten i Sverige under 75 år," *Nationalekonomiska föreningens förhandlingar 1952*, pp. 17–18. See also the obituary by Erik Lundberg, where he recalls how Heckscher tried to dissuade young scholars from losing the independence of their views by entering into various organizational connections. *Dagens Nyheter*, December 23, 1952.

† See Erik Lundberg, *Konjunkturer och ekonomisk politik* (Stockholm, 1953), p. 265.

horizons, monopoly, and the general disadvantage in the market of earners of low incomes.* It is further true that Heckscher had carried over from the earlier period in his evolution a good deal of sympathy for social reform and greater equality of incomes. In his book on Industrialism he gave a warm account of the course of social legislation in England;† to him the positive emphasis on social policies constituted the main distinction between the old and the new economic liberalism, a subject on which he published a booklet in 1921.‡ But, as Professor Montgomery has pointed out, the extent of what seemed to him feasible and rationally defensible in this field was limited.§ Too much of such policies seemed to him to run counter to his basic creed of individualism. For this reason, it was to the cooperatives, particularly the consumers' coöperatives, based on the "healthy element of self-aid," that he felt attracted; he regarded them as an emanation of the true liberal spirit, inherited from the nineteenth-century economic liberalism.‖

It is difficult, if not impossible, for an outsider to assay the extent of Heckscher's influence upon Swedish economic policies. It seems to have varied a good deal over the course of the years, but in certain periods, and particularly in the twenties, must have been strong indeed. A dramatic episode occurred when in an article published in *Stockholms Dagblad* ¶ in March 1920 Heckscher criticized the Central Bank for allowing a differential to persist between the official and the market price of gold in conditions of free convertibility, and for maintaining far too low a rate of discount. The effect of the article was to make the public aware of the existing profit opportunity and, by the same token, to force the *Riksbank* to take immediate corrective

* *Staten och det enskilda initiativet efter kriget,* Sveriges Industriförbund (April 23, 1918), pp. 9–12, 14, 17–18.

† *Industrialismen,* 4th ed. (Stockholm, 1948), pp. 161 ff.

‡ *Gammal och ny ekonomisk liberalism* (Stockholm, 1921).

§ Arthur Montgomery, "Eli Heckscher som vetenskapsman," *Ekonomisk tidskrift,* 1953, p. 158.

‖ See Eli F. Heckscher "Den ekonomiska kooperationens ideal," *Svensk tidskrift,* 8:512 (1918); also: *Industrialismen,* p. 168.

¶ This independent, but basically conservative paper, Stockholm's oldest morning paper, discontinued its publication later in 1920. In the summer of 1921 Heckscher published his first article in the liberal *Dagens Nyheter,* a paper that during the war had bitterly opposed the Conservative governments of Hammarskjöld and of his successor Swartz. The change seems to date Heckscher's shift in political allegiance.

steps including a raise in the rate.* Clearly no bold stroke of this nature could have been dealt by anyone but a person of complete independence, and Heckscher may have had this episode in mind when
he stressed the importance of free criticism of public policies by independent scholars.

At the same time, Heckscher's sustained preoccupation with
monetary policies may complete the picture of his views in the field
of economic policies. There is no doubt that in monetary matters
Heckscher's orthodoxy was far-reaching. He viewed with sadness
and disgust the collapse of the nineteenth-century monetary system.
He regarded the policies pursued during the war as a "rich record of
human folly," and he considered return to "sound money" an absolute
prerequisite of economic stability. He felt that Sweden should return
as speedily as possible to the old gold parity, because "its abandonment would make monetary stabilization impossible for years." In
these matters his views were far more extreme than those of his
teacher Davidson who contemplated Sweden's rush back to the
normalcy of the prewar parity with a good deal of scepticism.†

I have dwelt at some length on Heckscher's views and activities
with regard to current economic problems, not only because much of
Heckscher's personality was invested in them, but also because they
are by no means irrelevant for an appraisal of his role as an economic
historian. I said before that Heckscher's political interests competed
with his purely scholarly activities. This is only partly correct. The
two spheres were by no means unrelated to each other, and it is as
revealing to see in what way Heckscher's general philosophy influenced his research as to point to areas where, perhaps surprisingly,
Heckscher's general creed remained altogether inoperational.

## II

The men who over the last century or so have made important
contributions to economic history fall into two unequal groups. On

* Eli F. Heckscher, "Monetary History 1914–1925 in Its Relation to Foreign
Trade and Shipping," *Sweden, Norway, Denmark, and Iceland in the World War,
Economic and Social History of the World War* (New Haven and London,
1930), p. 244.

† See "Monetary History," pp. 247, 265; and Eli F. Heckscher, "David Davidson August 21, 1854–March 18, 1942," paper given before the Swedish Royal
Academy of Sciences, March 31, 1951, published in translation in *International
Economic Papers*, No. 2 (International Economic Association, London, 1952),
p. 134.

one side stands the vast majority of historically or juridically trained scholars who allowed themselves to be deflected into preoccupation with past economic events. They brought to the nascent discipline the canons of critical historical research and the subtlety of a lawyer's mind as applied to legal documents. On the other side stand those for whom exploring the course of economic development essentially meant thinking about it in terms of economic concepts and economic models. This is still an exceedingly small group and some claims to membership in it are rather ill-founded. One must exclude from it those for whom empirical material served merely to verify certain lines of theoretical reasoning. Furthermore, there are those whose claims are based on intentions rather than results. Here Werner Sombart is probably a case in point. He liked to repeat again and again that all economic history must be based on economic theory. And yet beyond developing some Marxian intuitions and asking a few relevant questions, not much theory and still less any competent handling of theoretical problems is discernible in the imposing structure of Sombart's work. In fact, to this day serious and sustained application of economic theory has remained a hope, and, as was true before, the bulk of young economic historians nearly everywhere comes from the study of history rather than of economics. The exceptions are important, but their number is pitifully small, and among the great economic historians Heckscher's figure occupies a solitary and uncontested place.

It is clear that Heckscher himself regarded his use of theoretical tools as the very essence of his own contribution. In a *Student's Guide to the Study of Economics,* published in 1945, he described himself — or suffered his collaborator to describe him — as having primarily striven to inject economic theory into economic history.*
In a sense, the claim is *more* than justified. For what makes Heckscher so altogether unusual as an economic historian is the fact that he succeeded in making some significant theoretical contributions of his own. By his article on "The Effects of Foreign Trade on the Distribution of Income," in which he dealt with the problem of relative scarcities of the factors of production in international trade, he had most fruitfully stimulated Professor Bertil Ohlin's fundamental work. In Heckscher's modest words:

* Eli F. Heckscher and Carl Erik Knoellinger, *De ekonomiska studierna och deras hjälpmedel, En handledning* (Stockholm, 1945), p. 71.

# ELI F. HECKSCHER

My then pupil, Bertil Ohlin, followed up my attempt and reshaped it, especially through an application of the general price theory of Walras in the form which it had received at the hands of Gustav Cassel. My . . . treatment . . . does not contain much of any value over and above Ohlin's books, while the latter have removed numerous blemishes in the earlier treatment and, still more important, have brought the theory in connection with actual conditions and problems of the interwar period.*

"This does not prevent," Heckscher went on to say, "my attempt from being one of the first in the field." Undoubtedly his was a significant initiative toward a generalization of the theory of international trade.

In some respects, his second major theoretical article, on the problem of overhead cost, is even more revealing.† This article, the original version of which was written without knowledge of J. M. Clark's study, addressed itself to a complex of problems of central theoretical relevance. By fastening his attention to a situation where in his parlance "unfree [meaning scarce] factors create [temporarily or intermittently] 'free' capital," by seeing this as a loss to society, and by posing the problem as to how at least a utilization of such capital to capacity can be achieved, he boldly entered the sphere in which the price system as a regulator of economic activities becomes problematic. In fact, he felt that the whole area was so much *sui generis* as to stand outside the normal purview of economic theory, perhaps a not unnatural attitude to take in the early twenties. In dealing with these problems, and in considering the danger of monopoly and below capacity output, he stumbled upon the solution of public ownership: socialized enterprises could cover their fixed cost by taxation and maintain output at capacity. It is true that in a concrete case Heckscher is likely to have hesitated before recommending socialization for fear of reduced efficiency. Enough has been said

---

* Prefatory remark to the English translation. The article appeared first in *Ekonomisk tidskrift*, 1919, pp. 1–32, in an issue dedicated to Davidson: "Utrikeshandelns verkan på inkomstfördelningen, Några teoriska grundlinjer." It was republished thirty years later as "The Effects . . . ," *Readings in the Theory of International Trade* (American Economic Association, Philadelphia, 1949), pp. 272–300.

† The article was published in revised form in German: "Intermittent freie Güter," *Archiv für Sozialwissenschaft und Sozialpolitik*, 59:1–31 (1928); its original version appeared as "Intermittent fria nyttigheter," *Ekonomisk tidskrift*, 1924, pp. 41–54.

above to show that Heckscher regarded public ownership with great diffidence. But considerations of this sort would never give him pause in the midst of a theoretical argument or even influence his choice of subjects. In this sense, his political views and his general philosophy never were allowed to influence his work. For him more important than drawing political inferences was emphasizing the value of free and undogmatic theoretical reasoning. "Here lies a justification for socialization which is not seen at all by the socialists whose theorists continue to adhere to a distorted version of classical economics that becomes more and more obsolete from day to day." *

In concluding this listing of Heckscher's theoretical contributions, reference might also be made to his critical analysis of Gustav Cassel's theory of purchasing power parity, contained in his previously quoted work on *Sweden's Monetary History, 1914–1925*.† It is true that Heckscher tends to go much too far there in his assertion that purchasing power parity has meaning only if costs of carriage do not exist at all, so that *all* goods enter into international trade and are either exported or imported. Apart from such exaggerations, which seemed to flow with some ease from his pen when Cassel was concerned, his discussion is probably the best statement of limitations upon the theory of purchasing power parity, enriched and enlivened by practical applications to the case of Sweden. The relevant pages would still make most useful collateral reading in any course on international economic relations. It may be added that Heckscher's doubts about the concept of purchasing power parity did not prevent him from using it at least loosely in concrete cases. Thus, for instance, he attributed the fall in the Russian exchange rate in the first decade of the nineteenth century to the course of the Russian inflation rather than to the development of her balance of payments.‡

One must agree with Professor Ohlin when he points out that it was not given to Heckscher to erect a comprehensive theoretical system§ or rather perhaps to relate his thoughts to an existing body of doctrine. It is true that there is something inchoate, perhaps even impressionistic, about his theoretical contributions. But it is equally

* "Intermittent freie Güter," p. 24.

† Pp. 151 ff.

‡ Eli F. Heckscher, *The Continental System, An Economic Interpretation* (Oxford, 1922), p. 317.

§ Bertil Ohlin in *Stockholms Tidningen,* December 23, 1952.

true that his was an imaginative theoretical mind, fertile with new ideas and quite unreluctant to pursue them toward new and startling conclusions. As Professor Montgomery justly points out, it is surprising how persistently Heckscher's theoretical thought revolved around matters which in due time came to constitute important portions of modern economic theory.*

A few words on the source of Heckscher's theoretical interests may be in order. Davidson's role has been mentioned before and there is no doubt that it was he who first introduced Heckscher to economic theory, put him through the mill of theoretical training, and taught the ways of rigorous casuistic thinking. In the long run, the influence of Alfred Marshall, to whom Davidson seems to have borne some spiritual resemblance, became decisive and Heckscher himself in the Introduction to his *Mercantilism* acknowledged his debt to the *Principles* which, as he said, had "profoundly influenced my approach to economic history." † Finally, there was the personal contact with Wicksell, and traces of Wicksell's thought appear in many of Heckscher's writings as they do in the previously quoted article on the "Free Goods" and also in the present volume.

Without wishing to detract from the importance of the influences just mentioned, one may surmise that even in this respect Hjärne's influence was present, though not, of course, in any substantive sense. Hjärne was exclusively concerned with political history and seems to have been blissfully free from knowledge of, and even interest in, economic problems. His theoretical luggage in the subject seems to have been light indeed and apparently consisted of the curious combination of Bastiat and Marx whom he had read during his student days.‡ There seems to be another though indirect connection: Hjärne used to place strong emphasis on the need of theory in dealing with political history. A historian, he said, must start from a general conception of a political body and of its objectives and he must make his concepts so general as to have room within them for all the multifarious nature of political events.§ Translated from the context

* Montgomery, "Eli Heckscher," p. 160.
† *Mercantilism*, I (London, 1935), 13.
‡ Eli F. Heckscher, "Harald Hjärne," *Ekonomisk-historiska studier* (Stockholm, 1936), p. 174.
§ Harald Hjärne, "Om politiska omdömen i historien," *Samlade skrifter*, Vol. IV: *Samfundsliv och tankevärld* (Stockholm, 1940), p. 114.

of political history into that of economic history, this meant substitution of Hjärne's insistence on political theory by Heckscher's insistence on economic theory. There is, apparently, no direct evidence to support this supposition, but indirectly the connection is well stated by Heckscher in the following passage: "The relation of theory to the study of history is not peculiar to the field of economics. On the contrary, it is necessary to historical study to base all along the line upon what has been found with regard to the general character of those phenomena which are studied." * In a sense, this paraphrases Hjärne's remarks quoted above.

On the other hand, all this should not imply that Hjärne actively encouraged Heckscher's interest in economic history, let alone in economic theory. If anything, the opposite seems to have been true. The best Hjärne could do in this respect, was to supply a grudging appreciation of economic history as he did in his letter to Heckscher, written in the penultimate year of his life (1921).† In retrospect, the manifold difficulties which confronted Heckscher tend to appear small in the light of his eventual success. In reality, however, they were very considerable. To obtain recognition of economic history as an independent discipline, Heckscher had to overcome a good deal of resistance. One of the reasons was, he felt, the country's active political past. The Age of Empire left an almost indestructible academic legacy. Political history had traditionally played a dominant role, and Hjärne's work was, of course, entirely encompassed within that tradition. In fact, Heckscher's repeated warnings against the disadvantage of concentrating the historians' interest in the area of political, and particularly diplomatic, history seem to contain an implicit criticism of Hjärne.‡ What has been — and will be — said of Hjärne's influence on Heckscher's work must not conceal the creative independence of Heckscher's mind or his role of a bold innovator in radically transforming the character and the status of his discipline.

* Eli F. Heckscher, "A Plea or Theory in Economic History," *Economic History* (Suppl. to the *Economic Journal*, 1926–29), 1:525–534; reprinted in *Enterprise and Secular Change,* eds. Frederic C. Lane and Jelle C. Riemersma (Homewood, Illinois, 1953), pp. 421–430.
† "Harald Hjärne," p. 174.
‡ See Eli F. Heckscher, *Historieuppfattning, materialistisk och annan* (Stockholm, 1944), p. 25; and "Den ekonomiska historiens aspekter," *Ekonomisk-historiska studier,* pp. 16–17.

## III

Heckscher's main work in the field of economic history belongs to two spheres: first, the series of studies on the attempts of the State to regulate economic life; second, his monumental study of Swedish economic history to which he devoted the last two decades of his life. In the former group the big two-volume work on *Mercantilism* stands out as the best-known piece of Heckscher's writings. But preceding it there are at least three other books which may be regarded as being loosely but importantly related to the great work. Into this category fall the previously quoted studies on the *Continental System*, and the *Swedish Monetary Policies, 1914–1925,* as well as *The World War Economy.** Viewing these studies together may help to a better understanding of Heckscher's processes of subject selection and, by the same token, of Heckscher's personality. As Goethe once remarked, the choice of subjects always tends to reveal the real quality of a man's mind.†

It is true that Heckscher's interest in the study of mercantilist policies goes back to a fairly early point in his career. In 1908, he published a study on the Swedish equivalent of the English Navigation Acts, his first effort at delving into a somewhat more remote period of economic history. It seems, however, that the great experience of the First World War and the sudden resurgence during the conflict of measures of government policies which seemed to have belonged to a long bygone age, decisively determined the continuation of Heckscher's interest in the subject of mercantilism. In this significant fashion Heckscher's basic political interest and his constant preoccupation with the problems of the day asserted themselves in his historical work. This has basic methodological connotations and Heckscher was fully aware of them. At one point, late in life, he wrote: "Since for all earlier periods of human history we know not only what took place but also what came after it, we have possibilities of choosing our facts, not only in relation to the actual situation in the period in question, but also with regard to the significance of these facts, their relation to later developments, which

---

* *Världskrigets ekonomi. En studie af nutidens näringslif under krigets inverkan* (Stockholm, 1915).

† Goethe, *Gespraeche mit Eckermann,* January 25, 1830.

is, of course, impossible when we are concerned with our own day." *
One might recall that Huizinga, the great Dutch historian, used to say that the peculiarity of the historical method consisted in viewing the events from the vantage point of the moment when they occurred.† That, to his mind, distinguished history from sociology. I doubt that Heckscher ever agreed with this view, even though he may have found it useful at times to think in those terms as a safeguard against deterministic temptations. Because interest in current affairs was to him a major source of inspiration in scholarly research, he understood well that the historian's vantage point in reality was his own time. Both the nature of questions that were raised and the direction into which the answers pointed were intimately related to that vantage point.

*The World War Economy,* published in the second year of the war, was not a study of economic history in the accepted sense of the word. It was a review of current economic developments, in which economic war measures were placed under the light of a rather merciless theoretical analysis. To some extent, incidentally, the purpose of the book was to refute the then frequent view that economic theory had nothing to contribute to the understanding of the interventionist war economies. At the same time it is astonishing how much historical thought entered into, or rather emanated from, the book. It shows in particular that preoccupation with the war forced Heckscher's mind back to the period of the Napoleonic Wars, giving rise to a number of stimulating comparisons.‡ He witnessed with surprise the emergence of views among German economists which were an uncritical repetition of the least justifiable ideas of the mercantilist period.§ And it is even more interesting that he found it useful to discuss the world war economy in terms of a shift back toward "Provision Policy" which he considered peculiar to the period of the Middle Ages. The dichotomy between "hunger for goods" and "fear of goods" which, fifteen years later, was to play a central part in his *Mercantilism* and thus to serve as a basic tool of a *historical*

---

* Eli F. Heckscher, "Quantitative Measurement in Economic History," *Quarterly Journal of Economics,* 53:168 (1939).

† See J. Huizinga, *De Wetenschap der Geschiedenis* (Haarlem, 1937), pp. 63–64.

‡ See, for example, pp. 5, 32.

§ P. 153.

interpretation is already fully contained in this survey of acutely "modern" happenings.* It is, therefore, not at all surprising that *The Continental System, An Economic Interpretation* was the first large work published by Heckscher after the end of the war. The subtitle chosen by Heckscher throws an interesting light on his historical method and may be used as a point of departure for a brief discussion.

By describing his book as an economic interpretation, Heckscher did not mean to refer to the materialistic conception of history and to suggest that the diplomacies of the Continental Blockade should be explained by relating them to the basic role of economic factors. Heckscher was too careful and too modest a scholar to accept the idea of an all-determining economic causation. If one probed deep enough into any sequence of phenomena, economic causes must be discovered somewhere along the road. But to conclude therefrom that these causes were the only decisive ones would be highly arbitrary. Moreover, he never exaggerated the historian's ability to follow through long chains of historical causation and he emphasized that in doing so the chances of error must grow *pari passu* with the plausibility of alternative explanations.†

Just as he rejected interpretations of all historical change in terms of migrations and no doubt would have rejected any "martial" interpretation of history, he could not accept the one-sidedness of a single factor or set of factors. In addition, his strong sense of historical relativity suggested to him that the "predominant factor" itself was subject to a continual change. It is in this sense that one must take Heckscher's remark that only in the nineteenth century did economic factors acquire an ascendance which they had not possessed in previous centuries.‡ Above all, the disciple of Hjärne and the student of mercantilism knew full well that power as an independent factor deserved an attention which it never could receive at the hands of the adepts of the materialistic conception of history. About that more will be said later.

Thus, to embark upon an "economic interpretation" of the Continental System meant something entirely different to Heckscher.

---

* P. 235.
† *Historieuppfattning, materialisk och annan*, pp. 16–18.
‡ P. 28.

The fact is that the question of economic determination of, say, political history simply was not within the immediate purview of his interests, and he commented once upon the insignificance of the Marxian contribution to economic history: the excessive eagerness to explain the "superstructure" of social life had paradoxically led to a neglect of its "base." *

If economic history was to be considered an independent discipline it had to address itself to the relevant *economic* questions. That meant essentially the question as to how, in different historical periods, scarce economic means were used to satisfy given ends: "The object of economic history," he wrote, "is to show how scarce or insufficient means have been used for human ends throughout the ages; how the character of this problem has changed or 'developed'; what these situations and changes in them have been due to; how they reacted upon other sides of human life and human society. As far as I can see, this covers the whole field, and nothing but the field, of economic history." † This statement, which he would repeat time and again, sometimes verbatim, is a concise expression of his scientific creed as an economic historian.

Such a conception of the field of economic history naturally was most suitable for the application to it of theoretical reasoning and, in fact, made such an application indispensable. Once the scarcity relations were placed at the center of the historian's attention, it became, for instance, impossible, in treating earlier economic periods, to remain content with references to vague concepts such as tradition or inertia. If wages did not rise in the wake of a mass destruction of the labor supply, the theory forced the historian to investigate the exact mode of allocation of the labor force under such circumstances.‡

At the same time, to circumscribe economic history in this manner did not mean at all to confine explorations in economic history to those areas which lent themselves to theoretical treatment. In other words, the delimitation of the *field* did not, in Heckscher's view, entail

---

* Eli F. Heckscher, "Quantitative Measurement in Economic History," *Quarterly Journal of Economics,* 53:169 (1939).
† "A Plea for Theory in Economic History," p. 423.
‡ Eli F. Heckscher, *Ekonomi och historia* (Stockholm, 1922), p. 19; and "Den ekonomiska historiens aspekter," pp. 22–23.

the adoption of one *method* to the exclusion of others. Methodological limitations of this sort were quite alien to him, and he not only upbraided those who were "nothing but theorists," but once even defined economic history as a study of the "interplay of economic and other influences on the actual course of events." * The "events" had to be "economic" in the sense just described; otherwise they could not constitute a legitimate object of economic history. But, obviously, the study of "other influences" could not be conducted with the methods of *economic* theory. The basic methodological "impurity" of economic history was thus fully recognized.

It is true that at times Heckscher may have seemed to push his enthusiasm for the use of economic theory too far and to become guilty of confusing the appropriate area of study with that of the appropriate method. Certainly, his brusque retort to Vinogradov that legal history had "no business" to be included in the treatment of economic developments might appear surprising.† But the confusion is apparent rather than real. What it denotes is not so much an unwillingness to include legal measures among the "other influences," but a basic diffidence on Heckscher's part against bland acceptance of statute for an economic fact. In this respect, the German historical school came in for severe criticism:

> Hundreds of volumes, especially those written by the pupils of Gustav Schmoller and other members of the German historical school have been filled with the contents of laws, ordinances, and government regulations, without inquiring in the least whether these represented more than pious wishes or beliefs of their originators.‡

In one of his curious excesses of argumentative zeal, Heckscher even went on to say that the existence of legal stipulations only proved that the reality differed from what they were intended to bring about; otherwise it would not have been necessary to issue them in the first place. Such exaggerations must be taken with a grain of salt. The fact is, of course, that time and again Heckscher himself was compelled to rely on legal materials, as he does for in-

---

* "David Davidson," p. 126.
† "A Plea for Theory in Economic History," p. 426.
‡ "Quantitative Measurement in Economic History," p. 170.

stance in this book with regard to Swedish Provincial and National Codes.

Nevertheless, the negative attitude toward the use of legal documents as source material in economic history is basic to Heckscher's views and must be emphasized because of both its probable origin and its consequence. As to the former, one could not go far wrong in assuming that Heckscher's fundamental creed of economic liberalism had a good deal to do with his attitude. The laissez-faire creed, in rejecting government intervention, claimed that such intervention must needs be either superfluous, or detrimental, or ineffective. The bulk of emphasis traditionally rested on the last member of the triad, the Marxian veneration of the inexorable economic law, like so much else in Marxism, springing from the same source. Just as it was natural for the anti-liberal members of the German historical school to identify legal prescription with economic fact, it was natural for a liberal historian to be highly suspicious of the effectiveness of government regulations.

On the other hand, once serious doubts had been cast upon what used to be regarded as a primary source of economic information on remote periods, the search for other methods of research became imperative. The result was Heckscher's great stress on the usefulness of statistics, of quantitative measurement, in the field of economic history. This connection is perhaps best stated in Heckscher's last methodological pronouncement — the Postscript which he added to his Introduction to the present book.

It might be said that with respect to both the possibility of theoretical application and employment of quantitative methods in economic history, Heckscher's optimism apparently kept increasing throughout his life. As late as 1922, he still felt that the earlier periods of history were less amenable to theoretical treatment.* And Arthur Montgomery points out that similarly Heckscher at the beginning of his career viewed the use of statistics in history with some scepticism.† In both respects the later change in emphasis was very considerable and it might be said that Heckscher through continuous application of both theory and statistics succeeded in dispersing his own initial doubts in the matter.

* *Ekonomi och historia*, p. 24.
† Montgomery, "Eli Heckscher," p. 175.

With regard to statistics, Heckscher came to understand that what mattered least was whether or not trustworthy statistics were available for earlier periods. The answer to that, of course, had to be negative. But from the point of view of creative scholarship the real question was: "Does your problem admit of collection of materials from which statistics may be *computed?*" * As one who had to spend some time in dealing with Soviet statistics, I find Heckscher's formula surprisingly applicable to the latter area. Here, too, what was given was, in a sense, less important than what could be done. And I found it even more surprising that Heckscher without ever having devoted much attention to the problem of Soviet statistics was very much aware of the basic similarity that existed between the quantitative exploration of earlier historical periods and that of modern dictatorships.†

Heckscher's study *The Continental System* was written at a time when the methodological views just described were still in the process of formation and formulation. Nevertheless it reveals these influences with considerable clarity. His sophisticated attitude to legal acts prompted Heckscher to devote much attention to the evasions of the Napoleonic decrees and their implementation. The theorist was able and willing to deal with the effects of the Blockade upon price developments in terms of demand elasticities and substitution possibilities. He treated effectively the relationship between prices, exchange rates, and balances of payments. Above all, he was very much alive to the basic inconsistency of a policy which aimed at French industrial supremacy in Europe and wished to base that supremacy upon an industry raised in a protectionist hothouse. In general, the masterly pages dealing with the manifold inconsistencies of the Blockade policies could not have been written without much theoretical insight.

At the same time, the book is wonderfully impartial. Chaptal's "miracles" are indeed placed in the proper perspective, but there is no attempt to play down such attainments as were made. Writing at the end of the First World War, Heckscher felt and resented bitterly the deterioration in the standards of scholarship that resulted

---

* "Quantitative Measurement in Economic History," p. 180.
† See "Samhällshistoria och statistik," *Historieppfattning, materialisk och annan,* pp. 68–69.

from the War when "scientific work was transformed into a species of propaganda with a great show of learning." * When it is finally mentioned that Hjärne's student showed a great deal of zest and perception in dealing with the diplomatic aspects of the period in their effects upon economic problems, it is not surprising that a generation has passed since the publication of the book without impairing in the least its position as the standard work on the subject.

As previously said, *The Continental System* naturally adumbrated the comprehensive study of *Mercantilism*. An economic war on a grand scale and the use of economic means for political purposes inevitably constituted a resurgence of mercantilist purposes. In addition, the policy problems which arose in the Napoleonic days bore in so many respects detailed resemblance to the problems of the earlier period, as for instance in the perennial conflict between fiscalism and protectionism. It was owing to the burden of academic work and the manifold involvements in current discussions and committee work during the twenties, that such a long time was allowed to elapse between the completion of the two studies. But for the acceptance of the Research Professorship in 1929, the interval may have been even longer.

The two-volume work appeared first in Swedish in 1931; the next year brought Gerhard Mackenroth's translation into German; and, in 1935, the English translation by Mendel Schapiro was published. At least from a non-Swedish point of view, *Mercantilism* must be considered Heckscher's most important work, although in sheer pagination it is belittled by the four volumes of *Swedish Economic History since Gustavus Vasa*. It is, of course, impossible within the scope of this Preface to give an extensive account of the monumental work. I must confine myself to a few significant aspects, designed to cast light more on Heckscher himself than on his work.

Hjärne's influence upon Heckscher has been frequently mentioned here. It is, however, fair to say that it reached its acme in the study on *Mercantilism*. Harald Hjärne's approach to history was profoundly influenced by his basic belief in the unity of the European civilization. The Greek legacy absorbed in Christianity, the Church, and the Empire of the Middle Ages had created a homogeneous Europe as a cultural entity which the modern system of sovereign

* *The Continental System*, p. 3.

states had transformed, but not eradicated, the system rather than its members being considered by Hjärne as the fundamental political reality.* Despite all anarchy, Europe through long centuries had grown to be a "real historical community." † As a result, Hjärne felt, historical problems of individual countries could not be meaningfully treated except against the background of the European community as a whole. Thus, even when Hjärne went about preparing a course outline on an "Introduction to Scandinavian History," that outline was surely dominated by the urge to see Scandinavian history as a unity, but only "within the European cultural world." As Heckscher once pointed out, any distinction between "Swedish" and "general" history was an "abomination" in Hjärne's eyes.‡

It was probably quite natural for a man who was so deeply interested in the history of international political relations to develop that particular emphasis. The concept of the *communauté du droit des gens,* of the family of nations, based upon Western culture, has been traditionally regarded as the central concept of international law.

It was this message that Hjärne's students received. Heckscher heard it first, when as a high school boy of 15 he attended Hjärne's Summer School lectures in Uppsala, and he retained it to the end of his days. It is nowhere more clearly reflected than in his *Mercantilism.* The book was designed to be a "contribution to the history of economic policy as a *common European problem.*" § As a result, Heckscher deals with the problem of mercantilism "by selecting typical aspects in the economic policy of typical countries." || This is a crucial statement for the methodology of the book. It is based on the view that "when all is said, economic development followed similar lines all over the world." ¶

It is clear that once Heckscher decided to operate with the "instrumental tool" of a general concept of mercantilism, it was bound to contain some generally applicable elements. To say this is not to

---

* Harald Hjärne, "Nya problem för världshistorisk framställning," *Samlade skrifter,* IV (Stockholm, 1940), 271–272.

† Harald Hjärne, "Karl XII från europeisk synpunkt," *Samlade skrifter,* II (Stockholm, 1932), 279.

‡ "Harald Hjärne," p. 171.

§ *Mercantilism,* I, 13 (Italics mine.)

|| P. 23.

¶ Eli F. Heckscher, "Mercantilism," *Economic History Review,* 7:44 (1936).

preclude great divergences of emphasis. More or less stress could have been laid on the differential development in the individual countries concerned. One of the most characteristic features of Heckscher's book is the relatively narrow scope assigned in it to such differences. To be sure, a good deal is said on policy differences between France and England with regard to the practice of industrial regulations, and from time to time brief references are made to still other deviations in countries like Germany and Austria. What matters is that there is no attempt to bring these differences themselves into a systematic form, thus providing an explanation for them. The main weight is thrown behind an effort to establish mercantilism as a common emanation of the European community.

Some of the strictures to which Heckscher's work on mercantilism has been exposed have their root precisely in this main emphasis. Marc Bloch deplored Heckscher's failure to pay sufficient heed to the role of class interests as determinants of economic policies.* This criticism, I believe, must be interpreted as a reference to the fact that in different countries, depending largely on the degree of their economic backwardness, the ability of vested interests to assert themselves and to determine policies varied widely. In general, as one moved from West to East across the Continent, the importance of vested interests tended to decline and the State pursued its policies unbothered by the necessity to give in and to compromise. Russia which remained almost entirely outside the scope of Heckscher's treatment is perhaps the clearest example of an area where for a considerable time government policies proceeded in a vacuum of vested interests.

Incidentally, Heckscher did *not* inherit Hjärne's interest in Russian history. But Hjärne was driven into concern with Russia by his studies of the period of Charles XII. In addition, Hjärne did not consider Russia a member of the European community and he viewed the problem of Russo-Swedish relations of the period as a decision on Russia's admission to that community. Here may lie the source of Heckscher's reluctance to turn to Russia while he was investigating a common *European* problem.

Heckscher's preference to see mercantilism as a problem of Euro-

* Marc Bloch, "Le mercantilisme: un état d'esprit," *Annales de l'histoire économique et sociale,* 6:162 (1934).

pean unity *tout court* rather than as one of unity in diversity probably has much to do with what he had to say on the basic ends of
mercantilist policy. The basic inclination on his part was, I believe,
to view mercantilist policies as essentially serving the power of the
State. From this point of view the complex of internal unification
policies, to which the whole first volume of the work is devoted, was
just an attempt to strengthen the internal and, indirectly, the external
power of the State.* And yet in his treatment unification *and* power
are placed side by side as two independent elements of mercantilist
policies. The answer is that Heckscher could not fail to be impressed
by the fact that wealth as an independent end seemed to compete
with power effectively. Time and again, he felt, he had to weaken
his emphasis on power in favor of opulence. Some critics were quick
to regard this as a fundamental difficulty. Jacob Viner, in some measure, but particularly T. H. Marshall claimed that since both mercantilism and *laissez faire* were interested in power and wealth,
Heckscher had failed to establish a sufficiently distinctive concept of
mercantilism.† In replying to this criticism, Heckscher was surprisingly restrained and largely confined himself to the remark that even
though both mercantilism and *laissez faire* aimed at power and
opulence, the scale of priorities as between the two systems was completely reversed.‡ Heckscher may have been more forceful in stressing what after all, despite all qualifications, pervades his book,
namely that "power for the sake of power" was still crucially significant for the understanding of pre-laissez-faire policies, as it is for
the understanding of modern dictatorships. Power meant something
quite different to Gladstone, even to Disraeli, than to Colbert or
Hitler and Stalin. Furthermore, Heckscher may have emphasized
something else which too is richly contained in his book, although in
a less explicit fashion, that is, the specific interrelation of ends and
means with regard to power. The problem was not just that mercantilism and *laissez faire* used different means to attain certain ends.
It was Hjärne again who knew well that power can be coterminous
with its exercise; in other words, that power is acquired and main-

---

* *Mercantilism,* I, 25; II, 15.
  † Jacob Viner, "Heckscher's Mercantilism," *Economic History Review,* 6:100
(1935); T. H. Marshall, "Review," *Economic Journal,* 45:717–719 (1935).
  ‡ Eli F. Heckscher, "Mercantilism," *Economic History Review,* 7:48 (1936).

tained through commanding and regulating.* Thus, mercantilist regulations were not just a means for increasing the power of the State. In a very real sense, to regulate meant *eo ipso* to be powerful. To desist from giving orders meant relinquishing power. Again, a reference to the Soviet dictatorship which tends to order and to regulate much more than is economically necessary or even undetrimental, seems quite pertinent.

The main difficulty, however, remains that previously mentioned. By pursuing perhaps too relentlessly, the common nature of the phenomenon Heckscher found it difficult to observe that mercantilist policies in different countries were actuated by a different mixture, as it were, of different basic ends. By concentrating much attention on the most advanced countries, France and England, with their well-developed and articulate vested interests, Heckscher was forced to concede more than was necessary. On the other hand, an attempt to discover some regularities and uniformities in the spatial and temporal variations in mercantilist policies might have served to throw Heckscher's concept of mercantilism into bolder relief.

In stressing power and unification as basic elements in mercantilist policies, Heckscher no doubt was greatly influenced by William Cunningham and Gustav Schmoller. It is curious that, while acknowledging his indebtedness to Cunningham and Marshall, he failed to mention Schmoller in a similar fashion although there are of course plentiful references to Schmoller's work throughout the book. Schmoller, more than anyone before Heckscher, had stressed the unification aspect of mercantilist policies. Presumably, his general adverse judgment of the German historical school, very likely reinforced by a wartime interview (1915) with Schmoller and his distrust of Schmoller's Prussian bias, had something to do with it. In general, Heckscher felt a strong intellectual obligation to England: "British culture," he wrote, "has given me more than any other outside of my own country." † It may be added that at the turn of the century, Hjärne was one of the very few in Sweden who took a pro-English attitude in the Boer War.

On the other hand, both Cunningham and Schmoller showed little

---

* Harald Hjärne, "Nya problem för världshistorisk framställning," *Samlade skrifter*, IV, 275.

† Letter to the writer, August 12, 1952.

interest for the protectionist and monetary aspects of mercantilism, while Heckscher devoted to them large portions of the second volume of his study. It seems fair to say that it was Adam Smith who was Heckscher's main antecedent in this respect.

Like Adam Smith's, Heckscher's over-all appraisal of the mercantilist system was unfavorable. He could not but stress how small on the whole was the harvest of the unification policies, and how painlessly and efficiently the job was accomplished in the age of *laissez faire*. He stressed, too, that there was nothing distinctive, that is, original, in the spirit of the mercantilist legislation with regard to industrial regulations and that it had in this as in some other respects simply adopted the principles of the medieval system.* On the other hand, it cannot be denied that Heckscher, unlike Adam Smith, by stressing the importance of power and unification, tended to impart a good deal of meaning and rationality to the economic policies of mercantilism: "If we keep in mind that power was considered an end in itself, and that economic life was mobilized for political purposes, much becomes clear in mercantilist outlook." † And in dealing with mercantilist monetary policies he came to the conclusion that, surrounded as it was by a veil of erroneous notions, "the mercantilist idea of the stimulating effect on economic life of an increased quantity of money, was, for the most part, correct, and incidentally an important deduction." ‡

It is interesting to note that only a few years earlier Heckscher had expressed considerable doubts on the possibility of stimulating effects having been produced by the price revolution and, like Schumpeter in the *Business Cycles,* he referred to the effects of the runaway inflations after the First World War to corroborate his point.§ I cannot judge whether the appearance of Keynes' *A Treatise*

---

* *Mercantilism,* I, 233.
† *Ibid.,* II, 23.
‡ *Ibid.,* II, 236.
§ "Den ekonomiska historiens aspekter," p. 59. This essay was first published in 1930. The Swedish edition of *Mercantilism* not being accessible to me, I do not know whether the sentence quoted in the text above is contained in that edition, though it appears in the German edition. Curiously, Schumpeter, too, changed his mind on the subject and his remarks on the price revolution in his *History of Economic Analysis* (New York, 1954), p. 144, differ radically from those made in the *Business Cycles.*

*on Money* in 1930 did in any way influence Heckscher's views in this respect. On the other hand, it is my impression that Keynes' use, in the *Notes on Mercantilism*, of Heckscher's findings seemed to go much too far for Heckscher's taste. In particular, Heckscher had explicitly denied what Keynes just as explicitly stressed, namely that a justification of mercantilist monetary policies could be derived from the special circumstances of the period.* Nevertheless, in his article on the *General Theory* Heckscher rightly took its author to task for his "unhistorical doctrinarism" while, I fear mistakenly, upbraiding Keynes for the use of non-operational psychological concepts; but he did not seize upon this opportunity for protesting against the use Keynes had made of his analysis of the monetary theories of mercantilism.†

Whatever the reasons for this restraint, when all is said and done, mercantilist policies do emerge from Heckscher's analysis as a complex containing many a rationally defensible action, and adumbrating in several important ways the policies of the subsequent period. The two chapters in the concluding part of the work on the "Concord" and the "Contrast" between mercantilism and *laissez faire* stand out as a fine example of Heckscher's sense of both continuity and change in economic history. It is useful to remember at this point what has been said before on Heckscher's own most orthodox views in the matter of monetary policies. The system of mercantilist policies, however interpreted and reinterpreted, doubtless was profoundly repulsive to Heckscher's general philosophy. Under these conditions, the balanced impartiality of his treatment and conclusions is both an admonition and a source of inspiration.

Finally, a few words on the present book. It was published in Sweden in 1941 under the title *Svenskt arbete och liv* (*Swedish Work and Life*). Covering as it did a long period of Swedish economic history from the Middle Ages to the end of the interwar period, the book was both a summary of the preceding and a plan for further research. For after he had completed the work on *Mercantilism*, Heckscher embarked upon a new and no less ambitious

* *Mercantilism*, II, 202; J. M. Keynes, *The General Theory of Employment, Interest and Money* (London, 1936), p. 335.

† Eli F. Heckscher, "Något om Keynes' General Theory ur ekonomisk-historisk synpunkt," *Ekonomisk tidskrift*, 1946, pp. 161–162, 180.

venture: a comprehensive economic history of Sweden from the early sixteenth century on. By 1937, two large volumes had appeared, carrying the story until 1720. Two further volumes, dealing with the eighteenth century and continuing to the end of the Napoleonic Wars, were not published until 1950. The work on the nineteenth century was never finished. Thus, the present book is not simply a condensation of material published elsewhere. It is, in important respects, an independent and unique presentation of Heckscher's views on the economic history of his country.

Perhaps the most outstanding characteristic of Heckscher's work on Swedish economic history is that in this field as nowhere else was he able to satisfy his urge to use quantitative measurements for elucidation of long-term economic change. The availability of excellent statistics in Sweden over a comparatively long period has rendered it possible to deal effectively with questions such as the relation between population changes and harvest fluctuations, revealing the impressive intimacy of the connection between the two factors in eighteenth-century Sweden; and leading *inter alia* to the surprising discovery that even then birth rates were more sensitive to harvest fluctuations than marriage rates. The reader's attention is especially called to the pertinent diagrams and to the creative idea of using the data on taxable population for the purpose of a prosperity index.

The student of economic history has good reasons to be interested in the course of Swedish economic development. True, in many respects Sweden differed little from the Continent. The mode of land utilization and the organization of agricultural production carried over from the Middle Ages bore few, if any, specific traits. At the same time many striking differences emerge from Heckscher's presentation. There is, first of all, the absence in Sweden of serfdom and feudal disintegration. Heckscher provides a number of interesting and convincing reasons in explaining the phenomenon. Sweden shows clearly that a given mode of production did not of necessity lead to a specific political organization. Quite the contrary, it tends to reveal the independent importance of the political factor in influencing economic conditions.

Secondly, there is that most curious episode of the eighteenth century when the alienation of crown lands took place. This development closely paralleled similar processes in Russian economic history. In both countries the necessities of power policies decisively determined the change. But what followed in Sweden was not the belated enserfment of the Swedish peasantry but the surprising turnabout of the reversions. These portions of Swedish economic history are likely to give much food for thought to those concerned with the relations between economic development on the one hand and the behavior of political bodies on the other. There is no question that the alienation *cum* reversion episode in Swedish economic history casts, by contrast, a most interesting light on processes of economic development in a number of major European countries.

Finally, as Heckscher points out, "it is a fundamental fact that Sweden is economically a young country," which at present, through a faster rate of growth, has caught up with the more advanced countries. In this respect the Swedish case is particularly instructive to those concerned with the patterns of economic development which result from varying degrees of economic backwardness. In viewing the relative painlessness of Sweden's way of overcoming her economic disabilities, and particularly in comparing it with the Russian counterpart, one cannot fail to attribute a great deal of importance to the strong cultural tradition in Sweden; to the fact, that is, that for centuries Sweden has been a member of the European community of nations in a sense in which Russia never was. In an inobtrusive way this point — Hjärne's point — emerges with great clarity from a perusal of the book.

Heckscher did not wish to have the last chapter of *Svenskt arbete och liv*, which dealt with the interwar period, translated for the present edition without considerable revisions, but this intention could not be carried out. Except for occasional excursions, therefore, Heckscher's text in the present book does not go beyond 1914, but Professor Gunnar Heckscher has written for this edition a survey of Swedish economic development from 1914 to date. This survey, "The Disintegration of Nineteenth-Century Society" is here published as a Supplement to Heckscher's text.

*Note:* Readers who are less familiar with the political history of Sweden may find it useful to refer to the Chronology of Main Events in Swedish History and the list of Swedish Kings and Regents, appended to this book. Furthermore, the reader's particular attention is called to the map of Sweden which appears on page 2 and contains the place names mentioned in the text.

## IV

Heckscher carried on with his work almost to the last day of his life. On December 14, 1952, just eight days before his death, he said in his last letter to me:

I very much regret to say that I have now become doubtful about my ability to send you the last chapter of the book before the end of the year. I have had a relapse and have been unable to do more work for the last fortnight. But I hope to improve shortly. Please, do not give any time to the last chapter as it stands, because it will have to be rewritten in its entirety. I am very sorry indeed to disturb your time-table and must beg you to excuse me.

In those days, when his body was ready to give up the hopeless struggle, Heckscher still prepared for *Dagens Nyheter* an article on Macaulay which appeared in that paper several days after his death. There he expressed the hope that a future age might find more merits with the Victorians than has our own. In a sense, Heckscher himself was a great figure of the nineteenth century. His immense erudition, his classical background, his modesty, his fierce independence, his willingness at all times, in the words of his beloved Horace, to step on the treacherous ashes covering the smoldering fire of conflict and controversy, and, above all, his severity to himself, his supreme sense of duty — these qualities of a very great scholar are less readily produced by our age of anxiety and instability. To the very end he remained faithful to his mission and continued to labor in the knowledge that the night cometh when no man can work.

Alexander Gerschenkron

*Harvard University*

# AN ECONOMIC HISTORY
# OF SWEDEN

Bön med lyfta händer är ej nog
lantman, då du ber för jordens gröda.
Bed med handen på din plog,
då välsignar bönens kraft din möda.

Viktor Rydberg, *Hesiodos' råd.*

Farmer, do not fold your hands to pray
Asking for the gift of fruitful harvest.
Pray with hands upon the plow:
Toil itself will speed and bless your praying.

Translated by Archibald MacLeish

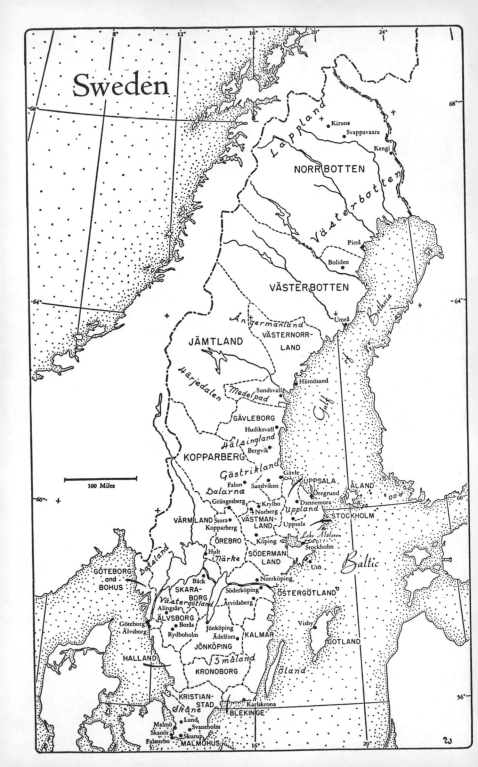

# ECONOMIC HISTORY *

IN PRINCIPLE, the relation between economic history and general history is a simple one. Economic history is concerned with one single aspect of historical development, and in this respect its position is similar to that of literary history, art history, military history, intellectual history, and so forth. But the subject matter of economic history is satisfaction of human wants. Hence it deals not with a specific set of social phenomena, but with one aspect of all human life. While everything has an economic aspect, nothing, not even phenomena generally classified as "economic," such as commerce or money, can be entirely explained in economic terms. If that is kept in mind, the borders between economic history and general history are clear. The problem thus is not one of delimitation. It arises from the fact that economic thought requires a fairly high degree of theoretical abstraction; this very sharply distinguishes it from the study of history which must strive for synthesis rather than for isolation of specific aspects of the historical process. More than other branches of history, economic history expects its adept to be both theorist and empiricist. This is a challenge for which the human mind appears none too well equipped. Perhaps that explains why the study of economic history, despite extended growth, has so far yielded a good deal less than the two sister disciplines on which it borders. Few students of economic history have combined keen powers of abstraction and mastery of empirical data, the two qualities which their subject matter would ideally require.

A far more difficult problem is the relationship of economic history to economic theory. This needs a somewhat more explicit treatment.

* These introductory remarks are devoted to some general problems of the study of economic history. They are not indispensable for an understanding of the rest of the book.

In the past, economic theory was clearly static. It attempted to explain positions of equilibrium and the mechanisms causing a return to such positions in case of disturbances. The time factor was not normally included within this framework. Even less attention was paid to consequences of changes in the basic conditions of economic activity. It might seem as if this theoretical approach had little to contribute to economic history which essentially focuses on the study of change. But this is not so. In the study of economic history great attention must be given to different stages of development, the tendency being to view these as closed entities. As a matter of fact, research in economic history has been most concerned with various stages and relatively little with modes of transition from one stage to another. This is not desirable, but it is probably inevitable, since transitions are much more difficult to explore. Moreover, the study of continuous change encounters serious difficulties of presentation.

In dealing with a given stage of economic development, static economic theory is a most useful tool, however great its limitations. A truly general economic theory would encompass that which all stages hold in common. If one could separate from the traditional body of economic theory those elements which pertain to specific periods and which played such a large part in its formation, the remainder would clearly be applicable to all economic epochs. Such a liberation of theory from its dependence on historical circumstance is actually not very difficult. But what remains is too little to make this procedure worth our while. We must, rather, bring out as best we can the historical conditions upon which the various assumptions of static economic theory are based, and then change those assumptions according to the nature of the society under study. If this is done with some skill, economic theory of the static variety remains an indispensable aid in the study of economic history — not as a substitute for the quest for facts but as a tool for the interpretation of the significance and interdependence of those facts.*

* Inspired by Wilhelm Roscher's voluminous but otherwise perhaps not particularly inspiring *System der Nationalökonomie,* I have tried to outline such a theoretical treatment of economic history in my paper, "Den ekonomiska historiens aspekter," which is included in *Ekonomisk-historiska studier* (Stockholm, 1936). [*Translator's note:* A condensed version of this paper has appeared in English under the title, "The Aspects of Economic History," in *Economic Essays in Honour of Gustav Cassel* (London, 1933).]

In the last few decades, however, economic theorists have attempted to transcend the confines of static theory. A new approach has been introduced which, somewhat questionably, has been claimed to be "dynamic." At first glance this development would seem very promising to economic historians; for economic development, the object of their study, is obviously a dynamic process. But actually the dynamics of the economic theorist is not the dynamics of the economic historian.

This type of theory, just as its predecessor, usually starts by assuming an unchanging framework for economic activities. The departure from static theory consists in the inclusion of the time factor while institutional conditions are still conceived as given. Such a theory has no room for the study of transitions from one set of underlying institutional conditions to another, nor for the study of the interaction between changes in those conditions and changes in the economic variables. Its only noteworthy results so far have been attained in the field of business cycles. Until very recent times these have been viewed as perpetually recurring processes, without asking whether or not the processes themselves are subject to irreversible change or irreversibly affect other phenomena.

At the same time the so-called dynamic theory has tended to become rather more abstract than the static theory; presumably because of the difficulty of mastering all the new variables required by the dynamic approach. For this reason it is far more casuistic and based on more limiting assumptions than the static theory. The latter essentially offers an answer to well-defined logical problems as, for example, that of allocation of resources. Such an answer has general validity in spite of the theory's disregard of a great many realistic factors.

If we add that the practitioners of the "dynamic" theory have often shown an almost complete lack of interest in their institutional assumptions, it will be clear that the range of their theory is fairly limited. However, a critique of that theory in relation to the purpose for which it was designed is not intended here. We are only concerned with its usefulness for economic history, to which it apparently does not have much to contribute beyond what is already contained in static theory.

The discipline of economic history is dynamic in a different sense.

Its "dynamics" is concerned with changes in the basic conditions of economic activities. In this sense the term is one of long standing in the tradition of economic thought. For instance, it is used in this way in John Stuart Mill's *Principles of Political Economy.*

Unlike economic theory, economic history therefore deals with unique historical sequences. This does not preclude more or less far-reaching similarities between individual historical sequences. For the essence of economic phenomena is simple. It lies in the scarcity of resources in relation to human wants, and this very simplicity leads naturally to the emergence and reëmergence of similar patterns.

Such similarities have been frequently studied. Strictly speaking, studies of this kind belong perhaps less to economic history and more to what should be called historical sociology or sociological history, a discipline of which Max Weber was undoubtedly the greatest protagonist. In those studies there have been attempts to trace the same pattern or sequence of patterns of economic phenomena within different and mutually independent societies. Where such similarities have been demonstrated with regard to a specific feature (the prevalence of barter or money economy, for example) one must beware of the common but fallacious notion that similarities in one area are necessarily paralleled by similarities in all other areas, thereby making these economies essentially identical. This has never been the case; in that sense history, as far as we know, never repeats itself.

Economic history usually asks three questions with regard to any given situation: how it develops, how long it lasts, and where it is likely to lead. This raises the problem of prediction, about which a few words may be said. Obviously, our ambitions here must be modest. Prognostications, to be scientific, require a degree of invariance that is essentially missing in economic behavior, as in human action in general. Among the sciences which engage in prognostication, on the whole only one, astronomy, has reached any considerable degree of perfection, and its subject matter is of course as far removed from human affairs as it could conceivably be. In economics, more rigorous forecasting is done by what the statisticians call extrapolation. That is to say, a development of which the past course is known to us is assumed to continue in a certain fashion during the near future. Among the natural sciences, meteorology is the one that invites immediate comparison — which, by the way, is none too flattering for economic history. Modern meteorology may foretell tomorrow's weather with some accuracy, but is hardly able to make long-run predictions, at least in its present state. Still, a careful study of the way in which a given stage of economic development has arisen and the direction in which it tends to move enables us to acquire some grasp of its further evolution. At any rate, it will lead to a deeper understanding of the shape of things to come than can be reached merely by studying a given and unchanged set of economic conditions, as the economic theorist does. In other words, the economic historian must direct his attention to the temporal determinants of economic activity.

Quite apart from what this approach might tell us about the future as seen from the vantage point of the present, it also has definite implications for the study of the past. It implies that the conditions of the past are to be considered *sub specie futuri,* or with a view to their development up to the present, so that the present is understood in terms of the forces by which it was shaped. Even when dealing with individual stages of the past rather than with sequences or processes, economic history must study those stages with a view to their subsequent transformation. This is a somewhat different matter from the conception of such stages as closed and isolated entities.

In economic theory it is of decisive importance to know on what points to focus our attention and how to distinguish between the relevant and irrelevant aspects of a certain stage. The treatment of economic theory frequently suffers from an inadequate sense for this distinction. Theory often becomes *l'art pour l'art,* an opportunity to poke with sharp analytical tools into matters which have significance only because they lend themselves well to this operation. It has rightly been said that such an intellectual game may be justified in pure mathematics for example, where it can be played with superb elegance, but that it is out of place in a discipline which is of necessity as crude and imprecise as economics. For such tendencies historical research is an indispensable remedy.

Historical research is even more indispensable for economic theorists when they base their argument on assumptions as to actual courses of events. Among modern theorists this was particularly true of Lord Keynes. His ingenious and in part pioneering work, both in monetary theory and in his theory of employment and interest, was often founded on a great number of assumptions about actual developments. But he neglected any attempt to verify those assumptions, although some of them probably have only a very slender basis in historical facts.*

In an earlier paper ("Den ekonomiska historiens aspekter") I have attempted to show how individual areas of economic theory can be adjusted to specific conditions prevailing in different historical periods, and I shall here briefly recapitulate some of those possibilities.

For instance, in price theory we may distinguish between the cases of directly controlled demand (rationing), free competition, and what is nowadays called imperfect or monopolistic competition. In wage theory we differentiate between cases where labor is free and mobile, free and immobile (serfdom), or, finally, unfree and immobile (slavery). In monetary theory, we distinguish between a single metallic standard, a bimetallic standard, and paper currency, all of which may be further subdivided.

Transformations in those and similar basic conditions of economic activity may have different causes. They may be caused by changes in the natural environment, which can be of general significance or remain more or less confined to a particular country, such as alluvial and climatic change, fish migrations, volcanic eruptions, etc. Generally, though, human or social changes are far more important: economic organization is a social phenomenon, and its natural environment is only a conditioning factor. Social change may be of a more external, political nature, as in the case of war, territorial change, change in government institutions, and so forth. Or it may be essentially internal or psychological. As a matter of fact, most social changes have their origin in changes in psychological attitudes which in turn may be traced back to a great many other phenomena such as religion, philosophy, literature, art. Obviously then, thousands of ties link economic history to all the other social sciences, and particularly to all the other historical disciplines. Insularity would be

---

* *Translator's note:* For a presentation of the author's critique of Keynes's work from the point of view of economic history, see his article "Något om Keynes' 'General theory' ur ekonomisk-historisk synpunkt," *Ekonomisk Tidskrift,* 1946, p. 161.

as obnoxious or even impossible in economic history as in the history of literature, art, or war. Conversely, general historical research must pay close attention to economic factors, lest it remain hopelessly truncated.

The following work is a study not of general economic history but of Swedish economic history. Yet it must be strongly stressed from the outset that the history of any individual country of the West is inseparably connected with the historical development of the West as a whole. And what is true of any Western country applies with particular force to a *small* Western country and to the *economic* history of such a country.

## A POSTSCRIPT

A few remarks may be in order concerning the application in this study of the general methodological principles just discussed. A relatively short volume like this gives few opportunities for explicit methodological statements at every stage of the process. I believe that my methodological principles are more clearly in evidence in the more detailed account on which this book is based — the four volumes of my *Economic History of Sweden Since Gustavus Vasa.**

The first of these principles has been to make use, wherever possible, of economic theory. More modestly put, this meant not to be satisfied with mere description of facts but to ask at all times how these facts were interrelated. Only from the logical patterns called economic theory can such questions be formulated and directed to the available material.

The second principle refers to the attitude toward historical sources. Many of our sources, after all, reflect what erring human beings thought and felt about contemporaneous events which they may have misunderstood or misrepresented. The critical judgment of the historian must separate the wheat from the chaff; Lord Keynes's treatment of mercantilism to which I have just alluded offers a recent and outstanding example of how dangerous it is not to exercise this critical judgment. Similarly, the most common and insidious error is to confound economic legislation and regulation with economic reality. The gap between policy and reality has

* *Translator's note:* Eli F. Heckscher, *Sveriges ekonomiska historia från Gustav Vasa* (Stockholm, 1935–1949).

usually been enormous. An efficient, honest, and incorruptible administration is a rare and recent historical phenomenon; even in large countries ruled by strong governments, economic statutes and laws have ever so often remained pious wishes exerting little or no effect on the course of economic development.

The only way to avoid such pitfalls is to trace sources which throw light on actual conditions. These sources must not be too different in character from those on which the study of present economic conditions is based. General judgments by contemporaries can hardly suffice, for few men were ever in a position to observe more than a minute fraction of even a small community, let alone a large territory or a country. The proper method, therefore, to be applied wherever possible, must be mass observation, that is, the use of statistical estimates.

Many students of economic history seem to believe that the statistical method is inapplicable to periods in which no statistics were compiled. I think this is a serious mistake. In very many cases it is possible for the historian to construct statistical estimates from nonnumerical sources. Such estimates might even be more reliable than those handed down to us in finished form, but their preparation obviously requires a great deal of time and care.

The type of source material most urgently desired, in my opinion, is that which yields secular statistical time series. Social change cannot be studied except on the basis of such data; and if reasonably representative, they may be highly illuminating though still incomplete. Time series of this sort may be misleading because of changes in methods of collection or presentation. One must keep constant vigil against such errors, but if the defects are not too serious they must not deter us from using that kind of material. We cannot afford to renounce the only source that reveals something about the proper subject of our study, which is social change.

The student of Swedish economic history is, I believe, especially fortunate in the quest for the requisite sources. The principal reason for this is the continuity of Swedish administration. A number of the central administrative agencies have been in existence for centuries, receiving and collecting similar data throughout their history. As a result, Sweden is an ideal object of study for the economic or social historian. This gives Swedish social and economic history a significance that would not otherwise be attached to the case of a comparatively small European country which has not usually been in the forefront of social change. I have attempted to avail myself of this opportunity.

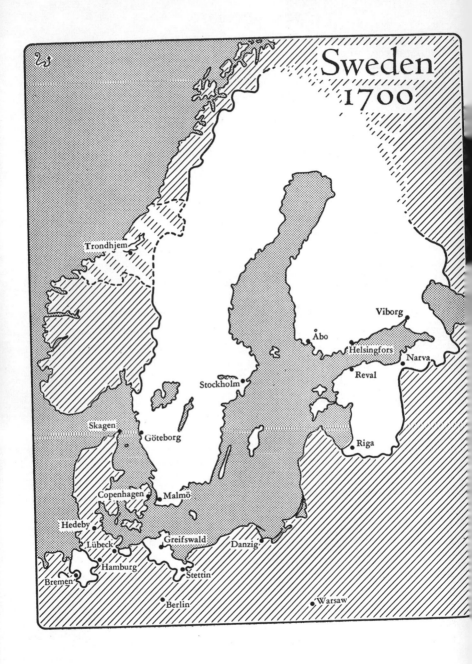

Sweden
1700

Trondhjem

Viborg

Åbo

Helsingfors

Narva

Reval

Stockholm

Riga

Skagen

Göteborg

Copenhagen    Malmö

Hedeby

Lübeck

Greifswald    Danzig

Hamburg

Bremen

Stettin

Berlin

Warsaw

# CHAPTER I

# STAGES OF SWEDISH ECONOMIC HISTORY

THE FIRST PROBLEM faced in a historical presentation usually concerns the choice of appropriate periods. But it must be clear from the beginning that such a division into stages is a concession to human weakness: usually it is too difficult to conceive of a historical process as the indivisible entity it really is. Yet for this very reason it is impossible to call any one division correct or incorrect, and it must be possible to resort to different divisions for different purposes. The problem is a heuristic, not a theoretical one.

Social change generally tends to be slow and gradual. Thus, in the selection of stages or periods in economic history, it often does not matter if the lines of demarcation are drawn twenty or even fifty years sooner or later, although frequently a specific and isolated event might be especially appropriate to mark an "epoch." Political history, on the other hand, particularly as conventionally presented, is primarily devoted to a chronicle of events and is therefore more easily divisible into periods.

In principle, the economic history of Sweden would probably best be separated into two periods only: *l'ancien régime* and *le nouveau régime*. If the line is to be drawn between the predominantly new and the predominantly old society, it will be a very late one, considerably later than the corresponding line for Mediterranean and West-European countries, though not much later than in Central-European countries. The line could not be drawn before the early nineteenth century and should perhaps be pushed up to around 1870. But this would obliterate the distinctions between very important earlier stages of development and give an inadequate picture of the manner in which the present is rooted in the past. Hence it seems preferable to make a much more thoroughgoing division based upon the gradual introduction of essentially new elements rather than upon the continued predominance of old ones. One must nevertheless keep in mind that the boundary lines are not all equally distinct, and it is also possible to consider all these early periods as sub-divisions of the *ancien régime*.

It is important, however, never to forget the artificial nature of almost all divisions of this kind. The past will always survive as a component of the new, and the seeds of the new are always sprouting in the past, long before they come to exercise any determining influence. The survival of old patterns is particularly noticeable in Swedish agriculture; but even in an area characterized by such early and profound change as the iron industry, we do not have to go very far back to find remnants from the past. The medieval technique for processing iron, the so-called *osmund* forging (*osmunds-smide*), disappeared as a predominant method of ironmaking as early as the seventeenth century, but occasional residues of it were to be found in the province of Dalarna in the late 1870's.

I shall now briefly define the periods into which I have divided Swedish economic history. Prehistoric time has been left outside the scope of this study. It seems to me more appropriate to refer this era to a discipline of its own, which might be called economic archeology as distinct from economic history. Such a discipline is undoubtedly of great importance, and has not been wanting in con-tributors. To arrive at the very beginning of things we would have to go back still farther, for if the theory of evolution has any validity, pre-human organisms and even inorganic matter must have had an economic aspect. What is called the ecological problem, that is, the problem of the relations between plants and animals and their location and environment, is closely related to the problem of satisfaction of their needs. However, since we do not retreat to such early starting points — which would require an equipment entirely different from that normally applied in economic or his-torical research — I have found it most reasonable to draw the line at the time when mankind began to leave its first written testimonies. But this is an arbitrary choice.

For our first period we might choose the early Middle Ages, the time from which the oldest written Swedish legal sources stem, the so-called Provincial Codes (*landskapslagarna*). Here we find an economically undifferentiated society without any actual division of labor. That society did present very sharp social differentiation, between freemen and serfs, although serfdom was by then already on the wane. But presumably this differentiation did not correspond to an economic differentiation of remotely the same importance. In other words, there was no real division of labor between the free and the unfree. Yet, it would be wrong to say that there was no division of labor at all. Functions were divided within individual households, particularly between men and women. It might be preferable to describe this stage as a society without exchange. Not even that, however, should be taken in a literal sense, since commerce had attained the status of a separate occupation at a much earlier time.

In its most important sector, agriculture, the conditions characterizing medieval society survived for many centuries. As late as the beginning of the nineteenth century, the overwhelming majority of the Swedish people lived under conditions which in many respects closely resembled those prevailing as early as the thirteenth century, probably even earlier. Consequently we can, in the case of agriculture, combine the epoch marked by the Provincial Codes with what in other respects is a subsequent period, and treat the Middle Ages as one unit.

As a second period, I take the time dominated by the emergence of a division of labor, the rise of the crafts and the towns. These closely interrelated institutions attain full development in the two last centuries of the Middle Ages, even though their history extends much farther back.

The third period must almost inevitably open with the accession of Gustavus Vasa (1520). This may seem strange, since that event marks no radical change in the social structure of Sweden. As we shall show, Gustavus Vasa, on the contrary, strove successfully to preserve and reinforce the medieval economic system. But he endowed this economy with a strength and a sharpness of contour it had not previously possessed, and his administrative activities provide us with a wealth of material for its study incomparably richer than any source material which has survived from the Middle Ages proper. I have chosen, therefore, what seems to me the obvious title for this period, the Maturity of the Medieval Economy. The appropriate range of this period would be 1520–1600, even though new and important changes appeared soon after Gustavus' death in 1560.

The next period is also fairly self-evident: In Swedish political history the years 1600–1720 are customarily called the Age of Empire (*stormaktstiden*). It was a time of manifold innovation under strong foreign influence, and might well be designated Foreign Influences and Economic Change.

Whereas the dividing line between the last two periods is fairly diffuse, the one between *stormaktstiden* and its successor is much more distinct. The entire political background underwent a sudden transformation.* The name of the period beginning in 1720 must be fairly arbitrary. I have chosen to call this stage The Foundation of Modern Sweden because of the rather conspicuous modernization which characterized it. As its end I have selected the year 1815, although in certain areas, particularly perhaps in that of economic thought, the year 1809 would offer a better closing point.

The time between 1815 and 1870 may be named the eve of the Great Transformation. In those years the ground was prepared for the disappearance of the *ancien régime,* most patently in the legal field, but also in technology and organization. In Sweden, this period comes to a fairly obvious end around 1870. The years 1870–1914, preceding the outbreak of the First World War, may be described as those of a mature nineteenth-century economy. For expediency's sake the last two phases will be combined, since the process of change in very many areas was continuous from the beginning of the nineteenth century, and a separation of the two periods might blur the picture.

It will be seen that this choice of stages largely coincides with that of political history. Our subject matter is, of course, intimately related to changing political institutions; but it could be that the necessity of relying on public archives as the main source has made me ascribe an undue significance to the nature of those institutions. Although far from excluding the possibility of other arrangements, this classification seems suitable for the purpose of the present investigation.

* One qualification must perhaps be made: the later part of *stormaktstiden,* beginning with the reversion of Crown property under Charles XI, was, in important respects, a period of transition.

# CHAPTER 2

# THE MIDDLE AGES

## GENERAL CHARACTERISTICS

THE SOURCES OF Swedish economic history in the Middle Ages are as inferior to their counterparts in many other countries as those of later periods are superior. So it appears today at least although research on the sources of the period is as yet too incomplete to warrant a definitive judgment. The main deficiency in the material is the lack of quantitative data. Without such data, it is in my opinion practically impossible to make any significant statements about social conditions. Various accounts and rolls still in existence do permit quantitative inferences, but those are isolated cases and rarely illuminate the general development clearly enough to offer any more profound insights into its nature and interdependence.

There is indeed no shortage of foreign sources: in particular, the accounts of the Lübeck customs supply material of the greatest importance for the history of Swedish foreign trade in certain periods. But foreigners tended to make acquaintance only with the surface layer of Swedish society, so that on the whole foreign records do not contribute much to our knowledge of the general features of the economy.

As far as our present knowledge goes, there are in the main two genuinely medieval sources which throw light on the salient characteristics of medieval Sweden:

(i) Early legal texts, primarily the Provincial Codes from the thirteenth and fourteenth centuries and the national codes. (There were two national codes for the country, one superseding the other. In addition there was a national code for the towns, which was much less important because of their relative insignificance. The town code as well as the earlier code for the countryside were compiled at about the middle of the fourteenth century; the later code for the countryside is approximately one century younger.)

(ii) Public records and diplomatic documents which, for the major part of this period, have been published in the collection *Svenskt Diplomatarium*. We may hope that more intense study of this voluminous collection will add considerably to our knowledge of the Swedish economy in the Middle Ages.[1]

Swedish sources, as well as foreign ones, flow much more richly for the relatively less important cities than for the rural areas, at least in the late Middle Ages. Most useful in this regard are the city chronicles called *tänkeböcker* ("memorandum books").[2] These are the records of city courts and magistrates, and their accounts of the variety of cases submitted to them give a very illuminating and variegated picture of urban life in that period. The most important of those books are those of the city of Stockholm, which run from 1474. Rolls and accounts of various kinds are also in existence, again particularly for Stockholm. All the medieval material from Stockholm has now been published, and *tänkeböcker* from several other cities have been or are being published.

Owing to this situation, the following presentation is largely based not on strictly medieval sources but on sixteenth-century material which is very rich indeed. Of course, this material can be applied only to those areas of the medieval economy which were not subjected to considerable changes by the public policy of the subsequent period. It is also possible that further scrutiny of Swedish medieval sources, the study of which is still in its infancy, will lead to more or less drastic revisions of the picture to be outlined here. But this can be the case only for the early Middle Ages; for the last few centuries of the Middle Ages the general features of the economy cannot be expected to differ greatly from those of the early sixteenth century in any pertinent respect.

At the outset, at least three characteristics of the Swedish economy in the Middle Ages must be noted. The first is the insignificance of foreign trade, that is, the autarky of the country; the second, the somewhat weaker self-sufficiency of households; and the third, the overshadowing importance of agriculture. But it should be emphasized that these are initial generalizations. There was in fact no such total absence of exchange as they would suggest, but for the time being we may disregard domestic as well as foreign commerce, and return to the subject later on.

Basically, this Swedish society was not particularly different from other contemporaneous societies, although on many points there were considerable differences in degree. If Sweden is compared to Central Europe, the difference reflects above all a time lag. It is a fundamental fact that Sweden is economically a young country. When we consider that her economic maturity is now equal to that of almost any advanced country, this means that her development, particularly in the last century, has been more rapid than in most other European countries.

The more self-sufficient an individual or a country, the more decisively all economic activity will be determined by consumption. Naturally, the necessity to provide for all consumption through domestic activity will force an autarkic economic unit into activities for which its natural conditions may be very poorly suited; nothing but exchange with other countries or individuals can alleviate that. Where there is no exchange, every productive individual will be a jack-of-all-trades, although there will be some division of labor within households, the men tilling the land and doing heavier work, the women tending to the cattle, cooking, and weaving. In later years, economic legislation and economic policy were to turn against this inevitable consequence of a self-sufficient economy, but for centuries they remained ineffectual for the very reason that the entire social structure would have had to be altered before another solution could be found.

The fact that non-agricultural activities were carried on within individual households did not detract in the least from the overwhelming predominance of agriculture in the medieval economy. Long historical periods had to elapse and great increases in the levels of consumption had to take place before Adam Smith could observe:

The desire of food is limited in every man by the narrow capacity of the human stomach; but the desire of the conveniencies and ornaments of building, dress, equipage and household furniture, seems to have no limit or certain boundary.*

* *The Wealth of Nations.* Book I, ch. XI, Part II, p. 164. (The Modern Library edition, New York.)

The fewer wants man is in a position to satisfy, the greater the importance of the production of food. Hence, in a country which does not carry on an extensive foreign trade in foodstuffs, a rough indication of the total satisfaction of wants may be derived from the relative importance of agriculture.

It is thus quite natural that the large majority of the Swedish people in the Middle Ages had to be primarily farmers and that at the same time they could not possibly be merely farmers.

The nature of Swedish agriculture and the living and working conditions of the agricultural population remained largely unchanged not only through the eighteenth century but well into the nineteenth. Insofar as this is true, we shall have no cause to return to the matter immediately in the ensuing periods; what is said in this section must hold for more recent times as well. However, we must distinguish clearly between the problem of agricultural organization and the problem of land ownership, which underwent far more rapid changes in various directions. Its study, unlike that of agricultural organization, cannot therefore be based on data pertaining to the sixteenth century alone.

### STORAGE ECONOMY

In an economy dominated by agriculture the problem of food preservation was necessarily of paramount importance. A modern economy is characterized by a continuous flow where consumption does not primarily draw on accumulated stocks of finished goods but is more or less simultaneous with production. Exactly the opposite was the case in the medieval economy, which may therefore be described as a "storage economy." It is literally true that in the old days normally no food was eaten fresh, whether animal or vegetable. Exceptions were made at weddings, funerals, and other festive occasions, and the somewhat macabre conception of a funeral as festive is explained by the fact that this was the most frequent and important opportunity for fresh food and drink. Something similar could be found until quite recently in untouched peasant communities, vividly described by August Bondeson in his story "Butter-Lars' Funeral" (*När Smör-Lars var död*).

Conditions may be illustrated by a reference to the sixteenth century. In 1573, about 5,300 persons were employed in the royal castles and on the domains of the crown. They were fed a total of 101.6 kilograms (224 pounds) per capita of meat and pork, of which 99 kilograms (218 pounds) were salted and dried.[3] Thus, practically nothing was fresh. The letters of Gustavus Vasa frequently refer to butter and pork which had been collected in taxes during the previous year, and at times produce reached even more respectable age before it was consumed. On one occasion, for instance, the thrifty monarch ordered three-year-old tax butter to be served to the hired men at the castle, "since this behooves them well";[4] and on another he ordered the sale of four-year-old malt, "since the moth is settling therein."[5] The subjects of the king, buying such goods, must likewise have been affected by the spirit of frugality. What held for meat and butter also applied to fish; in fact, even in fairly recent times any reasonably well-run farm kept a supply of round cakes of hard bread hanging down from the ceiling instead of using fresh bread. In one of the books on his Swedish travels Linnaeus found it noteworthy and almost improper that in parts of Skåne bread was baked as often as once a week, which presumably meant that soft bread was eaten. Gustavus Vasa explicitly ordered not only his own officers but the peasants as well to store meat and butter in the fall, after the slaughter, and to live on the produce of yesteryear during the following twelve months.

A natural consequence of this arrangement was an enormous thirst: food simply had to be washed down with fabulous quantities of beer in order to be edible. Beer consumption, in spite of strong fluctuations, always was many times higher than nowadays, on the average perhaps around forty times as high, not only for men but also for women. One of Gustavus' sons, Prince John, once wrote his father that his soldiery were not provided with enough beer "to help themselves to their subsistence."[6] They had been allotted a tankard of about 2.75 quarts (*kanna*) a day, but through the intervention of the prince this was to be raised to one-and-a-half such tankards a day and two on Sundays, equaling approximately 1,600 quarts a year. And there are many instances of a far higher consumption of beer. At the same time it should be mentioned that the quality of the beer was no different from that of the solid food. The beer too was stored and certainly often sour, since even Gustavus himself sometimes complained of being served sour beer.

As to the demand for other commodities, the most noteworthy consequence of this economic order was to accord to salt a position which nowadays can hardly be grasped. Since it was not to be found within the country, salt was the significant item in foreign trade for the mass of the people. To be cut off from the import of salt was a calamity; it became a weapon which was used by Sweden's warring enemies and its occasional foreign rulers such as Eric of Pomerania. Hops were grown in the country, but not in sufficient quantities, so that this also was an import of concern to most people.

Still another implication of storage economy was the great prominence of spices both in folklore and reality. The colonial wars, which were carried on for centuries, were largely "spice wars," and the spice market was one of the most coveted prizes of commerce. Nowadays, although economic causes of war are far from absent, the spice trade is not one of them, simply because spices have become so insignificant. But in times past, food was so unpalatable, if not downright spoiled, that it had to be very heavily seasoned to be at all edible, and the same was true of beer.

### THE AGRARIAN SYSTEM

In the main, storage economy stemmed from the peculiarities of medieval agriculture. There was constant fear of a grain shortage; accordingly fodder was hardly ever raised on arable land. The only exception, to judge from the Provincial Codes, was that oats were sometimes raised as horse feed. As a result, cattle did not derive any appreciable nutriment from arable fields but were grazed either on village meadows and enclosed pastures, as in the lowlands, or else in the forest which was then much more extensive than now. The forest pastures were considered particularly succulent and it would have seemed wasteful not to make use of them. The only way this could be done was by keeping the cattle in the woods, so that hardly any animal produce appeared during the summer. Milk had to be converted into butter, and butter had to be salted in order to stay fresh. In fact, the same usage prevailed in the lowlands, where the bulk of the population was settled. In the sixteenth-century food budgets which have been richly preserved, we very

Storage sheds from a sixteenth-century farm in Dalarna. The two sheds in the corner bear the dates 1585 and 1588 respectively. *Now at Skansen, Stockholm.*

The interior of a store-shed with barrels for beef, pork, and beer. Dried meat and sausages are suspended from the ceiling. Värmland.

Gathering of bog ore on a frozen lake in Småland. The ore was piled up under a hole in the ice by means of a rake and hauled up in basket-like sieves. The screens served as protection against the wind. Ink drawing by Kilian Zoll in 1852. *Privately owned.*

Bog ore from Småland. *Tekniska Muséet.*

The oldest documentary evidence of Swedish mining: a contract of 1288 concerning a one-eighth share of a mine at Stora Kopparberg. *Riksarkivet.*

The house of a prominent medieval merchant at Visby, Isle of Gotland. Water color
Ferdinand Boberg.

rarely find any mention of milk except in trifling quantities; butter was practically always salted, and so was meat.

There was no slaughter during the grazing period in the summer. Slaughter took place in the fall. In the winter the cattle produced practically nothing, which was not surprising in view of the low nutritional content of their fodder. Toward the end of the winter the cattle approached a state of starvation. In the sixteenth century Gustavus Vasa found it necessary to upbraid the peasants severely for still adhering to such practices. But the remedy he recommended to ensure provident husbandry is even more illuminating: peasants were told to gather "straw, leaves, reeds, bark." [7] Similar feedstuffs were also used, such as spruce twigs and nettles, not to mention horse dung. There is evidence from many countries that by springtime the animals were so emaciated that they often could not stand upright but had to be pulled on sledges or by the tail to graze the first grass. And their size was no better than their diet. Hans Forssell, who may be regarded as the first Swedish economic historian, has demonstrated this by pointing to the low weight of slaughtered cattle and the low milk yield, as well as to bones of domestic animals which have been preserved. He noted that the jawbones of hogs were just barely half the size of those of the 1870's, when he was writing, and that "the milking cows in the barns of King Gustavus were of a size which we would nowadays consider appropriate for a year-old calf of a good breed." [8]

One result of these features of the Swedish economy, which at first glance is rather surprising, was a sizable export surplus of butter — sizable, at least, when compared with the total exports. Thus, in the accounts of the Lübeck customs in the 1360's, the export value for Swedish butter appears larger than that of iron and copper, the two basic staples, taken together. It must be added that at other times butter was entirely absent, although it reappeared as a normal export item in the sixteenth century. This situation is of great interest as an illustration of the relation between exports and conditions of production. It was because milk and butter could not or were not supposed to be consumed while fresh that a surplus was available for exportation, in much the same way as, for instance, the grain exports from Czarist Russia in the 1890's were explained by the fact that so little of the grain was at the disposal of the peasants. "We must starve but export," was a Russian minister's pungent pronouncement. An additional explanation of medieval conditions is that, although the animals were very small and by present standards unproductive, their numbers were very large, not only in relation to the area of arable land — which is less relevant, since cattle were not fed on crops — but also by other standards. The size of the herds resulted from the desire to utilize the rich wild pastures and to cut grass on even very remote meadows. This also explains why at times hides and skins were chief items among Swedish exports; the very leanness of the animals gave a high ratio of hide to meat.

Thus, some of the features of storage economy were well rooted in the nature of the agricultural system. But this cannot be the whole story; other factors must have also been at work. As we have noted, fish, though unconnected with agriculture, was treated the same way as meat in that it was dried and salted. Similarly, the general use of hard bread remains unexplained. If we look for rational motivations for behavior of this kind, it is perhaps plausible to assume that there was a wish to avoid extravagant consumption by making food none too appetizing. (We recall similar efforts from the First World War.) Gustavus' austere instructions that fresh food was to be stored in larders and consumed only when a year old definitely give the impression that he found it morally reprehensible to eat fresh food. This was certainly a notion of long standing, even though its origins remain obscure. Clearly, however, modern consumption habits are not *per se* more self-evident or reasonable than those of former times.

On the whole, reluctance to raise forage crops on cultivated land tended to increase rather than decrease the scarcity of grain, since arable land was largely deprived of manure when cattle were pastured away from the village. Actually this was not merely owing to agronomic ignorance. When at length the change came, it was entirely empirical and well in advance of the emergence of agricultural science in the modern sense of the word. That the supremacy of the old agricultural techniques was not challenged until so late was the consequence of the medieval social order and particularly of the form of land tenure which prevailed in Sweden as in most other European countries.

## Village Organization

The organization of the communal village is usually known in Sweden as *bytvång* ("village compulsion") or *ägoblandning* ("intermixed ownership"). Distribution of land was that of the open-field system, in Sweden generally called *tegskifte* (*teg:* strip of land; *skifte:* partition); a common variant was called *solskifte* (*sol:* sun). *Tegskifte,* however, appears to have been preceded by a mode of settlement usually called *hammarskifte* (*hammare:* hammer); the ancient code of the province of Uppland mentions villages divided into the ancient partitions of hammers ("*i hambri och forni skipt*").[9] The real nature of the *hammarskifte* can probably not be ascertained, which inevitably has given rise to many different but equally weak interpretations. That it was more irregular than the *tegskifte* is suggested by various provisions of the Provincial Codes which aimed at a transition from *hammarskifte* to *tegskifte*, just as the reforms, which many hundred years later put an end to the *tegskifte*, brought about a still more regular land distribution.

The general features of the Swedish open-field system are known to us primarily from the large number of land maps prepared by government surveyors beginning with the last decades of the seventeenth century. Since those maps were often made following readjustments of individual holdings in the open field, we must conclude that the organization in the Middle Ages was even more irregular than the one we find in the maps. This rich material permits a fairly detailed study of the various patterns of settlement, and may also make it possible to estimate their prevalence in different regions. At the present time, however, we know very little about the latter problem, so that we must confine ourselves to a description of characteristics of the types of land systems.

The organization generally assumed to have prevailed in the early settlements — at any rate it is well represented in the maps — had the following features. The dwelling lots of all the villagers were arranged along the village street, on one or both sides of it. The arable land was divided into a number of fields (*vångar*), and each villager held a strip (*teg*) in every field. The individual strips were not necessarily equal in size. They were arranged in the same order as the dwelling lots along the village street; the Provincial Codes used the terse expression, "lot is acre's mother." But this was by no means the end of it. One villager might hold several non-adjoining strips in the same field. Since there was almost always a tendency to let the strips extend along the whole field, the strips often tended to become extremely narrow, both absolutely and in relation to their length. Instances occurred of villagers holding more than one hundred strips in the same village, in some cases even considerably more. A very striking and graphic example is found in the village of Gessie in the *härad* (approx. "district") of Oxie in Skåne, a map of which, dating from 1705, is reproduced in this book.

There the partition had been driven very far; in all the fields, large and small (and in subdivisions of the fields corresponding to the English "shots" or to the German *Gewanne*), we find an enormous number of regular narrow strips allotted to the villagers. The strips appear to have been only about ten to eleven yards wide and as a rule eight to ten times as long.

In addition, we find a great many other types of settlement. In smaller villages the division of land was sometimes simpler, while in some of the large villages individual holdings were more consolidated. On the other hand, at times we see an irregularity and a dispersion that almost defy description. A good example is the village of Bäck in the district of Vartofta and the province of Västergötland. Here there was neither a village street nor any systematic partition of the land. Every villager's holding was divided in a different way, and at the same time the number of strips was very large.

The *tegskifte* or open-field system originally must have been designed to insure equality in the allotment of land of different fertility and location. The introduction of bare fallowing (two- or three-course rotation) may also have made for the division of every holding among two or three fields. But these conditions alone could not possibly account for the extreme dispersion which is so often found. Presumably it must be explained by two other factors — continued subdivision among heirs and subdivision for sale. Since the new owners likewise wanted holdings in all the different fields, the original strips were usually cut up lengthwise into even narrower strips. When waste land was converted into arable land, the new fields were similarly partitioned. If parts of a subdivided holding were again brought under one ownership, this did not necessarily reduce the dispersion unless the reunited strips were adjacent.

*Bytvång* or "village compulsion" (like the German *Flurzwang*) was a telling name for this arrangement, for it tied the individual villager into the strait jacket of a rigidly communal system. The separate strips were far too narrow to be cultivated independently. Consequently, although the land was subjected to individual holding, the entire village had to be managed as a unit. Guided by the rules contained in the Provincial Codes or, at a later time, by the village bylaws based on these codes, a reeve or an alderman, possibly the village assembly, determined the time to plow, to sow, and to reap. After the harvest, the livestock was driven onto the stubble of the arable fields. All this made necessary a uniform method of cultivation. Nobody could raise crops different from his neighbors' or introduce a different rotation. Winter grain could not be used if the neighbors used spring grain because they would have to be sown and harvested at different times. As a vivid, although somewhat biased illustration of the system, we may quote an article which appeared in 1755 in the *Lärda tidningar* (Scholarly Discourses), published by Lars Salvius.

The sharing of fields, meadows, woods, and wild lands is but the nurse of a country's poverty. For as long as no one looks after his own, all husbandry is capricious as the moon, though rather on the wane than on the wax. I shall mention one or two of the innumerable abuses to which it leads.

Where neighbors are sharing fields and pastures, the fields are often not plowed or else they are not plowed in time. One must sow when his neighbor sows, whether the soil be ready or not. One must cut when his neighbor cuts, whether the crop be ripe or not. One must not change his crop to refresh the soil and the corn lest the neighbor protest it. One must make his hay when his neighbor does, most often unripe and in its best growth. One must, to his great harm, let the cattle graze the fields in springtime and fall, as the neighbor may please.[10]

Under a despotic government, such as that of Soviet Russia, even very radical changes might have been introduced into a system of this kind. But the reeve and the village council merely followed the codes or the village bylaws. Few other aspects of medieval agriculture could have contributed as much to the conservative character of the system with its nearly complete rigidity and resistance to change.

In the days of the Provincial Codes, however, we already find isolated lands outside the village communities, although the villagers appear to have looked askance at them; they often remained uncultivated. In early village maps, we even find individual farms predominating in certain places, particularly in the west and north. In some parts of the country this might possibly have been the original type of settlement, antedating the *tegskifte*. But no general inference with regard to the origins of *tegskifte* should be drawn from these facts, because at least some of the areas of individual farms were of recent settlement and were rather unimportant in the Middle Ages.

The crops raised in those villages were almost exclusively cereals. Judging from sixteenth-century conditions, the principal crop was barley which has since been gradually disappearing from Swedish agriculture, its production and consumption lingering in the north much longer than in the rest of the country. The barley now remaining is used principally for brewing and other purposes, and is actually an entirely different grain from the old six-rowed barley which was used for human food. Some of the Provincial Codes mention, beside barley, all the other major grains, such as rye, oats, and wheat. Oats are generally believed to have been the last crop to be introduced; as late as the sixteenth century it was still missing in many provinces. Insofar as it was grown, some of it apparently was used to feed horses. Wheat seems to have appealed to the popular imagination, for its mention is conspicuous in letters, legal texts, and chronicles of the period, though in reality its share in total crops was quite insignificant.

At the time of the Provincial Codes two-field husbandry already existed in some provinces; in other words, half the land was left fallow every second year. Whether any three-field husbandry occurred in medieval Sweden is not known. At any rate, it is most probable that systematic fallowing was the exception rather than the rule, and that the predominant practice was the one-field system, so that the same crop was planted on the same land year in, year out. In the words of the critic who was quoted earlier, one did not "change the crop to refresh the soil and the corn." But the perennial shortage of manure made it impossible to maintain cultivation on the same field indefinitely. The solution tended to be that parts of the plow land more or less irregularly were turned into pasture when yields had declined too much.

Outside the arable land and the meadows were the commons or wastelands. The meadows were probably normally subject to private rights, but not the forest which, presumably with very few exceptions, was held in common. This too raised difficult problems. Thus the article from 1755 continues:

Sharing in woods and wild lands is equally if not more harmful. Here everyone follows the old rule, "One shoots and another snatches; everyone keeps what he catches."

In practice this meant that the individual villagers could not be prevented from taking more than their share; in particular, it is likely that villagers with small holdings transgressed the requirements of the law and used the commons in excess of the share to which they were entitled by the size of their arable holdings. It also happened that squatters settled on the commons with a few hogs and geese or chickens. All this appeared unsound to the stronger individualism of a later period, and it is fairly clear that such communism in many cases led to neglect and decay. But in the case of the forest, common use initially mattered little, for its expanse in most parts of the country was enormous. It was also a great advantage that the forest lands were not partitioned; this occurred later and turned out to be of considerable harm to Swedish forestry.

## LAND OWNERSHIP

Rural organization, as it has now been described, must be kept carefully apart from the question of land ownership. Proprietorship actually was of a slightly different nature from that now suggested by the word. When, for instance, Bo Jonsson Grip, the *riksdrots* ("Steward of the Realm") and actual Swedish ruler under Albert of Mecklenburg (1365–1388), is said to have owned extensive lands in almost all the provinces and is described as the greatest landlord of the kingdom, one is tempted to imagine him as the owner of a large number of manorial estates. Nothing could be more incorrect. Though there were manorial demesnes as well as demesnes of the crown, their share in total land was negligible. From time immemorial, the overwhelming part of Swedish soil has been cultivated by peasants; ownership by others did not exclude this. In the majority of cases, in other words, the landowning nobility and gentry merely collected their fees from the tenants; they were absentee landlords or rentiers, not agricultural managers.* It also followed from this that no initiative to reform methods of cultivation was to be expected from the landowners, except to the very limited extent that they really administered their own farms, and probably not even then. Among the landowners, the monasteries probably contributed most to agricultural innovation and progress, especially in horticulture.

An important distinction must be made between four different categories of land or homesteads (*hemman*), a distinction which, at least for three of those categories, persisted down to the present century. It had been introduced for fiscal purposes and remained primarily an administrative classification, but it had a considerable impact on the entire legal development of rural Sweden. In many respects it shaped the old Swedish property law.

The four different classes of land were:

(i) Land owned by the crown — so-called *kronojord*.

(ii) Land owned by the church and the clergy — *kyrkojord*. This was exempt from taxation, a privilege generally designated by the term *frälse;* the church was said to enjoy "spiritual *frälse.*"

(iii) Secular tax-exempt land — *frälsejord*. This was essentially land owned by the nobility or gentry, the exemption being granted in return for military services.

(iv) Taxable land — *skattejord*.

The last category comprised the land owned by small proprietors or "freeholders," although their proprietorship at that time was not yet unqualified since only the three other classes possessed full rights of ownership. The freeholders' land was called *skattejord* or "tax

---

* *Translator's note:* It is virtually impossible to find an adequate terminology in English for Continental and Swedish conditions regarding nobility and gentry, because English and Continental systems are quite different. In England, a nobleman is a peer and as such always holds a title; according to circumstances, none, one, or more of his descendants also hold titles and are considered noblemen; but the great majority of the offspring of noble families hold no titles and fade into the gentry. Untitled persons can never be called noblemen in England. On the Continent, on the other hand, all children of a titled nobleman inherit his title and are counts or barons; and — even more important — a much greater number hold patents of nobility without any personal title at all. Whatever terminology may be chosen, it is therefore apt to be misleading.

land" because it was subject only to payment of fees to the crown as ruler of the realm, whereas tenants on other lands paid their rentals to their respective owners. The tenants on *kronojord* owed their dues to the crown, but to the crown as landowner rather than as ruler of the realm.

The relative extent of these categories of ownership in the early Middle Ages is unknown, but on the threshold of modern times the distribution for Sweden proper (excluding Finland) was as follows: *kronojord* 5.6%, *kyrkojord* 21.3%, *frälsejord* 20.7%, *skattejord* 52.4%. In Finland practically all the land (96.4%) was *skattejord*.[11] Part of the land which at that time was owned by the clergy and the nobility and gentry had at first belonged to the crown. The original magnitude of the crown holdings is unknown, but in any event figures show that they had been greatly reduced. On the other hand, a conspicuously large share remained in the hands of the peasants, that is, the freeholders, which considerably attenuated the government's loss of revenue, for its incomes from *skattejord* and from *kronojord* per unit of land were fairly equal. From the tenants of the crown only a few fees were exacted in excess of those paid as taxes by the freeholders.

*Frälse* meant exemption from taxes, or at least from land taxes, which were by far the most important ones. Its rationale lay in the commutation of the tax liability into other services. Temporal *frälse* depended on the provision of mounted soldiery. As long as this order prevailed, it was in principle possible for any peasant to obtain the privilege of frälse simply by providing a number of horsemen corresponding to the size of his holdings. Such circumstances obviously precluded the existence of a closed aristocracy.

On land which was exempt from taxation, dues corresponding to the taxes paid by the freeholder were levied by the respective owners. In addition, wide areas were assigned in fief by the crown, generally in exchange for services, but sometimes for specified payments, and sometimes even "for accounting," which meant that the holder had to account for taxes levied and deductions for services to the crown. The feoffee in those areas collected the fees due to the crown from both the tenants on the *kronojord* and the freeholders on *skattejord*. At the same time, the feoffee's obligations to the crown were given a very lenient interpretation, at least in the late Middle

Ages, so that the net revenue from his fiefs was actually not very different from that of his own possessions. This practice served to reduce considerably the crown's revenue from taxable land.

## NATURAL ECONOMY

The conditions we have described were largely the concomitants of a system in which payments were effected in kind rather than in money, and it seems appropriate to analyze the scope and significance of this system.

The introduction of money into economic relations and its repercussions in other areas of the community have been conveniently described by German authors as the transition from *Naturalwirtschaft* to *Geldwirtschaft*.* The most significant function of money in this connection is to serve as a generally accepted medium of exchange, that is to say, as a means of payment in all transactions. By a "natural economy," we mean a condition where the use of such an instrument of payment does not prevail. A reasonable interpretation of the term does not require that money be entirely non-existent in such a system. So rigorously defined, the term "natural economy" would hardly be applicable to any historical period. As the expression generally is and ought to be used, it simply means that payments in kind are common, or at least more common than payments in money.

There has been no real study of the extent of payments in kind in medeival Sweden. Nor would such research be easy, although a thorough scrutiny of the documents would probably add considerably to our present knowledge. At any rate, the legal codes of the Middle Ages contain many explicit references to payments in kind. Moreover, objects which could be used as tender or money equivalents were often referred to as *värdöra* (*öre*-worth or "pennyworth"). So, for example, Chapter XVI of the Commercial Code (*Köpmålabalken*), adopted in the middle of the fourteenth century and made to apply to all cities of the realm, specified which commodities could be used for transactions aboard ship. And Chapter V of the Land Code (*Jordabalken*) stated in detail:

* *Translator's note:* There seems to be no satisfactory rendering of those terms into English. In default of a better choice, the expressions "natural economy" and "money economy" have been used in the text.

These are the *värdöra* in which a lot shall be paid . . . gold, silver, ready cash, corn, cattle, pork, butter, seal, wadmal, linen, cloth, and other *värdöra*.[12]

This generous sample of commodities which might be used in exchange by no means exhausts the whole list.

In some cases legal texts speak of payment in money as opposed to other forms of payment. Thus they might speak of payment "in land or money." But closer scrutiny of the text usually suggests that "money" stands for any other object of value, as in the case just cited, for anything except land. Here it is by no means certain that payment in cash was at all intended. Nevertheless, there are instances where we must assume that medieval legislators wished to prescribe payments in cash and nothing but cash. Yet even then it is doubtful whether this intention was really carried out. We must expect that payment in kind was at least as prevalent in the Middle Ages as in the sixteenth century. If so, money cannot have been commonly used in transactions, except possibly in combination with other means of payment.

But money has functions other than that of a medium of exchange, which in the Middle Ages was quite subordinate. By contrast, money was particularly important as a standard of value. When the Provincial Codes prescribe fines of thirty or forty *mark*, this does not imply that the culprit had to surrender that amount in silver and coin. He paid up in so-and-so many bushels of corn, heads of cattle, etc., but all those commodities had been evaluated in terms of money. A great many other commodities also served as value standards, but at an early stage money proper was fairly generally adopted for this purpose. In fact, calculation in money terms was so widespread that it tended to supplant physical units — one would speak of "*öre*-land" and "*örtug*-land," "a *penning* of corn," "a *mark* of wadmal," etc.*

Finally, coins, along with precious metals in plate or other form, served an important function as a store of value, particularly in turbulent times when wealth had to be both easy to hide and easy to move. Hoards of medieval coins recently discovered in various places must have served this purpose.

To return to the problem of exchange, the concept of "natural

* Normally 1 *mark* = 8 *öre* = 24 *örtug* = 192 *penningar*.

economy," a system where payments in money are non-existent or negligible, actually comprises three different forms of economic organization.

First of all, a system of self-sufficient households is a form of natural economy. In the absence of any exchange whatever, money is useless. This is not a particularly significant case, since the completely closed household is rarely found within our historical experience. A second form, usually thought to be the very essence of *Naturalwirtschaft,* is barter, in which goods and services are exchanged directly. Presumably barter must at one time have played a prominent part, though it naturally involved a great many difficulties. For this type of exchange requres the singular fourfold coincidence that each party desires to forego what the other party wants and *vice versa.*

The reign of Gustavus I provides us with the first exhaustive picture of Swedish natural economy; and by this time it appears that a third variety of economic organization frequently prevailed, in which an "intermediate commodity" was introduced in the transaction. To obtain a desired good, one first had to acquire another, the intermediate one, which could in turn be exchanged. Sometimes the transaction would be completed only after a whole sequence of barters in such intermediate commodities. Of course, money is the ideal commodity for this purpose and might be defined as a generally accepted intermediate commodity. But the exchange of goods and services without the use of money was slow in disappearing, and the result was an indirect exchange. It was certainly this practice that largely induced early economic legislation to pay such close attention to the middleman's trade.

Let me take a concrete example from the sixteenth century.[13] The peasants in the province of Dalsland, having butter to spare, wanted to get fish from the fishermen on the North Sea coast in the province of Bohuslän. But the fishermen had no need for butter, so the peasants had to turn somewhere else where their butter would be in demand. They traveled inland to the miners in the province of Värmland in order to trade their butter for iron. The iron was then transported down to the coast where at length it was exchanged for fish. Similar patterns were repeated all over the country and often a great number of middlemen were required to complete a transaction. This indirect arrangement for payment in kind was immensely more inconvenient than payment in money, but at least it removed the fundamental disabilities of direct barter.

The common effect of all forms of natural economy was very considerable rigidity. A natural economy clearly does not permit the same degree of consumers' choice as does a money economy. This might be illustrated by the case of domestic servants, where payment in kind still occurs. In a prosperous modern home in a high-cost residential area in Stockholm, a domestic servant might receive twice as much of her pay in board and lodging as in cash. But the employee has no influence whatever over the disposal of these two-thirds of the wage. She has to accept the chambers and fare that her employer provides, although she would probably prefer cheaper housing and food if she could receive the difference in cash and dispose of it at will. Such restriction of consumers' choice characterized all economic relationships under natural economy.

Natural economy also had a considerable impact upon public administration. The very institution of *frälse* might be seen as a form of barter, an exchange of tax exemption for military services. Similarly, enfeoffments made it possible for the crown to obtain services by renouncing its revenue from the fiefs. But in addition, peasants as well as everybody else generally paid their taxes and dues in kind, that is, in corn, malt, butter, meat, fish, cattle, hides, or iron. Thus, the crown came into possession of a variety of products and had to use them as best it could. To a large extent they were consumed directly by the crown; bailiffs and governors would feed their soldiers and clerks out of this revenue. No town could be the permanent capital of the realm, for the king and his retinue were supported in the same way, and transportation difficulties were such that it was far easier to move the entire court on horseback to the various castles and estates where the revenue was stored than to collect it all in one central depot. This is one of the reasons that medieval rulers were continually on the move. Inevitably, however, revenue from the peasants was often of a different composition from the consumption of the crown, in which case the crown had to arrange for exchange transactions.

The other receivers of dues from the peasants, the spiritual and temporal lords, were in the same position, though to a lesser degree.

And the peasants themselves were forced to perpetual exchange of commodities. Under conditions of natural economy, trade was thus in some degree a universal occupation, which is one of the reasons for the relatively great importance of commerce even in very primitive stages of economic development.

## THE ABSENCE OF FEUDALISM

In many countries, the character that natural economy imposed upon public administration was an important factor behind what is generally, albeit somewhat ambiguously, called feudalism. Since most of the revenue raised by the state was disposed of by bailiffs and governors in the provinces, local officeholders were largely self-sufficient. The regional administrations were autonomous financial units, managing their own revenue and expenditure. This is obviously not the way in which public finance is organized in a money economy where revenues are easily allocated to whatever purpose without regard to their origin. In contrast to officials in a unified system of public finance, the regional functionaries in the Middle Ages were essentially independent of the central administration, which, for that matter, was not even "central" but followed the ruler on his travels. This had far-reaching consequences for the whole social order. Protected as they were by the lack of adequate communication facilities, local power holders were often tempted to assert their independence and to act on their own behalf rather than on that of the state.

Such decentralization, if not disintegration, went very far indeed. Provinces would raise their own taxes, introduce local currencies, and charge tolls on the goods carried through their territories. These practices, although sometimes an entirely legal result of enfeoffments from the state, worked toward the dissolution of the country into smaller political entities. In the same way the Holy Roman Empire of the German nation, about which Voltaire made his famous remark that it was neither holy, Roman, nor an empire, was split up into a number of separate states. In France, such tendencies toward disintegration were overcome at a much earlier stage than in Germany, but at one time very similar conditions had prevailed west of the Rhine to a varying degree. Other Continental countries underwent the same experience.

In Sweden also one might have expected to find a fully developed feudal order of this kind. Natural economy was as widespread in Sweden as in western and central European countries, and certainly far more persistent than in those more rapidly developing regions. Moreover, the road system was less extensive and the condition of the roads worse, if possible, than on the Continent. Oddly enough, there were few signs of comparable disintegration in Sweden, and even those disappeared very early. The only area in which unification lagged badly was that of weights and measures.

As for the coinage system, early regional differences went out of existence in the Middle Ages, and local tolls and other economic barriers between the provinces seem to have been rarer than in any other country, including England. The reasons for this singular development have never been thoroughly analyzed, but a few immediately spring to mind. On the one hand, political interest in unification was much stronger than in most other countries. On the other hand, such political ambitions found a much more propitious environment.

First of all, the estates and fiefs of the landed nobility were scattered over many different provinces. This made for an interest in communications between the provinces and for a far stronger national orientation than would have been possible had the holdings of the aristocracy been confined to individual provinces. As an example one might refer again to the powerful figure of Bo Jonsson Grip. Many of his estates were concentrated in the province of Östergötland, but nevertheless he held land all over the country. He therefore did not aim at becoming, say, Duke of Östergötland, but strove for a dominating influence over the policy of the country as a whole. Another important factor is that enfeoffments in Sweden were never quite hereditary; consequently to preserve large landholdings intact from generation to generation was a difficult task. Here, too, the case of Bo Jonsson is illustrative, for his enormous holdings were divided upon his death.

While these conditions might account for the interest in national unity, they do not explain how it was actually attained. To understand this one must consider the nature of Swedish communications. In this respect, Sweden was actually more favored than the large Continental countries, even though Continental highways were probably far superior to those in Sweden, and Continental waterways immensely so. But both highways and rivers could be easily blocked. The large navigable rivers of the Continent were virtually studded with toll stations at intervals of five to ten miles: the burgs on the Rhine which every tourist now admires are monuments to that state of affairs. At practically all of them tolls were levied at one time or another. There was no counterpart to that in Sweden. Instead, the country possessed two methods of communication which were more difficult to block.

One was offered by the long coasts. Other countries with long coastal strips, like England, Norway, and Denmark, likewise succeeded in avoiding feudal disintegration. The coast of England is much longer in relation to the area of the country than that of Sweden; but, on the other hand, the important trading centers along the Swedish coast are shielded by archipelagoes which make blockades extremely difficult. If anyone had attempted to collect a toll somewhere in one of the island groups, the small vessels of those times could easily have evaded it by slipping through the maze of sounds and straits.

Secondly, there were the winter roads which had no counterpart in more southerly climes. The snow and ice offered a rather unique opportunity for easy transportation in spite of the extreme difficulties in constructing and maintaining ordinary highways. In winter, such small hauls as might be called for in the medieval economy were easily carried on sledges across land and water even without any ordinary roads. Should it occur to some lord to levy a toll along such a winter track, nothing could be simpler than to open up another one. In consequence, transportation of heavier goods in particular was almost entirely limited to the winter months. Summer transport took place only when delay was absolutely impossible. This remained the practice until the introduction of railroads. It is actually difficult to see how medieval Sweden could have achieved an even remotely comparable economic development without the boon of its winter roads. This mode of transportation is largely accountable for the absence of feudal disintegration in Sweden.

### DOMESTIC TRADE

We have previously emphasized the degree to which the autarky of the country and the self-sufficiency of the households characterized the medieval economy. The time has now come to qualify the previous statement by a description of such exchange as did occur. The procedure used in this trade has already been touched upon in connection with the concept of natural economy; we must now take a closer look at its extent and nature.

In many important respects, rural households were not self-sufficient. First of all, we must not infer that a farm, just because it produced a quantity of food sufficient for the subsistence needs of the household, produced the specific kinds of food that the household actually needed or wanted. Geographically, there was a difference between the agriculture of the lowlands and that of the forest regions, with emphasis on cereal produce in the former and on animal produce in the latter. At a very early stage an exchange of grain for animal foods must therefore have taken place. Animal products were generally more easily transported. In 1759 the first Swedish professor of economics, Anders Berch, wrote that "livestock farming promoted its own transport." Butter had a fairly high ratio of value to volume, and cattle, generally oxen, transported themselves either at the cost of fodder (the quantities of which may have been considerable) or at the cost of a weight-loss. There is little doubt, then, that Sweden in the Middle Ages was crisscrossed by drives of oxen and by hauls of butter and grain. This alone was an important modification of the self-sufficiency of the households.

Another object of trade was fish. Even after the Reformation in the sixteenth century fish consumption was many times larger than nowadays, and it might have been higher yet during the Catholic period with its many fasting days. Although a great deal of fish was caught in rivers and brooks all over the country, many farms were without any access to fishing waters. On the other hand, coastal fishing communities had to dispose of their catches. Again we must infer that exchange took place.

Third, there was the practice of rural handicraft, an ancient tradition, especially in poorly endowed regions where the land did not fully support a household. The peasants themselves must then have bought foodstuffs, paying for them with the products of their craft, in most cases probably iron and wood products, but possibly also textile and leather goods.

So far we have dealt with exchange transactions within the agricultural (and fishing) population. There was in addition the traffic between those basic strata of medieval society and the non-agrarian "superstructure." First, there was the exchange of iron for food; but the peasants also purchased imported commodities like salt, hops, spices, and to some extent cloth, for all of which they had to pay with foodstuffs. This was a source of quite diversified trading.

Our attention, however, should not remain limited to the conventional type of exchange. To do this would be to overlook the unilateral payments of taxes and dues by the peasants, which were far more important than most of the forms of bilateral exchange. With some good will, one might possibly consider payment of such dues as a *quid pro quo* for the services of the state, but it would hardly be worthwhile to pursue this argument very far. Compulsory payments are always different from voluntary transactions and, at any rate, we are only interested in the immediate impact of those payments upon agricultural households. The recipients of their services were on the one hand the king and his retinue, his bailiffs, officers, soldiers, and clerks, and on the other hand the temporal lords and the church. The obligation to support those groups implied that the peasants in all circumstances had to produce in excess of their own consumption. In a sense, this meant that the degree of self-sufficiency within the country tended to be reduced. *Pro tanto*, it should become impossible simply to identify the Middle Ages with a system of "closed economy."

If the recipients of rents and taxes had no immediate use for the goods received, unilateral payments from the peasants would give rise to chains of barter transactions. When this was so, payment of taxes and dues in the form of food was one of the channels whereby food was transmitted from surplus to deficit areas. Conversely, if payments were made in other forms, such as iron or manufactures, these might be exchanged for food. Finally, a relatively large share of the crown's revenue was exported, thereby initiating international trade.

The upshot of all this was that the economy, even though almost the entire population was tilling the soil, was in many respects an *open* economy in which movements of goods played a considerable role. Those who supported themselves on the land produced not only for their own consumption but also for the market or else they marketed the products of others and provided for the support of the ruling groups.

It now only remains to consider what I have called the "super-structure" of this economy, that is, its non-food producing segments, of which the principal one was mining.

## MINING AND METAL MAKING[14]

Among the metal industries, ironmaking was to rise to unchallenged predominance and assume unique importance for the economy. A few exceptions apart, it probably always was predominant; at any rate, it was certainly the oldest branch of metal production. In the beginning, ironmaking was based on the use of lake and bog ore which were to be found in most regions of Sweden, particularly in the province of Småland. Those ore supplies were especially easy to extract and also had the advantage of being continually replenished by the precipitation of iron in the water. Although nothing is known about it, we may assume that such extraction was undertaken by the peasants since it cannot have demanded a great deal of organization or equipment. The exploitation of lake and bog ore had already occurred in prehistoric time and was still highly important by the beginning of the Middle Ages. Even in those early days, it seems, part of the iron production went into exports.

Comparatively early the exploitation of bog ore was supplemented by that of rock ore deposits. The exact age of this branch of the iron industry is uncertain. It must have been considerably older than the early fourteenth-century documents in which it is first mentioned; the reference there is to the mine at Norberg in northern Västmanland. The only other reasonably reliable evidence of early mining of iron ore has been discovered at Visby, on the island of Gotland, and, to judge by its site, ought to belong to the twelfth century. Archeological finds reveal ore and slag, the analysis of which makes it almost certain that they derive from the mines on the island of Utö in the southern part of the Stockholm archipelago. It seems reasonably safe to assume that those mines had been worked as early as the twelfth century, at which time other mines of which we know nothing might also have existed.

The introduction of rock ore mining fundamentally changed the structure of the iron industry. As soon as this type of mining attained any considerable proportions, it called for a much more elaborate organization than did extraction of bog ore, and therefore almost necessarily developed into an independent industry. Not only the mining of the ore but also its further processing became locationally bound to the mining districts in *Bergslagen* where the industry has essentially remained to the present day. This gave rise to communities legally as well as socially very different from the agricultural villages. Their legal status was defined by the medieval term "immunities," which meant that they enjoyed privileges which exempted them from the general law of the land.

At an early stage Swedish iron came to be known by the name *osmund*. It is now generally assumed that the term was derived from the personal name *Åsmund,* but neither its origin nor its exact meaning have been sufficiently clarified. I believe it probable that *osmund* originally denoted the shape of the product, regardless of the method of production. It is therefore possible that bog iron was called *osmund;* at any rate, this was the case with iron extracted from rock ore.

By the middle of the thirteenth century we find the word *osmund* in a Dutch tariff list, indicating that such iron was exported at that time. In the last third of the fourteenth century, exports of iron from Stockholm to Lübeck rose from 275 to 900 (metric) tons per annum; toward the end of the next century the figure had risen to 1,100–1,300 tons.[15] These quantities may now seem ridiculously small, but they mark the beginning of a momentous change. We have reason to assume that iron became a regular item in Swedish exports at an early date. It is also evident that Swedish iron, commanding as it did a price 50 per cent higher than German iron, was held in high esteem in Europe in the last centuries of the Middle Ages. It seems to have been almost the only kind of iron that reached the Baltic ports on the Continent, and in England *osmund* was sold at the same price as steel — that is, it was valued much higher than ordinary iron. There can be no doubt that this was partly the result of the quality of the ore which, of course, is the more important the more primitive the processing technique. Whether the processing was also superior is impossible to say. At any rate Spanish iron was at least as widely spread as Swedish and had penetrated into Western Europe and perhaps farther than that.

The furnaces for smelting osmund iron were equipped with very weak bellows. An important characteristic which distinguished this method from all more recent processes of any significance was that the product was immediately malleable; technically it is therefore known as the direct process. Nevertheless, osmund iron was not normally used in the form in which it emerged from the furnace; as a rule it was cleansed from some impurities. Possibly this also reduced the carbon content and made the iron more malleable.

A change of far-reaching consequence occurred when those small and low osmund furnaces were raised and equipped with stronger bellows which increased the temperature of the charge. In the old furnaces the iron had remained a doughy mass which prevented it from absorbing a great deal of carbon from the fuel. At the higher temperature, however, the iron assumed liquid form which increased its carbon content to a point where it was no longer malleable. The product of this change was pig iron; and in all probability the change was unwelcome, perhaps even the result of an untoward accident reminiscent of the alleged invention of blotting paper. For without further processing pig iron could be used only for casting, whereas the primary need was for wrought iron. Otherwise, the innovation brought conspicuous advantages; production could be made continuous and the product may have been purer. The blast furnace was undeniably superior to the old type, but the need to submit pig iron to subsequent treatment definitely introduced the indirect process into ironmaking. The pig iron was at first refined in the same way as the osmund, and the final product therefore retained this name. Since *osmund* referred to the fact that the iron was cut into pieces of a certain weight and form called *osmundar*, the name remained applicable although the product was now derived from pig iron.

Exactly when the blast furnace was introduced in Sweden is a moot point. There is no documentary evidence of it until the middle of the fifteenth century.[16] Indications that blast furnaces had existed in Sweden at a much earlier time are not particularly convincing. Even such traces as were left by the blast furnaces of the second half of the fifteenth century are very few. Not until the sixteenth century did the blast furnace attain a position of consequence. Thus it belongs essentially to the modern era, but its appearance in the late Middle Ages marked the start of one of the most significant developments in Swedish economic history.

Besides iron, two other metals were produced in the Middle Ages, silver and copper. Silver came essentially from two mines, East and West Silvberg (Silver Mountain). But there is no evidence that significant amounts of silver were extracted until the mine at Sala was discovered in 1510. For about half a century thereafter the Swedish silver trade enjoyed a period of prosperity which was brought to an end by the influx to European markets of large silver supplies from Mexico and South America. The silver industry then became an unfortunate legacy, since the rulers refused to recognize the transient nature of the boom and for centuries kept on sinking capital into an activity which seldom even returned expenses.[17]

Far more important, particularly in later times but probably also in the Middle Ages, was the copper industry.[18] The oldest public documents testifying to its existence, likewise the first evidence of any Swedish metal trade, stem from the 1280's and concern Stora Kopparberg (The Great Copper Mountain) at Falun, which until very recent times remained the only important copper mine in Sweden. In all probability operations began earlier, for the documents suggest that the mine was already a going concern. How much earlier is impossible to tell, just as in the case of the iron trade, but quite clearly a new activity needs some time to attract governmental attention and regulation before its first traces are left in public documents. Copper, too, was exported early, and sources from the late Middle Ages even indicate that the exports of copper exceeded those of iron. But the heights that the Swedish copper industry would eventually reach were not yet in sight.

## THE HANSEATIC LEAGUE

The emergence of no fewer than three metal industries, at least two of which were partly oriented to exports, raised problems of finance and trade beyond the capacity of the Swedes. Assistance came from the most prominent merchants in contemporaneous northern Europe, the Hansards, and particularly from Lübeck, the leader of the Hanseatic League. In the early fourteenth century, traders from Lübeck were already co-owners of the mine at Stora Kopparberg. From then on, German influence became noticeable all over Bergslagen; even today it is expressed in place names like *Garpenberg* and *Garphyttan* since *garp* was a nickname for German; or like *Saxhyttan,* referring to the Saxons.* This was the first foreign influence of essential significance for Sweden's economic development, and it was an influence by no means confined to the metal industries.

The Hansa's and especially Lübeck's main traffic plied between the Baltic and the North Sea — more precisely, between the southern coast of the Baltic and Flanders. The location of Lübeck was extremely favorable for such trade, whether by land or by inland waterways, especially after the completion in 1390 of the Stecknitz Canal between Lübeck and Hamburg. This waterway not only shortened the distance between the Baltic and the North Sea; it also offered a perfectly safe connection, whereas the detour of the so-called *Ummelandfahrt* around Skagen (Denmark) ran through the perilous waters of the North Sea. When the Hansards and the Hanseatic cities are mentioned as buyers and sellers of goods, it must be remembered that they were intermediaries between areas of production and consumption and that they consumed only a trifle of what they bought. A large part in that trade was played by the herring fisheries off the southern tip of the Scandinavian peninsula. The neighboring towns of Skanör and Falsterbo on the coast of Skåne constituted one of the foci of medieval international trade, however remarkable this may appear to anyone visiting those tiny communities today.

Lübeck was in a particularly good position to control this trade, thanks to the salt supplies in nearby Lüneburg. It tried to extend its control over salt too, since the herring were salted down on the spot, and the herring fishery required immediate access to large quantities of salt. Skåne was then not part of Sweden, and we must not be tempted to conclude that Swedish trade was the main concern of the Hansards. As a rule this was not so.

Nevertheless, the Hanseatic influence in Sweden became considerable and had many lasting effects. It affected the entire non-agrarian

* *Berg:* mountain; *hytta:* foundry.

superstructure of the economy, not only the mining industries but also commerce, shipping, and manufacturing; and it put its stamp on the emerging towns. Nothing could be easier to explain. Even if we disregard the political power of the Hansards, which of course contributed to their economic supremacy, they were certainly enormously superior to the Swedes in mercantile affairs. And despite their ruthless monopolism they did, in all likelihood, organize the carrying trade more efficiently than the Swedes themselves would have been able to do. Gustavus I rescinded the Hansards' extensive privileges; yet they maintained their position for another two-thirds of a century, practically until the end of the sixteenth century. Characteristically, by the end of the sixteenth century the Hansards were supplanted not by Swedish merchants but by other aliens, primarily Dutchmen and to a lesser extent Scots.

Through their commercial preëminence the Hanseatic merchants influenced Swedish civilization in general to a degree which may appear surprising in view of what I have said about the weakness of the "superstructure" in medieval Sweden. The reason evidently was that the thin crust of the non-agrarian population constituted an indisputable elite. The Swedish language itself remains the most telling proof of the impact of the Hansards. The great number of German, especially Low German, idioms and constructions irrevocably adopted in the late Middle Ages produced a language which differed in important respects from the Swedish of the Provincial Codes and the early Middle Ages. Attempts made toward the end of the nineteenth century to restore Nordic purity to the language were many centuries too late and remained completely ineffectual.

At this point let us anticipate later developments and raise the question as to why, beginning at the end of the Middle Ages, the Hansards, particularly the Lübeckers, were at length displaced by the Dutch. Transfer of leadership from the merchants of the Baltic to those of the North Sea might suggest that North Sea trade had superseded Baltic trade, but this can hardly be the explanation. Trade between the shores of the Baltic and the North Sea continued briskly. What happened was that Lübeck's geographical superiority was greatly reduced so that the Dutch were able to conduct their trade with the Baltic on an equal footing. This came about when the herring schools shifted their spawning grounds from the coast of Skåne into the North Sea. At the same time North Sea salt, the so-called bay-salt from the French Atlantic coast, began to be used extensively, replacing Lüneburg salt in importance. But Dutchmen continued to go into the Baltic, exchanging the products of West European countries for Baltic wares, among which corn from Prussian and Polish ports was becoming an increasingly important commodity. Geography as such did not discriminate against the merchants of Lübeck. If anything, it favored them. The Dutch conquered this trade, nonetheless, probably simply because they were better merchants and shippers. Apparently it was especially significant that the Dutch were able to master the *Ummelandfahrt,* a route the Hansards had always tended to eschew. This enabled the Dutch to break the Hanseatic monopoly in so far as it had rested on Lübeck's ability to control the route from Lübeck to Hamburg.

Swedish foreign trade, whether transacted by Hansards or Dutchmen, was what has been called "passive trade." [19] In other words, Swedish merchants did not themselves carry their goods overseas, nor did they fetch back foreign wares. Instead, the transactions took place in Swedish ports. Today such an arrangement would probably be held to be unfavorable. In the late Middle Ages passive trade was, on the contrary, considered a great advantage, particularly by Gustavus Vasa, who had checked the political power of the Lübeckers. The argument was that passive trade offered a favorable strategic position and secured advantageous terms of trade, since the foreign merchant was compelled to buy and sell, lest his voyage be in vain. Possibly also an old tradition, derived from the commercial policy of Venice, contributed to this view. The argument for passive trade was not unreasonable, even though it could not have claimed validity for every time and place.

Some indication of the range of commodities handled in foreign trade may be obtained from the traffic between Stockholm and Lübeck. It is the only segment of medieval foreign trade which can be followed in detail, and this for only two periods, the 1360's and the last years of the fifteenth century. We must, however, emphasize that the lack of continuous data makes it impossible to say whether those figures represented normal conditions. Thus, in the year 1368, for which the composition of trade is given in Table 1, the ratio of salt to cloth was much lower than for other years in the same decade;

and toward the end of the fifteenth century the export side consisted almost exclusively of copper and iron, whereas butter had completely disappeared.

It has already been mentioned that the principal, and for the Lübeck trade the exclusive, source of cloth was Flanders. Salt was

TABLE 1.  COMMODITY COMPOSITION OF THE TRADE BETWEEN STOCKHOLM
AND LÜBECK IN 1368

*Percentages*

| Exports | | Imports | |
|---|---|---|---|
| Butter | 44.6 | Cloth (including a small quantity of linen) | 51.3 |
| Iron | 20.1 | | |
| Copper | 17.5 | Salt | 22.9 |
| Furs and hides | 16.0 | Miscellaneous (spices, oil, wine, beer, etc.) | 25.8 |
| Miscellaneous | 1.8 | | |
| Total | 100.0 | Total | 100.0 |

Source: W. Koppe, *Lübeck-Stockholmer Handelsgeschichte im 14.Jh.* (Neumünster-Holstein, 1933), Chapters III to V.

first obtained from Lüneburg, but after 1370 bay-salt appeared, from the Bay of Bourgneuf on the Atlantic coast of France. In the sixteenth century a source was found even farther south, at Brouage by Ile d'Oléron. It is peculiar that no mention is made of imports of herring, and that hops do not seem to have been bought from Lübeck.

GROWTH OF THE TOWNS

Needless to say, this commercial development was closely interrelated with the rise and growth of towns in Sweden, although actually commerce as well as town life existed there long before the Hansards.

The Vikings and even their predecessors had carried on an extensive overseas trade, active as well as passive. An early destination for this trade was Hedeby, a town in South Jutland which also went by the name of Slesvig; later there was direct commerce with the empire of the Franks. But as far as we can tell, the eastern routes leading through Russia to Byzantium and central Asia were more important. Alien merchants handling the western trade were mainly Frisians. From the east, too, foreign tradesmen came, some belonging to the Khazars, the strange merchants on the Caspian Sea, who demonstrably visited Sweden — one of them is even supposed to have been buried in the town of Birka, not very far from the present site of Stockholm. However, the eastern trade was largely active; it was conducted by Swedish wayfarers going east, not merely as Vikings but also as merchants, perhaps as a rule combining the two callings. The indisputable base for this trade was Gotland, as evidenced by the enormous quantities of foreign coins that have been found there; but the population along the Baltic coast of the Swedish mainland also took part in those exploits. In all likelihood, Swedish merchants turned southeast when the Arab advance barred the direct Mediterranean routes from central and southern Europe to the Orient. A quantitative estimate of this trade probably cannot be made. The only quantitative data relate to findings of coins, and to convert those into estimates of trade turnover is hardly feasible. Among the commodities in this traffic were two which have not since then been of consequence in northern countries — slaves and amber.

By the close of the Viking Age this trade came to a virtual end; practically no trace of it exists in the Middle Ages proper — hence the summary treatment it has received here in spite of its rather substantial significance in an earlier time. It is not easy to explain how the Swedes came to rid themselves so completely of their early commercial tradition and to become so dependent on the merchants of other nations. But that is what happened, and so we cannot, in a study of Swedish economic history, assign much importance to the mercantile ventures of the Vikings. The historical process must possess continuity in time and cannot be said to have been appreciably affected by isolated episodes which have left no legacy to the future.

Although the earliest Swedish towns grew out of the commerce of the Vikings, we find in the development of the towns themselves the continuity that was lacking in the development of foreign commerce.

The definition of a town is far from unequivocal, and the enormous literature on urban history, especially with reference to the rise of the towns, is actually concerned less with the economic or social aspects of the towns than with their juridical and political aspects. From an economic point of view a town may be adequately defined as a community which is dependent upon exchange with the outside world, primarily with the surrounding countryside but, in the case of the larger cities, also with more remote places. A town, in other words, is a community which is not self-sufficient, particularly with regard to food. But some communities of this kind are never conceived of as towns, so that for more precise identification we have to apply social criteria. Socially, towns are densely populated communities where the ratio of population to area considerably exceeds the average for the country as a whole. This very fact makes it impossible for the town to satisfy its own food requirements, for the production of food almost always requires more space. than other branches of industry. Such communities had been distinguished, legally and administratively, from the rural countryside and had been accorded the status of "immunities" even before comparable privileges were granted to the mining communities mentioned above.

Interest in urban development steadily increased until the middle of the seventeenth century, and privileges of township were conferred upon a great number of communities which were without any potentialities for urban economic development. These communities remained rural settlements equipped with the legal status of a town. Medieval cities rarely belonged to this category. Unlike many of the foundations of a later time, they had risen spontaneously, reflecting an existing need of one kind or another. Consequently, they possessed powers of survival frequently lacking in the more recently founded towns, of which few were destined ever to flourish.

For centuries to come, however, even the spontaneously rising towns were to preserve many rural features. Not only large numbers of livestock but also cultivated fields were often found within the town limits. In the reign of Gustavus Adolphus (1611–1632) and even later, Stockholm still had a large and varied animal stock. In the 1620's, for example, there were not only 300 horses and about 750 heads of cattle, but also a number of sheep and goats and almost 1,400 hogs.[20] Although it is difficult to estimate how many of those animals were kept on the island, "within the bridges," which constituted the nucleus of old Stockholm, undoubtedly most of them were. Hogs occupied a special position in view of their contribution to the problem of garbage disposal, if not necessarily to general cleanliness. Such conditions were apt to debase further the standards of hygiene which, hogs or no hogs, were highly unsatisfactory by modern tests. To accommodate the motley animal population, the narrow streets, still to be seen in the old parts of the city, were obviously inadequate. But other towns were even more rural in character, particularly where actual farming was practiced. In Härnösand, for instance, in the early years of the nineteenth century, the inhabitants neglected to ring the hogs, so that the animals rooted up the main square. In Piteå there were complaints as late as 1836 that "whole squads" of goats were roaming around the city, ruining, of all things, the rye fields.[21]

The oldest town on the Swedish mainland was Birka, situated on Björkö, an island in Lake Mälaren. Although its history falls almost entirely within the Viking age, the town is fairly well known through excavations. Birka was visited by Ansgarius, a missionary dispatched by Louis the Pious, on his two Swedish voyages around 830 and 850. It was probably founded earlier, though not before the late eighth century. After a few centuries it seems to have disappeared, leaving no trace above ground, to be succeeded almost immediately by nearby Sigtuna which still exists today as a tiny place where no one but schoolboys and tourists disturb the peace of monastic ruins. Other towns followed in relatively large numbers. In addition, there was Visby, on the island of Gotland; but Visby lay outside the main current of Swedish municipal development. It rapidly became the foremost commercial center of the Baltic, no doubt because of the Gotlanders' ancient position as leaders of Swedish merchants under the Vikings. Visby also was the site of a very early German settlement, probably the first within the area which now constitutes modern Sweden. The Germans, presumably attracted by opportunities for trade with the East, had arrived there by the twelfth century.

In the early Middle Ages municipal progress received new impetus. According to a tradition based mainly on the so-called Eric's Chronicle (about 1330), the regent Birger Jarl founded the city of Stockholm in the middle of the thirteenth century, though the evidence on this point is not at all conclusive. It is clear, however, that he conceived of a city plan which was to put its stamp on the city for a long time to come and that the city, if not newly founded, was much enlarged under his regency. The emergence of the mining industry in this period also contributed to the growth of towns throughout Svealand.

It would be highly interesting to know something about the size of those nascent towns, considering the fundamental importance of demographic conditions for the entire social framework. Unfortunately, no economic or social factor is harder to estimate; there are more pitfalls in census-making than a non-statistician could possibly imagine. The official Swedish vital statistics, which are by far the oldest in the world, lead back only to 1749, while estimates based on earlier materials will not carry us beyond 1720. For earlier times we have only farfetched inferences from scanty and inadequate data. This is particularly the case with regard to the population of entire provinces, though not even the population of smaller regions can be estimated on any but the weakest foundations. Still it may be mentioned that Henrik Schück has estimated the population of Stockholm in the fifteenth century, when in all probability it was the largest city in the country, at "a few thousands," which is unlikely to mean much more than four to five thousand.[22]

The main influence on the development of Swedish towns came from the Hanseatic merchants. At quite an early stage, many a townsman's name suggested German nationality. The Germans' interest in the Swedish mining industry caused them to settle inland as well as in the coastal towns. Thus all Swedish towns in the Middle Ages were under some German influence, and the increasing urbanization should probably be related to the Hansards' ever more extensive penetration inland. Characteristic of this situation is a proviso in the national City Code, adopted some time in the middle of the fourteenth century, according to which half the members of the town councils were to be Germans. Possibly the actual meaning of the provision was that *no more than half* of the councilors were to be German; hence it may have been designed to protect the interests of the Swedes. As a matter of fact, allegedly Swedish mayors and town councilors were often in reality German.

The Germans in Sweden showed neither eagerness nor ability for assimilation. Many of them continued to regard themselves as citizens of their German home towns and returned to spend their old days and be buried there. Those who remained were also very much inclined to emphasize their exclusiveness; even today the high-spired church of the German congregation in Stockholm stands as a memorial to that colony of aliens. The Germans' attitude reflected a strong sense of superiority; to the Hansards in general and especially to their powerful leaders from Lübeck, Sweden often appeared to be a colonial territory fit for exploitation only.

The growth of nationalistic sentiment in Sweden in the fifteenth century was accompanied by increasing resentment against foreign rulers. In the 1460's, a critic wrote: "The Master of the Mint is a German, the Collectors of Duties and Tolls are Germans, the Collector of Taxes is a German, so that for Swedes no office is left or open but that of executioner and of gravedigger." Eventually, in the patriotic fervor after the victory over the Danes at Brunkeberg in 1471, the old proviso about German magistrates was repealed. Probably, however, this did not greatly affect the Germans' commercial position. Throughout most of the sixteenth century the bulk of Swedish trade was with Lübeck and Danzig, and German merchants retained their lead for a long time to come.

Domestic trade was undoubtedly much more important than foreign trade although it has not attracted the same attention. In principle the right to trade was a privilege reserved for the burghers of the towns. Actually, domestic trade was largely carried on by peasants dividing their time between trading and farming, or traveling most of the time, leaving the care of the farm to the women and children. Rural trading or *landsköp*, as the phrase ran, was repeatedly outlawed ever since Magnus Ladulås (1279–1290), which probably did not affect its scope in the least.

## THE HANDICRAFT SYSTEM

The last sector of the superstructure of medieval economy was manufacturing. Handicraft, in the sense of industrial processing of raw materials, clearly antedates historic times; human needs for shelter, clothing and tools were satisfied even under the most primitive conditions. In a narrower sense, by the origin of crafts we mean the emergence of specialized artisans for whom the craft was an independent occupation rather than an occasional activity. Such specialization, too, is a very old phenomenon. The oldest of the artisans is probably the blacksmith whom ancient folklore often endowed with magic powers. In Sweden early manuscripts of the Provincial

Codes make relatively frequent mention not only of blacksmiths and locksmiths but also of silversmiths and goldsmiths, indicating their presence in the countryside as well. Other craftsmen, like carpenters, bakers, tailors, and shoemakers, are mentioned only in relatively late manuscripts of the Codes. Insofar as these occupations existed in rural areas, they indicate a division of labor within the rural community. The peasants were so many and the towns so few that the rise of specialized craftsmen in the villages themselves could not be prevented in spite of repeated serious attempts in this direction.

But craftsmen were, relatively speaking, far more numerous in the towns. Artisans probably constituted the largest occupational group in the cities. So it is not surprising to find much more frequent reference to crafts in the town laws. In the towns, particularly in Stockholm, differentiation into separate crafts was already so extreme in the early Middle Ages that for centuries there were comparatively few additions of new occupations except when new trades arose or some additional function was transferred from households to professionals. Presumably, town craftsmen did not cater to the farmers except when the latter visited fairs and marts in the towns. Otherwise their customers were the burghers of the town, the nobility and the gentry, and the clergy. Even in the towns, professional bakers and brewers did not for a long time put an end to the corresponding domestic work, and the same may have been true for butchers. In the countryside, these and other functions were retained within the household to a much larger extent. Thus, despite the weakness of specialized rural handicraft, there was no large rural demand for products of the towns.

Professional craftsmen operated on an extremely small scale. As a rule, a medieval craftsman presumably had no helpers outside the family, and for a fairly long time after the end of the Middle Ages it was quite exceptional for him to have both a journeyman and an apprentice. The prominence which our sources accord to the institution of apprenticeship results primarily from the fact that the exceptional cases attracted attention and regulation.

One must not confuse the discussion of handicraft with that of craft organization. The organization of Scandinavian crafts was a late phenomenon in comparison with central and western Europe and hardly ever attained the strength which characterized the guilds

Coins from the Vasa period. *Kungl. Myntkabinettet.*

Gustavus Vasa. Portrait by anonymous artist.

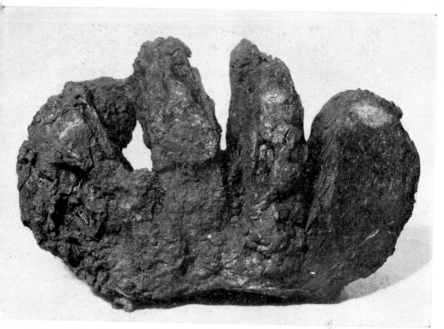

A lump of malleable iron ("freshed") found in Småland. *Kalmar Museum.*

Copper making at Stora Kopparberg. From a map of 1683.

From the copper mint at Avesta: furnace (A), various hand tools, and an anvil (K) for the finishing of coins stricken under a water-driven hammer (not shown). Detail from ink drawing by Anton Swab, 1723.
*Kungl. Biblioteket.*

in other European countries. For natural reasons, craft organization was practically non-existent in rural communities where each village would have, at most, a single artisan in the more basic crafts; and rural life remained more fundamental to Sweden than to most countries in central and western Europe. But even in the towns guilds were late to develop. The national City Code does not mention them, and, as further indication of their subordinate position, the same code delegated the task of industrial regulation to mayors and town councils, though this was one of the main functions of the guild system elsewhere. The oldest preserved charter for a Swedish craft guild, granted to the tailors in Stockholm, dates from 1356. The *universitas sartorum,* as the tailor guild is referred to in the Latin text, was by no means a sartorial academy, but the Latin description of the guild is a useful reminder that our universities are the only surviving organizations to have preserved the corporate features of the medieval guilds. Toward the end of the Middle Ages we find twelve to fifteen craft guilds mentioned in the city chronicles (*tänkeböcker*) of Stockholm, so that by then the institution had evidently become fairly well consolidated.[23]

## MONEY

A country's monetary system generally occupies a rather special position among its economic institutions. As we pointed out in connection with natural economy, money has repercussions in all areas of the economy while at the same time it is more purely economic in character than any other social phenomenon. Hence it calls for separate treatment.

The Swedish monetary system in the Middle Ages was not very different from that of other countries.[24] Swedish coins had been minted under Olof Skötkonung in the Viking Age, and we can assume that his coins really served as a medium of exchange, although their quantity was insignificant. But this was a short episode and it was not until the end of the twelfth century under Knut Eriksson that domestic coinage was resumed.

Although domestic money was issued only sporadically, we cannot assume that there was no currency in circulation during the long spells when Swedish coins were not available. Foreign currencies circulated freely ever since money came into general use, in part owing to the mechanics of foreign trade, and particularly to the absence of credit transactions. Sweden was a remote country, and bills of exchange did not make their appearance until a late date. Since imported goods could not be paid for indirectly by exported goods through bills of exchange, both types of goods had to meet at the same trading place at one and the same time. In reality, however, foreign coins often had to be accepted if no suitable counterparts in goods were to be found.

The same thing occurred in countries with domestic coinage, which produced a mixed circulation of foreign and domestic currencies. In addition, foreign coins of high quality were much in demand for hoarding purposes. But if money in circulation tended to become short because of insufficient coinage, foreign money would be deliberately imported in exchange for goods. Such an import of money would take place either spontaneously, by an increase in exports and a decline in imports in consequence of the low domestic price level (the classic case of the specie-flow price mechanism); or else, if exports could not or were not allowed to expand, by the authorities' decision to acquire foreign money and to curtail importation of goods. One way of implementing such decisions was to force merchants to surrender part of their customs duties in silver (the so-called *silver-växel*).

The demand for money, in turn, depended on two factors — the extent to which payments in money had displaced barter economy, and the general level of prices. It is true that constant complaints about scarcity of money must be interpreted with the greatest caution; they might often indicate mere dissatisfaction with levels of personal income. More convincing evidence of scarcity of money in the proper sense is the complaint that money was so short that people "could not get away from each other," that is that they were unable to make their wealth transferable, the low liquidity thus constituting various restraints upon mobility.

Under this arrangement the supply of money must have been very irregular, and the supply of Swedish currency even more so. Coins from Gotland were used in Östergötland and the southern stretches of the Baltic coast; Danish coins were used in Småland and Västergötland; coins from Reval were current in Finland. The only regions where domestic Swedish currency predominated were Svealand and

Norrland. The absence of national Swedish coins in other sections of the country doubtless stemmed in part from the existence of local currency systems in the individual provinces.

As far back as monetary denominations are known to us, the *mark* was the basic unit as well as the highest. Practically always, it contained eight *öre*, and one *öre* contained three *örtug*. The lowest unit was always the *penning*, but the size of the penning varied in the individual local currency systems. In Svealand there were eight penning to one örtug, in Götaland sixteen, and on Gotland twelve. The Svealand system was to become generally accepted in the beginning of the fifteenth century.

Originally the mark was a unit of weight, just as the pound (*libra*) which was the base of the old French *livre* as well as of the still surviving pound sterling. The weight of the mark is nowadays always assumed to have been 210.6 grams (somewhat less than seven Troy ounces), or almost exactly nine-tenths of the widely used Cologne mark. Most writers have assumed that the coin was initially identical with its weight in silver, in other words, that the mark piece contained about 211 grams of reasonably fine silver.

But it is quite certain that a coin weighing almost half a pound of highly valued silver was never used. In fact, mark pieces were never struck as long as this standard prevailed. In the Middle Ages mark coins appeared in circulation only once (in 1512), and only after the debasement of the currency had greatly reduced the weight of the mark. For a long time the only pieces struck were penning coins.

Whereas this currency was at least conceptually related to the unit of one mark of fine silver, there is no evidence in historical time of any correspondence between mark pieces and mark weights. On the contrary, a passage in the code of the province of Östergötland indicates that in Birger Jarl's reign (in the middle of the thirteenth century) two marks in coins made one mark in silver. The result was an utterly confusing double standard which prevailed as long as the mark was the basis of the currency. From our point of view the system has an advantage, for the changing ratio between the two standards provides us with a simple measure of the silver content of the coins. Occasionally the expression *mark lödig* (mark sterling) was used for the standard weight in silver, and *mark penningar* for the currency unit. When the örtug became the standard piece, *mark penningar* was replaced by *mark örtug*. These units of reckoning represented, in accordance with the relations mentioned above, 192 penningar and 24 örtug respectively.

The debasement of the currency which took place in Sweden, as practically everywhere else, found expression in the increasing number of mark penningar or mark örtug contained in one mark lödig. To trace the course of this debasement in full would serve little purpose. Yet it may be pointed out that immediately before 1520 no less than sixteen to eighteen mark in coin were required to make one mark in silver, which implies a decline to one-eighth or one-ninth of the relation prevailing in the thirteenth century. This measure, paradoxically enough, more clearly reveals the economic significance of the process than a mere analysis of the silver content of the pieces which were in fact struck. For reasons to be explained shortly, the purchasing power of the coins in actual trading transactions may have been higher than their silver content alone would indicate.

Those who debased the currency in the Middle Ages faced a task infinitely more difficult than their modern successors. A German mark note issued in 1913 and one issued in November 1923 look almost identical. But in 1923 the old note was worth no more than the new one, although it originally had had a purchasing power about 1,000,000,000,000 times higher than in 1923. In other words, it had become completely worthless without any particular change in its appearance. This was achieved simply by printing a great many similar notes, and the result was possible because the face value of paper money bears no relation to its intrinsic value. When, on the other hand, the value of the currency is related to its substance, new coins with a lower metal content than the old ones will not depress the value of the old issue to the level of the new.

The rulers who were perpetually debasing their currencies therefore had to take care to call in the old coins and to convert them into new and inferior issues. Otherwise gains from the debasement would have remained limited, and the difficulties in finding sufficient raw material for new coinage would have been formidable. To the extent that the old currency was not entirely withdrawn, as was certainly the rule, old coins were melted down into plate by the holders and either exported or hoarded. But old coins might also continue to circulate, at a premium. This made it necessary to specify whether payment was to be made in old or new coin, or in the coin of a certain regent or of a certain year. And even more important, it would now take a larger number of the new coins struck to equal an undebased unit, whether it existed only ideally, for accounting purposes, or was actually coined. Thus the örtug would be worth ten or eighteen newly struck penning but only eight of the old. Hence the techniques and effects of debasement were enormously complicated in comparison with modern nominal currencies, so that the very difficulties in debasing the currency tended to prevent inflations of such excessive dimensions as paper money has occasionally given rise to.

Generally, the value of coins on a metallic standard cannot greatly deviate for any length of time from that of their metallic content, but one exception is worth mentioning. The right of coinage was the prerogative of the Royal Mint, and individuals possessed no right to have their plate struck into coin. In such conditions, the minter was in a position to raise the value of the coins over and above their metallic value simply by curtailing the issue. Certainly this was not common practice, for usually the minters were too pressed for money to feel tempted to restrict the issue. However, there is at least one important instance in which such a restriction was undertaken, toward the end of the reign of Gustavus Vasa, after his last depreciation of the currency in the 1540's.

## SUMMARY

To summarize, it may be said that medieval Sweden was in a far more primitive stage of economic development than most countries in western and central Europe. This relative backwardness was to be diminished in the following periods. The use of money as a generalized medium of exchange was steadily increasing elsewhere in the last centuries of the Middle Ages, in England even earlier; but there is no indication of any similar development in Sweden. It is perhaps still more significant that in the rest of Europe the late Middle Ages were a time of rapidly expanding navigation, communication, and commerce, domestic as well as international. On these foundations arose what might be fairly called the early capitalistic era or the period of commercial capitalism. Sweden was almost entirely barred from the Mediterranean and Atlantic commerce which provided the stimulus for those mercantile advances. The Swedish share consisted in the crumbs that fell from the table of the Hansards. To them Sweden was a trading area rather than a trading partner. Except for the Hanseatic League, the only source of foreign influence was the church, the only substantial international power of the Middle Ages. In the main Sweden led an isolated existence. Nevertheless, foreign impact did produce important changes, particularly with regard to the development of the towns, the emergence of specialized crafts and craft guilds and of a mining industry based on domestic resources but organized and financed by the Hansards.

Generally speaking, Sweden had apparently relapsed into stagnation after the Vikings' era of vigorous activity, when ties with other countries must have been quite strong, although nothing is known about the actual extent of commerce in that period.

A final, fairly self-evident observation is that the devastating feuds raging throughout the late Middle Ages* must have retarded the country's economic development and prevented the undisturbed growth of industry and trade. This question is still entirely unexplored; even the pertinent problems have hardly been formulated. It may be quite difficult to find a satisfactory basis for any clear-cut answer, though intensive research should certainly add considerably to our knowledge of this period. Until then we must assume, if merely on the basis of sweeping analogies, that the wars of independence wrought great hardships for the masses of the Swedish people.

* *Translator's note:* After the conquest of Sweden in 1389 by a Danish-Norwegian army under Queen Margaret, the three Scandinavian countries were united under common rule, the so-called Kalmar Union. The predominant partner was Denmark, and Danish bailiffs, sent to Sweden, made themselves hated by the peasants who in the 1430's rose against foreign rule. For the better part of a century the struggle for independence flared in repeated revolts followed by Danish retribution. The Kings of the Union thus alternated with Swedish Lord-Protectors as rulers of the country. After the execution by the Danes of Swedish nationalist leaders in the "massacre of Stockholm" in 1520, a national rebellion broke out which resulted in the final defeat of the Danes, the dissolution of the Union, and the elevation of the Lord-Protector, Gustavus Vasa, to the Swedish throne.

# CHAPTER 3

# THE MATURITY OF THE
# MEDIEVAL ECONOMY (1520–1600)

## GENERAL FEATURES

PARADOXICALLY, the era of Gustavus Vasa, with its deliberate and systematic attempts to preserve and reinforce the basic character of the medieval economy, opens up a new page in Swedish economic history. It is precisely the government's sustained and vigorous effort to strengthen the existing structure of society that separates the sixteenth century from its predecessors.

In all probability, the new policies were associated with a rapid rise in levels of consumption, particularly around the middle of the century. It is natural to assume that a period of prolonged peace should materially increase standards of welfare as compared with the devastating effects of the wars of independence. Nevertheless, as was pointed out at the end of the last chapter, our knowledge of the previous era is so negligible in this respect that no quantitative conclusion can be expected.

The reign of Gustavus may have brought a prosperity unknown under the earlier rulers, something the king never allowed his subjects to forget. But those improvements were attained within the essentially undisturbed framework of the traditional economy, and economic policy continued to be guided by a strictly medieval conception of economic life. The economic views held by the rulers of the country were hardly more advanced than those of the population at large; if anything, economic ideology tended to lag behind economic reality. This is especially true of Gustavus Vasa himself, and somewhat less so of his three sons. There was a good deal of the Renaissance about Eric XIV (1560–1568) and John III (1568–1592); and Charles IX (1604–1611), who was a Calvinist, differed from his father not only in his religious orientation but also in his strong dependence upon German economic thought, presumably because of his two German marriages. The last decades of the century, therefore, brought substantial changes. I have chosen, however, to relegate at least some of those to the following period so as to simplify our bird's-eye view of the sixteenth century.

NATIONAL SELF-SUFFICIENCY

There was no particular change in the degree of national self-sufficiency during the sixteenth century. The following table of the composition of imports through the ports of Stockholm, Gävle, and Söderköping, in 1559, may be taken as a fairly accurate picture of the country's total imports. Corresponding figures for 1928 have been introduced for the sake of comparison.

TABLE 2.   COMMODITY COMPOSITION OF SWEDISH IMPORTS IN THE
REIGN OF GUSTAVUS VASA AND IN MODERN TIMES
*Percentages*

| | Via Stockholm, Gävle, and Söderköping, 1559 | | Total Imports, 1928 | |
|---|---|---|---|---|
| Salt | 24.7 | | 0.2 | |
| Hops | 18.8 | | 0.2 | |
| Dry goods and spices | 11.8 | | 7.9 | |
| Textiles | 35.8 | | 10.7 | |
| Cloth | | 25.1 | | 1.7 |
| Wadmal and linen | | 6.4 | | |
| Silk, etc. | | 4.3 | | 0.8 |
| Beverages | 3.9 | | 1.1 | |
| Beer | | 2.4 | | |
| Wine | | 1.5 | | 0.5 |
| Total | 95.0 | | 20.1 | |

Source: Customs Accounts, first collected by Hans Forssell, but amplified and elaborated in Heckscher, *Sveriges ekonomiska historia från Gustav Vasa*, I:1, p. 39, and Appendix V, pp. 19–29.

Whereas the prominence accorded to salt and hops has of course no counterpart in modern times, between the fourteenth and the sixteenth centuries not much had changed. (See page 48.) The proportion of salt in 1559 was practically the same as in the table for imports from Lübeck to Stockholm in 1368. That table contained no reference to hops, probably only because hops were not taken from

Lübeck. On the other hand, textiles, which claimed by far the major share in 1559, seem to have grown in importance, although there is no certainty that the figures for 1368 represented normal conditions. Besides those three main items, spices were the only import commodity of any consequence in 1559. In 1928, the four items (salt, hops, textiles, and spices) taken together represented less than one-fifth of all imports, in other words, less than salt alone in the sixteenth century.

Aside from salt and hops, most imported wares in the sixteenth century were essentially luxuries, consumed by the court and the aristocracy. Silk, for instance, occupied a conspicuous position, considering the small volume of trade. The royal family's and the court's demand for imported articles was probably a significant factor in Gustavus' absorbing interest in foreign trade and in Sweden's "liberation" from the Lübeck merchants. Nowadays, Swedish imports consist mainly of raw materials and semi-finished goods, while imports of consumers' goods have been reduced to relative insignificance.

The composition of exports shown in the following table reveals a much closer resemblance to modern conditions, at least for the most important item which, then as now, was iron. Exports of this metal accounted for one-fourth to one-third of all exports. On the other hand, by-products of livestock farming, such as fats and hides, were far more important, partly for the reasons referred to in connection with medieval agriculture.

In exports as in imports the composition of trade in 1559 was fairly similar to that of 1368 (page 48), although in the meantime, toward the end of the fifteenth century, Sweden had exported practically nothing but metals. On the whole, however, the export structure from the Middle Ages to modern times shows much more stability than the import structure, thus reflecting the degree to which Sweden's economy has been shaped by her natural resources.

The "liberation" from the Hansa did not alter the fact that foreign trade continued to be handled by foreign merchants with their own ships and to move, by and large, within the Baltic basin. Nor was Gustavus anxious to see any change in this. A believer in passive trade, he discouraged rather than promoted Swedish navigation and was fairly indifferent to the prospect of trading across the

TABLE 3. COMMODITY COMPOSITION OF SWEDISH EXPORTS IN THE
REIGN OF GUSTAVUS VASA AND IN MODERN TIMES
*Percentages*

|  | 1559 |  | 1928 |
|---|---|---|---|
| Copper | 5.6 |  |  |
| Iron | 28.7 |  | 28.3 |
| Osmund |  | 23.9 |  |
| Bar iron |  | 4.8 |  |
| Fats | 24.7 |  | 3.4 |
| Butter |  | 17.5 |  |
| Oil, lard, suet, tallow |  | 7.2 |  |
| Hides, skins, and furs | 22.8 |  | 2.0 |
| Hides and skins |  | 18.7 |  |
| Furs |  | 3.5 |  |
| Grain and flour | 4.0 |  | 1.4 |
| Fish | 1.4 |  |  |
| Wax | 0.3 |  |  |
| Textile raw materials | 0.2 |  |  |
| Wood | 11.6 |  | 43.1 |
| Tar | 1.1 |  |  |
| Thaler coins | 0.2 |  |  |
| Total | 100.0 |  | 100.0 |

Source: Customs Accounts, first collected by Hans Forssell, but amplified and elaborated in Heckscher, *Sveriges ekonomiska historia från Gustav Vasa*, I:1, p. 55.

North Sea. On the other hand, he probably did wish to pit the Dutch and the Scots against the Hansards. Presumably, he found it useful to hold a threat over Lübeck and Danzig without impairing their position as preëminent trading partners. A change did not occur until the end of the century, when North Sea crossings became common. The figures in Table 4 show the relative standing of North Sea trade in the imports to Stockholm between 1571 and 1620.

TABLE 4. STOCKHOLM'S IMPORTS FROM NORTH SEA PORTS
*Percentages of Stockholm's total imports*

|  | 1571 | 1581 | 1585 | 1590 | 1600 | 1610 | 1620 |
|---|---|---|---|---|---|---|---|
| North Sea trade | 4.8 | 8.4 | 9.7 | 11.9 | 19.6 | 29.6 | 31.7 |
| Of which from Holland | 2.7 | 7.4 | 4.8 | 9.5 | 10.3 | 16.6 | 26.6 |

Source: Customs Accounts, first collected by Hans Forssell, but amplified and elaborated in Heckscher, *Sveriges ekonomiska historia från Gustav Vasa*, Appendix V, p. 5.

THE GUIDING PRINCIPLES OF ECONOMIC POLICY

The purely medieval character of Gustavus' economic policy was fully reflected in his attitude toward natural economy. Money interested him mainly for the purpose of hoarding. At his castles in Stockholm and elsewhere he assembled a sizable treasure, which was to melt away rapidly under Eric XIV, because of the strain of the Danish war.* For spending purposes Gustavus preferred goods to money. When once he was faced with what he called a "huge outlay" he expressly decided to levy a certain fine in kind rather than in money. Treasure was not to be wasted on spending.

There was an illuminating contrast between this view and the one that would prevail with mercantilist statesmen like Colbert, the famous Minister of Finance of Louis XIV. Colbert undertook to determine French currency requirements on the basis of his sovereign's needs for expenditure. He assumed that government expenditure was limited by the available money supply, thus overlooking the velocity of money and many other complicating factors. The contrast between Gustavus' views and those of Colbert partly reflects the great difference between the Swedish economy of the first half of the sixteenth century and the French economy of the last half of the seventeenth century, especially with regard to the role of money. But it also denotes a fundamental difference in economic thought. Despite its complicated mechanics, natural economy offered a clearer view of economic problems. The veil of money did not obscure underlying realities. As a matter of fact, Gustavus Vasa often revealed an insight into economic processes unmatched by most of his successors.

The field of foreign trade is another case in point. The medieval attitude to foreign trade was in sharp contrast to that of mercantilism. As long as domestic commodities were directly exchanged for foreign goods, everyone was bound to understand the fact that importation was the sole purpose of exportation. Imports were the end, and exports nothing but a means to attain it. Gustavus always tended

* *Translator's note:* In 1563, conflicting land claims of Denmark and Sweden resulted in an attack by Denmark, then allied with Poland against Sweden. This so-called "Northern Seven Years War" was ended by a peace treaty in 1570, after the deposition of Eric XIV and the accession of John III.

to obstruct exports; export permits were granted only to those merchants who had previously imported useful commodities and promised to keep on doing so in the future. A mercantilist statesman would have acted in the opposite fashion.

In the finances of the crown Gustavus introduced a previously unknown rigor and precision, though still within the boundaries of natural economy.[1] He exercised incessant control over governors, bailiffs, and other officers, constantly impressing upon them their duty to promote the interests of the crown. Concern with the revenue of the crown and of the House of Vasa overshadowed everything else. Still, the population stood to benefit from the firm control over government finance. It had particularly far-reaching consequences in two main respects.

In the first place, the crown was continually seeking to sell the goods constituting its tax revenue at the highest price possible. A born merchant, Gustavus always eagerly followed price movements and supply conditions in different parts of the country, and when he discovered a favorable market he would order shipments to that area to be sold there to the highest bidder. Similarly, the king managed the country's export trade in a very personal manner. In selling the commodities of the crown which made up the bulk of total exports, Gustavus was an unscrupulous haggler, but so, presumably, were the foreign merchants with whom he dealt. He also tried to secure favorable bargains for his own subjects, although he had an extremely low opinion of their mercantile talents. Tartly he remarked that they "throng and battle for the goods that strangers carry into the realm as would starving pigs for draff and mash." This view probably contributed to his predilection for passive trade. As long as the aliens came to Swedish ports, he and his governors were able to keep the thumb on them and their Swedish colleagues in a way which would not have been possible abroad.

Gustavus' ceaseless trading throughout the country produced a vivid concern with internal communications. At that very time German princes undertook to obstruct interregional trade in foodstuffs, a policy which was initiated to prevent food shortages but in reality aggravated them. Gustavus was never tempted to imitate such policies which would have been in direct opposition to his own interests since trade in foodstuffs was one of his main preoccupations. It is not difficult to imagine what this policy meant for the internal trade of the sparsely settled country with its miserable roads.

In the second place, Gustavus' eagerness to promote the economic interests of crown and House led to the so-called reversion of church lands to the crown, probably the most important aspect of the Reformation to Gustavus. The church was deprived of all its landed property. To some small extent it was taken over by the temporal lords, but the major part was retained by the king, who offered the most tenuous arguments in order to prove that church estates originally had belonged to his family and therefore were his rightful possessions.

Distribution of land ownership by categories of owners at the end of the Middle Ages has already been discussed. The following table indicates the result of Gustavus' policy. (No distinction is made between the holdings of the crown, called the *kronojord*, and the personal possessions of the House of Vasa.)

TABLE 5.  DISTRIBUTION OF LAND OWNERSHIP IN SWEDEN
*Percentages*

|  | At the end of the Middle Ages | At the death of Gustavus Vasa |
| --- | --- | --- |
| Crown (*kronojord*) | 5.5 | 28.2 |
| Church (*kyrkojord*) | 21.0 | |
| Nobility (*frälsejord*) | 21.8 | 22.4 |
| Peasants (*skattejord*) | 51.7 | 49.4 |
| Total | 100.0 | 100.0 |

Source: Tables presented in my *Economic History of Sweden* on the basis of materials contained in Forssell's *Sveriges Inre Historia från Gustaf den Förste*, Vol. I (Stockholm, 1869), Appendix, corrected in accordance with later criticism. See *Sveriges ekonomiska historia från Gustav Vasa*, Vol. I:1, Appendix IV, p. 14.

The figures show that the lords had gained very little whereas the crown and the House of Vasa had increased their share fivefold. The peasants had actually lost somewhat in relative standing, but on the whole succeeded in maintaining their old position.

The qualities shown by Gustavus Vasa as a framer of economic policies, or rather, as a great business manager in control of the Swedish economy, are perhaps best epitomized by saying that he managed to combine an incomparable shrewdness with an almost complete lack of economic imagination. The type of society in which he had grown up was to him the only conceivable one. His thinking was shaped by it, and all his reforms were intended to perfect and to raise it to the highest possible efficiency, primarily for the benefit of the crown (including himself), and secondarily for that of his subjects. There was literally no sphere of economic activity which Gustavus did not claim to understand better than his subjects, be it agriculture, trade, manufacturing, shipping, mining, coinage, or anything else. Our knowledge of the Swedish economy in his days very largely relies on his own letters,[2] which sometimes makes it difficult to evaluate the quality of his judgment. The letters, by the way, which are distinguished by a sardonic and vituperative sense of humor, compare favorably with the correspondence of far more famous rulers. But although his vision was so often obstructed by preconceptions flowing from vested interest or prejudice, the total impression of an extraordinary and universal familiarity with the economy of the country is overwhelming. Considering that before his accession his opportunities to gain such insights had been quite limited, he must have spent his reign in study of nearly every single branch of the economy. No other Swedish ruler even remotely compares with him in economic understanding; more than anyone else he represents the practical economist on the throne. In consequence he occupies a unique position in the economic history of Sweden. His limitations were such as could be expected in these circumstances: a doctrinaire's — or an idealist's — adherence to the past, and a deficient sense for the requirements of foreign policy and conditions in other countries. For the economic policy of his time, however, the latter shortcoming was of no particular significance.

NATIONAL PROSPERITY

The upshot was a remarkable increase in the prosperity of the Swedish people. Unhampered by soldiers and bandits, the peasant was allowed to plow, sow, and reap his harvest. In the words of the Swedish poet Geijer, he could "till his blood-sprayed lands."

But though it was prosperity, in many ways it remained a very primitive prosperity. Food was still salted and dried and, what was worse, consisted of a very small number of foodstuffs which were consumed in enormous quantities: bread, salted and dried meat and fish, and salted butter. If it is correct that progress, material and also spiritual, consists in increased differentiation, then such a consumption pattern must be described as barbarous.

The most illuminating picture of sixteenth-century food habits is provided by the food budget for the castles and domains of the crown in 1573. It refers to consumption by as many as 5,675 in-

TABLE 6. FOOD BUDGETS FOR ROYAL CASTLES AND MANORS IN 1573, COMPARED WITH AVERAGES FOR SWEDEN IN 1912–13

*Calories per person and day*

| Commodities | Male and female agricultural servants | The royal court | King Eric (deposed) and his keepers | Duke Magnus and his court | Averages for total population 1912–13 |
|---|---|---|---|---|---|
| Cereals | 2,370 | 2,870 | 3,105 | 4,195 | 1,795 |
| Potatoes | — | — | — | — | 328 |
| Total | 2,370 | 2,870 | 3,105 | 4,195 | 2,123 |
| Sugar | — | — | — | — | 354 |
| Other vegetable foodstuffs | 40 | — | — | — | 138 |
| Meat and pork | 540 | 945 | 855 | 935 | 577 |
| Milk | — | — | — | — | 749 |
| Butter | 155 | 305 | 305 | 300 | 317 |
| Cheese | 5 | — | — | 10 | 39 |
| Eggs | — | — | — | — | 21 |
| Fish | 370 | 450 | 450 | 325 | 58 |
| Total | 3,480 | 4,570 | 4,715 | 5,765 | 4,376 |
| Beer | 835 | 1,815 | 1,815 | 1,670 | 26 |
| Grand total | 4,315 | 6,385 | 6,530 | 7,435 | 4,402 |

Sources: *Rikshufvudboken för 1573 jämte sammandrag av rikshufvudboken för 1582* (The National Ledger for the year 1573 and a Summary of that for 1582), published in *Historiska handlingar*, XII:1, 1883. Caloric equivalents and figures for 1912–13 from *Folknäringen vid krig* (The Food Situation in Wartime), Vol. IV of the reports of *Statens krigsberedskapskommission* (The Royal Committee on War-Preparedness), Stockholm, 1918.

dividuals and must without any doubt be considered quite representative. It also enables us to distinguish between the menial servants and various groups of higher status. In the following table the 1573 diet (in caloric values) may be compared with the corresponding averages for Sweden in 1912–13.

As the figures show, the diet of menial servants contained only a few per cent less calories than the average diet in 1912–13, and that of the court was almost 50 per cent higher. If beer is excluded, the picture becomes less favorable for 1573, but even then the servants' daily consumption amounted to almost 3,500 calories per person.

Considering that subsistence requirements are generally estimated as 3,000–3,300 calories per person a day, the food situation in the sixteenth century, on the basis of these figures, was apparently remarkably satisfactory. But the monotony of that diet is evident; and again it must be remembered that nearly all the food of the plain people was salted or dried. The court and the lords would eat mainly fresh food. The enormous quantities consumed must have included what was lavished upon their guests; on the other hand the members of the court were in turn entertained by the lords, and we are forced to conclude that the consumption of solid foods in this group was fabulously high. Similarly, beer consumption of the courts amounted to 1,700–1,800 calories a day, contrasting with an average of 26 calories in 1912–13. It is probable that the lords constantly reveled in food and drink in a way which was beyond the reach of the peasants except at special celebrations. The high mortality and generally poor health were certainly related to the gluttony of the age. For the peasants, a harvest failure would mean a reduction of the food consumption below its normal level; however, in the late sixteenth century famines seem to have been rarer than in many a later period.

## THE METAL INDUSTRIES[3]

The only field of economic activity in which an essential advance was made in Gustavus' reign was the iron industry. This was the sole area in which Gustavus wished for a departure from medieval tradition, but when he wanted something he wanted it badly — *quod vult, valde vult*. His eagerness was great, and he contributed not a little to the change by importing and employing German ironmakers who built both public and private ironworks.

We have already described how the blast furnace had been introduced by the middle of the fifteenth century, at the latest. The innovation promoted by Gustavus related to the second part of the indirect process of ironmaking, in which pig iron was "freshened" or "fined" into a malleable product. In contemporary eyes the reform amounted to the substitution of a new product for the old

Water-driven ore conveyor, designed by Christopher Polhem for the mine at Stora K

opparberg. Drawing by Samuel Sohlberg, 1731. *Kommerskollegii Gruvkartekontor.*

osmund iron. Since the new product was shaped into bars rather than *osmundar*, it was called bar iron. This was to become one of Sweden's most famous staples.[4]

The price paid for bar iron was about twice as high as that of osmund iron, and with Gustavus, as later with Charles IX, that seems to have been the main reason for their interest in the shift, although price alone is clearly not a criterion of profitability. Occasionally, bar iron is mentioned in the late 1520's; however, it probably did not come into its own until shortly after 1540. Toward the end of the century, the manufacture of bar iron was given new stimulus by a Dutchman named Willem van Wijk. Wijk was first in the service of the Duke of Södermanland (later Charles IX); after a disagreement with the Duke he allied himself with King John III. Under John he made his most important contribution, the organization of the ironworks at Dannemora in the province of Uppland where the purity of the ore was such that Dannemora iron established itself as the best Swedish iron by far. In comparison, the development of the iron industry in the province of Värmland, which was pressed by the Duke of Södermanland, remained fairly insignificant during the period. Värmland was to assume a dominating position in Swedish ironmaking, but not until the late seventeenth century; the praise that has so often and undeservedly been lavished on Charles IX for his policy on this point is merely another expression of a widespread tendency to elevate him at the expense of his brothers, Eric XIV and John III.

The transition to bar iron manufacture was far from rapid. Not until around 1600 did bar iron overtake osmund iron in export value, and since its price was twice as high the quantity exported amounted to only about half that of the older product. In aggregate production, the predominance of osmund iron was probably even greater because more of it was consumed at home. But there are no data to confirm this supposition. The better part of a century was to elapse before osmund disappeared.

The introduction of hammer works for bar iron production represented perhaps the first step toward a more capitalistic industrial organization. Private ironmakers still operated on a fairly small scale, although there had been a considerable increase in the size of their furnaces. However, a great number of hammer works were operated by the crown. That these establishments appeared quite large, even far too large, to Gustavus himself is evident from a letter to his principal assistant, the German ironmaster Markus Klingensten. Gustavus complained that Klingensten was proceeding "too rashly in proposing to place two hammers in one building, for which purpose you want to build a house large enough for a cathedral."

The copper industry received even more of Gustavus' attention than the iron industry, but it resisted his attempts at reorganization and presented the picture of an industry in decline. Yet in the last two decades of the century it recovered spectacularly under the impact of an enormous price rise, when Spain, the leading nation of the period and owner of the richest silver mines of the world, unexpectedly adopted a monetary system that for all practical purposes amounted to a copper standard. At the same time, the influx of silver from the New World depressed the Swedish silver industry even further. The expansion of the iron and copper industries resulted in an unprecedented upswing in exports and foreshadowed the industrial change of the following period.

## REGULATION OF INDUSTRY AND TRADE

In the field of economic regulation, Gustavus' notions were entirely in line with his general medieval orientation. He was a convinced exponent of the traditional principle that the so-called urban industries — commerce, shipping, and handicraft — should be confined to the towns. The perennial problem was how to suppress rural trade. The peasants had an ineradicable propensity to trade among themselves rather than to carry their products to the market towns and make their purchases there. But, despite his strong opposition to rural trade, Gustavus took no radical measures against it. Although he issued a torrent of decrees outlawing it, he would explain, as he once did in reply to a complaint from the burghers of Stockholm, that it was as difficult to exterminate rural trade as to "catch all the wolves of the woods." [5] Thoroughly realistic, he generally accepted the requirements of expediency.

Under his sons, particularly Charles IX, policies with regard to the cities became more and more consistent. To a large extent they were patterned upon North German municipal policies, but with an important difference. In Germany, privileges had been granted to individual towns separately, and the nature of the privileges differed, offering a fairly confused picture. Swedish policy was carried out on a national scale and followed a general plan.

This was especially the case with what was known as the staple policy. The principle of this policy was to make the town a staple (entrepôt). All trade had to pass through the staple; merchants had to offer their goods for sale there or use the services of the townsmen in having them carried on to other markets. Swedish cities were divided into two categories: staple cities and inland cities (*uppstä-der*), the right to oversea trade being reserved for the staple cities which were generally situated on the coast. The inland cities were allowed domestic trade only, and not even this without certain limitations. Magnus Eriksson's medieval City Code had already contained the germ of what was to be called the Bothnian trading restriction,[6] according to which Sweden's cities north of Stockholm and Finnish cities north of Åbo were enjoined from direct trade with the regions south of these two staple cities.

Under Gustavus Vasa the staple policy was not rigorously pursued. His successors applied it more systematically, until a definitive classification of staple and inland cities was finally laid down by Gustavus Adolphus in the early years of his reign (1614 and 1617). With few changes, that classification persisted until 1765 and, in some respects, longer than that; even today only certain cities are "staple cities" in the sense of being equipped with their own customs houses. Charles IX, father of Gustavus Adolphus and an extreme doctrinaire in matters of economic policy, made a few attempts (first in a memorandum of 1595)[7] to render the system still more rigorous. According to him, Stockholm was to be the only Swedish staple. This extreme plan was never executed, but the tendency of the ruler to favor Stockholm over the other staple cities remained as pronounced as the general inclination to favor staple cities at the expense of inland cities.

Another main field of municipal policy was the regulation of the craft guilds. Their position did not particularly change under Gustavus Vasa; however, in 1576 Prince Charles, Duke of Södermanland, introduced in his duchy a stern regulation[8] of the guilds which explicitly followed German models. He went so far as to prescribe a *numerus clausus* limiting the number of craftsmen in the different

trades so that no new masters were admitted except to replace va-
cancies. Prince Charles occupied a somewhat unique position as an
exponent of such monopolistic limitation on any competition among
craftsmen. When this question was raised again under Gustavus
Adolphus (1621 and 1622), there was far more apprehension lest
the privileges of the guilds be abused. The end result of municipal
policy in the sixteenth and seventeenth centuries was, nevertheless,
continuous growth of the guilds, although they had few supporters
and a great many opponents among the rulers after Charles IX.
They did not reach the smaller towns until the eighteenth century,
while in the countryside they were never really accepted.

In the Middle Ages, Swedish towns had been small and, except
for Stockholm, quite powerless. This presented a striking contrast to
the Continent. There influential cities arose in the Middle Ages under conditions of local disintegration. But the policies of Gustavus
Vasa and his successors equipped the Swedish cities with the same
economic functions as were performed by their continental counterparts. What happened, for instance, in Germany "from below" as
a result of an elemental development, took place in Sweden "from
above" through deliberate policies of the central government.

## THE DUKEDOMS

The power wielded by Prince Charles in his duchy during the
reign of his brother, John III, in the last decades of the sixteenth
century, seriously jeopardized the unity of the country. Faithful to
his German inspiration, Charles attempted to make his territory into
a closed, self-sufficient economic area, and to subject it to an economic policy completely independent of that in the rest of the country. Of course, what made this development at all possible was the
creation, by Gustavus Vasa, of the dukedoms with which he endowed
his sons. Originally, this measure was undoubtedly taken for administrative reasons, in order to attain a more efficient supervision
of local crown officials, since natural economy made it far from easy
to keep in touch with local developments from one central vantage
point. But for its success Gustavus' scheme depended upon absolute
harmony among his sons. This turned out to be entirely unrealistic.

If the dukedoms had survived for some time, the result might have
been the very opposite of what Gustavus Vasa had intended, and

if Charles had remained in his position for long, he would almost certainly have achieved a considerable measure of disruption. Relatively soon, however, he became the ruler of all Sweden; after that elevation he pursued a policy of national unification as firm and rigid as his previous policy of local autonomy had been. From then on, Sweden was to see only two other ruling dukes. They were too weak and their reigns too short to enable them to repeat Charles' early policies, so that Sweden escaped from the threat of a belated political and economic disintegration.

## THE COINAGE SYSTEM

There was no great change in the monetary system in the sixteenth century.[9] This is far from saying that there were no currency debasements. On the contrary, they assumed larger proportions than ever before, and on a few occasions it was necessary to undertake currency reforms and to recall the deteriorated money. Under Gustavus Vasa currency was repeatedly depreciated; on one of those occasions he remarked with characteristic pungency that too much pork in the stew was an unhealthy thing, and that the same was true of too much silver in the coins. His last debasement of the coinage, in the early 1540's, caused general unrest and concern over high prices. This, in turn, provoked the king to compose some of his more explicit manifestoes which were read aloud to the populace at fairs and marts. Needless to say, these skillful and persuasively written declarations made no mention of the debasement of the currency, but attributed the price rises to any number of more or less insignificant causes.

Thereafter Gustavus ruled for two decades without any further deterioration of the money, a feat remarkable enough to secure for him a reputation as a protector of monetary stability. Two additional factors probably contributed to that reputation. In the first place, the king succeeded, by limiting the coinage, in lifting the value of the currency above that of its metallic content. Secondly, and this was perhaps more important, debasement of the currency under Gustavus was a mere trifle compared with what took place under his sons.

Eric XIV, the first to succeed to the throne, annually issued no less than seven times as much money as his father; Gustavus' hoards of silver were sent to the mint. At the same time there was considerable deterioration of the coins. But the second son, John III, was to go still farther in that direction. A currency reform was found necessary in the very beginning of his reign, followed by an even more drastic debasement in his last years, and yet another currency reform after his death. This inflation produced what is perhaps the first explicit Swedish reflection on monetary policy, to be found in the city chronicle (*tänkebok*) of Stockholm for the year 1592–93. The city clerk, who must have been a man of exceptional intelligence, made the following entry: "In '91 and '92 too many bad coins were struck; the cost of all things and the contempt of money swiftly rose, and good money was drained away so that lately nobody has wanted to sell his goods for the bad and soft money." [10] In another passage, it is explicitly said that nobody took money in return for goods but that "those who were cautious exchanged goods for goods." Thus the destruction of the monetary system led to the resumption of barter just as money transactions tended to decline under the impact of inflation after the First World War. Before the end of the century, however, the currency had been restored.

Gustavus Vasa introduced an innovation of lasting effect in the field of foreign exchange. In addition to the ever-deteriorating currency which circulated within the country (*kurantmynt*), he struck a coin of stable value called the *daler*, which had almost exactly the same silver content as the many foreign *thaler* coins. It was already an established practice to seek protection from the continual debasement of the domestic currency by writing contracts and settling at least international payments in other currency units which were not affected by monetary upheavals at home. For this purpose, foreign coins of stable value had been used, but to Gustavus it seemed natural to replace those by a special domestic issue. Even in Sweden, the Swedish daler did not attain the same widespread use for this purpose as foreign coins. But the experiment was successful in that the daler remained unaffected by fluctuations in the value of other coins, and its metallic value remained constant.

In the last decade of the sixteenth century, however, a formal change was made in this arrangement when the daler was incorporated into the regular currency system bearing a fixed relation to the other monetary units. As a consequence, the daler, which was made to equal four marks, was deprived of its former stability and fluctuated with the value of the mark. Actually, the change amounted to nothing more than the introduction of a higher denomination, so that four marks came to be called one daler. The old daler coin itself and its metallic value remained the same, but was given a new name, the *riksdaler*. The *riksdaler* retained its original value for centuries, unaffected by the vicissitudes of the monetary system as a whole. This constancy made it possible to escape some of the worst consequences of the monetary confusion. Debts would be contracted in *riksdaler* with the knowledge that payment would be made in accordance with the parties' original intentions, although the sums would be paid in the currently equivalent number of daler or mark.

The price level is always affected by the monetary system, and it reacted accordingly to the many debasements of the currency. Prices in Sweden were essentially determined by domestic events and policies. However, a rise in the international price level started during the sixteenth century, primarily as the direct or indirect result of the influx of silver from Mexico and Peru. Economically, Sweden was fairly isolated so that the waves of price increases abroad did not reach her until very late, essentially not until the beginning of the seventeenth century. The main reason for Sweden's insulation from international price developments was that her foreign trade was extremely insignificant; another, that her terms of trade were deteriorating as the demand for Sweden's export goods tended to decline in relation to the demand for the commodities she imported. Not until these two factors were simultaneously removed by the increase in foreign demand for Swedish copper and iron and the consequent growth in the volume of foreign trade were the international price increases transmitted to Sweden. However, as soon as the effects of those changes were exhausted, domestic developments regained their dominant influence upon price levels. On the whole, the impact of the international price revolution was therefore smaller in Sweden than in most other countries.

SUMMARY

What is remarkable about the Swedish economy in the sixteenth century is not that at length there was a change, but that the change was so late in coming. Sweden remained essentially medieval throughout the period. Isolated as it was politically, economically, and intellectually, the country still looked to the past rather than to the future. The tasks performed by the government were still so minor that neither rulers nor taxpayers felt hampered by the continued existence of natural economy. Since the government did not defray any substantial expenses abroad, it had no need to acquire foreign currency through exports. The way of life of the population at large had remained so unchanged that, except for salt, import trade was of little general concern.

If one wished to provide attractive labels for historical eras, the later years of Gustavus Vasa's reign might perhaps be called the Age of Bliss in Swedish history. There is often a tendency to glorify the past; still, posterity was probably well justified in referring to his reign as a golden age. But it was an extremely conservative and static age, something which might well be true of most golden ages. For great changes never occur without causing great suffering, however much they may eventually improve the lot of the masses.

In the half-century following Gustavus' death this state of affairs was already undermined. Sweden was sucked into the whirlpool of political conflicts between the Baltic countries; seeds of internal unrest were sown, and the Renaissance entered upon the Swedish scene with its architectural extravagances swelling the needs for public revenue. Tradition was losing its hold. On the basis of the revolution in the metal industries, a large-scale production of bar iron and copper emerged, oriented toward the export markets. The rapidly growing iron industry called increasingly for a capitalistic organization of production. The decidedly medieval German influence was supplanted by impulses from Scotland and, more important yet, from Holland, which was to be the leading economic power of the seventeenth century. Thus a cornerstone, though no more, was laid for the developments of the next century. But change was still on the whole subordinate to permanence. Not until centuries later would the revolution in agricultural technique lead to the first fundamental transformation of the structure of the Swedish economy.

# CHAPTER 4

# FOREIGN INFLUENCES AND ECONOMIC CHANGE (1600–1720)

## The Burden of Power Politics

In the seventeenth century Sweden was confronted with political tasks more difficult than ever before or after. The Age of Empire (*stormaktstiden*), as the period is commonly called in political history, also became an age of change for the Swedish economy which now definitely moved away from its medieval framework.

In no other period of Swedish history has the entire economic system been so geared to political action. It absorbed the economic resources of the country to an unprecedented extent. Nevertheless, the economic structure still set fairly narrow limits to the extent to which economic resources could be placed at the service of power politics. An agrarian society in which domestic and international trade alike remained at a low level inevitably resisted rapid reallocation of resources which can be achieved with relative ease in a modern economy.

The impact of the political development was twofold. The interminable wars, raging for seventy-five of the one hundred and twenty years of the period (not to mention the last years of the sixteenth century), imposed a colossal strain on both human and natural resources. Furthermore, as a result of the wars fought on foreign soils, financial obligations were incurred abroad that had to be discharged in foreign currencies, the supply of which was limited in Sweden. The transfer problem induced significant changes in the economic structure of the country.

Sweden gained her first experience with this problem in the very beginning of the period after the Peace of Knäred in 1613, when she was required to pay redemption to Denmark for the fortress of Älvsborg, to be remitted in *thalers* "such as are current in Germany." [1]

The same task was later faced, for sustained periods of time, when foreign mercenaries formed the majority of the soldiery in the Swedish campaigns and could not be remunerated in the same way as the Swedish troops. How desperately difficult it was at times to find the wherewithal is seen from a letter written by Gustavus Adolphus to Axel Oxenstierna in the summer of 1631, before the battle of Breitenfeld:

We have often told you, our dear Chancellor, what misery, pain, and disturbance the maintenance of the army has been causing us. All our allies have deserted us, and we have been forced to conduct the war *ex rapto* (by rapine), much to the disgust and harm of our friends. We still have no means to support the troops but by their intolerable plundering and looting.[2]

On the other hand, the employment of mercenary troops obviously relieved the drain on Sweden's own human resources. Likewise, the fact that the campaigns were fought abroad eased the demand for her material resources, because warring armies in those days lived mainly off the fat of the land. This made for a difference between battleground and homefront that has largely been erased in the total wars of our times. The Swedish seventeenth-century wars could hardly have been fought if the troops had not been able to live off the land, and even despite that saving of domestic resources the small and economically backward country stood time and again on the verge of ruin.

No less important than the burden of warfare was the steady flow of foreign influences to which the country became exposed. Although it is rarely emphasized, military and political expansion obviously bring a country into intense contact with other nations. In a country as relatively backward as Sweden in the seventeenth century, such contacts inevitably accelerated the rate of economic and social change. The steady expansion of foreign trade tended to end Sweden's economic isolation and to lead the country into the mainstream of general European development.

ECONOMIC FLUCTUATIONS

The assessment lists of taxable individuals provides an unexpected index of economic fluctuations in Sweden.[3] Figures for the taxable population have often been used for estimating the total population;

but closer study has shown them to be fairly useless for that purpose, since tax collectors generally included in the assessment lists only those persons who were expected to be able to pay their taxes. While the figures do not correctly picture changes in total population, they may be assumed to reflect changes in prevailing economic conditions as appraised by the tax collectors. A careful study of the assessment lists has, with few exceptions, corroborated this supposition. Chart I of the assessed population in various counties, from the death of Gustavus Adolphus until the beginning of the nineteenth century, therefore throws some light on fluctuations in the level of prosperity in Sweden. A brief summary of the graph may be in order.

There is no obvious explanation for the sharp upswing in two counties in the late 1630's. But the deep trough in 1650–51 points to the overwhelming importance of the harvest. Those were years of bad crop failures, partly because of floods which were particularly devastating in Östergötland where the slump was most pronounced. The following period is one of upturn and growth, especially under the regency of Charles XI.* When the king reached his majority in 1672, the powerful steward, Per Brahe, who had been the most influential member of the regency, referred to the period as "truly a golden age" (*vere aureum seculum*).[4]

But the war with Denmark which followed coincided with severe crop failures, so that the troughs in the chart are then exceedingly deep, even strikingly so in the case of the country of Jönköping. The severity of this depression is peculiarly significant in view of the fact that the Danish war was practically the only one in that period to be fought on Swedish territory. This may serve to illustrate what has just been said about the division of the burden between the war theaters and the home territory.

The longest spell of sustained growth during this period began after the Danish war. It was also the longest spell of unbroken peace, and the explosively rising curves of those years are an eloquent commentary on the economic impact of war and peace. New troughs reflect the terrible harvest failures in the years prior to the death of Charles XI in 1697, even though the declines are smaller than may have been expected in view of the magnitude of the disasters.

---

* The regency, consisting of the dowager queen and five members of the Council of the Realm, served from the death of Charles X in 1660.

Taxpaying ( *mantalsskriven* ) Population in Selected Swedish Counties, 1634-1820

Ratio Scale

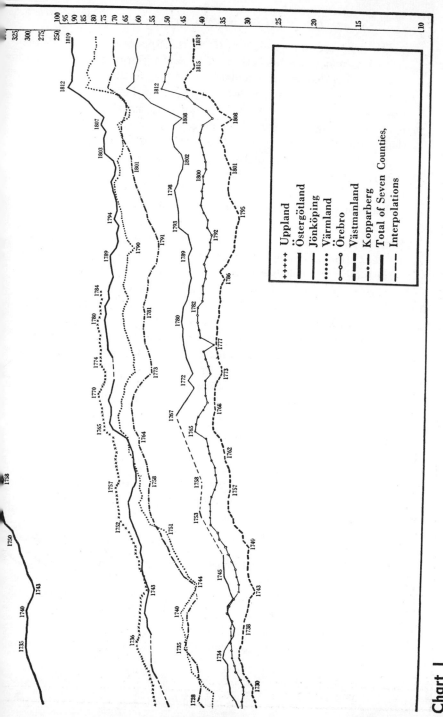

**Chart I**

Legend:
+ + + + +  Uppland
━━━━━  Östergötland
∙ ∙ ∙ ∙ ∙  Jönköping
∙∙∙∙∙  Värmland
─○─○─  Örebro
━ ━ ━  Västmanland
─ ∙ ─ ∙ ─  Kopparberg
━━━━━  Total of Seven Counties,
─ ─ ─ ─  Interpolations

The next upswing, which includes the first seven years of the campaigns under Charles XII, may be said to refute the very widespread notion that this particular part of the Northern War exacted a devastating toll from the Swedish people, an impression probably based on the desperate financial straits in which the government found itself from the very beginning of the war. The Council, in their letters from Stockholm to the absent king, continually presented the most dismal picture of the situation. However, as will shortly be seen, it was not the economic distress of the people but entirely different factors that made for those financial difficulties.

The slumps consequent upon some poor harvests were followed by the severe plague in 1710 and 1711 which resulted in troughs very similar to those in the later parts of the 1690's. The curves for the various counties actually reveal the order in which the plague visited them. Although an upswing followed, it was not sufficient to restore the prosperity experienced in the first years of the century.

Finally, in the last years of Charles' reign, another series of deep troughs slumped to levels even below those of the plague years. In some counties the depression persisted through the remaining war years after the death of the king. We may infer from this development that, although the early years of Charles XII imposed smaller sacrifices upon the population than is generally believed, the later phase of his reign undoubtedly did cause very severe hardships. It is striking that conditions at that time, when the war was fought in foreign territories and no epidemics were raging, were nevertheless as bad as in the worst years of the plague.

The conclusion of peace in 1721 ushered in a period of swift and at times truly breath-taking economic development. A sustained rate of rapid growth clearly distinguished the years after 1721 from the erratic development during *stormaktstiden*.

NATURAL RESOURCES

To meet the cost of prolonged warfare, Sweden depended, above all, on her natural resources. Agriculture remained the basis of the economy, but in wartime commodities other than foodstuffs were in most urgent demand. Export goods were particularly important since they were the only source of foreign exchange. In this respect Sweden was in an extremely favorable position, more favorable perhaps than at any later time. The force of circumstances had given her something of a monopoly in her three most important export commodities: — copper, iron, and tar. We shall now consider the conditions and the war-induced policies in those industries.

## Copper[5]

The copper industry was the strongest link between Sweden's political expansion and her economic development. No other Swedish industry was ever so intimately connected with the country's foreign policy.

The growth of the copper industry began with the turn of the century. As mentioned before, it received its first stimulus from the sudden increase in the demand for copper when Spain adopted a copper standard. In 1599 and 1606 the annual minting of copper in Spain was about twice as high as in any later period for which figures are known. Next came the redemption to be paid to Denmark, for the fortress of Älvsborg. This obligation was largely to be met in the following way. The government, which was by then in full control of the copper industry, sold the entire output to merchants who carried it to all the markets in western, northern, and central Europe, first and foremost to Amsterdam and Lübeck. The proceeds were received in *riksdaler,* originally intended to be used exclusively for the redemption of Älvsborg. Unfortunately, a large part was used to defray other pressing expenses, and redemption payments had to be covered from other sources (see below, page 105).

The financial reliance upon the copper industry aroused a desperate urge to increase output. Production continued to grow as the mine at Falun (Stora Kopparberg) was expanded. In fact, the need for government revenue remained so pressing that there was a tendency to step up production at any cost, without regard for sound mining principles. A peak year was reached in 1650, during the brief breathing spell which began with the Peace of Westphalia (1648). Even though output declined somewhat in the years after 1650, production still stayed at a high level. But in 1687 the excessive and predatory exploitation led to a terrible cave-in in the mines; despite rapid recovery the old levels of output were never regained. Under Charles XII production decreased further until, by the end of his reign, the industry had all but dwindled away, along with Sweden's political power. Although copper production did linger on throughout the following century, and Swedish copper retained a prominent position in foreign markets, its former glory was irretrievably gone. By that time Swedish copper had served its political purpose; that is, to provide the solid core of Swedish war finance in the Age of Empire. Without copper, presumably neither the redemption of Älvsborg nor Swedish participation in the Thirty Years War would have been feasible.

It remains to explain why copper rather than iron became the main prop of war financing, in spite of the vastly greater general significance of the iron industry. There were several reasons. First, the crown was a substantial co-owner of the mines at Stora Kopparberg, and therefore was in a far better position to control the allocation of copper than that of iron. Second, the copper industry was essentially concentrated in one place whereas the iron industry was scattered throughout Svealand. Third, the high value per unit of weight made copper relatively less expensive to transport than iron. Finally, demand conditions for copper were possibly more favorable than those for iron.

In order to raise the required amount of foreign currency the government attempted to dispose of the copper abroad, in the manner which had proved so successful in the case of the Älvsborg transaction. But completion of those transactions often took a long time, although the crown was represented by numerous agents abroad, especially in Amsterdam, who sometimes coöperated and sometimes competed with each other. The inflow of foreign exchange frequently failed to keep pace with the government's feverish need for foreign money, particularly during Gustavus Adolphus' temperamental reign. It was then necessary to borrow from one source or another, mortgaging the copper or using it as collateral in the hope of future deliveries. The ever-present problem was how to make the copper trade yield maximum profits in the shortest possible time. On two occasions, first under Gustavus Adolphus and then under the regency after his death, special copper companies were formed in the hope that they would prove more efficient than either the crown or the existing private groups associated with the mines at Stora Kopparberg.[6] The first company was not a complete failure but proved a thin disguise for the government's own operations and was therefore soon dis-

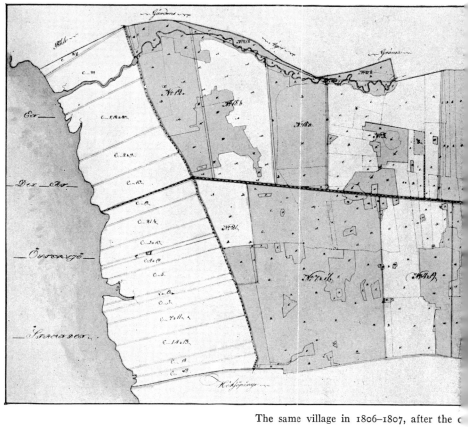

The same village in 1806–1807, after the c

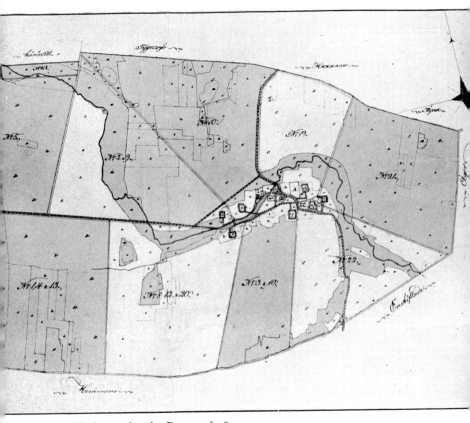

...mplete consolidation under the Decree of 1803.

continued. The second was a failure from the outset and lasted only a few years.

If the need for foreign exchange had not been so enormous, the Swedish situation would have been vastly more favorable. Sweden had an indisputable monopoly of copper in the European market which it retained through the whole century. The only other country that produced as much copper or more was Japan, and the quantities of Japanese copper reaching the European market were both insignificant and irregular. Although there were, of course, a few European copper mines outside Sweden, their output was small. In 1690, the foremost Swedish metallurgist of the time, Erik Odhelius (later given a nobility patent as Odelstierna), was dispatched by Charles XI to make a careful inquiry into all European metal production and trade. On his return, he submitted a report which is probably the most complete existing source of information about mining and metal trades in Europe in the late seventeenth century. Odhelius made no secret of the difficulties faced by the Swedish metal industry; but despite the fact that the Swedish copper industry was already in decline, his conclusion on the prospects for Swedish copper was as follows: "For the production of copper Sweden has always been like a mother, and although in many places within and without Europe some copper is extracted it counts for nothing next to the abundance of Swedish copper." [7] It can be imagined how strong the Swedish position must have been previously when the "abundance" was even greater.

Nevertheless, the scale of production was far from large by any modern standards. Not even the peak-year of 1650 yielded more than 3,000 metric tons, while over somewhat longer periods the highest average was about 2,100 tons a year. After 1665, the output was less than 2,000 tons a year, and from 1710–20 on it sank below 1,000 tons a year.[8] By way of comparison, the output of copper in the United States after the Second World War was about 800 million metric tons. Swedish copper production in the middle of the seventeenth century therefore amounted to about one-quarter of one per cent of the present American output. But according to Odhelius' meticulous estimates of European copper production in the early 1690's, Sweden then contributed about half of the European copper supplies, and presumably a much larger share at an earlier time.[9]

Sweden exploited her monopoly to the utmost, sometimes perhaps even too ruthlessly. Amsterdam in the 1620's was the headquarters of Louis de Geer, one of the shrewdest and boldest of Swedish agents in foreign markets, a man destined to play a unique role in Swedish economic life. A Walloon nobleman, born in the bishopric of Liége, he had established himself as a merchant in Amsterdam but later moved to Sweden, the first and the greatest bearer of a name now famous in Swedish history. De Geer on one occasion triumphantly reported that he had succeeded in raising the price of Swedish copper in Amsterdam from 45 to 72 *riksdaler* per *skeppund,** that is, by 60 per cent.[10] This report was confirmed by one of the competing Swedish agents. De Geer's technique was to buy minor amounts through straw men, thereby creating a "market expectation" of a price rise which enabled him to sell the bulk of his supplies at very high prices. The wisdom of his policy might be disputed. It caused violent price fluctuations in a market that was already highly speculative, while as the leading supplier Sweden probably had a long-run interest in price stability. The desperate need for foreign currency, however, made the government prefer the one bird in the hand to the ten in the bush.

### THE COPPER STANDARD

In 1625, the preoccupation with copper led to a measure which was to affect the Swedish monetary system for 150 years to come. Gustavus Adolphus then introduced a copper standard or, more precisely, substituted for the old silver standard a bimetallic standard based on silver and copper.[11] The intention was to raise the foreign price of copper without curtailing production. If part of the copper supplies were used for Swedish coinage, the price outside Sweden, it was

* *Translator's note:* The *skeppund* ("shipping pound") was the highest Swedish unit of weight, varying from commodity to commodity. With regard to metals, the peculiar feature was that a *skeppund* in the mining areas was heavier than a *skeppund* in the inland cities, and heavier yet than a *skeppund* in the coastal staple cities. By this allowance for transport cost it was intended to equalize prices per *skeppund* everywhere (a similar difference prevailed between the *skeppund* for pig iron and bar iron, one unit of pig iron supposedly sufficing to produce one unit of bar iron). For copper and bar iron the *skeppund* was: in staple cities 300 pounds (136 kg.); in inland cities 315 pounds (142.8 kg.); in the mining regions 330 pounds (149.6 kg.). *See* Heckscher, *Sveriges ekonomiska historia,* Vol. I, Book 2, pp. 670–671.

hoped, could be raised to the desired level. As long as high prices were maintained without supporting measures, coinage was supposed to be discontinued. A secondary argument was that the use of a domestic metal would make the import of silver superfluous. A prerequisite of this policy obviously was a Swedish monopoly in copper; if other suppliers could replace the Swedish copper withdrawn from foreign markets, nothing would have been gained.

The existence of monopoly was indubitable; yet the policy was not very successful. This should not have been surprising because the Swedish need for circulating currency was trifling. Once copper currency had displaced most or all of the circulating silver, no sizable quantities of copper could be absorbed by Swedish coinage. However, since the size of the coin issue was determined not by the need for currency but with a view to the effects upon the foreign price level, an overissue of coins resulted which depressed their value below that of the metal. As the next step, copper was exported in the form of coins, depressing foreign copper prices at least as much as if it had been exported in the form of plate. The scheme was therefore based on a miscalculation. This was soon widely admitted in Sweden. Axel Oxenstierna, for one, seems to have opposed the plan almost from the beginning, but Gustavus Adolphus refused to relinquish what was apparently a pet project. Thereafter, for one reason and another, no initiative was taken to return to a pure silver standard, and the copper standard survived until the currency reform in 1776, although it was largely put out of effect in 1745 when inconvertible paper money was introduced.

The copper standard was clearly a very serious inconvenience. The price of copper was barely more than one-hundredth that of silver, so that a copper coin would weigh about a hundred times as much as an equivalent silver coin. Both in weight and size these large rectangular metal slabs seem to have been unique in the history of coinage. The ten-daler piece weighed about 43 pounds (19.7 kilograms),[12] and the two-daler piece, which was the standard coin, measured about 9.5 inches (240 millimeters) diagonally. However, the greatest drawback was not so much the weight and size of individual pieces as the total metal weight required for a certain payment—hence the awkwardness of the transaction, regardless of the denominations of the single pieces.

That those conditions seemed no less grotesque to contemporaries than to later generations may be seen from the rather malicious comments made by a young Danish diplomat by the name of Bircherod, who in 1720 wrote back to Denmark:

A daler is the size of a quarto page . . . many carry their money around on their backs, others on their heads, and larger sums are pulled on a horsecart. Four riksdaler would be a terrible punishment for me if I had to carry them a hundred steps; may none here become a thief. I shall take one of these dalers back to you unless it is too heavy for me; I am now hiding it under my bed.[13]

His reference to the hardships of thievery was not without basis. In Viborg some burglars who had broken into a cellar and found there a small sum of money had to leave it behind because they could not lift it. More serious, however, was that transportation of any sizable sum required the use of wagons. This proved particularly obstructive to the treasury in its collection of tax revenue; the haulage of revenue from the provinces to Stockholm was among the matters considered by the Council in connection with organizing the transport system.

The copper standard also raised purely monetary problems. Gustavus Adolphus had intended the copper daler to equal the silver daler and had therefore affixed the same denominations to pieces struck from copper as to silver coins. But the metal content of the copper coins was based on a price far in excess of the market price. The copper daler was thus inferior to the silver daler, which created a most perplexing double standard, one of the best known curiosities in Swedish monetary history. The strains on public finances caused the government to reduce the metallic weight of the copper daler progressively, thereby steadily depressing its value below the silver daler. When, finally, three copper dalers exchanged for only one silver daler, the new copper pieces were stamped *daler sölff-mynt* or "daler silver." [14] Thus, a "daler silver," although cut from copper, was now simply a denomination equivalent to three "daler copper." The above-mentioned two-daler piece with a diagonal of almost ten inches was accordingly stamped "two daler silver," although it amounted to "six daler copper." At the same time, real silver coins were minted and issued, so that all the usual consequences of a bimetallic standard were apparent. As a rule, only the copper currency was in circulation and the silver coins disappeared, though it also happened occasionally that silver drove out copper. All this was in accordance with the so-called Gresham's law that bad money drives out good money, simply because the metal value of "good money" is higher than its face value, or, as we might also say, because it is cheaper to pay in "bad money."

It might be asked why the copper coins were made so heavy, since their bulk was the major practical inconvenience of the copper standard. The reason of course was that the whole scheme aimed at creating domestic outlet for Swedish copper. Token coins of copper with a metallic content far below that corresponding to the face value would not have served the purpose; therefore a coin with an intrinsic value roughly corresponding to its face value had to be issued. It is important to realize this, because during a short but eventful period an entirely different kind of copper money appeared, the famous token money coined by Charles XII in his later years. Those coins contained only one to one-half of one per cent of the copper corresponding to their face value and were in all respects equivalent to inconvertible paper money. They had nothing to do with the copper standard except perhaps that the choice of copper rather than of some other material might have been influenced by copper standard traditions. This token money, however, was short-lived and was withdrawn from circulation after three years.

PAPER MONEY

At least one of the consequences of the copper standard was quite unexpected. The inconvenience of copper coins facilitated the introduction of paper money, which is the more noteworthy because Swedish paper money was the first in Europe. The background was as follows:

In 1656, a Livonian of Dutch extraction, by the name of Johan Palmstruch, received royal permission to found a bank.[15] Five years later, it occurred to him to issue bank notes that possibly were modeled on the so-called copper bills in which the mining association at Stora Kopparberg had been paying the miners before the introduction of regular currency for that purpose. The issue of paper money was equivalent to receipt of interest-free deposits, which made them highly popular with the managers of the bank. In fact, the notes were received by the public with such enthusiasm that they passed at a premium over the awkward copper money. This was only to be expected. But as a result, the managers, who naturally had no experience whatever with paper money, issued an excessive volume of bank notes, presumably because the prevailing low interest rates had stimulated the demand for bank credit. Since the notes were originally redeemable in hard cash, their sudden depreciation now caused a run on the bank. This unprecedented phenomenon quite naturally produced a panic: the bank was closed and the issue of paper money interrupted. The fear of paper money persisted for almost a century, although Palmstruch's bank after its failure had been taken over by *Riksens ständers bank* (Bank of the Estates of the Realm), nowadays known as the *Riksbank,* which is the oldest existing bank in Europe.

## BRASS

In the course of the seventeenth century the copper industry was strengthened by the rapid development of the brass industry which, though founded in the previous century, now assumed significant proportions.[16] Brass is an alloy of copper and zinc, but since only small amounts of calamine, the ore of zinc, were produced in Sweden, most of it had to be imported. The Swedish superiority in copper, however, was such that zinc ore could be imported from England and the finished brass returned to the English market in the face of stiff competition from English brassmakers. As copper mining declined, there was growing enthusiasm for the "refinement" of copper into brass, until in the eighteenth century the brass works were the major consumers of Swedish copper.

## IRON AND STEEL

Although the advances of the copper industry, as we have seen, had momentous consequences in many fields, ironmaking remained the most important industry by far in terms of production. During the whole period, copper never succeeded in threatening the predominance of iron in the export trade. On the average, iron accounted for about 50 per cent of the total export value and copper for only 30 per cent.[17] Together they overshadowed all other items entirely. An expansion in iron exports, however, roughly coincided with the decline in copper exports; by 1720 iron alone accounted for 75 per cent of the total export value, whereas the share of copper had declined to about 10 per cent.[18]

It may be estimated that iron production increased fivefold between 1600 and 1720. Its relative importance in foreign markets also was considerable, but our information about the production of iron in the rest of Europe is so scanty that it makes a quantitative estimate of the Swedish share fairly worthless. All the same, we can safely say that Sweden's share in the over-all European production of iron was smaller than that of copper. On the basis of very dubious appraisals of conditions around the middle of the eighteenth century, when Swedish output was not much larger than in 1720, I have estimated the Swedish share of the world output of bar iron at about 35 per cent which may be on the high side.[19]

More important than Sweden's share in world output of iron was her position in world exports of the metal, and here her leadership was indisputable. Few other countries actually exported any but trifling amounts. Of the many markets which absorbed Swedish iron, the English market was incomparably the greatest. According to accounts of the English customs, no less than 82.5 per cent of the iron imports in the years immediately prior to 1720 came from Sweden.[20] The English iron industry had suffered a sharp decline, and domestic output probably did not exceed the imports, which means that Sweden provided about 40 per cent of all the iron consumed by England.[21] The absolute dependence upon Swedish iron is also illustrated by an episode which took place in those years. During the English, or rather, the Hanoverian war against Sweden, importation of Swedish iron was at first prohibited. The consequent shortage, however, was so disruptive that the ban was lifted and Swedish iron readmitted, provided it was shipped via Continental ports. Swedish export statistics show that the rerouting did not cause any drop in Swedish iron exports.

The importance of the iron industry for the Swedish economy of the period is obvious. Nevertheless, it is easy to exaggerate the international implications of Swedish supremacy in iron. A country occupying at present a position of the same relative superiority in iron and steel would be an economic and political power of the first rank. Yet one certainly must not conclude that Sweden was to the seventeenth century what the United States is to the twentieth. The situations are not even remotely comparable. Although Sweden supplied about 40 per cent of all the iron consumed in England, this amounted to only 4 per cent of the total commodity imports into England.[22] In those days iron did not play anything like its present part in economic life, and consumption of iron and steel was still very insignificant. Its present key position is the result of the Industrial Revolution which raised the production of capital goods to a dominant branch of the economy. Prior to the Industrial Revolution the position of machinery and communications which now absorb the bulk of iron production were as a rule quite subordinate.

Two other conditions served further to limit the advantages of Swedish supremacy in iron. In the first place, most machinery was built of wood, not iron. If iron was indispensable for some part of a machine, the rest was nevertheless made of wood. Remnants of wooden winches and power transmissions may be seen even now in various places in Bergslagen, and water pipes, so essential in the mining industry, were almost exclusively made of wood. When this was the case in the very heart of the Swedish iron districts, we can imagine what things were like in England where at that time iron was singularly scarce. Secondly, most countries in Europe, although they had no spare iron for exports, did not require any large iron imports either. England was the most significant exception.

But, all things considered, it still remains true that the Swedish position was quite prominent. In fact, it was stronger than was generally realized abroad at a time when production of a semi-finished product like iron was regarded as far less valuable than production of finished manufactures.

To what factors, then, did Sweden owe her prominence? Several such factors are readily apparent. Most important was the immense fuel supply in the rich forests. The iron industry of the time depended entirely on charcoal, since repeated attempts in other countries, particularly in England, to use coke and coal to smelt iron had not yet been successful. Referring to the eighteenth century's depletion of forest supplies in many European countries, Werner Sombart called it a great menace to *Frühkapitalismus*. This applied with considerable force even to the seventeenth century, particularly in England where the drastic decline in iron production was directly related to the exhaustion of the wood supplies.

A second factor was the purity of Swedish ores. We have already noted that primitive production techniques placed a particular premium on the quality of the ore. And finally, there was the entrepreneurial factor. It can hardly be denied that metallurgical and technological advances in Sweden had been very substantial, and that Sweden was somewhat of a pioneer in the processes of ironmaking. This may be illustrated in various ways. Swedish ironmakers and ironworkers were, for instance, brought to France by Colbert in order to modernize the French ironworks and cannon foundries.[23] French workers complained that the Swedes, who were jealously guarding the Swedish secrets of production, would order them to leave every time a critical stage in the production process was reached. Another episode, recorded by Coleridge, concerns one Foley, a member of the well-known family of English ironmasters, who was anxious to learn the secrets of the Swedish rolling and slitting mills but saw no other way to do so than to disguise himself as a wandering minstrel in the hope of gaining admission to a Swedish ironmill. The story may or may not be true, but its currency testifies to the high regard in which Swedish ironmaking was held. Undoubtedly, the meticulous precision that still characterizes Swedish ironmaking is a heritage from those days; it has been said to be managed with the care of a laboratory experiment. This was clearly not conducive to large-scale production.

As the preceding account indicates, the monopoly position of the Swedish iron industry did not breed neglect of quality. On the contrary, great attention was paid to improvement of the product even though the results were not always commensurate with the efforts. Thus, quality control (*järnvräkeri*) was instituted, following medieval patterns, for pig iron as well as for bar iron. Special checkers (*vräkare*) inspected the iron before it was exported and rejected substandard products.[24] Partly for this reason "iron stamps" came into use as early as the sixteenth century. Each iron producer registered his own stamp with the authorities to indicate the origin of his product; these stamps, which are still being used, stimulated competition in quality. Nevertheless, it can certainly be assumed that enlightened self-interest on the part of the ironmasters contributed more to the maintenance of high quality than the demonstrably impractical and planless control by the government.

These attitudes are partially explained by the general concern with quality inherited from the Middle Ages. One of the craft guilds' most essential functions had been to supervise production methods and quality. Another perhaps more important reason was that the Swedes never felt quite secure in their position. There was a constant fear that a deterioration in quality or a price increase would revive the closed-down ironworks in other countries and intensify foreign competition. This view was not shared in all quarters. Christopher Polhem,[25] for instance, advocated a firm monopolistic organization of Swedish iron exports in order to make iron "rare" and to raise its price.* Although this plan was never realized, it did exert some influence in a different form, as will be shown presently. That the quality of Swedish iron was so determinedly maintained was to prove extremely fortunate; it might even be said to have saved the Swedish iron industry in the fateful crisis still to come.

Technologically speaking, the excellence of Swedish iron was the result of a number of innovations introduced in the early seventeenth century. First of all, there was the so-called Walloon forge, which contained two hearths instead of one. One hearth was used to reduce the carbon content of pig iron in order to make it malleable, the second to beat it into bars. Walloon iron, though probably through no intentions on the part of its creators, turned out to be incomparably superior to any other iron for the purpose of steel production. Steel, that is to say, hard iron, in those days was produced by further processing of malleable iron. But the contemporaneous importance of the innovation should not be exaggerated, as is often done. Walloon iron really played a very small part in Swedish iron-making since steel output at that time was always extremely insignificant compared with the production of malleable iron. In the eighteenth century, for instance, Walloon iron made up only 10 to 12 per cent of the total exports of Swedish iron.[26] In England, Walloon iron was called Orground or Arground iron (from the Swedish place

* *Translator's note:* Christopher Polhem (1661–1751), the foremost scientist and inventor within the Swedish iron industry, whose innumerable projects, ranging from metallurgy to mining and mechanical engineering, excited considerable attention and admiration.

name Öregrund); but actually it became the specialty of the Danne-mora works in Uppland, where it benefited from the extraordinary purity of the Dannemora ore which naturally contributed to its rep-utation.

At the same time, other great technological changes were in proc-ess. The main result was the introduction of the German forge[27] which came to account for the production of all malleable iron ex-cept Walloon iron. No less important than the changes in forge technology were changes in the production of pig iron, particularly the introduction by the French-speaking Walloons of the so-called French furnace.[28] This was a blast furnace of stone which replaced the old constructions of lumber and earth (mulltimmershyttor). Taken together, all those changes laid a foundation for the Swedish iron industry that was to last into the early nineteenth century.

Within the country, Värmland now became the leading iron-pro-ducing region. An assessment for tax purposes made in 1695[29] re-vealed the following distribution of the total iron production between the more important provinces:[30]

| Värmland | 22% | Uppland | 14% |
|---|---|---|---|
| Närke | 17 | Dalarne | 7.5 |
| Västmanland | 16 | Gästrikland | 6 |

The main shipping port for Värmland iron was Göteborg, which consequently assumed an important position in the iron trade. In the period 1681–85, Göteborg's share of the combined exports of iron from Stockholm and Göteborg was 17.4 per cent; in 1716–20 that share had risen to 30.4 per cent or almost twice as much.[31]

## ORGANIZATION OF THE IRON INDUSTRY

Värmland's increasing prominence in ironmaking was the outcome of a policy deliberately pursued by the rulers since the regency for Queen Christine. Basically, this policy arose from the government's interest in the conservation of forest resources in the old mining regions. The aim was to reserve those forests for mining and pig iron production and to move the forges for bar iron production to the richer wood supplies in other areas where there were no mines. If successful, this policy would have broken up the vertical integration of the iron industry. Such a reorganization would have meant the end of a tradition which has actually proved invincible; and, in addition, it would have raised a host of practical difficulties. Bar iron works could not be moved out of the old mining region (Bergslagen) where the pig iron was produced except at the risk of disrupting the supply of the raw material. In fact, with one most important exception, the actual changes produced by the government policy were quite limited. A few works were founded in remote provinces in the western and northern parts of the country as well as in Finland, but all that did not amount to much.

The exception concerns Värmland, where the effects of the government's policy were momentous. Värmland's proximity to the mining region meant that her bar iron production could still be based on a steady flow of pig iron from Bergslagen. Thus the major obstacle to shifting the industry did not exist. Accordingly, western Värmland rapidly developed into one of the major ironmaking regions. The old mining districts of Bergslagen did not lose their lead in bar iron production, but growth was more rapid without than within Bergslagen: in 1636 the relative proportions were 22.4 to 77.6 per cent, in 1695 they were 37.7 to 62.3 per cent.[32]

For the rest, the government's policy aimed at a certain curtailment of total production, still prompted by its concern with the fuel supply. Although this was to have far-reaching consequences in our next period, prior to 1720 the effects were slight. A few works were closed down by Charles XI on the ground that they had been founded without due authorization or were inappropriately located,[33] but the new additions always exceeded the shutdowns.

The Swedish iron industry in this period assumed its present form of organization. This involved the creation of ironworks (*bruk*) requiring what were for that time substantial amounts of capital. Socially, the ironmasters (*brukspatroner*) of such works were the first secular group outside the nobility to assume the status of an upper class.[34] An outstanding student of the Swedish iron industry has claimed that no occupational title in Sweden ever enjoyed a higher prestige than that of ironmaster.* The traditional small ironmakers (*bergsmän*), who in contrast to the ironmasters be-

---

* *Translator's note:* Occupational titles, it may be mentioned, are extremely widely used in Sweden, sometimes even to the point where direct address is put in the third person, with the use of a title instead of a pronoun.

longed to the lower strata, were thereafter almost entirely confined to mining and pig iron production. Very soon the ironmasters began to displace the small producers even from the production of pig iron by equipping their works with blast furnaces of their own. These new ("French") stone furnaces were sometimes called ironmaster furnaces (*brukspatronsugnar*).

As already suggested, the organization of the ironworks required large amounts of capital. It is no exaggeration to say that this was the most crucial problem of all faced by the Swedish iron industry. It was solved more or less satisfactorily through a system of credit called *förlag* (German *Verlag*) which contained the essential elements of the merchant-employer system. Foreign importers made advances to the exporting merchants in Stockholm and Göteborg, who in turn gave credit to the ironmasters who, as the last link of the chain, made advances to their workers.[35]

This was, of course, a precarious system with many peculiar features. All parties were bound to their creditors. The workers were usually indebted to their employers, often increasingly so, and could not change their employment unless they were able to settle their debts or find another employer willing to take over the loans granted by his predecessor. This easily led to intensified local rigidities and immobilities. The ironmasters in turn were tied to the merchants in the export cities and could not shift to new buyers unless they had cleared their debts. And, although less is heard about it, the exporters may have been similarly tied to the foreign importers. When an ironmaster defaulted on his debt to the creditor, the latter was entitled to operate the works himself until the debt was paid. The advances were made either in money or in kind, which caused great complications in accounts between ironmasters and merchants. Either the prices of future deliveries of iron were set lower than those of "ready" iron, or else fabulous prices were charged for commodities which the lender shipped to the ironworks. Thereby the distinction between price and interest tended to become very much blurred. The elements of natural economy were stronger yet in the relationship between the ironmasters and their workers. The workers generally drew their credits in the form of commodities from the master's store. That could hardly be avoided as the works usually were situated in isolated places in the country. The evils of the truck system were often felt; at times prices charged may indeed have been lower than market prices, but when the opposite was true there were serious complaints.

Compared with the production of bar iron, further processing, including steelmaking, was distinctly secondary. Swedish steel never gained the same repute in foreign markets as Swedish bar iron. It was regarded as inferior to steel from Styria, Remscheid, and Solingen, and even to English steel, which was produced from Swedish bar iron.[36] Other branches of the industry were more successful. Under Louis de Geer's management, a flourishing cannon manufacture shot up; and the production of small arms, largely by handicraft, gained a considerable reputation. These activities primarily supplied the Swedish armed forces, while a substantial part of the output also went into exports.[37] There was also a vivid interest in the manufacture of various other iron products, from simple hardware to more complex mechanical devices. In particular, the products of Christopher Polhem[38] bore witness to the mechanical genius of the man and baffled his contemporaries. But commercially this branch of the iron industry did not yet carry much weight.

## FOREST PRODUCTS

The third largest Swedish export commodity was tar (more precisely, tar and pitch), although it accounted for only 6 to 8 per cent of the exports,[39] a mere trifle next to iron and copper. Tar, which is nowadays mostly produced synthetically out of coal, was formerly always extracted from wood; the Swedish-Finnish tar industry was therefore based on their coniferous forest resources. Besides, tar possessed substantial advantages over other wood products as an export commodity. It was far more easily transported than boards and planks, and presumably more in demand, since for shipbuilding, particularly the construction of warships, oak was preferred to Sweden's spruce and pine. The navies as well as the merchant marines of all the seafaring countries were highly dependent on the supply of tar, so that the Swedish monopoly, which at times was virtually complete, was quite burdensome to England and France and, perhaps in lesser degree, to Holland.

The Swedish monopoly position in tar was exploited, possibly even more ruthlessly than that in copper. From the middle of the seventeenth century onward a number of tar companies were founded,[40] which by their pricing policy roused deep resentment among their foreign customers, especially the English. In the beginning of the next century the English at last decided to subsidize the production of tar in the North American colonies where wood was abundant. This, in combination with rumors of war and the final rupture between England and Sweden toward the end of the reign of Charles XII, served to remove Swedish tar from the English market. The strictly monopolistic policy was never resumed; but as long as it lasted it had been a rich source of revenue to the owners of the tar industry, most of whom were leading merchants in Stockholm and, to some extent, Göteborg. The actual distillation of the wood was a typical rural industry along the shores of Norrland and Finland, though the peasants had no reason to rejoice over the large profits earned in tar exports. If anything, their lot probably deteriorated as a result of the creation of the tar companies.

The lumber industry was definitely of secondary importance compared with tar manufacture.[41] As long as the Norwegian forests along the Atlantic coast remained undepleted, the Norwegians retained a competitive superiority in the West European markets. Moreover, this advantageous position proved a stimulus to technological progress in Norway, which further increased Norway's edge over Sweden. The sawmills in northern Sweden were still fairly inaccessible, and would remain so until, at a much later date, the rivers were cleared for flotage. The Swedish lumber industry was therefore located principally in Småland and along the western coastline. In earlier times, oak played a considerable role, but when the supplies of oak began to give out, spruce and pine grew in importance. This was a permanent shift, but as yet there was no other indication of the future significance or character of the lumber industry.

## FOREIGNERS

Most of the economic developments in the seventeenth century which have been described here cannot be fully understood unless account is taken of a vitally important group: the foreign immigrants to Sweden. It can safely be said that neither before nor later did foreigners contribute more to Swedish economic development.

Almost every innovation in the Swedish economy had its origins

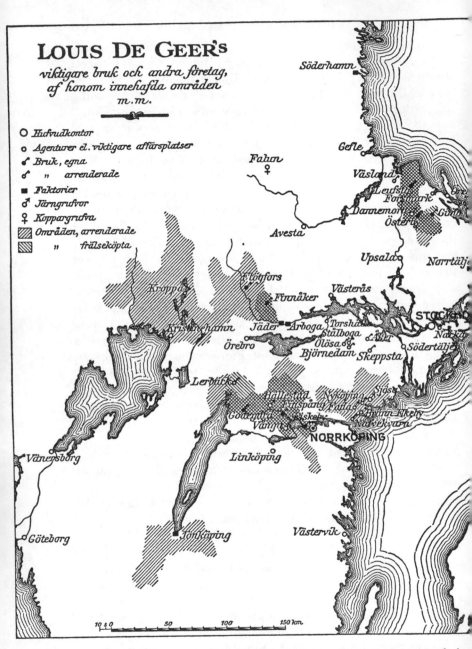

Map of Louis de Geer's establishments in Sweden. From the top down the legend reads in tion: Main Office; Agencies; Mills owned by Louis de Geer; Mills leased by him; Manufa Iron mines; Copper mines; Leased properties; Purchased properties. Reproduced from E. W. D *Louis de Geer.*

in the initiative of the immigrants. Foremost among them all was undoubtedly Louis de Geer,[42] a descendant of an old Liége family which had settled in Amsterdam. There was practically no field of economic activity with which de Geer did not at one time or another concern himself.

From the point of view of the government, his most essential contribution was to the procurement of government revenue. He was the leading exporter of Swedish copper, as well as the manager of the government's arms manufactories and thus the leading producer of guns and ordnance.[43] He was the greatest ironmaster of the country, and a pioneer in the modernization of the Swedish iron industry. He produced all kinds of manufactured goods: brass, steel, tin, wire, paper, cloth. He was a big shipper and a shipbuilder; during the Danish war in 1644–1645 he succeeded in leasing a fleet of Dutch vessels which he put at the disposal of the crown. His other activities ranged from an attempt to colonize the Gold Coast to the operation of a retail store at Norrköping. For his transactions within the country he maintained a system of banks designed to facilitate payments between distant places. In return for his steadily increasing financial claims on the government he received large estates, thus becoming a big landowner as well.

A variety of interests does not of itself result in prosperity; it might easily lead to ruin. But in the case of de Geer it seemed to have no untoward consequences. In relation to the size of the national product, de Geer's income was probably larger than that of any Swede today — it would be a mistake to believe that income distribution in the past was more egalitarian than in recent times. When we also consider that de Geer's demeanor was often far from tactful, as witnessed by his voluminous correspondence,[44] it is not surprising to find that he was quite unpopular in many quarters, including the government. This was of small moment, however, since his help was constantly needed, both as creditor and as councilor in economic matters where his experience was unsurpassed. But although he became the founder of one of the most renowned families of the Swedish nobility, it is doubtful whether he ever felt himself to be a Swede. Through the years he kept his house in Amsterdam where he died; and presumably he never learned to write the Swedish language since all of his letters to royalty or to the Council in Stockholm were in

Dutch, German, or French, of which languages he was in perfect command.

At de Geer's death in 1654, there was no one of similar stature to succeed him, but shortly after the mid-century two brothers from Aix-la-Chapelle were for some time intensely active in commerce and industry: Abraham and Jacob Momma (later raised to nobility as Counts Reenstierna).[45] Of their numerous ventures only the most famous may be mentioned: they opened up the iron mines at Kengis and the copper mine at Svappavaara in the province of Norrbotten in the very north of Sweden. In contrast to Louis de Geer, they ran out of luck and ended up in a resounding bankruptcy.

There is little point in listing all the foreigners or Swedes of foreign descent who reached high prominence in the seventeenth century. Suffice it to mention explicitly the Geijers, two Austrian brothers who immigrated under Gustavus Adolphus in order to engage in ironmaking; one of their descendants was later to take over the famous Uddeholm ironworks.[46] Christopher Polhem[47] was probably also of Austrian descent although his family had temporarily halted in Pomerania on their trek to Sweden.

The origin of the immigrants was varied. Of the over-all number of aliens the Germans were in a large majority, particularly if the Austrians are included with them. They excelled less in business than in other pursuits; Germany of the period could hardly be considered a pioneering country economically speaking. Still, there were many west Germans, particularly those from the brass center of Aix-la-Chapelle, who were quite active. But the chief source of entrepreneurs was Holland. Many factors contributed to this condition. Sweden and Holland, the two leading Protestant powers on the European mainland, kept in intimate political touch, although their friendship was not at all times free from strain. Important above all was the economic expansion of the Dutch in the seventeenth century, one of the great miracles of economic history. Only a few decades earlier the Netherlands was a small and powerless country engaged in a seemingly hopeless struggle with Spain, Europe's strongest power. Now it was the master of Europe's mercantile and military navigation, of colonial trade and of the most valuable colonial territories. It controlled European commerce in grain and in most other commodities as well. Yet the Dutch were more than mere traders; they also made themselves known as pioneers in a variety of other fields, such as, for instance, agricultural improvements. The human resources and impulses flowing from such a country were invaluable to Sweden's economy, and thereby, indirectly, to her political exploits. Dutch financial resources were also drawn upon in a number of cases, especially in the payment of the Älvsborg redemption, which was completed with the help of a substantial Dutch loan that was never entirely repaid.[48]

Though far less numerous than the Dutch, the Scots and the English were not to be overlooked. The French, on the other hand, were very few; possibly Sweden's impact upon the French economy was greater than *vice versa*.

Among the industries in which the contributions of foreigners were particularly significant, the iron industry held first place. Technical terms reveal that Walloon iron and the so-called German iron were made by imported techniques. The Walloons had been brought to the country by Louis de Geer from his homeland, the bishopric of Liége. Probably numbering not more than a few hundred families, they nonetheless laid the foundation for the triumphant upswing of the Swedish iron industry. Apart from the Walloon forge, the French-speaking Walloons also introduced the masoned blast furnace frequently called the "French" furnace. Their language also left other enduring marks. The name of one of the iron centers founded by de Geer is still spelled in French fashion (Leufsta, where the Swedish spelling would require Lövsta), and not a few Swedes today bear names of Walloon origin: Gauffin, Hybinette, Sporrong, Lemoine (or Lemon), Guillaume (or Gilljam), Blanc (or Blanck), etc. Throughout the eighteenth century Walloon ironworkers were still manning the ironworks in Uppland.

But not only the Walloons were active in the iron industry. From Austria or southeast Germany came the German forge, and a Dutchman, Reinhold Rademacher, founded the famous iron manufactories at Eskilstuna. Among the leading ironmasters we find, besides de Geer and Messrs. Momma-Reenstierna, a Frenchman, Claude Roquette (later Hägerstierna), "tailor by appointment" to Queen Christine. Then there were the many foreign merchants of Stockholm and Göteborg who later entered the group of ironmasters, such as the distinguished Tham (Tamm) family, and the even more distinguished though now extinct family of Amya, to mention only a few.

The other metal trades likewise profited from the aliens. In the copper industry an improvement in the later stages of the liquation process, the so-called *gårmakeri,* was introduced by Govert Silentz (later de Silentz) from southern Holland. Minting, closely connected with the copper industry, was taken over by a Dutchman named Marcus Kock (later, Cronström), whose descendants played a prominent part in Swedish business for some time. Even the tar trade was in the hands of foreigners or their descendants. Needless to say, commerce in general was in their hands. So, for instance, three of the four directors of the first semi-governmental copper company were foreigners. As we have already seen, the founder of Sweden's first bank and the creator of Europe's first paper money was another Dutchman, Johan Palmstruch (whose name before he was raised to nobility had been Wittmacher). Palmstruch, incidentally, was the brother-in-law of Rademacher, the aforementioned founder of the Eskilstuna manufactories.

All those fields of activity, however, were overshadowed by the foreigners' contribution to government finance, and in no other sphere was their role more essential. For, prior to the creation of commercial banks in the late nineteenth century, the international capital market was operated largely through personal contacts between the various capitals, based as a rule on family ties. To supply governments with foreign credits, family connections were therefore almost indispensable. The most illustrious example from a later period is of course the House of Rothschild, "the five little Frankfurters," who maintained the most intimate contacts among the five financial centers in which they resided. Two similar cases, though by no means so famous, occurred in Gustavus Adolphus' reign: the five Spierinck brothers (in Swedish, Spiring) from Holland, one of whom, later raised to nobility and given the name of Silvercroon, was the excellent administrator of the very profitable Swedish war-tolls in Prussia in 1629–1635;[49] and the four Wewetzer brothers, one of whom, given the name of Rosenstierna, was Secretary of the Treasury. Louis de Geer also coöperated with Dutch relatives, particularly the Trip family. In addition, there was an almost endless number of foreign financiers among the creditors and financial advisers of the government until the end of the century, whereas very few Swedes belonged to that category except a few aristocrats like Axel Oxenstierna and Jacob de la Gardie, the Lord Constable. Most of the capital raised for the first copper company was contributed by foreigners, primarily by Louis de Geer; Axel Oxenstierna was the only Swede to participate on any sizable scale.

Conditions in the city of Göteborg are illuminating.[50] It was almost planned as a Dutch colony. The first City Council contained ten Dutchmen, one Scotsman, and seven Swedes. The second Council was even more heavily dominated by foreigners: there were five Dutchmen, two Germans, two Scotsmen, and only three Swedes. Characteristically, the highest office of the city, that of the burgrave, who was the city's link with the national government, was filled by foreigners, first a Dutchman and then a Holsteiner, for the first thirty years after the city's founding in the 1620's. That the local mayor should also be a foreigner was almost taken for granted. In the city's affairs the Dutch — and for that matter the foreigners in general — were completely dominating. Construction of the port was directed by two Dutchmen who were even authorized to hire Dutch labor; the fishery, particularly the herring processing, was regarded as one of the perquisites of the Dutch; a Dutchman was the head of the first tar company of the city; the fields of the city were accorded to immigrating Dutch peasants; the physicians were usually Dutch, and when the city considered employing a mid-wife it was found necessary to import a Dutch widow. Naturally the same held true in commerce, except that there was a prominent Englishman among the merchants, and later quite a few Germans.

Faced with conditions of this kind, we might be tempted to conclude that the seventeenth century was merely a repetition of the Hanseatic period in Swedish history. Actually, there was a fundamental difference. The Hansards regarded themselves as the agents of a more advanced civilization and Sweden as a colonial territory; they remained thoroughly German and were never assimilated. But it did not even occur to the aliens of the seventeenth century that the country might have belonged to them, and they, or at least their children, acclimatized with almost incredible speed. As a rule, the second generation was Swedish by language as well as by custom.

A typical example is that of two brothers named de Besche, whose forefather had arrived in Sweden some time around 1600. The two brothers, third-generation Swedes, were the leaders of the group of Swedish ironmakers hired by Colbert,[51] and although the family, like de Geer's, originally hailed from the French-speaking bishopric of Liége, one of the brothers complained that he lacked a writing knowledge of French.

While the immigrants were rapidly assimilated and after a generation not to be distinguished from Swedes of ancient stock, nevertheless they brought many changes to Swedish society. But there was no trace of any particularism. Although Gustavus Adolphus, in his eagerness to attract Dutch immigrants to Göteborg, had promised the city its own jurisdiction,[52] much in the fashion of German cities, no such arrangement was ever put into effect. Evidently this was an expression of the strength of the Swedish state. The immigrants were satisfied to accept its rule and to become its loyal servants. In the Hanseatic era, on the other hand, the state had been powerless and completely unable to deal with the arrogance of foreign merchants.

The governments of the seventeenth century also pursued a deliberate policy aimed at absorbing foreigners. An indication of this policy was the extent to which they were raised to knighthood and thereby to membership in the First Estate of the realm. Even today, no less than 42.5 per cent[53] of all the families on the rolls of the Swedish House of Lords (*Riddarhuset*) are of foreign origin, excluding descent on the distaff side. The foreigners were certainly no less numerous as members of the Third Estate, that of the burghers of the towns, although no exact figures are known. Generally speaking, we might say that whereas two of the Estates, the clergy and the peasants, were almost exclusively Swedish, foreigners and their descendants were as common as Swedes in the other two Estates, that is, among the nobility and the burghers.

Any ambitious foreigner thus found the doors wide open, and there was no pressure on him to acquire any external Swedish characteristics. The age of nationalisms was yet to come; Europe still enjoyed the legacy of medieval universalism as epitomized by the Holy Roman Empire and the church. The situation was so remote from the reality of the present day as to appear almost shocking to a modern observer. Thus respect for the purity of the language was practically nil. Even Axel Oxenstierna, although a Swede, wrote a language which was an unashamed hodgepodge of Swedish and Latin with a dash of German; and he was far from alone in this habit. Foreigners were free to use their own language when it suited them. A very good illustration is provided by a debate in the House of Lords which was opened by no less than four speeches in foreign tongues[54] — three in German and one, by Louis de Geer, in Dutch. We have already mentioned how de Geer also corresponded in foreign languages with royalty and with members of the Council. The same practice was followed by people in far more official positions.

That the strong foreign influence was not exclusively to the good is fairly self-evident. Most serious was the attitude toward the peasants which foreign immigrants brought along with them from their feudal homelands. This constituted a grave threat to the traditional freedom of the Swedish peasantry, to which we shall return presently.

## Towns and Town Policy

Foreign influence on economic policy in seventeenth-century Sweden is more difficult to ascertain than the foreigners' contribution to industry and commerce. For the most part, economic policy bore the imprint of the government's general policy with which it was inseparably connected. However, it was also largely influenced by ideas of essentially foreign origin, particularly with regard to the cities. Charles IX, as we have seen, had been an ardent advocate of the extension of the power of the cities. With few changes this policy continued to be pursued throughout the seventeenth century when the area to which it applied was formidably widened by the foundation of new towns on a scale unprecedented in earlier centuries and, in fact, unparalleled until our own age. But quite unlike modern urbanization, the foundation of new cities in the seventeenth century was still inspired by the traditional principles of town policy, which purported to reserve all urban industry — commerce, shipping, and manufacture — to the cities and to prevent its exercise in the countryside.

The number of cities in Sweden was roughly doubled as a result of this policy — to thirty-three old cities, thirty-one new ones were added.[55] Nevertheless, the effects of that urbanization must not be overrated. Rarely did the new creations manifest much vigor and vitality. Unfortunately, no statistics of the urban population of Sweden are available until 1800; but a glance at the situation in that year shows that the new cities had not withstood too well the test of time. Almost half of the cities existing in 1800 had been founded in the seventeenth century; yet their inhabitants were only about 28 per cent of the total urban population. Whereas the average population of the older towns amounted to 1,600, that of the new towns was 1,000, while two-thirds of the new towns still had a population of less than 1,000.[56] A few had grown to considerable size; otherwise the average for the new towns would have been even lower. Nor were the contemporaries satisfied. Swedish cities came in for a great deal of sharp comment in the Council at the time of Gustavus Adolphus and the regency which succeeded him, although criticism was directed against the old towns as much as against the new. Gustavus Adolphus himself called the cities "devoid of commerce, rotting, and decrepit," and the Lord Councilors used unflattering terms such as "peasant villages" and "thieves' dens."[57]

The reasons are easy to see. Above all, the new towns and, for that part, some of the old ones served no real economic purpose. The functions which the so-called urban industries were supposed to perform were in reality more conveniently discharged by the peasants themselves, whose primitive agriculture left them with a great deal of spare time. The peasants were also extremely reluctant to move to the cities. A group of peasants compulsorily removed to the city of Umeå petitioned for relief, calling themselves "townsmen by command,"[58] and they remained ever ready to escape at the first opportunity. The same lack of enthusiasm characterized dealings between the peasants of the countryside and the townsmen. A peasant made the irreverent comment about the city of Sundsvall, "It should have been in Hell, but they put it between Hudiksvall and Härnösand."[59] By and large, the towns, especially the new ones, remained rural settlements equipped with town charters.

Municipal policy itself was to a great extent responsible for the weakness of the new towns. With few exceptions, they were in the category of "inland cities" (*uppstäder*), while national policy drastically favored the staple cities at the expense of the inland cities. The town toll[60] introduced in 1622, called the "petty toll," further discouraged trade between the countryside and the towns. The peasants were anxious to eschew both the dues and the chicanery of the toll officials.

Most important, however, was the government's overriding desire to favor the capital at the expense of all other cities. Axel Oxenstierna, for instance, had an almost touching confidence in Stockholm's future. One of the darkest moments of his life was the day Sweden was forced to renounce the Swedish war-tolls levied in Prussia during the Thirty Years' War. "Half the power and strength of the realm is lost," [61] he complained. "The best we can hope for is the growth and enlargement of the towns, especially of Stockholm." On a later occasion he remarked, "All our measures should aim at the settlement and growth of Stockholm. Thereafter Stockholm should be able to put the others on their feet." [62] Comments on this subject in the Council were to the same effect.

Stockholm actually did expand very fast, although deliberate governmental policies had little to do with the rise of the city. As the center of the rapidly growing iron export trade and the seat of the central authorities, Stockholm developed quite spontaneously. Peasants throughout the country evidently preferred to trade with Stockholm[63] where the merchants with whom they dealt were subject to vigorous competition, rather than to be caught within the trammels of some monopolistic trader in the nearest small town. Even from very remote parts of Norrland peasants would deliver their produce to Stockholm, by-passing all the small towns in the North. It is difficult to estimate the population of the capital, but it was obviously growing rapidly. For 1676 we have a probably incomplete estimate of 42,000–43,000[64] which was quite impressive.

From the time of Queen Christine's regency to the end of the period, the major share of the country's foreign trade, no less than two-thirds to three-quarters, passed through Stockholm. This left a mere trickle of trade to be split up between all the other staple cities; it is not surprising, therefore, to find that the latter remained quite insignificant. Apparently none of them exceeded 5,000 inhabitants. Particularly Göteborg must have been a disappointment to the government. When it was founded, the city was intended for a glorious future; it was even expected to become the grain staple of northern Europe and a successful competitor of Amsterdam. Instead, it never grew beyond the size of Norrköping,[65] which was one of the medieval towns, and its share of the country's foreign trade tended, if anything, to decline until it was stimulated by the iron exports from Värmland. Apart from Göteborg, the only new city to acquire any importance in the course of the century was Karlskrona, which sometimes led Göteborg in growth. The reason for this was that Karlskrona became the country's main naval base.[66]

## MERCANTILISM[67]

The seventeenth century introduced one new feature into Sweden's economic policy — mercantilist ideas replaced the "policy of provision" of natural economy, which had aimed at promoting imports rather than exports. Beginning with the regency under Queen Christine, a decisive emphasis was placed upon the achievement of a "favorable" balance of trade. Although it seems not to have been generally realized by contemporaries, the export surplus which gradually developed was actually caused by factors that were anything but favorable. Foreign borrowing eventually resulted in considerable interest payments which could be transferred only in the form of an export surplus. Especially beginning with the reign of Charles XI, an orthodox policy of protection of manufactures was also carried out. "Manufactures," as the term was used, included finished products but not the prominent export commodities such as metals or forest products. The main emphasis rested on textiles. The textile industries were granted a number of privileges and reached a certain prosperity in Stockholm and Norrköping. Norrköping is still the center of the Swedish wool industry; Stockholm, however, lost most of its textile industries in the course of the nineteenth century.

But mercantilist policies were, generally speaking, of very limited scope in Sweden, and their fruits as a rule few and insignificant. Ideologically, nonetheless, Swedish mercantilism is of great historical interest as an indication of the Dutch and general West European influence on Swedish intellectual life. Mercantilist thought in Sweden was akin throughout to mercantilist principles current in western Europe. It laid heavy stress on what it called "freedom," and there is little doubt that Axel Oxenstierna as well as most other leading politicians attempted to achieve their results with a minimum of coercion, that is of prohibition and sanction. The prime instruments of policy were tariff protection at first and creation of industrial privileges later on. Even more important was the almost unexceptional aversion to government-conducted enterprises. Private businessmen were to be induced to engage in such activities as served the general interest. German mercantilism, which on the whole developed somewhat later, was to put a very different emphasis on coercion and state enterprise.

Among the more abortive features of this economic policy was the interest in colonization. The most famous of the colonies was New Sweden, on the shores of the Delaware, founded in 1638.[68] It survived for eighteen years, without ever having attained any particular importance. The other colonial ventures were of even less consequence.

In the field of business organization the most remarkable achievement of mercantilism was the creation of trading companies.[69] This innovation was eagerly received in Sweden, though the results were much poorer than, for instance, in England and the Netherlands. Only the tar companies were really successful. We have already mentioned the two copper companies, of which the first survived for just a few years and the second proved a failure from the outset. Repeated attempts to found iron companies resulted in stillborn ventures. In the import trade, which dealt with a wide range of commodities in small lots, the corporate form of organization proved too inflexible; salt and tobacco companies were the only ones to acquire any significance.

In shipping, too, trading companies were active, although this form of organization remained quite secondary compared with the standard form of partnership through which individual shippers held shares in a large number of ships in order to distribute their risks in the absence of maritime insurance.[70] Their customers, incidentally, did the same so that cargoes as well as ships had a great many part owners.

Swedish shipping at times underwent a fairly considerable expansion which was largely politically determined. Whenever Sweden was able to stay neutral in the many naval wars of the period, much of the immense Dutch shipping in the Baltic was taken over by the Swedes.[71] In part this was mere camouflage, as when Dutch ships were registered under the Swedish flag, but sometimes the shifts in ownership were real. In the boom of the 1690's, the Swedish mercantile fleet counted no less than 750 ships,[72] a size it did not reach again until more than a century later.

Shipping policy was in one respect closely related to mercantilism as a system of power. It occurred to Gustavus Adolphus that the building of armed merchant ships, designed to serve as a naval reserve and to defend themselves against attackers, should be encouraged.[73] This gave rise to the so-called "mounted" or armed merchantmen which carried a certain number of guns and satisfied various other military requirements. Such a vessel seems to have been a Swedish innovation, although it was later imitated elsewhere. In Sweden it became the basis for a discriminatory tariff policy, which was one of the chief features of Swedish shipping regulation. Armed merchantmen enjoyed what was somewhat exaggeratedly called *helfrihet*, or "total exemption," entitling them to a reduction of their customs duties by one-third. Other Swedish ships were subject to *halvfrihet* ("half exemption"), a customs reduction by one-sixth. Foreigners paid the full amount. This policy was not entirely successful, partly because the size of the men-of-war was rapidly increasing. Merchantmen would have had to follow suit if they were to hold their own, but such increases in tonnage would have rendered them too unwieldy for commercial purposes. Nevertheless, the system was retained from its inception in 1645 until the reign of Charles XII, when it was suspended never to be reinstated.

Under the influence of mercantilism, the first Swedish writer on economics emerged. He was Johan Classon Risingh,[74] first Secretary of the Board of Commerce (*Kommerskollegium*) established in 1651, and Governor of New Sweden during the last few years of the colony's existence. His chief interest, however, overshadowing all his other activities, was the *magnum opus* which he planned and only partially finished. This obsession was mainly responsible for his death in misery in 1672. His book, of which even the finished parts are still unpublished, was called *En Tractat om Kiöp-Handelen* (A Tract on Commerce). A short *Uttogh* (excerpt) was published in 1669, through the intervention of Magnus Gabriel de la Gardie. In this work, as in his many likewise unpublished pamphlets, Risingh appears as an orthodox though slightly old-fashioned West

European mercantilist, strongly influenced by Dutch and, to a somewhat lesser extent, English thought. Having spent some years in Amsterdam, he was actually a product of the Dutch intellectual climate and paid little heed to the facts of Swedish economic life. Thus, he presents a very vivid picture of a merchant's life, which, though a rather accurate description of a big merchant in Amsterdam, was certainly quite inapplicable in Sweden. It is mainly as an exponent of the Dutch influence rather than as an original thinker that he deserves our interest.

The chief difference between the various mercantilist schools of thought, at least in the eyes of contemporaries, was that the "bullionists" advocated export prohibitions on precious metals in order to create a favorable balance of trade, whereas later mercantilist writers wanted to create an export surplus through commercial policy which, by stimulation of exports and prohibitions on imports, would result in an automatic influx of precious metals. On this point, Risingh belonged to the older bullionist tradition, and his book contained few novelties. On the other hand, he showed a good deal of balanced judgment, tended to avoid exaggerations, and was well-informed on conditions in Holland.

## AGRICULTURE, STANDARD OF LIVING, AND POPULATION

Although many changes took place in the Swedish economy in the seventeenth century, one must not infer that there was anything like a basic transformation of the economy. No such thing occurred in any country, despite the fact that the impact of change in countries like the Netherlands, France, and England was much stronger than in Sweden. The main obstacle was the extreme agrarian traditionalism. Old agricultural methods persisted with practically no change, foreign influence was small, and the continuation of the strip-system constituted an almost insuperable barrier to reform. This did not mean that agricultural output did not increase; considering the growth in population, stability in output would have been catastrophic. But the increase came from the cultivation of new land rather than from gains in productivity.[75]

One aspect of the cultivation of new land attracted great attention and continued to do so for a long time. That was the settlement of

Finns in the forest areas of mid-Sweden, begun under Charles IX when he was still the Duke of Södermanland, and carried on into modern times.[76]

Swedish cultivation was now extended to the moraines above the line of glaciation where, unlike the once submerged lowlands, the land was not covered by sedimentary deposits from the receding waters. The Finns cleared the land by burning it over (*svedjebruk*), and sowed in the ashes; huge forest areas were devastated, often because the fire got out of hand. On the ash-covered fields first-year yields were enormous compared with those in traditional agriculture, but after a couple of years the Finns would leave their settlements and move elsewhere. The growing concern over the wood supply for the metal industries made the government apprehensive of further deforestation. The Finns, who had originally been encouraged to immigrate, were now sometimes even persecuted by the government. In addition, bitter antagonism often prevailed between the Finns and the native farming population. Actually, reclamation of farm land by the Swedes themselves was probably more extensive than that by the Finns, particularly as the iron industry spread over previously unsettled forest regions.

Even with the extension of cultivation by internal colonization, increases in food production were insufficient. If food budgets from the seventeenth century are compared with those from the sixteenth, an unmistakable although not uniform decline appears. The average decrease in per capita food consumption might perhaps be estimated at one-third. An example from the manor of Gripsholm for which data are available for both centuries may be cited. Consumption in 1555 had been 4,166 calories per day and person. In the years 1638, 1653, and 1661, it was only 2,480, 2,883, and 2,920 calories respectively.[77] In composition the diet remained almost exactly the same as in the sixteenth century. For the upper classes, however, the Thirty Years' War and the immigration of German nobility led to almost unbelievable gluttony as well as to a general luxury which in some respects was quite barbarous.

Nothing would be more helpful for the study of social conditions of the time than some knowledge of its demographic situation. Unfortunately, our data are sparse as well as unreliable. An exceptionally thorough investigation of conditions under Gustavus Adolphus has resulted in an estimate for the total Swedish population of about 900,000.[78] This may be on the high side, but presumably it is impossible to arrive at a more accurate estimate. From 1720 on, the size of the population in Sweden proper is known with fair precision. In 1720, it amounted to 1.44 million.[79] However, the area of the country had then been enlarged considerably by the acquisition of new provinces, and it is difficult to ascertain the population in what had been the Sweden of Gustavus Adolphus. A careful reckoning might put the population of this area in 1720 at approximately 1.12 million.[80] If those estimates are reasonably correct, there had been an increase of roughly one-fourth in about one hundred years, which corresponds to an annual rate of growth of .22 per cent. That is more or less what can be expected for those years, considering the generally low rate of population growth in pre-modern periods and also, in this case, the hardships to which Sweden was exposed in the seventeenth century. In the nineteenth century, the Swedish population doubled in only eighty years,[81] which means that it grew at an average annual rate of .87 per cent, but this was an unprecedented phenomenon.

## ALIENATION AND REVERSION OF CROWN LANDS

The economic development so far described coincided with two momentous transformations relating to the distribution of wealth. One was the alienation of crown lands and revenues to the nobility; the other was the reversion of this process, which was described by the technical term "the reduction" (*reduktionen*).

The lands and revenues alienated from the crown ever since the death of Gustavus Vasa (1560), but especially during the seventeenth century, came almost exclusively into the hands of the aristocracy which then rose to the peak of its power. The transfer of property was so extensive that holdings of the nobility increased some two and a half times. By 1652, only about 28 per cent[82] of the total land holdings remained in the possession of the peasants and the crown. The redistribution of property and income was so tremendous that it is difficult to convey all its implications to the modern reader. Its scale may be illustrated by the fact that the annual revenue from alienated property held by twenty-two families of the aristocracy corresponded to the combined salary of five hundred assessors, that is, civil servants of medium rank, or about 8 to 8.5 per cent of the total revenue of the crown.[83] Alienation also had a great many other consequences.

First of all, the crown lost most of its estates. At best the land was sold in regular fashion, but as a rule it was simply given away. Almost all the estates Gustavus Vasa had acquired from the church were transferred to the aristocracy and many more besides. Secondly, a great many of the freeholding peasants were, in a sense, deprived of their ownership by the so-called alienation of rent. This transfer of crown revenue was even more important than the transfer of crown land, and calls for a word of explanation. The land in this case was owned not by the crown but by the peasants. But, as mentioned previously (page 30), the ownership of the peasants was not unqualified. The superior ownership (*dominium directum*) or, in the view of many people, the real ownership, was held to be vested in those to whom the peasants paid their taxes, which were commonly called rents. Alienation therefore meant something more than mere transfer of the tax rights from the crown to the aristocracy.

That the transfer of tax rights was also thought to imply a transfer of property rights is clearly seen by a few examples. Even such a conservative and moderate man as Axel Oxenstierna called the recipients to whom the taxes from the peasants had been transferred "the lords and masters of the peasants."[84] The documents of alienation conferred upon the recipients the right "to enjoy, use, and retain" these estates "in everlasting ownership (*sic*), as do others their hereditary property (*sic*)."[85] When Per Brahe, the most masterful of the landed aristocrats, made a remark in Council to the effect that only the nobles were the immediate or direct subjects of the crown, the peasants being *mediate subditi*, that is subjects under the nobility and only indirectly under the crown,[86] he was obviously introducing in Sweden a purely feudal conception. It is no wonder, then, that the peasant representatives in the Estates declared themselves fearful of the fate which had reduced free men to serfdom in other countries.

Whereas the conveyance of land and land rents to the nobility was quantitatively the most important change in land ownership, another development, much less conspicuous, was to have far more lasting effects — namely, the emergence of large-scale farming. Manorial estates (*säterier*) enjoyed more complete tax exemption than other *frälse* land, which was one reason for the interest the aristocracy now manifested in agricultural management. In addition, there were also other social and personal advantages in the possession of a country residence. In comparison with earlier periods, the formation of manorial estates was extraordinarily rapid. In Uppland, where the change was probably more drastic than elsewhere, their number increased eightfold during the period of alienation. In the famous work by Erik Dahlbergh, *Suecia antiqua et hodierna,* the architectural splendor of seventeenth-century manor houses and castles is vividly illustrated, although it should be remembered that Dahlbergh's drawings were often based on architectural designs that were never carried out. There can be no doubt that this was the time when the country estate became an institution.

The factors behind the alienation of crown property and revenue were many, some of them quite evident. For its tremendous military exertions the crown disposed of no other assets than its estates and taxes from the peasants. Sheer financial pressure was thus the main factor, especially during the regency under Queen Christine. Transfers were partly in the nature of repayment of old debts; this was the case with Louis de Geer's land acquisitions. In other cases, salaries of civil servants had been withheld for long periods, accruing to a considerable sum. Sometimes, alienation was in return for real services, whether in war or peace. But in addition, most notably during Christine's own reign when alienations reached their peak, many instances of sheer squandering occurred.

Yet there was also a deliberate policy behind the alienations, particularly under men like Gustavus Adolphus and Axel Oxenstierna. They were both confirmed adherents to the view that natural economy should be replaced by a money economy, especially in the field of public finances as well as in the country at large. This, incidentally, was one reason for the policy of enthusiastic urbanization. For townsmen could pay in money, while the peasants paid in kind. The great emphasis on customs duties was rooted in the same notion. In the case of alienations there was a wide discrepancy between the aim and the result. Payments of rent continued to be in kind. The only difference was that they were made to a new recipient. At best, the crown acquired a claim which was to be rendered in cash or in services for which, in absence of alienations, the crown would have to pay in money. But time and again alienation was in the nature of a pure grant so that no payment to the crown resulted from it. Even where land was given away for a consideration, the crown was in fact renouncing a permanent revenue in return for a single sum paid once and for all.

In such cases the only justification for the transfer was the notion that the land would be much more efficiently administered by the recipients than by the crown. The same view also made for a general tendency to transfer various activities from public to private enterprise. But it would be naive to believe that there was no more to alienations than just a preference for private enterprise. One must not forget that land was conveyed to the aristocracy by governments closely associated with the aristocracy.[87]

All the same, the alienations were merely an episode in Swedish history. A second momentous redistribution of wealth and income followed. In the long run, the drawbacks of alienation were such as to become intolerable from the monarchy's point of view. A strong king on the throne was bound to attempt to undo the harm that had been done. Thus, under Charles X to a very moderate degree, and under Charles XI in a far more drastic fashion, the policy was reversed and a large-scale restoration of the alienated lands was carried out. This process came to be called "reduction" or reversion (*reduktionen*).[88]

Although reversion aimed principally at the restoration of whatever alienation of land had taken place without equivalent compensation, in its extremely ruthless and merciless execution, which was directed by the king himself, there was a general tendency to minimize the value of the services that had been performed by the recipients. To that extent, the intention was to reduce the aristocracy to its position before the time of the large alienations. But in one very important case — that of the manorial estates — that was not done. Formally and legally the reason was that the amount of land to be reversed was stated in value terms computed as capitalized rents, which meant that the recipients were not obliged to return to the crown the same lands they had received but could substitute lands from their original holdings. Obviously, they found it generally preferable to renounce scattered holdings where they collected the dues from the peasants but did not exercise managerial functions. The exchange of such scattered holdings for compact manorial estates was profitable for the landlords since the estates enjoyed almost complete tax exemption while the scattered holdings did not. In fact, it may appear strange that Charles XI did not oppose such exchanges. At any rate, the consideration which probably carried most weight with the aristocracy was that they were far more intimately attached to their domains than to their other holdings; often expensive manor houses had been erected on the former to serve as their main residences.

The government had a very limited interest in the acquisition of manorial estates. Presumably this was behind Charles' failure to insist upon return of the land attached to manorial estates. Such estates had to be operated on a larger scale, and large-scale agriculture by the crown had practically disappeared by that time. Consequently, preservation of manorial estates was in the interest of both the government and the landlords. The actual outcome has so far been studied in only two provinces, Uppland and Södermanland; there most of the estates remained in the possession of the nobility and the gentry. Alienation had thus resulted in one definitive change that was not undone by reversion. Since, on the other hand, rent-paying holdings were extensively restored to the crown, the result of the two-staged process (alienation *cum* reversion) was to make the Swedish landlords owners of compact and often self-managed estates, but also to weaken their position as a rentier class.

While there is no doubt that the aristocracy was dispossessed of the larger part of the holdings it had acquired through alienations,[89] one must not imagine that the landlords were submitted to terrible suffering and deprivation. The main inconvenience of the confiscation was the confusion in property relations: titles to land were sometimes disputed for decades, and endless litigations were necessary in order to decide whether a certain piece of land belonged to the noble or to the crown. To be sure, some cases of real hardship occurred, although by no means as many as the outcry with which the reversion was received might suggest.

As a matter of fact, only one aristocratic family was deprived of *all* its landed possessions, the family of de la Gardie, but it was a family which in the preceding era, through descent, court connections, and offices held, had stood at the very top of the hierarchy. Hence it almost appears as if Charles XI were deliberately striving to ruin Magnus Gabriel de la Gardie, the king's uncle by marriage and in his day the most magnificent among Swedish noblemen, whose revenue might easily have made him an object of envy for many a ruler of a German principality. His major-domo died of starvation, while de la Gardie himself sat out the rest of his days on an estate which once had been his own but now belonged to the crown. Even that shelter was a special favor accorded to him by what he called the *"malitieuse pouvoir* of Mr. Wrede,"[90] the chief reversion administrator in the final phase of the reform. His wife, Countess Marie Euphrosyne, was allowed to keep another estate for her lifetime, and his sons fared no better — they all had to affirm their impoverishment under oath (*juramentum paupertatis*) in order to be released from the claims against their father. However, those claims arose not only from the reversion of alienated crown land, but also from another of Charles XI's blows against the nobility, the so-called Regency Inquisition (*förmyndarräfsten*). The king thereby called to account the regents who had ruled the country during his minority and forced them and their families to refund large amounts of money they were said to have personally appropriated. De la Gardie had been one of the principal regents, which contributed to the downfall of the family. Moreover, the de la Gardies, unlike many other families, did not hold medieval title to any land; all their holdings stemmed from alienation and were affected by reversion.

The other members of the *haute aristocratie* were in a much more favorable position, despite all their clamor and lamentation. Anecdotal history would have it that when treasury agents wanted to cut the shining buttons off his coat, Gustaf Otto Stenbock,[91] Lord Admiral and later Lord Constable, broke into tears, saying that now there was nothing left and that his wife would have to support him. But such stories are sheer fiction. Actually Stenbock kept no less than six large manors; his wife had at least one and subsequently bought numerous others. The case of his nephew, Lord Marshal Johan Gabriel Stenbock,[92] is even more striking. He was very close to Charles XI, and in a letter to the king claimed that he no longer owned an acre, that all his lands, entailed or not, were gone. It is true that at the time the title to a great many of his estates was not yet cleared; still, the ultimate result was very different. In Uppland alone he came to own, though at various times, no less than twenty-five different estates, among which were some of the largest in the land. He became a sort of wholesaler in manorial estates, was appointed to serve on the board which administered the reform, and ended up as one of the greatest landlords in Uppland.

Another spectacular case was that of Nils Brahe, who was burdened with the debt of both his uncle, the Lord Stewart Per Brahe, Jr., and his father-in-law, the Lord Constable Carl Gustaf Wrangel, both of whom had been members of the regency council. He was forced to surrender fabulous sums, but nevertheless managed to salvage all the large family estates.[93]

At the same time, however, that a great many landlords were dispossessed of their holdings, large estates were assembled in the hands of new owners. This is not an unusual historical occurrence. On the contrary, almost all economic revolutions with which we are familiar have created opportunities for rapid personal enrichment. The Swedish social and political framework was such that even after reversion it was the nobility that was offered this opportunity, at which it did not fail to grasp. The notion that Charles XI himself should have been hostile to nobility *per se* is entirely unfounded. In fact, no other ruler, including Queen Christine, created more noblemen. The new landed fortunes fell into the hands of the reversion administrators and the king's favorites. We have cited the case of Johan Gabriel Stenbock, but a few others were perhaps even more noteworthy. Thus, the competent and merciless Fabian Wrede[94] was among those who benefited most from the reversion which he himself administered. Another gainer was Charles XII's Foreign Minister, Carl Piper,[95] and especially his widow, Christine von Törne, who was probably Sweden's wealthiest woman, the owner of innumerable estates of which a great many were entailed. By a remarkable quirk of circumstance, which Linnaeus would certainly have attributed to *nemesis divina*,* Fabian Wrede's acquisitions were later to be used to redress the family which had been hardest hit by reversion. Magnus Julius de la Gardie,[96] Lord Councilor and

---

* The book Linnaeus published under that title was intended to show the retribution falling upon evildoers through their becoming victims of the same sort of disaster they had themselves created for others.

High Marshal in the early eighteenth century, married Wrede's fourteen-year-old granddaughter, thereby acquiring no less than eighteen of the Wrede estates; hence the de la Gardies once more became one of Sweden's wealthiest families.

The riches assembled by the reversion administrators are not difficult to explain. Their influence upon the king who had become an absolute monarch, the corruption for which both Wrede and Piper were famous — or infamous — together with their access to inside information, enabled them to profit from the situation.

But those who had ready cash and knew how to use it also saw their chance for large acquisitions. In particular, the wealthy nobles of Skåne seem to have put the opportunities to account. Debt-ridden property was bought at auctions on easy terms, for often enough those with ready money did not hesitate to avail themselves of the distress of their brethren. Naturally, this aroused deep resentment. One of the unfortunate victims remarked in the House of Lords in 1689: "Our lands are taken away for a penny; what is worth 70,000 riksdaler is sold for 7,000." [97] An example on a large scale was Roslags-Näsby, a prosperous estate with a "well and opulently appointed" *corps de logis* (manor house) and barns, purchased by J. G. Stenbock for the absurd sum of 1,368 daler silver.[98]

The chief conclusion must be that the reversion by no means reduced the Swedish nobility to complete ruin. Although growth of the mining and metal industries and of commerce was already creating a certain wealth outside the ranks of the nobility, for a long time to come the great riches remained in the hands of the nobles.

The economic and social effects of the reversion were manifold. Its only purpose, which had been to reclaim the sources of crown revenue, was attained. But the recovery of alienated property had another far-reaching consequence. The increasing use of money in public finance so vigorously promoted by Gustavus Adolphus and his Chancellor was checked, and a deliberate return to natural economy took place. Once more the revenue of the crown consisted of grain, meat, iron, and scores of other commodities. The result of this retrogression was that natural economy in Sweden persisted longer than in any other comparable country. This was especially true of public finance where it might even be said to have lingered on until the beginning of the present century.

The renaissance of natural economy was most clearly reflected in the organization of the armed forces.[99] Rents accruing to the crown were assigned for definite purposes, especially for maintenance of the cavalry. The infantry, on the other hand, was maintained by peasants organized in permanent groups, each of which set up a farm for cultivation by a soldier. Consequently, the army tended to be composed of peasants rather than of warriors. Civil servants, too, were assigned specific shares in the crown's revenue from the peasants. It may sound strange to the modern reader that the early nineteenth-century poet, Esaias Tegnér, should complain about low grain prices, but the reason was simply that his salary as a professor at the State University of Lund was paid in grain. Apart from such allocations of tax revenue, estates belonging to the crown were directly assigned as residences to officers of the army as well as to civil servants, for their operation and usufruct.

Though all this was doubtless quite medieval in character, it created a security for public officials that had long been wanting. From the government's point of view, it was an advantage to have them closely bound to the soil and producing their own sustenance. On the other hand, this very fact tended to make both the civil service and the army much less flexible. In the past Sweden's political strength had largely rested on her aristocratic absentee landlords and her cash-paid army; those assets were now lost. Charles XII, it is true, pursued an aggressive foreign policy and embarked upon vast military ventures, but the intolerable strains to which the public finances became subject within three years of the death of Charles XI were largely due to the rigidities of natural economy. It is also characteristic that, whereas previous wars had been financed in part through extensive domestic and foreign loans, the twenty years of the great Northern War (1700–1720) resulted in only very slight foreign borrowing. The Swedish government was simply not in a position to offer adequate security to lenders, once its revenue had all been assigned for specific purposes.

The reversion obviously had momentous consequences for the peasants. Freeholders and tenants on crown land who through alienation of their taxes and dues had been submitted to the rule of lords, regained their old status. That their general position was thereby improved is quite evident, particularly with respect to the freeholders.

They no longer could be said to be subjects of "lords and masters," and no one could thenceforth call them *mediate subditi.*

Whether their economic conditions were actually improved is far more dubious. Although this large problem has hardly yet been investigated, it seems that the king's tenants had fared as well, or better, under the lords as they did under the crown, so that they really did not benefit from reversion. But it would seem plausible, though far from proven, that the opposite was true of those freeholders whose taxes had been leased out to the lord. The latter cannot be presumed to have been as interested in their welfare as in that of his own tenants; their gain might therefore well have been economic as well as social. Whatever benefits the peasants re-

TABLE 7.  DISTRIBUTION OF LAND OWNERSHIP IN SWEDEN
*Percentages*

|  | At the end of the Middle Ages | At the death of Gustavus Vasa (1560) | Charles XII's reign (1700) |
|---|---|---|---|
| Crown (*kronojord*) | 5.5 | 28.2 | 35.6 |
| Church (*kyrkojord*) | 21.0 | — | — |
| Nobility (*frälsejord*) | 21.8 | 22.4 | 32.9 |
| Peasants (*skattejord*) | 51.7 | 49.4 | 31.5 |
| Total | 100.0 | 100.0 | 100.0 |

Source: Heckscher, *Sveriges ekonomiska historia från Gustav Vasa*, I:1, Appendix IV, Tables 1 and 2. See also note to Table 5.

ceived were tempered by the subordination to military and civilian functionaries of the state to which they now owed their payment of dues and taxes.[100] Yet, although the system caused some friction, in the last analysis the status which reversion bestowed upon the peasants was surely the prerequisite for their liberty and subsequent rise to power. Already in the following century they were to reap the fruits of the social transformation which grew out of the land reform.

As to the quantitative aspects of the changes wrought by alienation and reversion, the distribution of land ownership in Sweden proper in 1700 appears in the following table, along with previously cited figures.

As those figures show, reversion resulted in a fairly even distribution among the crown, the nobility and the peasants, although the shares declined somewhat in that order. Thus the peasants did not return to the relative position they occupied in the sixteenth century. The crown was better off than ever before and the nobility too was in a better relative position than at the end of Gustavus Vasa's reign. The figures, however, do not reveal the tremendous shift in favor of the nobility which had taken place in the meantime, only to be revoked through reversion; no comparable figures for that intermediate period are available. Instead, the absolute land holdings of the nobility at different times are presented in the following table, which also includes Finland.

TABLE 8. Landholdings of the Nobility, 1527–1700
*Hemmantal* *

|  | Sweden | Finland | Sweden and Finland |
|---|---|---|---|
| 1527 | 14,822 | 215 | 15,037 |
| 1560 | 15,075 | 327 | 15,402 |
| 1652 | 32,887 | 10,758 | 43,645 |
| 1700: revised * | 15,754 | 1,296 | 17,050 |
| 1700: unrevised | 19,582 | — | — |

Source: Heckscher, *Sveriges ekonomiska historia från Gustav Vasa*, Appendix IV, Table 3.

The table reveals the magnitude of the shifts. It shows also that even after reversion the nobility in Sweden retained more land than it had possessed before the alienations of the late sixteenth and the seventeenth centuries. In Finland, alienations were immensely more extensive, relatively speaking, than in Sweden; and although no exact comparison in stable units can be made, the very low figure

\* *Translator's note:* The inclusion of Finland introduces a complication related to the peculiar Swedish land measure *mantal* or *hemmantal* ("man tale," "homestead tale"). This flexible unit which was first introduced in the assessment lists made up in Gustavus Vasa's days represented the "normal" holding of one peasant household (not the average holding for beside the "full peasants" [*helbönder*] with a *mantal each*, there were "half peasants" [*halvbönder*] with half a *mantal*). The share of holdings below one *mantal* was in 1566 only something like 6 per cent of the total for Sweden (and even less than that for Finland), but in later centuries it grew to more than 50 per cent in Sweden proper. Especially under Charles XI, the assessments in *mantal* were reduced, in other words, the size of the average *mantal* increased, in order to provide a conservative basis for the assignment of revenue for governmental purposes. Comparable post-reversion figures in old, unrevised, *mantal* are available for Sweden but not for Finland.

in revised *hemmantal* units suggests that reversion was also far more thoroughgoing than in Sweden proper. As a matter of fact, it was even more drastic in the trans-Baltic territories, particularly in Livonia and Pomerania — but developments in those areas fall outside the scope of this study.

## SUMMARY

What was then the economic heritage left by the Age of Empire? We must distinguish between the decades before and after the accession of Charles XI.

The first part of the period realized a territorial expansion of permanent importance through the acquisition from Denmark of several provinces* on the Scandinavian peninsula. The economic advantages of those acquisitions were soon evident. With improvements of land transport outstripping those in sea transport, the territories on the Scandinavian land mass were able to make a far more valuable contribution to Swedish economic development than could the trans-Baltic territories which were soon lost. Skåne was later to replace Livonia as the granary of Sweden. Economically, the most important achievement of the time before Charles XII was probably the transformation of the iron industry and the introduction of capitalistic forms of organization. The emergence of the ironmasters as a high-status group beside the nobility was an important social change. The foundation was laid for monopoly in that most important export industry, a policy which came to fruition in the eighteenth century.

But the reign of Charles XI and particularly the reversion was responsible for many more of those nascent social changes that were to mature in the following century. Deprived of their extensive land holdings, the nobles tended to become gentlemen farmers rather than rentiers. While they were more productive perhaps than previously, they contributed less to the government of the country. Also, the civilian and military officials of the crown, whether nobles or not, were tied to the soil from which they received their remuneration. For the peasants the change was even more drastic. The perils of serfdom had been warded off and the foundation for their future rise to political power had been laid. The government, which by its

* Jämtland, Härjedalen, Gotland, Halland, Skåne, Blekinge, Bohuslän.

return to natural economy had radically weakened its capacity for power politics, nevertheless restored to public administration the stability which the earlier part of the period had lacked.

Thus Sweden emerged from its long century of warfare. Though the social and economic developments of the period had vastly improved the country's capacity to solve its internal problems and to raise its prosperity, they also spelled the end of what to this day remains Sweden's most grandiose contribution to European politics. The retreat from power politics called perforce for an attitude of resignation. That peaceful attitude, though not always equally well maintained, marks the birth of modern Sweden.

# CHAPTER 5

# THE FOUNDATION OF
# MODERN SWEDEN (1720–1815)

## GENERAL CHARACTERISTICS

OUR NEXT PERIOD roughly coincides with the eighteenth century, although its beginning is strictly marked by the year 1720 which in Sweden's political history clearly separates the Age of Empire from the era usually described as the Age of Freedom. Surely, in the decades to come more important changes, particularly more important economic changes, occurred than the introduction of the constitution of 1720. But in Swedish economic history that year still stands out as the sharpest dividing line between the new and the old. The sudden change is visible in Chart I, showing the taxable population (pp. 82–83). Upon the conclusion of the Northern War, the curves rise explosively in a way which belittles altogether the corresponding episode in the seventeenth century, when a period of peace had been ushered in by Charles XI. In Chart II, showing Swedish vital statistics, the mortality rates between 1720 and 1735 are amazingly low. Not until the 1840's was mortality again reduced to this level. What happened after 1720, therefore, was not only an increase in general welfare as shown in the increase in taxable numbers, but also a rise in life expectancy. Nor was the improvement merely temporary; a good deal of it remained permanent in spite of a certain setback after the first ten or fifteen years of peace.

The nature of the social change occurring around and after 1720 may be summarized in a few observations, partly amplifying what has already been said about the previous period. While these observations refer especially to the Age of Freedom (1720–1771), which is the most characteristic and best-known part of the eighteenth century, essentially they apply to the succeeding Gustavian period as well

The entire population was affected by the transition from war to peace. The burden that had lain so heavily upon the nation was now lifted. The people could settle down to peaceful pursuits. The economy was given new objectives — peace instead of war, prosperity instead of power. A new spirit descended upon the country. To an astounding degree, even by modern standards, all eyes were upon "utility," all minds concerned with material improvement. The utilitarian craze undeniably created a narrow-minded, petty-bourgeois atmosphere; yet it was by no means incompatible with a genuine enthusiasm for the arts and sciences. The Swedish Academy of Science, founded in 1739, was one product of this intellectual climate with its seemingly contradictory components.

During the Age of Freedom, a fervent interest in social problems developed, especially on the part of the educated classes. We shall come back to this when we discuss the economic literature of the period. Anyone who could wield a pen felt himself called upon to contribute his pennyworth, well aware that the new constitution saddled every citizen with the responsibility for good government. Although in the latter half of the period the return to a strong monarchy under Gustavus III was to change all this, passionate concern with the social question smoldered under the surface and blazed forth at every opportunity.

New elements of the population were rising to leadership in the economy. In the preceding chapter we touched upon the position occupied by the prominent merchants of the cities and by the iron-masters. Those groups constituted a new upper class, mostly untitled, which not only proved able to attain considerable economic power and develop a dignified way of life but in many respects even came to play a part in the intellectual and artistic awakening of the time. This was not true of another group that now acquired a new and increasing significance — namely, the peasants. Nevertheless, the shift in the social status of the peasantry was the most important of all.

By and large, the untitled upper class did not fit into the traditional political system of the four estates, while the status of the peasants in the old system was far below their aspirations in the changing world of the eighteenth century. The new social groupings cut across the old distinctions between nobles, burghers, clergy, and peasants. Many of the ironmasters were nobles, but they shared in a community of interests with both the ironmasters of the gentry, who were not represented at all in the Estates of the Realm, and the merchant-ironmasters, who belonged to the burghers. Thus, in this period the foundation was laid to the new Swedish society, a society based on class rather than status.

In sharp contrast to the earlier period, the dominant impulses now were almost exclusively domestic in origin. Sweden no longer had any ambitions beyond its own borders, and the influx of foreigners was of negligible importance, especially compared to that of the seventeenth century. In one sense national sentiment was therefore strengthened considerably, although its scope was more limited than when the country still aspired to a leading position in European politics. One can hardly imagine Swedes of the eighteenth century using foreign languages in parliamentary debates, though this had been fairly common practice in the preceding era. Nobody would have wanted to use a foreign language for such a purpose and nobody would have tolerated it. Nationalism in the narrow sense of the word, that is, a strong sentimental attachment to that which distinguishes one's own country from all other countries, also made its appearance, although it was to blossom forth in full strength only with the spread of early nineteenth-century romanticism.

Finally, it is impossible not to sense what might be called the modernity of this period. We may be impressed and even fascinated by the men of the seventeenth century, and yet they remain distant figures, quite unlike ourselves. But for the men of the eighteenth century we readily develop an intimate understanding, not because they were greater in stature — this they were not — but because they are so much nearer to us in spirit. In the eighteenth century, for instance, Swedish literature assumed a form familiar and accessible to anybody in command of modern Swedish, whereas considerable effort and historical training are required before one can enjoy the writings of the seventeenth century. At least one of the reasons for this lay in the general absence of foreign influences. The new age was distinctly Swedish in customs, language, and spirit. Even the Gustavian era, for all its borrowed rococo, was not at heart under foreign sway, and its great poets, Kellgren, Bellman, and Lidner, belong to the living tradition of Swedish literature.

## POPULATION

Descending from the heights of intellectual activity to the prose of economic life, the student of the eighteenth century finds himself in possession of material he has badly missed in his scrutiny of earlier periods. Vital statistics are now available, shedding light on that fundamental aspect of social history, the growth of population. Starting in 1721, the data remain fairly meager until 1750, but they nevertheless enable us for the first time to follow the basic trends of the development. From 1749 on, official publications of vital statistics begin to appear. This remarkable and truly pioneering achievement represents by far the oldest regular compilation of its kind. It was from the very beginning characterized by extraordinary thoroughness and almost inexplicable maturity. The credit goes primarily to the Swedish clergy, for the compilations were based entirely on the parish registers which had to be carefully kept and adequately processed.

The development of Swedish vital statistics since 1720 is represented in Chart II to which the following discussion should serve as commentary.

In the last chapter, the total population of Sweden proper in 1720 was estimated at 1.44 million. In 1750, the figure had risen to 1.78 million. By the turn of the century, it had grown to 2.35 million; and in 1815, the end of the period, it had added another 100,000 and was approaching 2.5 million.[1]

In all probability this population increase was unprecedented in magnitude. Table 9 demonstrates the rate of increase throughout the period. We have previously estimated the rate of growth during the century prior to 1720 at .22 per cent; this is a lower rate than for any decade of the present period, except 1801–10, when the Finnish war caused heavy losses even within Sweden proper, mostly through dysentery. Of the five-year periods, not only 1806–10 but also the peaceful years 1771–75 show absolute decreases. But taking a long view, the contrast between the eighteenth century and the previous one was enormous. Although our knowledge of the development in other countries is more limited, we may well assume that the Swedish population increase in the eighteenth century kept pace with that of most other countries; in England, where rapid indus-

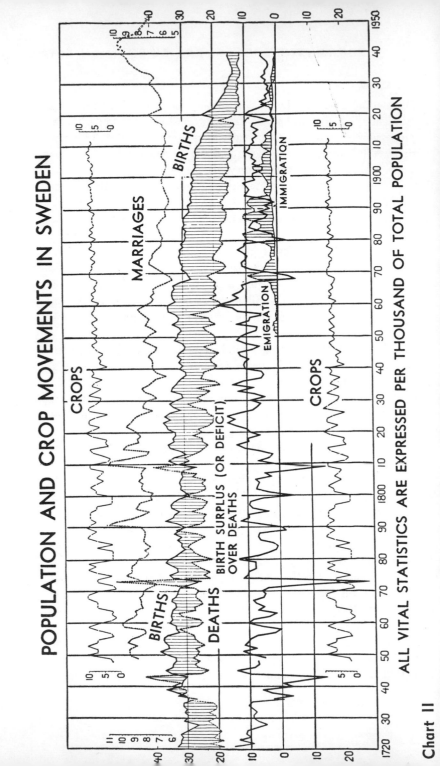

POPULATION AND CROP MOVEMENTS IN SWEDEN

ALL VITAL STATISTICS ARE EXPRESSED PER THOUSAND OF TOTAL POPULATION

Chart II

trialization was setting in, the population naturally grew much faster.

TABLE 9.  GROWTH RATES OF THE SWEDISH POPULATION, 1721–1935
*Average annual percentages*

| Years | Marriage rate | Birth rate | Death rate | Excess of birth over death rate | Net increase or decrease of population |
|---|---|---|---|---|---|
| 1721–35 | — | 3.24 | 2.12 | 1.12 | — |
| 1736–50 | — | 3.34 | 3.04 | .30 | — |
| 1751–55 | .92 | 3.71 | 2.63 | 1.08 | 1.03 |
| 1756–60 | .88 | 3.43 | 2.82 | .61 | .53 |
| 1761–65 | .88 | 3.46 | 2.90 | .56 | .53 |
| 1766–70 | .83 | 3.37 | 2.62 | .75 | .65 |
| 1771–75 | .81 | 3.13 | 3.29 | −.16 | −.22 |
| 1776–80 | .89 | 3.47 | 2.49 | .98 | .94 |
| 1781–85 | .78 | 3.17 | 2.78 | .39 | .29 |
| 1786–90 | .80 | 3.21 | 2.80 | .41 | .35 |
| 1791–95 | .91 | 3.39 | 2.51 | .88 | .84 |
| 1796–1800 | .80 | 3.27 | 2.56 | .71 | .57 |
| 1801–05 | .79 | 3.13 | 2.44 | .69 | .63 |
| 1806–10 | .86 | 3.04 | 3.20 | −.16 | −.21 |
| 1811–15 | .89 | 3.29 | 2.70 | .59 | .57 |
| 1751–1800 | .85 | 3.36 | 2.74 | .62 | .55 |
| 1801–1850 | .79 | 3.22 | 2.39 | .83 | .81 |
| 1931–35 | .72 | 1.41 | 1.17 | .24 | .35 |

Source: *Statistisk årsbok* 1952, Table 39.

A closer study of the components of this development clearly reveals the eighteenth century's intermediate position between the *ancien régime* and the *nouveau régime*. What immediately strikes the eye is the difference between the trends in birth rates and mortality rates, both of which were much higher than in our times. The birth rate remained fairly stable, over shorter periods as well as in the long run; only the strongest economic disturbances were able to influence it noticeably. The birth rate was in fact the most constant factor in all early societies; while it did vary from country to country or even from province to province, relatively speaking it was far more stable than nowadays. The mortality rates, on the other hand, showed violent fluctuations from year to year, immediately reflecting variations in the food supply. Consequently, the net increment, the surplus of the newly born over the dead, essentially expressed changes in mortality, although usually accentuated by some variation in the birth rate. Except for birth rates, all the vital statistics were extremely unstable in comparison with modern conditions, as appears from a cursory glance at the diagram. Before 1721, the birth rate was probably even more stable, which, incidentally, is most advantageous for economic research. Once the absolute number of newborn infants is known over a considerable period of time, and the birth rate can be assumed to remain constant, the size of the total population can be inferred with a fair degree of reliability.

Another demographic peculiarity of the period was the absence of any trend, rising or falling, in either birth or mortality rates. Variations appear only in the short run; long-run averages remained essentially unchanged. Both fluctuations from year to year and stability over longer periods were highly typical of the *ancien régime*. Some cyclical fluctuations may perhaps be discerned, but it is probably impossible to say whether they bear any resemblance to modern business cycles. The fluctuations derive from changes in mortality rates which, with few exceptions, show a period of five to six years from peak to peak. This is so much more remarkable since the harvest fluctuations (represented twice in the diagram, on top as well as on the bottom) are much less regular. Whether the same regularity appeared in earlier periods is an open question.

The diagram, nonetheless, clearly demonstrates how erroneous it is to believe that the preindustrial economy was characterized by great stability. Changes in the social structure were much slower than in more recent times, it is true; but short-run fluctuations were much more violent. This is immediately seen by a comparison of the left and the right portions of the diagram. Economic fluctuations in preindustrial times were entirely dominated by natural causes and human action was of slight import. Modern trade cycles are of the opposite type; they are far more dependent on social than on natural causes. The diagram seems to indicate, in contradiction with what is usually asserted, that the instability of society tends to be less than the instability of nature.

The main factor in population fluctuations was the harvest. If harvest and mortality figures are compared carefully, a marked covariation is found, although as a rule mortality changes tend to follow harvest changes with a lag of one year. A general exception must be made for severe calamities other than crop failures, mainly wars and the smallpox epidemic of 1778–79. On the whole, the curve for the net increase in population moves in the same direction as the harvest, and mirrors the mortality figures.

The significance of this is that the population still lived so close to a subsistence minimum that a bad harvest immediately resulted in an increase in mortality. It did not necessarily mean that people usually died of starvation, for the majority survived in spite of under-nourishment; but critical cases — the ill, the old, and the infants — did not survive. By and large, the process undeniably followed the Malthusian model in the sense that population tended to increase faster than food supply and suffered fairly frequent setbacks.

Two features in the demographic development especially serve to illuminate its Malthusian character. First, an increase in mortality generally took place before external events occurred that might be expected to lead to such a result. Particularly striking in this regard were the years after 1735, when a period of extraordinarily low mortality gave way to one of rising death tolls culminating in the first Finnish war. To a lesser degree, the same phenomenon is observed in connection with the severest visitation of them all, the crop failure in 1772–73, which was preceded by some, albeit slight, increase in the mortality rate. A second trait, even more conspicuous, is that after a temporary increase the mortality rate would recede with remarkable abruptness. Thus, in 1743 the mortality rate was 4.37 per cent, but in the following year it was 2.53 per cent, and in 1745 only 2.33 per cent, so that there was now a net *increase* in population as large as the *decrease* had been just two years before. The same tendency is even more pronounced in the seventies. In 1773, the mortality rate reached the fantastic height of 5.24 per cent, while in the following year it dropped to 2.24 per cent, the lowest since 1735.[2] In line with what has already been said, the high mortality must have served to weed out the least fit members of the community. Those who survived were probably in no worse condition than before the ordeal; perhaps they had even been hardened. Some of the data on Russian famines in the post-revolutionary period would suggest the same effect and could perhaps be said to confirm the Malthusian thesis.

It has been indicated that the birth rate did not remain entirely unaffected by harvest fluctuations, although this has often been overlooked. The diagram would tend to suggest that particularly severe crop failures resulted in a declining birth rate, operating partly but not entirely through a decline in the marriage rate. The effect was naturally reinforced wherever two bad years came in succession. This is most clearly evident in the difficult years 1772 and 1773, when the marriage rate dropped from .78 per cent in 1771 to .68 per cent in 1772, and the birth rate from 3.22 per cent in 1771 to 2.89 per cent in 1772 and 2.55 per cent in 1773.[3] At the time, and perhaps even in more modern times, greater attention seems to have been given to the opposite phenomenon, that is to stimulating marriages and birth rates in prosperous times. Thus, *Tabellkommissionen,* the authority in charge of the early Swedish population returns, made a characteristic statement in its report of 1761, a year of good crops: "Boys and maidens were instantly ready for the bridal bed, and even the love of the married ones was burning brighter." [4]

It might be tempting to regard epidemics as a cause of population movements that was independent of the food supply. Without doubt they took a heavy toll; normally ten to twelve thousand people died annually of typhoid and smallpox. But the question in this context is really whether the incidence of epidemic diseases varied from year to year, along with mortality rates. This was not the case. The conclusion must be that epidemics, although never absent, affected the mortality rate only in conjunction with harvest fluctuations with which they correlate in a striking fashion. Thus, epidemics were an instrument for checking the population rather than the basic cause of its reduction.

Apart from harvest fluctuations, other economic factors seem to have been of fairly small consequence in determining the size of the population. An illustrative case is the great depression of 1767 and 1768, brought about by the *Caps,* who appreciated Swedish currency with strong adverse repercussions upon the export industries.* From

---

* *Translator's note:* The *Caps* and the *Hats* were the names of the two parliamentary parties during the Age of Freedom. The *Hats* whose economic policy was essentially mercantilistic pursued a foreign policy which initially aimed at revenge against Russia and the restoration of the Baltic Empire; they were largely supported by the nobility, the army, and the protectionist interests. The more liberal *Caps* relied increasingly on the commoners, showed

reading the contemporary pamphlets one might feel that the country was on the brink of ruin and destruction, but vital statistics reveal an entirely different picture. In 1767, the mortality rate was exceptionally low at 2.56 per cent; it rose slightly in 1768 but reached only 2.72 per cent, which was below the long-term average and also below rates in the pre-appreciation years of 1764 and 1765.[5] One might possibly claim that good harvests ought to have resulted in a declining mortality in 1768; the slight increase which actually occurred can then be ascribed to monetary policy and to the export slump it had caused.

On the other hand, a tendency toward an incipient loosening of the tie between population and crop movements is clearly visible. As we shall see, it is fairly evident that there had been a permanent improvement in the level of output since the previous century. Such an improvement can always be used either to increase the population while maintaining the standard of living or to raise the standards for a constant population. The two alternatives, which obviously leave room for many intermediate possibilities, can perhaps be roughly translated into two corresponding historical tendencies. Essentially, the former tendency, which Malthus observed and regarded as the normal state of affairs, was characteristic of early times. The increasing predominance of the latter tendency is of more recent date. In this respect, as in so many others, the eighteenth century was a transitional period, although increases in numbers still overshadowed increases in levels of consumption. The fact that the birth rate was more sensitive to harvest fluctuations than the marriage rate indicates that some kind of birth control took place, though probably there was no use of contraceptives in the technical sense. Yet since the mortality rate followed the harvest much more closely than the birth rate, what birth control there was cannot have been very extensive.

Thus, the data assembled in the diagram reflect a fairly complex development which might be summarized in the following way. While increase in available resources permitted a faster growth of popula-

---

greater restraint in the field of foreign policy, and vigorously opposed the inflationary war finance of their opponents. The *Hats* were in power from 1739 till 1765 when they were replaced by the *Caps*. The *coup d'état* of 1772 temporarily put an end to parliamentary government in Sweden.

tion, by and large the increase in population exhausted the growing supplies, so that the majority of the people still lived close to subsistence. Nonetheless, as will be seen presently, some room was left for an increase in prosperity. Such an increase required adjustments in the birth rate. That the fertility of married couples began to follow crop fluctuations was therefore a fact of paramount importance.

On the whole, the data show how quickly the strains and sufferings of the long war period had been overcome. This is an illustration of what was said in the last chapter — the resources of an agrarian non-exchange society cannot be engaged for war purposes to anything like the extent that is possible in a modern economy. From this point of view, the fifteen years between 1720 and 1735 are of special interest. True, the low mortality in this period was also the result of the harsh weeding-out process of the preceding years, but the favorable death rate could not have been sustained for so long unless it had been supported by the tremendous improvement of living conditions that occurred as soon as the pressure of war was lifted. Chart I, of the changes in the taxable population, reveals an even more stupendous increase. It is hard to imagine that recovery could have been so rapid if the war had greatly depleted the country's resources.

However, the advent of peace did not immediately remove all traces of the war. They remained most clearly discernible in the sex ratio which gave women a preponderance unequaled in any later period.

TABLE 10.   SWEDISH POPULATION: NUMBER OF WOMEN PER 1000 MEN,
1750, 1780, 1939

| Year | In the total population | In the population over fifty years of age |
|------|------------------------|-------------------------------------------|
| 1750 | 1,127 | 1,445 |
| 1780 | 1,082 | 1,285 |
| 1939 | 1,018 | |

Source: *Statistisk årsbok* 1952, Table 12.

Between 1750 and 1780, the ratio of women to men in the total population declined by 4 per cent; for the population over fifty years of age the corresponding decline was no less than 11.1 per cent. That the decline was so much stronger in the higher age groups, which had been directly affected by the war, suggests that the ratio in 1750 must be essentially attributed to the war. This is fully confirmed by a closer study of the sex ratio in the various age groups. The rapidity of the recovery nevertheless remains much more striking than the lingering imprints of the war.

SOCIAL STRUCTURE

In addition to vital statistics, we also possess data on the social composition of the population. Table 11 shows the distribution in 1760 of the population in Sweden proper and in Finland. The available material arranges the population by estate, or by occupation, or by a combination of the two.

TABLE 11. COMPOSITION OF THE POPULATION IN SWEDEN PROPER
AND IN FINLAND IN 1760

|  | Sweden | | Finland | |
|---|---|---|---|---|
| Nobility | 8,918 | .5% | 1,727 | .4% |
| Clergymen and teachers | 14,705 | .8 | 3,592 | .7 |
| Gentry | 26,943 | 1.5 | 5,039 | 1.0 |
| Servants | 39,745 | 2.1 | 6,966 | 1.4 |
| *"Gentlefolk" and servants* | *90,311* | *4.9* | *17,324* | *3.5* |
| Soldiers | 154,208 | 8.4 | 66,365 | 13.5 |
| Court and church servants, etc. | 26,013 | 1.4 | 6,067 | 1.2 |
| *Lower state employees, etc.* | *180,221* | *9.8* | *74,432* | *14.7* |
| Merchants | 10,500 | .6 | 2,726 | .6 |
| Manufacturers | 14,431 | .8 | 738 | .1 |
| Craftsmen | 38,786 | 2.1 | 3,967 | .8 |
| Shippers and sailors | 5,704 | .3 | 782 | .2 |
| Other burghers | 32,894 | 1.8 | 7,120 | 1.5 |
| Servants | 20,055 | 1.1 | 3,440 | .7 |
| *Townsmen and their servants* | *122,370* | *6.7* | *18,773* | *3.9* |
| Iron and metal makers, miners | 58,033 | 3.2 | 4,898 | 1.0 |
| Rural craftsmen | 39,532 | 2.2 | 11,027 | 2.5 |
| Millers | 10,708 | .6 | 1,639 | .3 |
| Rural shippers and sailors | 6,699 | .4 | 912 | .2 |
| Peasants | 888,793 | 48.2 | 243,005 | 49.7 |
| Cottagers | 195,557 | 10.6 | 51,694 | 10.6 |
| Paupers and crofters | 236,873 | 12.9 | 67,697 | 13.8 |
| Lapps, settlers, etc. | 8,514 | .5 | 407 | .1 |
| *Rural population (except soldiers, nobility, etc.)* | *1,444,769* | *78.6* | *381,279* | *77.9* |
| Total population | 1,837,671 | 100.0 | 489,808 | 100.0 |

Source: Heckscher, *Sveriges ekonomiska historia från Gustav Vasa*, II:1, page 130.

Even a cursory glance at the table shows that the great majority belonged to the rural population and was engaged in agriculture. However, the exact size of the farming population cannot be ascertained. The figures usually quoted are demonstrably faulty. One of the main difficulties is that a substantial but indefinite number of the soldiers as well as many of those included under "gentlefolk with servants" actually were farmers. Furthermore, even some of those who were reported as active in mining and metal making as well as in rural handicraft should be included in the farming population. At the maximum, one can assume that agriculture supported about three-quarters of the population in Sweden proper. Remarkably enough, this share remained almost constant for more than a hundred years; as late as 1870 it was 72.4 per cent, which again points up the virtually completely agrarian character of Swedish society.

The numbers engaged in mining and metal industries appear surprisingly small. Even if we forget that some of them really belonged in agriculture, employment in these industries was out of any proportion to their general importance and to their impact on the country's economic development. The aggregate for mining and metal industries, handicraft (urban and rural), and manufacturing, is no more than 8.3 per cent for Sweden (without Finland). The corresponding share according to the 1930 census was 35.7 per cent, and according to the incomplete census for 1936, 37.2 per cent. Industrialization had thus made very small headway even by the middle of the eighteenth century. The importance of rural compared with urban handicraft (2.2 vs. 2.1 per cent) is noteworthy in view of all the attempts to suppress the former. Still more so is the figure for manufacturing (.8 per cent), which appears grotesquely low considering the role it played in the social thought and legislation of the time.

Finally, the number of "gentlefolk" (*ståndspersoner*) is quite remarkable. This group, possibly with the addition of some merchants and manufacturers, might be called the upper class. Obviously the definition of such a class will be more or less arbitrary; what distinguishes a social class from an estate (*stånd*) is the absence of legal criteria. A social class must be defined in terms of social criteria. In one of the first reports of the Swedish statistical office it is noted that in the country anybody who dressed in a coat of cloth classified himself as a gentleman (*ståndsperson*); the rest of the rural population presumably still wore wadmal.[6] While this criterion might have served fairly well to identify the upper class in the country, it is likely that in the cities, in addition to noblemen, clergymen, and teachers, the category included all untitled civil servants, officers, etc. — everyone, that is, who was regarded as the "equal of a noble." Not only the size of this group is remarkable, but also, specifically, the number of persons who were included without belonging to the two estates of the nobility or clergy. Their number is larger than that of the two estates taken together; in other words, the class society had already superseded the estate society. This numerical reduction of the role of the estates within the upper class is the statistical illustration of the development that has already been discussed in general terms.

So far we have been primarily concerned with Sweden proper. Finland's agrarian character was even more extreme than that of Sweden; the share of the population engaged in mining, handicraft, and manufacturing was barely more than half that in Sweden. Finally, the role of the upper class was also much smaller. Essentially this probably expressed an even more archaic social structure than Sweden's. Undoubtedly the absence of natural resources like iron and copper ore was a contributing factor. So was the fact that the center of government and administration was located in Stockholm on the other side of the Gulf of Bothnia.

COUNTRY AND TOWN

An important aspect of Swedish society in the eighteenth century is disclosed by the distinction between rural and urban population in Table 11. Unfortunately, no complete estimates of the urban population can be found until 1800, but figures for the city of Stockholm are available as far back as there are figures for the total population of the country. In addition, it has also been possible to locate various eighteenth-century data for a number of other towns.

The numerical and economic insignificance of most cities remained as pronounced in the eighteenth century as in the seventeenth; in fact, in this regard there was little change until around 1850. A reasonably reliable estimate shows that in 1760 no more than 9.4 per cent of the population lived in towns; as late as 1800 this figure had not reached 10 per cent.[7] That the share of the urban population did not increase appreciably did not mean, of course, that the numbers of townsmen remained constant: at the very least, they kept pace with the total population which, as has been said, grew at a fairly high rate. But the implication is that the agricultural sector had to provide for much the same share of the population until the middle of the nineteenth century or even until around 1870.

Among the towns, Stockholm completely dominated the picture. This had been so in the seventeenth century, and had not changed much by the middle of the eighteenth. In 1757, for instance, 39.4 per cent of the urban population resided in Stockholm, and the city's rate of growth had been very impressive indeed. In 1720, there had been 45,300 inhabitants; in 1757 there were as many as 71,900, an increase of more than 50 per cent in less than forty years. Strangely enough, from then on the population remained at a standstill. In 1820, it was 75,600, or about the same as sixty years earlier. This is explained by several factors. While it is quite possible that the increase in the first half of the eighteenth century had exceeded the growth of the city's economic capacity, it is also true that thereafter the manufacturing industries which, in Stockholm and only in Stockholm, employed a great many workers not only stagnated but even receded. In addition, the discrimination in favor of Stockholm in maritime trade — the Bothnian trade compulsion — (see page 73) was abolished in 1765, thus enabling the cities of northern Sweden and Finland to by-pass Stockholm. Probably most important of all, exports of iron, the largest item on Stockholm's export list, virtually ceased to grow in the 1740's. Finally, the loss of Finland in 1809 was a hard blow for Stockholm which had a far greater attraction to the Finns than Åbo, the trading center on the Finnish side of the Gulf of Bothnia. The immediate result was an absolute decline in the population of Stockholm.

In relation to the total urban population, the decrease was even stronger. From the 39.4 per cent in 1757, Stockholm's share had fallen to 32.9 per cent at the end of the century, and, surprising though it may be, it continued to fall throughout the nineteenth century despite the city's rapid growth. For the eighteenth century the year 1757, in which Stockholm's share in the total population was 3.8 per cent, represents a maximum. Thereafter it dropped to

3.2 per cent in 1800, 2.9 per cent in 1820, and 2.7 per cent in 1850. But this marked a turning point; now it is no less than 10 per cent.[8] Yet even the increase in Stockholm's share since 1850 has not stopped the fall in her share in urban (as distinct from total) population. That Stockholm's relative position vis-à-vis the other cities has declined means only that urbanization has become more diffused.

Stockholm apart, most Swedish towns have developed essentially within the last two hundred years, a fact often concealed by the incompleteness of existing municipal histories. For instance, Göteborg, the history of which has only been completed through 1718, probably had a population of only 4000–4500 in the 1670's, or about 10 per cent of Stockholm's population. In 1757, the ratio had risen to 11.4 per cent; in 1800, to 17.0 per cent, and in 1850, to 28 per cent; it has now reached 48.1 per cent.[9] Malmö's development in the nineteenth century was even more spectacular; in 1800, the ratio of Malmö's population to that of the capital was about one-twentieth, whereas it is now more than one-fourth.

TABLE 12. POPULATION IN CITIES OTHER THAN STOCKHOLM
*Sweden, excluding Finland*

| Year | Population | Per cent of | |
| | | total population | urban population |
|---|---|---|---|
| 1760 | 110,500 | 5.8 | 61.4 |
| 1800 | 153,920 | 6.6 | 67.1 |
| 1850 | 258,460 | 7.4 | 73.5 |

Source: Heckscher, *Sveriges ekonomiska historia från Gustav Vasa*, II:1, page 88.

In spite of its arrested development, Stockholm remained the unrivaled center of the country; it is therefore gratifying that its development can be studied in detail in a way not always possible for the other cities. In itself, however, this development was far from gratifying. It is no exaggeration to say that social conditions in the capital were appalling. This was of course true of all big cities of the time; Rousseau's eulogy of rural life rested on a sound appreciation of reality. An English observer said of Paris immediately before the French Revolution that her streets were trenches drawn through dungheaps;[10] Berlin's stench could be felt at six miles' distance; and Linnaeus found that the beautiful town of Hamburg smelled like a latrine.[11] Under such circumstances it is not surprising that conditions in Stockholm were far from perfect. In fact, the mortality rate appears to have been considerably higher in Stockholm than in the much larger foreign centers. For them, the mortality rate was commonly estimated at 4 per cent. Though this rate is fantastic by modern standards, in reality the mortality rate in Stockholm was not brought down to such an average until the 1870's. Generally it was about 4.5 to 5 per cent, and sometimes for whole decades the average would climb to 6 per cent. During the entire period 1731–1760, no quinquennial rate ever fell below 5 per cent. In Sweden as a whole, the mortality rate was excessive; in Stockholm it was generally almost twice as high as the national average. Nowadays, it is even somewhat below that average. Although birth rates in Stockholm were very high and exceeded the average for the country, the result was a continuous excess of deaths over births, so that the city could not even maintain its population without continual immigration. This, too, was in sharp contrast to the situation for the country as a whole where a strong excess of births over deaths was the rule and the opposite situation a rare exception. This is clearly seen from Table 9 and from Chart II.

From the many contemporary descriptions of sanitary conditions in Stockholm a sordid picture emerges. There were fen waters everywhere, even in the center of the town, large "reservoirs filled with putrid sewage" overflowing into the streets at various points; latrine dumps were scattered all over the city.[12] Worst of all were conditions in South End with its motley population of industrial workers.

In the countryside the open air and the low density of the population acted as a check upon epidemics. But Stockholm was an unfortunate combination of the old and the new. It was highly industrialized and extremely crowded, but had as yet seen no sign of the great sanitary reform which was to transform it into one of the healthiest places in the world. The public health situation of the capital was perhaps the darkest side of eighteenth-century Sweden.

The occupational distribution of the urban population is known for Stockholm and a few other cities. Stockholm's lead in economic development is evident from the relative size of the manufacturing population. In 1760, it amounted to 12.6 per cent in Stockholm (in 1763 even 14.8 per cent) but to only .7 per cent in the country as a whole and to less than 5 per cent in most other towns.[13] This serves to explain the difference in sanitary conditions between Stockholm and the other towns. At the same time the relative strength of the upper class was far higher in Stockholm than in the country as a whole; in 1760 it was 14.4 per cent in Stockholm but 5.2 per cent in Sweden proper.[14] The presence of "gentlefolk" did not seem to better the sanitary conditions.

## THE CHANGING PATTERN OF RESOURCES

Before passing to economic conditions in a narrower sense, we should inspect the basic prerequisites for economic progress as they existed during the eighteenth century.

The first thing to consider is the effect of territorial changes. The peace treaties after the death of Charles XII had deprived the country of vast territories, although, from the vantage point of the present day, Sweden would seem to have kept everything worth keeping. All the Baltic provinces, the possessions in north Germany as well as the province of Kexholm in Finland, were lost; and if ever a territorial reduction brought unfavorable economic consequences, they should have been expected in Sweden after 1720. A closer inspection, however, will reveal that the strictly economic loss for that part of the population which remained within the boundaries of Sweden cannot have been very great.

Of the surrendered provinces the one which had contributed most to the Swedish economy was Livonia. In the seventeenth century, around the mid-eighties at the latest, Sweden had become dependent upon small but regular imports of grain from that province. But the loss of Livonia would have been severe only if the grain trade were not allowed to continue on the same terms as before. The Treaty of Nystad provided for free exports of grain to Sweden in quantities which remained sufficient for a long time and were later permitted to increase with the growth of demand. Thus, in giving up Livonia, Sweden did not sever connections with her granary, nor did she have to pay export duties to Russia.

The losses to the Swedish treasury were more important, though since Sweden no longer ventured any large-scale military campaigns abroad the need for revenue had been considerably reduced. Still the change was drastic. If Livonia had been ceded before Charles XI's reversion, it would have been a hard blow to Swedish nobles who held especially large possessions in trans-Baltic provinces; as it was, the loss was carried by the crown. No less than three-fifths of the holdings recovered by the crown through reversion were actually located there. Those two items, treasury revenue from Livonia and the government's estates in the Baltic provinces and north Germany, probably constituted the heaviest economic loss imposed by the peace. On the other hand, economic dislocations such as usually result from territorial changes and are likely to do most harm were almost entirely absent. Aside from grain exports, economic ties between the main territories (in Sweden and Finland) and the trans-Baltic provinces were too weak for any such disturbances to arise. The severing incision was made where it hurt least.

Within the new borders, the greatest change in the transition from the seventeenth to the eighteenth century was the steep decline in the copper industry. This, like the loss of Livonia, was mitigated by the reduced need of revenue for political purposes. Practically all other fields showed marked though not spectacular advances.

The iron industry, although it did not expand significantly after the 1740's, remained extremely profitable throughout the century; in agriculture at least the first signs of progress were noticeable. An increase in aggregate available resources must have occurred. But on the other hand, the population was growing rapidly, certainly more rapidly than in previous centuries, and it is not immediately clear whether or not there was any substantial increase in the standard of living.

The development of *per capita* levels of consumption may be studied by comparing the food budgets of various estates with the same sort of data from the two preceding centuries.[15] Possibly the standards of living enjoyed by laborers on such estates were higher than those of the peasant population, but there is little doubt that the relative changes in their consumption from one century to another should indicate the development of the prosperity of the agricultural population as a whole.

In the seventeenth century, there had been a drop of perhaps as much as one-third below the standard of the mid-sixteenth century. The postwar upswing of the eighteenth century made good a large part of the decline, although it did not fully restore the levels of consumption reached under Gustavus Vasa, during that age of bliss in Swedish history. There were, however, marked changes in the composition of the diet. Especially the consumption of animal foods showed a considerable decline, below the levels even of the seventeenth century. Under Gustavus Vasa, the laborers had received about four times as much meat and pork; the same was true of fish, and butter consumption apparently all but disappeared in the eighteenth century, although the same may not have been true of milk. There was less difference with regard to cereal foods: their consumption seems to have been roughly the same as in both the previous centuries. In the consumption of beer there was an enormous decline. On the other hand, a substitute was provided by the appearance of hard liquor, the consumption of which kept growing well into the nineteenth century — at what cost to society it is impossible to say.

Using again the calory supply *per capita* and *diem* for our yardstick, the following picture emerges: around the middle of the sixteenth century, the caloric supply had amounted to somewhat more than 4,000; but in the course of the seventeenth century it had dropped to 2,500–2,900 calories. For the eighteenth century, about one-half of the food budgets indicate around 3,000 calories, but at least one-fifth of them yield more than that and the rest less. In the previous centuries, the accounts did not distinguish between male and female farm workers, but in the eighteenth century a distinction was made in the ledgers revealing considerable differences in consumption between the sexes. On the average the ratio was about 4:3, but sometimes it was as much as 3:2 in favor of the men. Generally speaking, the figures are higher than those for the previous century, but the failure to attain the levels of the sixteenth century is striking. In addition, the quality of the food had deteriorated and its vitamin content had probably declined. In view of the unprecedented population growth, this picture is hardly surprising.

It should be added that what has been said refers to years of normal crops. When, as frequently happened, the harvest failed, food resources available to the peasant population must have dwindled to practically nothing. The laborers on the large estates were more fortunate in this regard; there, stocks were often available and less was sold to the outside in such years.

Thus, throughout the eighteenth century the increase in resources appears to have been used to support a larger population rather than to create greater prosperity. In consequence, social conditions retained their old character. The seeds of economic development were indeed sown, but the process of germination was to take another century.

AGRICULTURE

Of the various industries, agriculture still has first claim on our attention. The main question is whether the eighteenth century produced any fundamental change in the organization as described in the earlier chapters. Basically, that organization remained the same; but nevertheless important shifts took place which mainly served to increase productivity but, at least in one respect, also proved a source of serious difficulties.

The first and most conspicuous change was the expansion of oats cultivation and the introduction of the potato. The increased popularity of oats probably improved cattle feeding, for although oats were also used for bread, it is likely that they went into the feeding troughs more often than the other crops. Oats had been grown in the west of the country for a long time and became quite common in Bergslagen during the seventeenth century. Now, however, the cereal spread to new areas in every part of the country and was grown on all kinds of poor soil. It was raised even in places where rotation was not practiced at all.[16] A great deal of new land was opened up during the period, much of which, we may assume, was given to oats.[17] This development probably at least partly remedied one of the gravest shortcomings of the old agricultural usages, the virtual starvation of the cattle, and additional supplies for human consumption may also have been quite important.

Far more momentous, even revolutionary, was the introduction of the potato.[18] The potato had been known in Sweden since the middle of the seventeenth century, but only as an exotic curiosity of the botanic gardens, although it is mentioned by Schering Rosenhane in his agricultural handbook, *Oeconomia*, completed in 1662. The potato was introduced on a large scale by Jonas Alströmer, a prosperous manufacturer who pushed it as vigorously as his own wares, with nothing like the same result. (An early Swedish name for potatoes

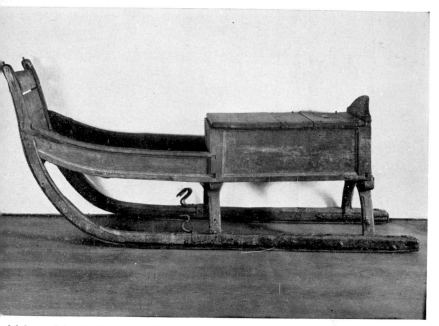

sleigh, used for the transport of heavy copper coins by smelters in Dalarna when making payments. *Dala Fornsal, Falun.*

coin sleigh and men carrying copper money on their backs. Detail from an etching of *Riksbanken* in Eric Dahlbergh's *Suecia Antiqua et Hodierna.*

A 25 copper daler banknote issued by Palmstruch's bank in 1663. *Kungl. Myntkabinet*

The interior of the "Big Forge" at Christopher Polhem's shop at Stjärnsund where mo
his inventions originated. Drawing by Carl Johan Cronstedt, 1729. *Tekniska Musée*

Riddareholm          Tyske Kyrckian.

holm and Göteborg were the centers of the iron export trade. On this detail from an
g of Stockholm in 1630 by W. Hartmann the iron porters are seen carrying bar iron
from the checking post to the quay.

Louis de Geer. Portrait by David Beck. *Leufsta*.

*nolor,* is thought to have been derived from the name of his farm, *Nolhaga.*) Though Alströmer's efforts attracted attention, by and large only some of the upper classes were ready to listen to his propaganda. We find, for instance, a minister in Dalarna who experimented with potatoes as early as 1728. The peasants, however, resisted the innovation stubbornly. As late as the mid-fifties, the county governors submitted pessimistic reports about their attempts to stimulate interest in the new crop although plants and instructions were provided freely.

At the time it was frequently suggested that the soldiers returning from Pomerania after the Seven Years' War (1756–63) had learned to grow potatoes in northern Germany, but that is far from certain. One might have at least expected to find that poor harvests induced the peasants to raise and eat potatoes. This sometimes did happen, but it was apparently considered a last and desperate resort. In 1764, it is reported that peasants in the county of Skaraborg "lacking grain, had sustained themselves on earth-pears." More often the situation remained like Kipling's picture of India in the late nineteenth century: "Men would die at arm's length of plenty, sooner than touch food they did not know." In Denmark it was said that people would change their religion more easily than their food habits. And reluctance to change production habits appears to have been at least as strong as resistance to new consumption habits.

Reports from the governors reveal that, between the 1770's and 1790's, opposition to the new plant began to break down;[19] curiously enough the crops were exceptionally good in this period. But it was not until the two first decades of the nineteenth century that potato growing was generally adopted. The development which definitely paved the way for the potato was its use for distillation into liquor. In 1748, the Countess Eva de la Gardie, wife of Clas Ekeblad, who was then President of the Chancellory, submitted a paper to the Academy of Science in which she emphasized the possibility of using the potato not for direct consumption but for cattle feed when mixed with oats and for distillation and powder manufacture — a performance which made her until 1945 the only woman to have been a member of that illustrious body.[20] The Board of Commerce (*Kommerskollegium*) publicized the suggestion the next year, and from then on there is frequent reference to distillation from potato.

The popularity of the root thus came to be based on the attraction of its "juices," which may seem paradoxical but is fairly easy to explain.

Hostility against the potato by no means extended to the distilled product. The liquor was easily transported and marketed, and the residue was used as feed. Under Gustavus III, private distillation for home use was restricted for fiscal reasons, which undoubtedly reduced drinking, although this was not the intention at all; in royalist circles drinking was even conceived as a patriotic duty. In 1800, the restrictions were lifted and a torrent of liquor burst forth, acting as a tremendous stimulus for potato growing. The temperance movement had not yet emerged; not until the following period, in the 1830's, was the battle against the bottle organized under Peter Wieselgren. Until then in most circles hard liquor was regarded as a perfectly respectable beverage. In the 1820's, for instance, the governor of Blekinge made the casual observation that distillation was "so-to-speak the real purpose" of agriculture.

As long as the potatoes were absorbed by the distilleries, they obviously did not increase the food supplies, but the general effect was to facilitate the introduction of the crop. Since the mash was used for cattle feeding, distillation became a substitute for food-crop raising and indirectly advanced livestock farming.

The quantitative effect is difficult to ascertain, for potatoes were not grown on the arable land; acreage therefore does not provide a very adequate measure. Such data are probably more reliable for oats and indicate considerable advances. Toward the end of the period, the situation in terms of acreage was as follows: the amount of land given over to oats was 71 per cent of that devoted to barley, 63 per cent of that under rye, and roughly double that for the mixed grains. The transformation of agriculture was under way. Although the immediate effect of the increases in oats and potatoes on the food supply was indirect, through improvements in cattle feeding, it was precisely here that change was most urgently called for. We shall return later to the ultimate effects on the aggregate level of food production (see pages 172–173).

The choice of crops was highly dependent upon methods of cultivation.[21] At the beginning of the period those were still extremely primitive. Three different methods prevailed, of which the most primitive was perhaps the most common. This was the one-crop system, which involved no rotation at all, nor any regular fallowing. Wherever supplies of manure were insufficient, the crops soon gave out, and the lands were then abandoned or used for pasture, until they would be sown again. Under this system spring grains were the principal crop — mostly barley but also spring rye and even some spring wheat. This mode of cultivation prevailed through a large part of southern Sweden, and was used on peripheral fields in other parts of the country as well.

The two-field system, where half of the land was left fallow every year, was customary in a large but fairly closed area including the eastern sections of the country — parts of Västergötland, most of Östergötland, the important provinces around Lake Mälaren, and the coastal strip in the south of Norrland. Its great advantage was the possibility of some rotation between spring and fall crops, though the practice was terribly wasteful in comparison with modern agriculture where fallowing is practically unknown.

The three-year cycle, which divided the land between fall crops, spring crops, and fallowing, was by and large the most advanced of the agricultural techniques, although one-third of the land was still left waste. It occurred in some districts in the south of Sweden (Skåne and Småland), along the shores of Lake Vättern, and on the island of Öland and Gotland. Skåne was already beginning to assume its position as the granary of Sweden and was so described by Linnaeus around the middle of the century. While in general some progress must be assumed to have taken place during the eighteenth century, the exact extent of the shift toward more advanced crop systems is unknown.

Nor is there any way of knowing what happened to the crop yields per acre, though considerable improvements in that respect seem unlikely; even in the first half of the nineteenth century yields were very slow to improve. At any rate, the bulk of the additional food supplies came not from increases in yields per acre but from the expansion of the area under cultivation. Since it may be assumed that the new lands were inferior to the old ones, even a constant yield per acre would indicate some improvement in agricultural techniques.

But the opening up of new land was the crucial factor.[22] It had already played a great part in the seventeenth century, but there was an important difference. The seventeenth century had been a period of internal colonization in which the forest regions had been put under plow. A hundred years later the additional land brought under cultivation was largely in the old and settled regions. This expansion which began in the eighteenth century was further accelerated in the early years of the nineteenth century under the stimulus of high grain prices. Ever since that time Swedish farmers — perhaps spurred on by the pride of ownership — have been somewhat more eager to acquire new lands than to improve the cultivation of those they already possess. In a famous report on the economy of Kopparberg County in 1818–22, Hans Järta, then governor, complained of this tendency because of the resulting shortage of manure.[23] Be that as it may, there is no doubt of the tremendous interest in reclamation. From the year 1779 we have the following observation which does not refer to any particular part of the country: "Everywhere the fields have been expanded and plowed, large stretches of wasteland enclosed and cleared, cottages built, meadows and pastures turned into arable land and often better cultivated than before."

An abundance of reports in the two first decades of the nineteenth century speak of clearing and tilling new lands. The Agricultural Society in Värmland, where expansion was particularly vigorous, reported in 1810 that the fields had now been extended even into the hills and that the pastures had been converted into arable land. In some places an increase of as much as one-fourth in the harvests is mentioned.

Along with the reclamation of land went the partitioning of the farms, another important development which will be discussed presently. Particularly in the regions where the large estate (*Gutsherrschaft*) prevailed, a rapid increase in the number of cotters occurred, which may, for that matter, have been going on long before our material enables us to discover it. In Kronoborg County there were 142 cotters in 1686, no less than 923 in 1766, and 1,828 in 1805. According to census material, there were two-and-a-half times as many cotters in the country as a whole in 1815 as in 1751.

Characteristically, however, this development, which was undoubtedly the most important single event of the period, could not proceed without endangering the structure of the whole agrarian system. The rigidity of the old system was incompatible with changes that made for increased production. The expansion of arable land, for instance, encroached upon the pastures, thereby further aggravating the shortage of feed stuffs. The old agrarian framework was obsolete and had to be replaced. But the transformation was a long, drawn-out process. The first step, which laid the foundation for all that followed, was the reform of the field system. The time was ripe for the Swedish enclosure movement.

## THE ENCLOSURES

The transformation of the agrarian structure had from the outset two very different, though interrelated aspects. One was the abolition of the *bytvång* ("village compulsion") and the strip system; the other, the distribution of the commons and wastelands to the individual villagers. It is easy to follow the actual course of the enclosure movement from literary and official publications of the time, but its effects are far from easy to appraise. Of all industries agriculture is perhaps the least amenable to statistical treatment. Still, a discussion of the impact of the enclosures must distinguish between the two aspects we have mentioned.

No presentation of the Swedish enclosures would omit the name of Jacob Faggot, head of the government's surveying bureau, and also a member and one time secretary of the Academy of Sciences, in which body he proved a valiant protagonist of economic progress. He was the first to raise the question of enclosures in a famous pamphlet, *Svenska lantbrukets hinder och hjälp* (The Obstruction to Sweden's Agriculture and Its Remedy), published in 1746, followed in 1755 by *Om allmänna tillståndets sjukdom och bot* (The Malady and Cure of Our State).[24] In the vast outpouring of pamphlets during the Age of Freedom, there are few items of comparable significance, although even Faggot's influence is easily overestimated. Faggot was in all respects very much a product of his age; as a surveyor he was of course especially interested in a reform which would create an almost unlimited demand for the surveyors' services. The extent to which Faggot was guided by foreign influence has not been studied and is difficult to determine. The only known comparable development before the middle of the eighteenth century was the English enclosures which had been going on for a long time but did not gain momentum before the eighteenth century. However, if Faggot was influenced by English events, the fact has not been proven. It is therefore not impossible that he deserves credit for considerable originality.

The first move toward a realization of the new ideas was taken very soon after Faggot's first proposal, with the Field Consolidation Act (*Storskiftesstadgan*) of 1749.[25] The act provided that in cases of advanced subdivision of the fields into narrow strips, government surveyors should "gently but firmly" impress upon the villagers the harmfulness of this state of affairs and then, if general consensus could be achieved, proceed to repartition the fields in such a way as to award to each farm one field or, failing that, as few separate acres as possible. In view of the ancient tradition of the strip system, such mild procedure could not be expected to be of much effect. A reform requiring general consensus was doomed from the outset, and Faggot from the very beginning had taken the opposite stand, suggesting that any single villager should have the right to demand that his holdings be consolidated. But this was almost revolutionary, aiming as it did at forced exchanges of land. The legislative development nevertheless proceeded in that direction with a new act in 1757, and finally resulted in the Surveying Act of 1783 in which Faggot's views were fully expressed. The individual villager could now demand consolidation of his holdings. However, in such a case only the claimant's own holdings were to be consolidated while the rest of the village holdings might still remain scattered. Since in practice it was impossible to consolidate one man's holdings without consolidating others, strong obstacles to individual consolidation continued to exist.

A long time was to pass before the enclosure movement came to anything approaching thorough consolidation. All that could be achieved at first was some reduction in the number of separate holdings belonging to one owner. This was a very gradual process, and little is known about its scope and speed. In Bäck, a village in the province of Västergötland, the maps of which are often used to illustrate the effects of consolidation, the number of separate holdings was by 1779 brought down to about one-half of what it had been; but how representative this case is no one knows.

It is certainly no surprise that resistance to redistribution was intense. The exchange of certain pieces of land for others was inevitably painful to a peasantry which for centuries had been tied to specific patches of land; all the ingrained notions of traditional ownership militated against the reform. To attain agreement on compensation or on the assessment of one strip in terms of another was difficult in the extreme. Perhaps the greatest trouble arose when some of the villagers were to be deprived of their houses and buildings in the village and to be settled on isolated homesteads. This made it necessary to erect new buildings but, more than that, it often left the farmer uprooted and broke up the communal life of the village.

In one part of the country, however, agricultural reform was carried far beyond what was envisaged by the fairly tame legislation of the initial stages. That was the work of a single man, Baron Rutger Maclean of Svaneholm in Skåne; it was begun in the 1780's.[26] Maclean was the descendant of one of the Scottish businessmen who settled in Göteborg; the family later became great landlords in Skåne. Rutger Maclean had studied agrarian conditions abroad, especially in England and Scotland, and was undoubtedly influenced by the enclosure movement in England. In all respects, he was an exponent of enlightened despotism — everything for the people, but nothing by the people — and possibly he was also spurred on by the Scottish rationalistic tradition. His achievement was probably more important than Faggot's, though it would have been unthinkable without the changes which had already taken place.

Maclean was the owner of fifty-one tenant farms, with forty peasants in four different villages in Skurup (Skåne), apart from the main farm which was worked by land laborers for him. The holdings, including the main farm, were intermingled but not with the land of other owners. Thus, being the single owner, he could dispose of the lands at will. This state of affairs obviously suited Maclean's character and predilections to a nicety. He had a map of the area drawn up and then parceled out the land into seventy-three farms, each of about forty acres (40 *tunnland*), in square lots with the buildings in the middle, special gardens, straight roads, and so forth. It was a perfect expression of the rationalist mentality of the Enlightenment. Then the peasants were to move from the old buildings to the new. They refused, and it is said that Maclean himself had to lead them by the arm to their new homes amidst loud wailing and general misery. The first reaction was not very hopeful. In 1785, there were 701 inhabitants on the lands of Maclean; next year there were only 603. But in 1787, half of those who had left had already returned, and in 1790, five years after the beginning of the experiment, the number had increased to 821. After this success, he undertook to redistribute the lands of his main farm which he combined into a number of large estates that he himself managed as model farms. The laborers on those farms were housed in the old village houses made vacant by the resettlement.

Naturally, such revolutionary measures could not but attract an enormous attention, particularly among Maclean's fellow landlords in Skåne. As a result, the western part of the province, Malmöhus County, was soon far ahead in field reforms; in 1822, nearly two-thirds of all the land in the county had been redistributed.[27]

On the other hand, Maclean's methods were obviously inapplicable in most parts of the country where the land was in the possession of the peasants. No individual was entitled to deal with other people's holdings as Maclean would with his own. Compulsory consolidation of the land into single parcels in Maclean's fashion therefore required intervention by the government. Probably because of strong influence from the developments in Skåne, a decree was issued in 1803 under the absolutist rule of Gustavus IV. This decree, which was initially valid for Skåne only, was promulgated without even consulting the Estates of the Realm and was supposed to have been written by Erik af Wetterstedt, head of the surveying bureau, and by Mathias Rosenblad, then Secretary of the Interior, later to be known as a diehard conservative, though evidently of a different bent in his younger days. The decree of 1803 for Skåne was followed by the decree of 1807 which applied to the country as a whole. But the obstacles to such extreme measures were not only legal and institutional. While the reform was feasible in the lowlands, it was hardly practicable in the hilly landscapes with their enormous differences in contours and quality of the land. In practice, the new legislation did little more than pave the way for somewhat less radical solutions which were eventually codified in the Redistribution Act of 1827.

The following quotations from an early nineteenth-century source give a vivid picture of how the repartitioning of a village proceeded:

On a little table the map of the village holdings is unfolded. On a bench or a wall, a figure is chalked up corresponding to the shape of the village land. It is then attempted to divide it into single holdings, according to the law as quadratic as possible, but still retaining the largest possible number of tenants in their old holdings . . . Then there is the fight to decide who shall have to move and who will be able to stay where he is. To soothe the tempers and to allow people to stay in the village, as many holdings as possible are made to converge narrowly upon the village . . . Thus prepared, the documents and the plan are sent to the Governor or the Governor General for his confirmation. In the field, the divisions look entirely different from what everybody had pictured when looking at the map in the dim room. All are dissatisfied, but there is no remedy . . . Thus began and ended many redistributions. Now comes the borrowing: those who have to move borrow to build their new houses; those who remain and have retained the better lands borrow in order to pay the heavy compensation to those who got the worse . . . He who now travels across the burgeoning fields of Skåne, enjoying the sight of the pretty farms, big and small . . . cannot picture the tears and the bitter worry out of which this loveliness has grown . . . But the great reform has been carried through, the achievement is completed.[28]

The most serious problem accompanying the enclosure reform was the disintegration of the village community. A way of life that had certainly not been free from friction but nevertheless had provided a good deal of neighborly solidarity and many a pleasant tradition was shattered when the villages gave way to homesteads located far apart. And the departure from the village was hardly ever a happy one even when the mover came into more land — because more land as a rule meant worse land. Though public allowances were paid to those who had to build new houses, what was paid was too little and often came too late, and many other expenses had to be incurred to make the new fields usable. One frequent complaint was that it was quite expensive to fence in the individual holdings, especially in regions where wood was scarce.

The enclosure movement was of course not peculiar to Sweden. It took place in most European countries; in England particularly it became the subject of much attention and strong criticism. For a long time the disappearance of the independent British farmer, the yeoman, was held to be the result of the enclosure movement. This has not been borne out by more recent research, which has shown that the large estates in England were older than the enclosure movement and did not even derive any increase from it. But certainly it cannot be denied that a system of peasant cultivation, as distinguished from peasant ownership, disappeared simultaneously with, and partly through, the enclosure movement. In Sweden, on the other hand, the enclosures were much less painful, and to a large extent their general effect pointed in the opposite direction. Neither a flight from the land nor a decrease in the small farmers' holdings occurred in Sweden. On the contrary, peasant farming tended to be stimulated by a peculiar aspect of the Swedish movement — the encouragement to parcel larger farms into smaller consolidated lots with independent owners (hemmansklyvning). This difference is striking enough to deserve closer study.

First of all, there was the tremendous difference in the cost of the reforms in the two countries. In England, every contested enclosure required a private act that had to pass both Houses of Parliament, a procedure involving the assistance of solicitors who, of all the English professions, have always enjoyed the reputation of charging the highest fees. In Sweden, the enclosures were handled by surveyors who were civil servants with a fixed salary and received a mere bonus for each transaction. The number of surveyors rose drastically with the beginning of the enclosure movement. In 1756, there were 86; in the following year, 141; and in another two years, 182; in the period 1815–27 there were about 300 of them.[29] That the enclosures were organized as a public service may not by itself have saved the Swedish peasantry, but it was certainly a powerful contributory factor.

There were also two fundamental economic reasons. The English development has been entirely misunderstood by those who have overlooked the strong attraction for the rural population of the rapidly growing industries in the cities; one of the main causes of the disappearance of the peasants was simply that industry offered them better terms. In Sweden it was the other way round. The only industry of a fairly modern structure, the mining industry, showed no expansion, for reasons that will be discussed later, while the manufacturing industries, still very small, were retreating rather than advancing, and offered miserable conditions to their workers. There were then no inducements for a flight from the countryside.

And, secondly, most of the factors that made for large-scale agriculture in England were completely absent in Sweden.

None of this, however, explains why the Swedish enclosures resulted in *hemmansklyvning*. Enclosure gave the English yeoman cause to go to the city; it made the Swedish peasant family split its farm. One reason was that once the traditional land distribution was destroyed on a national scale, there was less resistance to changes which were basically desirable. Another more positive reason was that the new land distribution lent itself to partition. Whereas the old narrow strips could not be further divided without great inconvenience, the consolidated fields now created were easily divided. In addition, the move away from the village resulted in the development of new land, new owners, new farmers. Finally, the improvement in the yields, which followed the reform, obviously facilitated division of the holdings among several owners. Thus, *hemmansklyvning* and enclosures were closely interrelated. And yet the extent of the connection should perhaps not be exaggerated. It might be more correct to say that the trends toward larger holdings in England and smaller holdings in Sweden had taken shape before the enclosures and independently of them, and that both transitions were promoted by the liberation from traditionalism which the enclosures encouraged.

So far the discussion has been deliberately confined to the enclosure of arable land. But the settling of people outside the villages, on lands previously in common use, naturally involved division of the commons. This led to complications of the same nature as those encountered in other countries, most notably in England. A considerable number of landless squatters had settled on the commons, keeping their swine, geese, and chickens there, and collecting wood in the common forests. The encroachment was illegal, but nevertheless tolerated. The new system tended to disrupt the very basis of their existence. Even though their numbers declined surprisingly little,[30] it is fair to say that those who suffered most from the enclosures were the squatters. But the poor among the villagers were also hit by the disappearance of the commons where they had been able to help themselves to considerable benefits. After the reform they were confined to what corresponded to their strict legal claims on the old commons. To them, the loss of security and mutual help in the village community must have been a severe blow.

## LAND PARCELING

For centuries, partitioning of farm property had been the subject of detailed restrictive legislation designed to ensure that a peasant should be able to discharge his obligations to the crown or, if a tenant, to the *frälse* owner. The taxes, and especially the land taxes, were levied according to flat rates that were imposed once a minimum ability to pay was reached. It was a curious "all-or-nothing" tax system. The unit of taxation was the farm, the *hemman*. It was also provided that too many peasants could not operate one unit jointly; the superfluous members of a family were supposed to found a new farm, which in due time could be assessed as a tax unit and increase the revenue of the crown. Gustavus Vasa in particular untiringly urged the peasants to create new farms.

Thus, legislation did not universally discourage the division of estates; when new land was brought under the plow no objection was raised, provided the conversion into arable land did not conflict with the mining industry's claims on the forest. By decisions in 1731 and 1740, cultivation of hitherto useless lands, fens and marshes, was even rewarded by tax exemption in perpetuity — without great effect, to be sure, since conversion of such land was practically impossible without application of mineral fertilizers. But partitioning of the existing arable land was generally frowned upon by the authorities. There was supposed to be one peasant to each *hemman*, or taxable farm unit, a relation that is also expressed in the alternative name of the unit, *mantal*. (See *Translator's Note,* page 127.) This was actually the rule under Gustavus Vasa, but under his successors frequent divisions took place despite all legal injunctions, so that with very few exceptions the farms were reduced to fractions of a *mantal*.

In the late seventeenth century it was still widely feared that the increase in population would lead to scarcity of land and pauperism. The Age of Freedom marked a great change in this respect. Enthusiasm for manufacturing was generally accompanied by an optimistic view of the population problem and, as in most countries under mercantilism, by an inclination to promote the growth of the population. Restrictions on land parceling were therefore relaxed. But although the new attitude to the population problem in general was one of the main causes of the new land policy, it was by no means the only cause; the pressure of circumstances was very strong. One of the county governors, Nils Reuterholm in Värmland, described the situation concisely in 1741, when he wrote that "the chief problem was where people should go." [31] It was, as we have seen, a time of rapid population growth; and almost inevitably efforts had to be made to find farmsteads for all those who wanted to make a living in agriculture.

With a stationary population there would have been no problem. Arrangements might still have been difficult on individual farms with many children, but if the total population had remained constant, corresponding openings would have appeared in other places, and the problem would have been reduced to one of migration. In reality, of course, the population did not remain constant but increased rapidly. It is true that to some extent the increase in population was the result of a policy which favored land parceling, since many of the young people in the countryside did not marry until they had a plot of land where they could settle. But any policy aimed at reducing the population or even at slowing down its growth would have been very unpopular and quite incompatible with mercantilist views. Growth of the population had to be taken as given; the question was where and how it could be absorbed.

If the population increase were to be absorbed by the agrarian sector without any parceling of farms, the consequence would perforce be greater landlessness and growth of the agricultural proletariat. This was not a desirable solution. On the other hand, a reduction in the size of the farms might make them too small to support a household, unless agricultural productivity could be raised to the point where the smaller units would become sufficient. An increase in productivity was assuredly the main answer to the problem.

But the peasants did not just work the land. Domestic manufacture, fishing, and illegal but nonetheless extensive rural trading were important activities in the rural community, forming a sizable sector within the national economy. To the extent that the lot of the farming population was improved by such activities, the limits of the rural population were no longer set by the productivity of farming alone.

It was also possible to transfer agrarian population to other industries, which was undoubtedly what the government had in mind. In practice, however, this solution had only limited possibilities of success. The mining industries were not allowed to expand, and the manufacturing industries were incapable of further growth.

What actually happened is not easy to study. The voluminous legislation, which constitutes our main source, was probably fairly ineffectual. A highly complicating factor was also the great difference between the various regions of the country. In forested areas or others with vast tracts of uncultivated land, parceling might result only in conversion of forest and pastures into arable land. The disappearance of grazing land was important enough, but the main problem was whether the forest resources were urgently required for some other industry; thus land parceling was restricted in the interest of the mining industries. Obviously, in the areas where arable land was divided, the problem was entirely different.

To begin with, an attempt was made to fortify the old customs which in the past had counteracted farm splitting, especially the tradition that the parents retired when the eldest son got married and that he was allowed to buy out his brothers and sisters on easy terms. This usage continued well into the nineteenth century, but hardly because it was favored by legislation.

The original assumption that the *mantal* should correspond to the normal size of a farm had, as we have said, become too unrealistic to be maintained even as an administrative fiction. When in 1684 the minimum area of a farm was set at a quarter of a *mantal*,[32] this could not be enforced, and from that time on legislation was progressively relaxed in order to catch up with actual conditions. In the mining districts, the forest areas, and the archipelagoes, parceling had generally proceeded much further; the normal lot was often below one-eighth of a *mantal*, sometimes far below it. In Värmland, where the process was probably carried farthest, lots of 1/240 or 1/288 of a *mantal* could be found.[33] On *frälse* estates parceling had not gone as far, although it was not legally restricted. The nobility were generally inclined to keep their tenancies intact, and the formation of large residential estates (*säterier*) even resulted in the emergence of some latifundia.

The definitive reversal of population policy took place in the

1740's, in the pursuit of "The Benefits Flowing to the Nation from a Large and Industrious Population," to quote the title of one of the pamphlets appearing at the time. Faggot was also an advocate of the new ideas when it came to land parceling. He wanted to abolish all restrictions on agriculture, to promote parceling and the creation of cottage farms, to lift the limitations on the number of laborers per farm, and to encourage early marriages. It was an expression of the optimistic pro-agricultural view of the population problem. Shortly after the publication of Faggot's first pamphlet, land parceling was allowed (in 1747) to proceed down to units of one-sixth and one-eighth of a *mantal,* and in some cases even farther. By 1756, farmers in Värmland were allowed to establish farms below one-twelfth of a *mantal,* which of course only legalized existing conditions.[34]

Data on the actual development during the period are most inadequate, but they seem to suggest that the number of farm units increased between 1751 and 1813 by at least 13.5 per cent, perhaps by as much as 21.5 per cent. However, those figures must be viewed against the background of the increase in total and rural population. The increase in rural population may be estimated somewhat more precisely than the number of farms; between 1751 and 1810 it grew by 31.6 per cent. Total population showed an increase of 31.9 per cent in the course of the same period.[35]

Thus, the rate of increase in the number of independent homesteads through land parceling was no higher than the rate of growth of the rural population. The number of landless households, on the contrary, kept mounting. According to the minimum estimate, the number of persons per farm unit grew from somewhat less than 7.5 in 1751 to 8–8.5 in 1810. One is therefore justified in saying that if the increase in population had to be accepted, nothing else could have been done but to allow at least as much land division as actually occurred.

To summarize, the growth in population raised the demand for new farms. The establishment of new farms was made technically possible by the enclosure movement, but was held in check by the limited extent of the enclosures, the resistance of custom, and, to some degree, by legal restraints. Hence, the number of farms did not keep pace with the growth of the rural population.

Whereas land belonging to small proprietors usually remained within the same families for generations, *frälse* land frequently changed owners. From the peasants' point of view, this mattered little, for as a rule the tenants probably remained and their leases were transferred to their heirs. Whether dues were paid to one nobleman or another generally made no difference to the peasant. But from the point of view of the gentry and nobility, trade in landed property was not unimportant; many gentlemen seem to have carried on a wholesale trade in large estates. Numerous instances are known of buyers who resold within one year, and the next owner sometimes did the same thing. This phenomenon was undoubtedly more or less stimulated by the administrative conception that landed property consisted of equivalent units, for example, *mantal;* the exchange of one plot of land for another in connection with reversion probably tended to implant the same attitude in the landlords.

The position of the landed aristocracy during the eighteenth century inevitably reflected the effects of reversion. But although the nobility, as previously mentioned, was allowed to exchange dispersed holdings for compact residential estates, large farms by no means constituted the major part of the nobles' land holdings. In the year 1772, for which a great deal of material exists, *frälse* land outside the estates proper and the immediately adjacent areas represented more than two-thirds of all *frälse* holdings. *Säterier,* that is, estates managed by noblemen, covered hardly one-fifth of the total. Thus, though the number of gentlemen farmers had increased, the aristocracy had not at all lost its position as an agricultural *rentier* class.

## REDEMPTION OF DUES

The position of the peasants had changed radically. Full ownership by an independent peasant was now generally recognized in practice, even though the notion of the *dominium directum* was still haunting the legal theorists. This development, more important perhaps than any letter of the law, imparted to the ownership of land an entirely new significance in the minds of the peasants. They themselves now recognized a profound difference between a taxpaying, independent farmer and a tenant on the crown's land. As a result, so-called dues redemption (*skatteköp*) became frequent in both the eighteenth and the nineteenth centuries. By this means crown tenancies were transformed into freeholds, and crown tenants into tax-paying proprietors. The importance attached to this change by all parties concerned is sufficient evidence of the high regard in which full proprietorship was now held.

Reversion, the principles of which were immutably upheld by all the regimes, might appear to conflict with the redemption of dues, by which the crown was again deprived of the land that had been returned to it. But this was not the case. The freeholder paid taxes almost exactly equal to the tenants' payments of dues, the only difference being that the tenants intermittently paid a certain fee in order to be entitled to retain the tenancy within the family. The main inconvenience of redemption from the point of view of the crown was that a freeholder could not be evicted for failure to pay his taxes whereas the crown's tenants could be evicted wherever it was found expedient to do so for one reason or another.

The real opposition to dues redemption, therefore, came not from the government but from the mining and metal industries. The ironmasters were interested in the acquisition of crown land, both in order to secure their forest supply and to exact dues from their tenants in the form of charcoal deliveries and freight services. However, if the ironmasters were to be entitled to redemption, the peasants in practice would be excluded from the competition. The ironmasters were in a position to pay many times as much as any peasant, probably more than any peasant would ever consider paying even if he had been able to do so. Since the crown had little or nothing to lose from redemption, it could accept a very low redemption rate, and the ironmasters' ability to pay more was the only factor that could have made for a high sales value of redeemed land.

It was in 1719 that the peasants were first entitled to redemption. The rates are said to have been very low during the first few years, sometimes even below the annual tax. In 1723, conditions were tightened and the minimum fee was set at a level six times the annual tax. It must be remembered, however, that tax assessments had remained unchanged in money terms and that inflation had reduced their burden considerably.[36]

Redemptions consequently became increasingly popular. But soon the growing concern for the metal industries worsened the position of the peasants. In 1770, redemptions were discontinued, first with some exceptions, then three years later altogether, and they remained in abeyance for sixteen years. In 1789, the split between Gustavus III and the aristocracy forced the king to lean more heavily on the commoners; in the same year he not only reinstituted the Act of 1723 but also granted the peasants several new privileges. From then on, redemption proceeded without obstruction.[37]

The land of independent peasant owners in Sweden proper amounted to about 21,000 full tax units — *mantal* — in 1700, after reversion had been completed. It rose to about 35,000 in 1815. Relatively speaking, this was an increase from 31.5 per cent of all holdings to 52.6 per cent. Hence, redemptions eventually restored the independent peasants to roughly the same relative position they had occupied by the end of the Middle Ages. The holdings of the crown declined correspondingly, from 35.6 per cent to 14.5 per cent.[38] Viewed over a long period, the ups and downs of the process are indeed striking. At the end of the Middle Ages, the crown's holdings had been practically non-existent; they grew through the addition of church property under Gustavus Vasa, disappeared again because of alienations in the seventeenth century; were returned by reversion; and were finally lost through redemptions of the eighteenth and nineteenth centuries. In 1878, the crown owned only 7.7 per cent of all farm land. The latter phase of this development laid the foundation for the dominating political position of the Swedish farmers in the latter half of the nineteenth century.

Long before that time, the administrative categories of land had lost their old meaning. As early as 1723, the two higher untitled Estates, the townsmen and the clergy, were granted the right to possess *frälse* holdings; in 1789 Gustavus III extended this right to all Estates, that is, also to the peasants. Whatever exclusive privileges the aristocracy still retained finally disappeared with the constitutional reform in 1810.

These developments, however, related only to administrative conditions of limited significance. From the point of view of economic history, the predominance of peasant farming was overwhelming; apart from all the freeholders, 87 per cent of all crown land and 80 per cent of all *frälse* land was cultivated by tenants. Putting the three categories together, no less than nine-tenths of all farm land in Sweden proper was cultivated by peasants. In Finland, the figure was higher, 96.3 per cent. For the two countries combined the average was 91.7 per cent. In all probability, those ratios had remained fairly stable since the reversion, but reversion itself is likely to have raised the peasants' share somewhat, since quite a few large estates (*säterier*) returned to the crown and thus to tenant farming.

## THE COMPOSITION OF THE AGRARIAN POPULATION

The predominance of peasant farming also indicates the nature of the agrarian labor force, which obviously was made up primarily of the peasants themselves. But the question remains as to the contribution made by the children of peasant households on the one hand, and by hired laborers on the other. While the statistical material is by no means satisfactory, it throws some light on those conditions in the period 1751–1815.

The number of adult children and hired helpers was, on an average, somewhat below 2⅓ per farmer proper, but falls to about 1⅓ to 1½ per independent cultivator (in other words, including cottagers' holdings, artisans' holdings, etc.). If only the men are counted, there was one helper per farm proper, and only .75 per independent cultivator. During the period when the statistical material distinguished between hired help and sons and daughters, there were only .8 to 1 hired helper, male or female, per cultivator. The regulations generally counted women as half units; on that basis the number of adult children and helpers may be estimated at 1¼ to 1¾ per farm and 1 to 1¼ per cultivator. Though those figures may not be very reliable, they certainly give the impression that hired farm labor played a very small part. The position of the hired laborers, which was the subject of a vigorous debate, was therefore fairly irrelevant insofar as the peasants were concerned, and the problem on the whole was confined to the large estates. Nevertheless, the legislation on this point deserves some attention.

The objectives of public policy were twofold. First, it was intended to put the entire population, except the "gentlemen," to work, a tendency which appeared in all countries. Underlying this attitude was the general view that laborers were a social asset that should be made available to other groups of society as well as to the state. In addition to principles, certain practical considerations naturally determined legislation; vagrancy, for instance, was dealt with by the Servants Act until 1833.[39]

The legislation was designed to support employers of all classes against the "licence" of employees. It was not altogether unopposed. A very illuminating debate in the late 1770's provoked Anders Chydenius into writing a celebrated pamphlet, *Tanker om husbönders och tienstehions naturliga rätt* (Reflections on the Natural Rights of Masters and Laborers), published in 1778, which effectively argues the position of the employees. It seems that its reception was cool. The ruling classes were of course in general sympathy with the employers, and cheap labor was held to be in the interest of the state. Anybody found to be without employment could be drafted into military service or into such civilian enterprises as canal digging and other construction work; alternatively he could be ordered to work for the informer for a wage below the going market rate. Coercion of workers did not stop at this. Well into the nineteenth century the law provided for corporal punishment by the employer, a barbarian custom to which Chydenius reacted with an indignation altogether modern in sentiment. Still, it should be remembered that the effectiveness of the many severe ordinances was another matter; in reality the situation was probably rather different from what the legal texts suggest.

Secondly, the law aimed at reserving the available labor force for the nobility and the gentry; consequently, legislation was directed against small proprietors as well as farm laborers. In earlier times, the retinue of a nobleman was excluded from military service, which made it possible for the aristocracy to attract the landless labor force. This privilege extended, with certain modifications, to all *frälse* land. Peasants within the *frihetsmil,* that is, a radius of one mile from the estate, were completely exempted, and other tenants on *frälse* land enjoyed a "half" exemption, in other words, twice as many peasants as elsewhere were allowed to join in the support of one infantryman. The nobility often permitted their tenants to be drafted in excess of this requirement, but never allowed their own servants and laborers to be drafted. A nobleman consequently always enjoyed a generous supply of servants, whereas the peasants were often in crying need of hired help. Except for vagrants, farm hands were the first to be drafted.

The reorganization of the armed forces under Charles XI changed the situation. It abolished the draft and therewith the old privilege. Instead, the Hiring Act of 1686 provided for direct limitations of the right to hire servants and workers. Since the servants and artisans of nobility and gentry were exempt from the limitation, the restrictions were aimed at the peasants only. The permissible number of employees depended on the size of the farm; there could be four to five adult workers per *mantal,* including sons and daughters, two women counting as one man. For a few years it was even held that peasants were not entitled to retain their own children in excess of those limits, but on this point, as on so many others, Gustavus III's reforms in 1789 relaxed the bonds of the peasants.

Quite certainly, the regulations were more a reflection of the prevailing mood of the legislators than a description of conditions as they really were. The figures already quoted show that the peasants had nothing like four or five farm hands working for them. Applying the standards used in the regulations, there were $1\frac{2}{3}$ to $1\frac{3}{4}$ per farm, and only *one* per independent cultivator. Those figures, it is true, were averages for farms many of which were smaller than one *mantal,* and it is not impossible that the law was a real hindrance to small farmers. But considering that the demand for labor on a small farm was correspondingly smaller, the difference between the legal limit and the actual average appears large enough to warrant the conclusion that the peasants were not seriously encumbered by this legislation. On the other hand, it almost goes without saying that the nobility hired the best laborers.

A special problem is raised by the rural proletariat, that is, the cottagers and the paupers. Combining the two groups does not seem entirely justified, since the cottagers were primarily independent producers like other servants. Yet the cottagers also supplied labor in the form of workdays to peasants as well as to the squires. The number of cottagers was not without importance for the labor supply of the small farmers, and during the period under review it changed markedly. In 1751, cottagers and paupers were a fairly small part of the rural population. Counted by heads of families, they were about one-fourth of all peasants; if the wives are included they were about one-third of the full-time labor force on farms. But while the peasants proper increased very slowly, the landless groups expanded rapidly until the middle of the nineteenth century; between 1751 and 1815 their numbers doubled and came to be about equal to the peasants proper. The increase in the number of cottagers took place chiefly in the second half of the eighteenth century; the increase in the number of paupers came later, starting mainly in the 1790's. Undoubtedly, this significant change in the composition of the rural population was related to the above-mentioned fact that the division of farm land did not keep pace with population growth.

From the point of view of the employers among the peasants and squires, the change meant that the ordinary laborers, whose numbers remained fairly constant, were supplemented by a growing number of cottages contributing workdays. This rise of a settled but at least legally landless agricultural population began well before 1815, although it was the great population increase in the 1820's that was mainly responsible for the pauperization of the Swedish rural population around the middle of the nineteenth century.

The large estates employed not only the landless groups but sometimes also hired tenants and freeholding peasants for part-time work. Still, this was far from being the rule. In Skåne, as in Denmark, the large farms were predominantly cultivated by peasants, though as early as 1662 Schering Rosenhane's *Oeconomia* had emphasized that the system was not suitable for the rest of Sweden. He was probably right, even though the apparent rise of peasant work on large estates in the eighteenth century requires further study. But by and large, the Swedish peasant had become too independent and too self-reliant to take readily to such work. The squire then had to resort to the same kind of laborers as the peasants.

## AGRICULTURAL PRODUCTION

The quantitative development of Swedish agriculture is reflected in the foreign trade statistics. At least since 1685, Sweden had been incapable of covering its own food requirements. This remained the case throughout the present period. However, on the basis of data on grain consumption which, according to the available food budgets, was very stable, it can be estimated that only a small fraction of total consumption was imported. In one ten-year period imports reached 9 per cent, but were generally much smaller, normally less than 5 per cent, which is even below the figure for 1685. It is of particular note that in the last two decades of the period (1791–1810), imports dropped to 2½ and 3⅔ per cent of consumption.[40] Considering the rapid growth of the population this must have required a remarkable increase in production, since there was no decline in per capita consumption. It compares quite well with an available statement by the clergy that 50 to 100 per cent more seed was used per *mantal* by the end of the eighteenth century than at the beginning. Only on the west coast was the increase less than 50 per cent. In the north twice or three times as much seed was used for sowing. Another interesting fact is that eighteenth-century food budgets without exception list peas, and in fairly large quantities at that; in the preceding centuries peas appeared only occasionally and then in small quantities. This would suggest a greater production of vegetables. Potatoes, by contrast, appear in those food budgets only around the turn of the century; even then they were not widely accepted as food.

The increased production of oats and other feed stuffs mentioned previously does not, surprisingly enough, seem to have been accompanied by any increase in meat consumption, while fluctuations in butter consumption which had already appeared in the seventeenth century were becoming even more striking. Oats were used for human consumption, and distillers' slop was probably not used as feed to any large extent. It must be added, however, that so far no food budgets have become available from western Sweden which was the principal wheat growing area.

## MINING AND METAL MAKING

The developments in agriculture, which have been presented in some detail, signified the most important advances within the Swedish economy of the period. But the second claim to our attention definitely goes to the mining and metal industries. In general, the eighteenth century marked the apex of an earlier development in this field rather than the beginning of a new era, and since the industry has been treated at length for the preceding centuries, a brief discussion should suffice now. For the iron industry, which had always been one of the main props of the Swedish economy, the eighteenth century was not the end of a chapter but rather a point of departure for its glorious performance in the following century.

Table 13, of the production of various metals and minerals around 1772, gives an idea of their comparative significance. As is seen from the table, gold was mined, although in very trifling quantities. Even the low figures for 1772 are about four times as high as the long-term average. The gold was extracted at Ädelfors, Sweden's only gold mine before the rich Boliden mine came into use. Ädelfors, located in Skåne, was discovered in 1738 and immediately aroused wild enthusiasm. It was hailed as a priceless addition to the country's national wealth; Linnaeus was one of those who described glowingly the benefits to be derived from it. In reality, things looked very different. Over eighty years of operations, the average annual output was just above one kilogram per year. In all, about 185 pounds (84 kilograms) were mined.[41] Needless to say, the value of output did not cover its cost by a long shot.

TABLE 13.  MINING AND METAL MAKING IN SWEDEN IN 1772
Riksdaler (rdr.)

|  | Value (added) | Per cent | |
|---|---|---|---|
| Gold: Approx. 20 *lödig mark* at 122 *rdr.* | 2,440 | | .08 |
| Silver: Approx. 1600 *lödig mark* at 8 1/5 *rdr.* | 13,120 | | .45 |
| Copper: Total output approx. 5500 *skeppund* at 50 *rdr.* | 275,000 | 9.40 | 11.66 |
| Approx. 3000 *skeppund* converted into brass at 16 2/3 unit value added | 50,000 | 1.71 | |
| Approx. 1600 *skeppund* consumed by the copper manufactories at 10 *rdr.* value added | 16,000 | .55 | |
| Iron: Approx. 368,000 *skeppund* bar iron at 5 1/2 *rdr.* (333,000 exported, 35,000 consumed in the country) | 2,024,000 | 69.21 | 85.34 |
| Iron manufactures: 54,000 *skeppund* at 8 *rdr.* (19,000 exported, 35,000 domestic consumption) | 432,000 | 14.76 | |
| Cast iron and munitions: approx. 5000 *skeppund* at 8 *rdr.* | 40,000 | 1.37 | |
| Alum: Approx. 7500 *skeppund* at 9 *rdr.* | 67,500 | | 2.31 |
| Vitriol: Approx. 700 *skeppund* at 4 *rdr.* | 2,800 | | .09 |
| Sulphur: Approx. 200 *skeppund* at 10 *rdr.* | 2,000 | | .07 |
| Total | 2,924,860 | 100.00 | |

Source: Prepared on the basis of Appendix to *Bergskollegii berättelse om bergverkens tillstånd*, April 29, 1773 (*Bergskollegii arkiv*, unpublished).

Compared to gold, even silver mining was of some consequence although it so happens that the table shows a subnormal output. Nonetheless, production was very insignificant at all times: during most of the period it hardly exceeded 650 pounds (300 kilograms) annually. In the early 1770's there was an upswing, when the output even doubled, but the boom was over before the end of the period under review.

Another branch of the mining industry, which does not even appear in the table, was coal mining. Coal had been mined in Skåne under Danish rule. From the end of the eighteenth century it continued to expand without ever attaining any special prominence.

Next to iron, the most important metal, as the table shows, was copper, which contributed 11.7 per cent of the total metal production. Until the 1770's it was also the second item in importance on the Swedish export list, albeit very far below iron. Then copper exports dropped, yielding their place first to fish and tar and then to lumber too. But, as we mentioned in connection with the seventeenth century, Swedish copper retained something of its former position on foreign markets. In Amsterdam, for instance, it was quoted throughout the period. Only Norwegian copper finally remained as a competitor, at prices far below the Swedish. Compared to the flourishing seventeenth century, however, copper was unimportant in this period. The output was about 800 metric tons a year as against an average of 2,100 tons around the middle of the seventeenth century. The story has already been told in the previous chapter: the mine at Stora Kopparberg was exhausted and the bitter end was accelerated by predatory exploitation resulting in continual cave-ins. The increasing depth of the mines and the drainage problem raised technical difficulties, and the fuel shortage was a further obstacle. Still, there was a slight increase in the output at Stora Kopparberg in the 1780's, at the same time that a new mine was discovered at Åtvidaberg in Östergötland which for a while contributed 100 to 150 metric tons a year. The five-year average for the whole country was thereby raised above an annual rate of 1,000 tons throughout the period 1781–95; in one of the three five-year periods it even reached 1,200 tons. But long before 1815 the decline was obvious. Stora Kopparberg yielded less than ever, and in spite of the new mines the total output did not reach 800 tons a year. The copper industry was inevitably on the wane. Still the industry's contribution to Sweden's power politics is undeniable.[42]

Stora Kopparberg is also of great interest from another point of view. Its development sheds some light on trends in business organization. Although externally the ancient institution retained the form it had assumed in the fourteenth century, behind this façade a significant transformation was taking place that was entirely spontaneous and bears witness to the force with which early capitalism could assert itself within a medieval form.

As time went by, the corporate nature of the institution began to disappear. Originally owned by the miners themselves, the shares in the mine were now diffused among all social classes and were no longer tied to participation in actual operations; they came to correspond almost entirely to modern company stock. A few miners with ownership rights still remained, but their position, too, was changed. They no longer worked either in the mine or in the smelteries; they became employers in the smelteries. The management of the mine itself was transferred to the corporation, the so-called *Bergslaget*, which paid the miners and distributed the ore to the smelters according to their shares in the mine. Thus, the organization came to resemble the modern stock company in that managerial functions were completely separated from ownership.

### THE IRON INDUSTRY

All other branches of the mining and metal industry were dwarfed by the iron industry. As Table 13 shows, bar iron alone represented more than two-thirds of the total value of the production of metals and minerals, while the total share of the iron industry was no less than 85 per cent.

The technology of the Swedish iron industry had crystallized in the seventeenth century. Despite many minor improvements and despite Sven Rinman's classical treatise on ironmaking, published in the 1780's, the new developments of the eighteenth century were in the realm of commerce and finance rather than in technology.

Incomparably the most important market for Swedish iron was England. The fuel shortage in that country was worse than in the preceding century, and attempts to substitute coal and coke for charcoal in iron smelting continued. In 1709, an English ironmaster,

Abraham Darby, had established coke-smelting of iron at Coalbrookdale in Shropshire. But for a long time the discovery remained secret, which precluded the diffusion of the new technique; moreover, the coke pig iron was at first very inferior and, above all, could not be successfully used for conversion into malleable iron. Its only use was in iron founding; for some time this branch of the industry experienced a tremendous upswing. Wares which had always been produced from wrought iron and could not profitably be manufactured otherwise, such as knives and scissors, were now made by casting. Sweden had never exported any but malleable iron, so that Swedish exports did not suffer from the introduction of coke pig iron; the competition from cast iron was too insignificant to depress the demand for wrought iron. Inasmuch as the English economy was rapidly expanding, the demand for imported malleable iron continued to grow.

The market situation for Swedish iron remained extremely favorable even after Darby's success. Around the 1750's, iron prices climbed to a higher level than ever before, remained there for about twenty-five years, and then continued to rise long into the next century. At the beginning of the present period, Sweden occupied an absolutely dominant position on the English market. No less than four-fifths of the English iron imports were fetched from Sweden. In Russia, however, Peter the Great had founded an iron industry, and in forest resources Russia was certainly not second to Sweden. On the other hand, Sweden was technically more advanced; moreover, the quality of the Russian iron was not equal to the Swedish. Nevertheless, export of Russian iron to England started shortly after Peter's death in 1725 and grew steadily until the early nineteenth century. For a short period toward the end of the eighteenth century, England even bought more iron from Russia than from Sweden, although total Swedish iron exports remained larger than the Russian. The slump in English iron prices which lasted for some twenty years until 1747 might possibly have been caused by the appearance of Russian iron on the market, though the quantities were as yet insignificant. At any rate, the market recovered, and from that time on until the first decade of the next century, Sweden never faced any but the most temporary difficulties in placing her iron in England on favorable terms. Nevertheless, there was no complacency in

Sweden; Russian competition caused grave anxiety. According to a Russian proverb which seems appropriate, "fear has big eyes."

Swedish policy in this situation was ruthless but profitable, at least in the short run. Already in the seventeenth century, the desire to avoid a fuel shortage had prompted restrictions on the iron industry, particularly in Bergslagen, although no attempt had been made to curtail production in the country as a whole. On the contrary, the purpose of the restrictions was to spread the industry more evenly over the forested areas. Production was continually growing until the 1740's when it reached 45,000 tons,[43] a very substantial quantity at the time, even though by modern standards the figure still is ridiculously low — in 1950 the Swedish output of iron was close to 1.5 million tons.[44] From the middle of the eighteenth century on, however, the industry remained practically stationary. The average annual rate of exports over five-year periods never exceeded 50,000 tons,[45] while total production was perhaps 10 per cent higher. This development was the result of a new policy designed not only to restrain the iron industry in certain districts, but to restrict total output as well. Various measures introduced during a twenty-year period beginning in the 1720's fixed the limits of output for each iron mill.[46] This policy, which was still generally justified as aiming at conservation of forest resources, in effect tended to amount to rigorous monopolization of the Swedish iron industry. At times, this was openly admitted, and it must have been fully obvious even when not explicitly stated. All Europe, especially England, was in a phase of vigorous industrial expansion; the demand for iron was increasing correspondingly. On the supply side Sweden at first stood alone, then was joined by Russia. The fruits to be reaped from deliberate curtailment of production and exports were clearly quite considerable.

The monopoly would have been even more profitable if the less efficient mills had been shut down. Production quotas imposed on each mill resulted in a cartel arrangement which prevented full utilization of the monopolistic possibilities. But a more drastic monopolization would have been quite incompatible with the economic views of the time, with the high regard for the social position of the ironmasters, and especially, of course, with the official justification of the policy.

Naturally numerous attempts were made to circumvent the restrictions. Individual entrepreneurs acquired inferior mills which were then closed down while their production quotas were filled from more efficient mills. There were also incessant applications for additional quotas. But by and large the policy was enforced with an efficiency that was rare in those days. The control of mining and pig iron production restricted the industry at the base. The establishment of new mills was discouraged, and applications for larger quotas for existing mills were rejected. Finally, the transfer of quotas from less efficient or closed down mills to more efficient mills was checked. Consistently applied, this policy would have resulted in an absolute drop in production, since some mills would always close down in the normal course of affairs. Though this was not allowed to happen, the regulations were eventually sharpened to the point where applications for additional quotas or transfer of quotas were made a criminal offense.

The supervision was efficient. Quotas could be exceeded temporarily if the surplus was made up by a curtailment below the quotas at some other time. But careful accounts were kept by the authorities, especially of export iron. No iron could be exported without passing through the iron wharves in the shipping towns, where it was weighed and checked off against the producer's quotas. Similarly, books were kept of the iron shipped to the manufactories for further processing. Only the iron that was sold directly within the country could evade the controls. The magnitude of this domestic consumption is not known with any precision, but it was certainly insignificant compared to the exports which probably absorbed as much as 85 to 90 per cent of the output. A study of the accounts of individual iron works reveals that the evasions must have been small indeed. Moreover, the loophole for domestic iron did not really affect the main object of the policy, which was to curtail supplies on the foreign markets.[47]

Special ledgers were kept where the iron mills were credited with their production quotas and debited with their exports and their sales to manufacturers. Overfulfilled or underfulfilled quota balances of one period could be carried forward into the next period. Thus, the system was flexible enough to permit the exports to follow trade fluctuations without exceeding the long-term quotas. Administratively, this whole attempt to monopolize the country's most important export industry was remarkably successful.

Quality control, which had always been one of the main features of the Swedish iron industry, was continued under the new system. There was still intense concern about potential foreign competition, and the existence of Russian iron exports served to prevent complacency. Interest in metallurgy was growing. It was furthered by the Iron Bureau (*Jernkontoret*), founded in 1747, which appointed technical directors and inspectors for the various branches of the industry.[48] One of those was the above-mentioned Sven Rinman, who not only was a pioneering student of metallurgical techniques, but who also pressed relentlessly for adoption of the highest quality standards that available knowledge permitted. Thus the Swedish iron industry avoided that ever-present danger of monopoly, quality deterioration. In fact, numerous technical advances seem to have been made. The Mining Board (*Bergskollegium*) reported in 1773 that where reasonably good ore was used coal consumption per ton of bar iron produced had been reduced by 40 per cent.[49]

Despite all this, toward the end of the century there was a change in the Swedish attitude. The years of booming trade created an illusion of security which tended to dull the awareness of the real threat to the Swedish position. This threat did not come from the east. A far greater menace, the one that was eventually to remove both Sweden and Russia from their leading positions, was the transition to mineral fuel for bar iron production.

Strangely enough, the awareness of this danger was stronger in the early half of the century than later. In 1727, for instance, Edward Carleson, then a clerk in the Board of Commerce and later its president, wrote in a report:

As to the ironworks here in England, there are certainly many mines and ore deposits, but for lack of wood and charcoal they are not being worked and could never do any particular harm to our trade. Somebody has recently submitted a project for the use of stone coal in iron smelteries and has been granted a Royal Privilege, but it is already certain to fail and would cost too much to ever be worth while.[50]

The author of this report was not a prophet, but his judgment was entirely correct for the immediate future. Swedish observers were also kept informed of the experiments with coke pig iron at a fairly early stage, despite the secrecy with which those were surrounded. In a report issued by the Mining Board in 1744 a summary of early English experiments is given, after which the following remark is made:

It has later been discovered at Coalbrookdale how to smelt with stone coal instead of charcoal, although not without various difficulties. Thus, twice as much stone coal has to be used, and the sulphur with which the coal abounds steals away much of the iron. Moreover, the iron which results cannot be wrought except when added in small quantities to better iron, although it is said to be well suited for casting.[51]

This statement too was remarkably correct at the time it was made. But from the mid-century on there were, as far as we know, no more Swedish reports on the English iron industry, and this was of course the time when the new methods of production matured, especially with the introduction of the puddling process in the early 1780's. This innovation was the harbinger of one of the most momentous technical revolutions in history. Not only pig iron but also malleable iron could now be made with mineral fuel. This was the beginning of the end for the Swedish and the Russian hegemony on the iron market, even though the puddled iron was inferior to the Swedish, especially in the beginning. The higher grades of Swedish iron, which were used for conversion into steel, were not seriously threatened; but this was only a small part of the Swedish exports. The bulk of Swedish iron was thus fully exposed to the pressures of the new competition. Puddled iron might be of inferior quality but it was nevertheless perfectly serviceable for many purposes where better grades had been used previously, "in default of something worse," as one might say.

Yet, twenty years were to elapse after the discovery of the puddling process before the blow hit the Swedish iron industry. In 1802 and 1803, one of Sweden's most intelligent metallurgists, Eric Thomas Svedenstjerna, visited England and was baffled and terrified by the advances made by the English and Scottish ironworks which, apparently, were as yet unknown in Sweden.[52] Upon his return he emphasized the menace. The new processes, he said, were designed deliberately to reduce English dependence upon Russian and Swedish iron. Prices remained high, however, probably for two reasons, both related to the Napoleonic wars. First, the war created a high level of demand; secondly, the operations of continental ironworks were seriously obstructed. Svedenstjerna called the previous twenty years the most prosperous in the history of Swedish iron exports, which was probably quite correct. But the peace of 1815 opened a new era of dire consequences for Sweden's oldest industry.

The Russians were much harder hit than the Swedes. The quality of Russian iron was not such as to warrant a premium over the cheap English iron, and Russian exports could not be maintained. Swedish iron, however, continued to find a place on the English market for uses where the cheap puddled iron was inadequate. After a slight decline for a few decades, Swedish exports were to recover and soon to exceed the limits that had been set in the period of monopolistic curtailment. Of course, prices were not the same, nor could the industry proceed as if nothing had happened; yet it was to show great resilience and to manifest unexpected powers of survival.

It would be a mistake to believe that the period of the Napoleonic wars was one of unmitigated prosperity. Shortly after the turn of the century, the iron industry ran into a few years of great difficulty. One important factor was a series of considerable increases in English tariffs on iron. In addition, the industry lost an important domestic advantage when the inflation that had proceeded practically throughout the eighteenth century came to a halt. If production costs had risen at the same rate as the price level for iron, the inflation would obviously have brought no gains to the industry. The price of charcoal kept pace, and the price of pig iron rose even faster than that of bar iron. But one important cost factor — labor — lagged behind. Throughout the period, the industry had derived part of its profits from the fact that wages were more sticky than prices. The fall of wages in relation to prices continued until 1765; and despite subsequent improvement the wage-price ratios of 1735–45 were never regained.[53] Most of the wages, though fixed in money, were paid in kind; as long as producers charged market prices for the commodities in which they paid their workers, the sluggishness of wages resulted in a reduction of real wages. Around the turn of the century, however, the workers began to demand that fixed prices be charged for the grain in which most of their wages were paid, and many mills, though not all, were forced to accede. Shortly afterwards a new wave of price rises occurred, but the workers now re-

In the second half of the seventeenth century, two-thirds to three-quarters of all Swedish foreign trade passed through the port of Stockholm. Detail from an etching in *Suecia Antiqua*.

Axel Oxenstierna. Portrait by David Beck. *Private collection, Stockholm.*

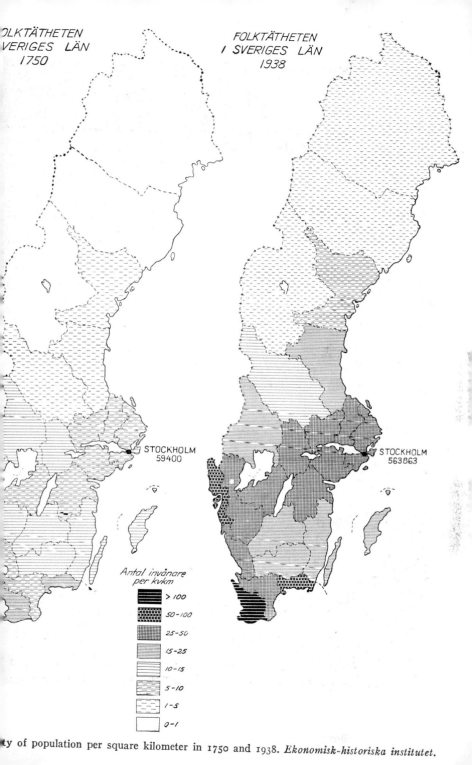

FOLKTÄTHETEN
I SVERIGES LÄN
1750

FOLKTÄTHETEN
I SVERIGES LÄN
1938

STOCKHOLM
59400

STOCKHOLM
563863

Antal invånare
per kvkm

> 100

50–100

25–50

15–25

10–15

5–10

1–5

0–1

ty of population per square kilometer in 1750 and 1938. *Ekonomisk-historiska institutet.*

*Dannemora Eld och Lufft Machin.*
Kongl. Maj:ts och Riksens Höglofliga Bergs Collegio
Underdån-ödmiukast Dedicerad af Mårten Triewald.

The so-called "Fire and Air Machine," an atmospheric steam engine, designed by Martin Triewald, was installed at the mine at Dannemora in 1728 and represented the first Swedish attempt — not very successful — to operate a minepump by steam. Etching by E. Geringius from a description published in 1734.

ceived full compensation. At the same time, prices for bar iron in Sweden declined, while in England tariff increases had raised the price level, so that Swedish producers were squeezed between rising wages and falling prices. This episode probably brought home the need for a reform in the Swedish iron industry before the competition from the puddling process made itself felt.

The prosperity enjoyed by the Swedish iron industry throughout the eighteenth century provides the fabric for an arresting chapter in Swedish intellectual history. We cannot describe here the great contribution which the ironmasters, whether noble or untitled, made to the country's intellectual development. Suffice it to say that they created an environment from which emerged much of what was best in the culture of nineteenth-century Sweden, including the two great Swedish poets, Gcijer and Tegnér. When all is said and done, this was perhaps the greatest gain of the Swedish iron monopoly.

And yet, the iron industry was never seen with unmitigated favor by the makers of economic policy in Sweden. The mercantilists who put their stamp on the eighteenth century as on no previous period were highly suspicious of an industry which was located outside the towns; and it did not improve matters that the interests of the iron industry inevitably clashed with some of the basic notions of the mercantilists, especially in the field of navigation.

## The Manufacturing Industry

The real favorite of the government was not the iron industry, but the manufacturing industry. It must be emphasized, however, that manufacturing, in other words, production of goods in "manu factories," was a very narrow concept. Literally all the main branches of the Swedish economy were excluded from this group, not only agriculture and handicrafts, but also the mining and metal trades, the tar distilleries and the sawmills. Within the group of "manufactories" belonged first the various branches of the textile industry, then the sugar refineries which were based on imported cane sugar, the tobacco industry, a small part of the iron industry, and miscellaneous trades of less significance. If one abstracts from the history of the last twenty-five years, it is correct to say that no other part of the Swedish economy has ever received the care and support that were bestowed upon those industries.

Table 11 on page 141 has shown how few people the manufactories employed; yet the year 1760, to which the table refers, was close to being the peak year for the whole period from 1720 to 1815. It is true that the table counts only fully employed workers, and that the total labor force was much larger, since it was chiefly made up of women who did part-time work for the manufacturers in their own homes but for whom work in the household remained the principal occupation. Their inclusion should increase the labor force to some 16,000–17,000 people at the peak. Normal level of employment must have been much lower, probably about 11,000–12,000. Toward the end of the period the figure dropped to the neighborhood of 7,000. While it is impossible to express the part-time work of these women in terms of full-time men's work and thus to estimate with any precision the combined labor contributed by the two categories of workers, nevertheless, even during their best years the manufactories cannot have employed much more than one per cent of the manpower of the country.

It is therefore hard to explain in rational terms why this branch of the economy enjoyed such special attention from the authorities and such undisputed priority in economic thought. In part the explanation was that the spirit of the time was technical far more than economic. The possibility of producing what had not hitherto been produced in the country was so fascinating that the suspicion that there might have been good reason not to produce it did not occur to anybody. For instance, attempts were made to plant mulberry trees and to give the silk industry a prominent position in the Swedish economy. Perhaps the main explanation of such ways of thought was that "finishing" was considered superior to production of semifinished products, no matter how profitable. Thus, production of bar iron, for which there was always a market, was to be retarded in favor of various iron manufactures which were in little or no demand. In practice, this view was even in conflict with one of the leading mercantilist tenets, that of the favorable balance of trade. Even the most generous export bounties could not evoke any sizable export of manufactured goods. The skill of industrial workers in Sweden was too inferior to that of other countries. Similar views prevailed in other countries; there, especially in France, they met with far more success.

Swedish textile manufacturers in particular were caught between the devil and the deep blue sea. In spite of all educational efforts, imported as well as domestic industrial workers were far too unskilled to be able to satisfy the demand for textiles among the upper classes and other exacting buyers. This demand was largely filled by foreign goods, the importation of which was prohibited but which reached the consumer through smuggling, as did almost all valuable goods in former times. Import prohibitions thus served as a tariff barrier corresponding to the fairly high cost of smuggling. On the other hand, manufacturers were not interested in the production of cheap goods for which the available skills might have been sufficient. Even when, as was sometimes the case, the attitude of the manufacturers was different, this had little effect, for the bulk of demand for cheap textiles seems to have been filled through domestic weaving, whether for home consumption or for sale.

Labor force figures indicate that the manufactories did not live up to expectations — no young plant this, growing under tender care into a mighty tree. Remarkable as it may sound, manufacturing activity, measured by employment, showed an absolute decline in the course of the period. Manufacturing was thus not ready to absorb the surfeit of rural population; in the words of Nils Reuterholm, it was certainly not the place "where people could go." The number of weaving looms in 1809 was as low as in 1745, when the reporting began, although in the meantime it had been more than twice as high.[54] The decline of the total industrial labor force has already been mentioned. Employment at the end of the period was less than half the peak figure. To some extent this decline was accompanied by rising productivity. Output per loom and worker doubled after the most inefficient workshops were weeded out following the crisis of the 1760's and the policy of subsidizing individual producers at any cost was discontinued.[55] Nevertheless, with very few exceptions, the manufactories could be kept alive only by permanent protection against foreign competition as well as by permanent domestic subsidy.

From the historical point of view, it is of special interest that the manufactories of the eighteenth century hardly ever were a point of departure for the industrial development of the nineteenth century. Nobody, to be sure, could have anticipated either the future importance of the forest industries or the rise of the Swedish engineering industry. But such an observation does not explain the industrial policy of the eighteenth century; if anything, it points to the general dangers of such a policy. For an unpredictable future development necessarily tends to aim its hardest blows at industries which have not been ruled by effective demand. The policy of the time was based on the assumption that certain branches of industry were especially indispensable to a flourishing economy, which was a complete mistake.

It is remarkable, however, that not even the rapid expansion of the textile industry in the nineteenth century was related to eighteenth-century manufactories. In the early period, the second most important branch of the textile industry was the silk industry, strange as this may sound. It was completely discontinued in the nineteenth century. In the eighteenth century, the wool industry centered around Stockholm, but in the following century it survived only at Norr-köping, an important wool town since the seventeenth century. Most indicative of all, the first mechanized cotton mill in Sweden, Rydbo-holm outside Borås, developed not out of manufactories but rather out of domestic industry. A peasant woman by the name of Mother Kerstin of Stämmemad had introduced the putting-out system in that part of the country; in 1834 her son, Sven Erikson, reorganized her establishment into a factory.

Contemporary opinion was equally deluded in the matter of the internal structure of the manufacturing industry. Through a talent for public relations almost unparalleled in Swedish history, Jonas Alströmer managed to convey to his own and later generations the impression that he was the founder of Sweden's manufactures, and that his establishment at Alingsås ranked foremost among the factories of the time. As to the first claim, we have already seen that as early as the seventeenth century many far from trifling establishments had been set up, often possessing far greater powers of survival than Alströmer's. As to the second claim, Alingsås was not even close to a leading position. Beyond any comparison, Stockholm was the most important industrial center; throughout the period the capital possessed at least two-thirds of all weaving looms; two-thirds of the total value of industrial output, often much more, originated there; and usually at least one-half of the total industrial labor force was employed in Stockholm. The second most important manufacturing town was always Norrköping. Alingsås ran third; it was prominent, if at all, only in the beginning of the period. In 1745, its shares in national totals were as follows: 4 per cent of the looms, 8.8 per cent of the workers, and 5.8 per cent of the value of industrial production. Even this modest showing was entirely dependent on the support Alströmer received from the government, and this exceeded the total subsidies to the rest of the manufacturing industry. When, after forty years, the subsidies came to an end in 1765–66, Alingsås sank into oblivion. In 1809, its shares amounted to only 1.5 per cent of the looms, 4.1 per cent of the workers, and, characteristically enough, only .3 per cent of the value of total industrial output.[56]

That even contemporary estimation of the quality of the textiles from Alingsås was fairly low is quite apparent from a report submitted to the riksdag of 1734 by three clothiers from Stockholm. They could not have spoken more frankly. Thus, four samples of barracan were said to be "coarse, unevenly woven, and badly dyed"; the Indian camlet "was of less than ordinary width, badly dyed and, as a result of inept weaving, quite streaky"; the damask was "thin and poorly manufactured"; the castor drugget "poorly made, in particular the gray which was badly dyed and calendered"; the black cloth was "of poor quality, since the fat had not been washed out of the wool, and the dyeing and calendering were similarly inadequate"; the blue cloth had "a whitish hue" and was "badly colored"; the blue baize was "too narrow to be double and too wide to be single width"; the red sarge was of "rather poor make and uncertain color and also considerably thinner than sarge should be," and so on.[57]

The manufactories were supported in almost every conceivable way. Competing foreign goods were generally prohibited, and subsidies were doled out in all forms, sometimes in cash, sometimes by donating buildings or other physical assets. A special tax was even levied for the benefit of the manufactories; to begin with, the proceeds went exclusively to Alingsås. The manufactories received their alms above all from the *Riksbank*, which contributed significantly to the ruin of the monetary system, to which we shall presently return. The straight subsidies were reduced when the bank could no longer continue this practice, especially after the victory of the *Caps* at the *riksdag* of 1765–66. The moment was unfortunate. An international crisis in 1763 had had its repercussions upon the Swedish economy and had shaken the position of the manufactories even before the change in support policy. The effect of the change, however, was highly exaggerated in the heated debate. In reality, most of the general supporting and protective measures were retained. As the ultimate decline of the manufactories testifies, their need for support continued to be so great that the reduced aid, though still large, was insufficient to enable them to hold their own, let alone to allow any further growth.

While the contribution of the manufactories to the national economy was much less significant than their contemporaries were ready to admit, one aspect deserves our attention, namely, their form of organization, which had arisen spontaneously and, as far as we know, unaided by government influence. This was the so-called merchant-employer or putting-out system (*förlag*) which historically links the medieval forms of industrial organization with the factory system. It was this system which became the characteristic industrial organization of early (or "commercial") capitalism. Though details of this form of organization varied from case to case, the general features were as follows:

The establishment was owned or financed by a merchant who received the finished product. Generally, he was also an employer, that is, he hired the labor force; but, unlike a modern employer, he had nothing to do with the production process as such. It was a natural form of organization in a situation in which working capital rather than fixed capital or management was what was desperately needed. The actual production was supervised by a manufacturer, or fabricant, who was sometimes more and sometimes less independent of the merchant-employer but always was his subordinate. Under the manufacturer were a number of craftsmen with their journeymen and apprentices. Each craftsman tended to be fairly independent of the others; hence the manufactory was hardly more than a loose aggregation of ordinary artisans. The craftsmen were treated as ordinary guild members in spite of the fact that they had been hired by the fabricant or by the merchant-employer and had lost all independence. In smaller firms it occasionally happened that the merchant-employer was also the fabricant or, more commonly, that the latter was himself a craftsman. In any case, the skilled guild artisans in the towns formed the nucleus of the organization.

The rest of the workers were in the countryside surrounding the cities. Usually, as many as three-fourths of them were women; they received their raw materials from the shop or factory in the city where they also delivered the products that were sometimes finished and ready for sale and sometimes required finishing or calendering in the factory. Most of them were married women from the lower classes, the wives of soldiers, sailors, and workingmen; but not a few were the impoverished widows and daughters of gentlemen. There were also cases where women were given full-time employment in the factory and, as was more often the case abroad, were quartered in the factory itself where they received "a warm bed and found their daily work." All this was of course completely different from modern forms of industrial organization. Yet, it was a workable system. If the Swedish manufactories had been built on firmer ground, the merchant-employer system as such would not have been a hindrance to further growth.

## DOMESTIC INDUSTRY

As already mentioned, the Swedish textile industry did not develop out of the manufactories. Rather it was rooted in the domestic industry, where textiles, especially linen and wool, were the main products.[58] But rural households also made wood, iron, and leather goods. Nor did they confine themselves to the production of small wares; thus, furniture and carriages were an important part of this trade. The scale of the domestic industry is revealed by the fact that it was often based on raw materials imported from other parts of the country; iron products, for instance, were turned out in places far removed from any iron supplies. Though statistically its extent cannot be ascertained, there are frequent references to domestic crafts in practically all the provinces; in certain regions like Västergötland, parts of Småland, Dalarna, and Ångermanland, it may even be suspected that the rural population devoted more time to crafts than to agriculture. Contemporaneous reports also agree that the domestic industry increased considerably during the eighteenth century. Especially weaving and spinning were taken up in province after province where there had been no textile crafts in the preceding century.

For this result the industrial policy of the time must be assumed to be largely responsible, although its aim was an entirely different one and, in fact, directly opposed to such a development. When protectionist policies raised the prices of foreign goods, the products of household industry rather than those of domestic manufacturers filled the void. Their qualities as well as the way in which they were distributed fitted the needs of the population far better. They were sold all over the country by traveling peddlers, traditionally from the province of Västergötland where the land was fairly barren; everywhere such salesmen are mentioned as *västgötar* or *boråsare* (from the town of Borås in that province). The peddlers were welcome guests who spared the peasants irksome and unpopular trips to town and who brought, along with their wares, tidbits of news and entertainment.

The market area of domestic industry, incidentally, was not limited to Sweden. There seem to have been considerable exports, particularly to Norway, but also, via Göteborg, to more faraway lands. It is rather significant that in the following century, when the factory system definitely made its appearance in Sweden, there were many who advocated an escape from the problems of an industrial civilization through return to the old household crafts. Such a solution was obviously impossible, but that the thought was put forward at all is quite illuminating.

The financial organization of domestic industry varied a great deal. Not only when they produced for their own use but also when they aimed to sell their products, rural craftsmen often got along without external financial aid. If they were processing their own raw materials, for example, wool, this could be done during the long winter months when there was no work to do in the fields. In the self-financing group we might also include the important category of migrant workers who were selling nothing but their own labor. Best known were the migrant laborers from Dalarna, men as well as women, who would walk all the way to Stockholm to seek menial employment, usually in heavy but well-paid work. By extreme thrift they would accumulate most of their earnings until they returned home, "with coins in their pockets and wedlock in their hearts."

In other cases the organization was clearly capitalistic. The putting-out system was practiced in all branches of domestic industry, as in the manufactories. Often manufactories and household industry were closely related, as when the former were based on home spinning by women in the surrounding countryside. When this was the case, the authorities had no quarrel with the domestic crafts; indeed, they even encouraged them by prizes and subsidies. But the sale of finished products from household industry was considered a highly inappropriate form of competition with the manufactories.

## HANDICRAFT

While handicraft was probably less important than household industry, nevertheless it represented the largest occupational group outside agriculture: according to Table 11 the number of craftsmen in 1760 was just a little over 3 per cent of the total population. The relative strength of rural and urban handicraft varied somewhat from time to time: in 1760, rural artisans seem to have been more numerous than urban and on the whole, though with some exceptions, they also seem to have been increasing faster in the course of the century. One must, however, remember that the rural craftsmen, or at least their families, devoted more time to farming than their urban colleagues; in a strict comparison their number probably should be scaled down somewhat. The most important rural craftsmen were the tailors and the shoemakers who were far more numerous in the countryside than in the towns, but blacksmiths and especially carpenters were almost equally important. More elaborate products were always turned out by urban artisans; luxuries were strikingly prominent in urban handicraft. A French writer has termed luxuries "very essential things," and that this was so — at least to the artisans — is certainly confirmed by the data. In most Swedish towns there were, for instance, gold- and silversmiths; a hatter was seldom absent and the wigmaker was common. The hatters actually ranked ninth among urban craftsmen outside Stockholm.[59]

The growth of handicrafts was also related to the decline in the self-sufficiency of the households. It is, for instance, apparent that, except for Stockholm, most of the baking in urban areas was done at home until the latter half of the century. Toward the middle of the century, half of the towns were without professional bakers; but there were bakeries in most of them toward the end of the century. The breweries, on the other hand, remained concentrated in Stockholm, which suggests surprisingly that home brewing persisted longer than home baking in the rest of the country.

The individual craftsman's scale of operations remained extremely small throughout the eighteenth century. Even in Stockholm where there were many more helpers per master than elsewhere, their numbers increased only from about three around the middle of the century to 3.6 in 1794.[60] This was partly due to the fact that a category called "servants" was no longer reported in 1794. Yet although the number of journeymen per master rose from 1.3 to 1.8, and the number of apprentices from 1.1 to 1.6, a craftsman's shop nonetheless remained a very modest affair. In the towns outside Stockholm the shops were even smaller, and their growth slower. According to estimates that may be a little too low, the number of journeymen per master rose from .5 to .6, and the number of apprentices from .7 to .8.[61] As a rule, the rural craftsman probably worked by himself; at any rate, the average ratio of assistants to rural craftsmen was less than one toward the end of the period.[62]

In the cities, especially in Stockholm, there was an important exception: builders sometimes employed as many as sixty workers, and by the end of the century even the average number of men per builder had risen to between 30 and 35.[63] Similar tendencies appeared in the other cities, although the average seldom rose to quite the same level. Contrary to what might have been expected, the explanation does not appear to lie in an exceptionally capitalistic character of the trade. The feature of "bigness" probably is accounted for in part by a particularly restrictive guild policy, but principally by the high skill required of the masters, who had to be their own architects. The masters may also have been eager to employ, more or less nominally, a great number of workers for reasons of prestige. The rapid growth, first of Stockholm and then of the other cities, likewise made for a considerable expansion of the building trades. Nevertheless, this did not change the general picture of the organization of the handicrafts.

The most important change in the organization of the crafts concerned the guilds. Throughout the preceding period the guilds had remained confined to the major cities. After the middle of the century, however, guilds had been organized in most of the small towns as well. The policy of the authorities was so unimaginative, that in spite of a basically unfavorable attitude to the guilds, the government not only tolerated them but even actively promoted their growth. It is true that the guilds did not lack an economic function. The shops were far too small and weak to be able to manage problems of organization and distribution individually, and in these matters the guilds played a vital part. On the other hand, their main contribution was to restrict competition and to limit the number of craftsmen; repeated attempts by the government to put a stop to such tendencies were seldom successful. The monopolistic positions do not seem to have resulted in higher incomes but rather to have been used to exclude from mastership those journeymen who were not sons or sons-in-law of the masters. But while monopolization provided a solution of sorts to the problem of entrepreneurial selection, at the same time it barred any development toward more efficient forms of organization so that, as a result, handicraft was no more successful than manufactories in providing a foundation for the industries of the next century.

It must immediately be added that the rapid expansion of the guilds after the middle of the century only concerned the urban crafts. In the countryside, most parishes probably had only one or two craftsmen in the same trade. A separate organization for those craftsmen was virtually impossible, and it seems to have been rather exceptional for rural craftsmen to be affiliated with urban guilds. This is worth emphasizing, since it is tempting to equate handicraft and guild system. If rural crafts are included, we can be reasonably certain that the majority of the craftsmen remained outside the guilds, even at the time when the latter reached the peak of their development.

## THE FOREST INDUSTRIES

The tar industry was a branch of the Swedish economy which, having emerged in the seventeenth century, persisted without any fundamental change. It was still essentially a peasant industry, concentrated in Finland, but very important also in Norrland. The industry soon recovered from the setback which had occurred under the reign of Charles XII, and great care was taken not to repeat the attempt at monopolization, although many circles showed deep interest in such a policy. Tar retained at least a constant share of the growing exports and must consequently have increased at least as rapidly as total exports.[64] In the 1770's, tar exports received a great impetus through the American War of Independence, for British premiums on colonial tar were then discontinued.

The timber industry expanded somewhat more rapidly, although it remained quite insignificant. Not until the beginning of the nineteenth century did its share in total exports exceed that of the tar industry, but once this had happened, further expansion was very rapid indeed.[65] In the beginning of the eighteenth century, after the end of the Nordic War, a first upswing in the exports of timber had taken place; but at that time Norwegian sawmills were still far superior to the Swedish. Technologically, the vital distinction was between saws with thick and saws with thin blades; the transition to finer blades entailed tremendous economies of wood. Thin saws, however, were not introduced in Finland until the 1730's, nor in Sweden proper until the 1750's. Most of the sawmills in Sweden were, as before, located on the West Coast; and development was very slow. In addition, it was only around the middle of the century that legislative policy accepted the timber industry's claim on the forest which had up till then been reserved for the mining industry. Eventually, restrictions on the timber industry were replaced by direct support, though only for mills with thin-blade saws.

Thus, there was as yet no sign of the future upsurge of the forest industries. Not until the middle of the century did any fundamental change in the timber industry occur, but when it happened it was a change of profound consequence for the country as a whole as well as for the relative position of the northern parts of the country.

## FOREIGN TRADE AND NAVIGATION

Second only to the manufactories, foreign trade and shipping attracted most of the interest in the debate on economic policy. Great importance was attributed to long-distance shipping, above all to the salt trade from the Mediterranean and the Iberian peninsula, which was the principal beneficiary of the so-called *produktplakat* (Commodity Act) of 1724.[66] Like the English Navigation Acts, the *produktplakat* barred foreign ships from Swedish trade except when carrying cargoes of products of the ships' own nationality. The measure was aimed chiefly at the Dutch who were the main international carriers. It succeeded in establishing a Swedish salt trade — in fact, while the law remained on the statute books Swedish shipping in the Mediterranean was more flourishing than it ever was afterward. But the result was also a considerable increase in the salt price and sometimes even a shortage of salt.

Such a development was especially inconvenient at that time. The rapid growth of fishing in the waters off the west coast had stimulated the demand for salt considerably, and the *produktplakat* therefore turned out to be a serious hindrance to the fisheries. On the other hand, the booming salt prices could be taken to justify the government's policy, since they made shipping appear extraordinarily profitable. Thus, Anders Nordenkrantz, author of the first major economic work to be published in the Age of Freedom, opposed the establishment of domestic salt factories, however laudable by ordinary mercantilist standards, on the ground that they might encroach on the salt trade and on Mediterranean shipping.

But more important industries than the fisheries were also hurt by the shipping policy. The *produktplakat* often forced foreign ships to sail empty to Sweden when they were not able to contract a cargo of their own nationality. This inevitably raised their freight rates. The Swedish carriers followed suit and raised their rates, which were already high because of the protection they received through partial customs exemption (see page 114). The ironmasters who represented the leading export industry were therefore from the beginning more or less determined opponents of the *produktplakat*. It was also attacked by two of the foremost economic writers of the time, both of whom argued the case for the iron industry. One was Lars Salvius, a well-known book dealer and book printer, who published his diatribe in the late 1730's; the other, Anders Chydenius, described the *produktplakat* in the title of his pamphlet The Source of Swedish Impuissance (*Källan til rikets wan-magt,* 1765). The attacks, especially that by Chydenius, caused a great stir, but the *produktplakat* remained unchanged throughout the period.

Mercantilist foreign trade policy manifested itself also in the trading companies and the colonial companies. The Swedish East India Company, first chartered in 1731 and surviving until 1806 (though not formally dissolved until 1813), was probably the most successful and certainly the most long-lived Swedish enterprise of this type.[67] In many of the small European countries at that time, ostensibly domestic companies were often chartered to accommodate those shipping interests of larger nations, especially England, who could not otherwise compete with the monopolistic companies of their own countries. Initially, this was the case with the Swedish company too; it was founded and managed by Englishmen. By and by, the Swedish element in the company grew, and was to make a considerable contribution to Swedish trade, first in Göteborg and later in Stockholm. It conducted what seems to have been a very profitable traffic in Chinese and East Indian wares, which were first carried to Göteborg but in most cases reëxported. Some of these commodities, however, remained in Sweden — in the first place tea, which in those days seems to have played a much larger part in the consumption of the upper classes than in later periods; also old china, silk and cotton cloth, raw silk, etc. To some extent such imports were frowned upon, as in other countries, on the ground that they threatened the balance of trade and encroached on the domain of domestic manufacturers. The spokesmen of the East India Company, however, always got the better of the argument, especially by emphasizing the profits of the reëxport trade. Though economically these imports were not very significant, they had a certain impact on the way of life of the upper classes.

We have already pointed to the social position of the merchants in the life of the eighteenth century, on which in many respects they put their stamp more than any other group. The merchants' strength derived from the urban predilections of mercantilism and in general reflected the rise of the bourgeoisie. In the early part of the century, English and Scottish merchants made a considerable contribution to Swedish trade; even among Swedish merchants at that time an interest in English civilization seems to have prevailed which was quite exceptional in Sweden. As a small but telling example, it may be mentioned that Jonas Alströmer and Niclas Sahlgren, a prominent merchant in Göteborg, corresponded in English between Göteborg and Alingsås.

The power of the merchants was primarily based on their position in the iron industry. They almost always provided the capital, they often took over the management, and without exception they were the exporters of the final products. Nevertheless, they did not specialize in the iron trade, although iron exports were the most vital part of their operations. Every merchant dealt in all commodities he could lay his hands on, usually importing as well as exporting. Toward the end of the period the leading house in Stockholm was indisputably Tottie & Arfvedson, and in Göteborg, John Hall & Co. Both were founded (or co-founded) by English merchants. The former was to keep its position for a long time, while a descendant of John Hall of the same name was to supply the outstanding Swedish example of a wastrel's decline from fabulous wealth to complete ruin.

## The Monetary System

The monetary system was one of the gloomiest parts of the picture of eighteenth-century economy. The difficulties which plagued it had their origin in the system itself and were not imposed from the outside. For most of the period the monetary system was characterized by more confusion than at any time before or after; no sooner had conditions stabilized after one crisis than another followed.[68]

The fear of paper money inspired by the collapse of Palmstruch's bank only persisted up till the Age of Freedom. The issue of paper money gained momentum particularly after the *Hats'* use of the Bank to finance the ill-fated Finnish war in 1741–1743. Subsidies to the manufactories had similar effects. The weight of the copper coins and their consequent export cost made it possible to depreciate Swedish bank notes considerably in relation to copper without unleashing any exports of copper coins that might endanger the convertibility of the paper money into copper. Nonetheless, bank notes were made irredeemable as early as 1745; unlike what happened in the previous century, this caused no panic. The authorities adopted a permanently irredeemable paper while retaining the denominations of the old copper money. The metallic value of the bank notes deteriorated incessantly, and a tremendous inflation got under way. No other economic problem attracted more attention during the Age of Freedom. Innumerable proposals for remedies were offered; they were the subject matter of the economic pamphlets which flooded the bookstalls.

Since it was evident to all that the deterioration was the result of the policy pursued by the *Hats,* the *Caps* were the chief critics of the prevailing situation. Returned into office in 1765–66, they quickly turned the rudder in the opposite direction and initiated a policy which almost provides a classic example of the consequences of excessive deflation. To contemporaries the most serious aspect of inflation appeared to be the fall in the external value of Swedish money, that is, primarily the rise in the rate of exchange between Hamburger banco and Swedish copper money. Futile attempts had been made to check this rise through manipulations by especially established exchange bureaus.

The *Caps* abruptly discontinued the exchange bureaus and decided instead slowly to depress the rate of exchange, in other words, to raise the foreign valuation of Swedish money, by a certain amount each year until the old par rate had been restored — to wit, thirty-six Swedish copper marks to one thaler Hamburger banco. The decision was supposed to be kept secret, but it soon became obvious what the government's policy was; hence violent speculation developed against the Hamburg thaler, which accelerated its fall in value beyond what had been intended. The export industries, above all the iron industry, found themselves in distress. Their prices in foreign currency remained unchanged, but in Swedish money their revenue dropped abruptly while raw material prices and wages lagged. Consequently, a serious crisis hit the whole iron industry; the disturbance was shrewdly fanned by the *Hats* who had influential and competent representatives in all the government agencies. The *Cap* Cabinet refused to summon the *riksdag* until the King, Adolf Fredrik, abdicated in order to force their hand. This desperate measure was successful; when the new *riksdag* convened in 1769, the *Cap* Cabinet fell, the old monetary policies were resumed, the paper standard retained, and the *Caps'* experiment turned into an episode of no permanent effect.

On the other hand, nobody considered an irredeemable paper money entirely satisfactory, and eventually a reform of the currency took place. This was mainly the work of Gustavus III's competent Minister of Finance, Johan Liljencrantz. Liljencrantz's currency reform in 1766–67 marked an epoch in Swedish monetary history. The old currency was depreciated by 50 per cent, so that the exchange rate was 72 rather than 36 copper marks to one thaler Hamburger banco. At the same time Sweden adopted a pure silver standard after one hundred and fifty years of allegiance to copper. The *daler* was also replaced as a monetary unit by the *riksdaler,* containing 48 shillings. For the time being, order had been restored.

But stability did not last long. Gustavus III himself showed scant interest in an orderly currency. On one occasion he wrote to his Minister of Finance, then Erik Ruuth, ordering him to provide money, adding, "I imagine the paper mills in Sweden have not yet burned down." [69] This was during his Russian war which naturally brought the same monetary strain as the previous one. In 1789 the paper money was again made irredeemable. But this time the Bank, which was under the management of the *riksdag,* treated the king's requests for loans with extreme coolness, and as a result the Bank's notes retained their value. The gains from this policy, though not altogether absent, were insignificant, for the king then resorted to the issue of Treasury notes, a policy which had gained parliamentary sanction when Gustavus succeeded in mastering the violent opposition of the *riksdag* in 1789. Treasury notes continued to circulate but at a discount in relation to silver and to the ordinary bank money which kept its silver value. The distinction between Bank *(banco)* and Treasury *(riksgälds)* notes was to survive for a long time in Sweden. Initially, the rate between the two kinds of money fluctuated widely. It was only under the reign of Gustavus IV that a new currency reform was undertaken (1803) which fixed the rate at the then prevailing ratio of 3:2. "To pay in banco" therefore meant to pay a premium of 50 per cent. Paper money was made redeemable, but return to specie payments was of even shorter duration than before, since the new Finnish war (1808–09) again caused a failure to redeem the notes. This time not only the Treasury notes were affected but also the bank notes which had been completely tied to Treasury money. The new irredeemable paper money was retained until the early 1830's.

Inevitably, the almost perpetual crisis characterizing the currency during the period under review had serious repercussions for all branches of the economy.

## Economic Thought

One of the most spectacular things about Sweden in the eighteenth century was the vivid debate and polemics on economic matters, which then aroused a great deal more attention than nowadays. There seems to have been, in the educated classes, a concern with social and economic problems to which no other period of Swedish history offers a counterpart. A great many of the publications that appeared were anonymous and brought no fame to their authors. On the other hand, many contributions clearly were made in order to promote the private interests of the author or his sponsor. Nonetheless, a large number undoubtedly sprang from no other motive than a desire to direct the nation to the road of prosperity. Purely theoretical economic studies, however, were rather rare; most of the writings dealt with the pros and cons of specific policy measures.

Although much of the economic literature of the time was of ephemeral interest and value, its sheer bulk was quite astounding. We have already mentioned, in the beginning of this chapter, that the constitution itself may have stimulated this activity; during the last phase of the Age of Freedom, the freedom of the press introduced by the *riksdag* of 1765–66 released a virtual torrent of publications. During the peak year of 1765 an economic pamphlet appeared every five days, while for the last decade of the Age of Freedom the annual average was about forty, not including newspaper articles.[70]

After Gustavus III's *coup d'état* and the restoration of the absolute monarchy, the freedom of the press was too curtailed to allow the lively debate to continue unchecked. But as soon as the restrictions were relaxed the debate picked up again, revealing that there was no loss of interest in the subject. This was a remarkable intellectual renaissance. The public had become aware that to accept the old order for merely traditional reasons was as impossible as to delegate the whole responsibility for the shaping of a new order to the rulers of the state.

Yet, the pamphlet literature does not seem to have exerted any great influence on economic policy, let alone on the economic development of the country. To the extent that the identity of the authors is known, they were generally members of the ruling classes, and their writings, especially during the Age of Freedom, primarily illustrate the views on which the government's policies were founded. Thus, the main significance of this literature lies in such documentation, and in the intellectual excitement it provoked and reflected. Under

Gustavus III, the views expressed in print came to be more often at variance with the policies of the government, and consequently less influential than before.

Except for one important interval, mercantilist ideas, often far more extreme than in the seventeenth century, were entirely predominating throughout this period, and for that matter even beyond it. The exception was the decade between 1755 and 1765, when an ideology which could be described as liberal made a short appearance. It is an episode of unusual interest, for among the advocates of liberal views were some of the most prominent Swedish economists of the time, whose work showed considerable originality and sometimes even anticipated the development of economic thought in other countries. Nevertheless, it remained an episode, of small influence even on Swedish economic thought. Eighteenth-century mercantilism, on the other hand, came to put its stamp on the teaching of economics at the universities, thus indirectly influencing Swedish economic policy until the middle of the nineteenth century, when mercantilist ideas finally lost their grip on public opinion.

The academic mercantilists in Sweden at that time differed from their foreign colleagues primarily in their interest in natural science and technology. As previously noted, scientific interest characterized the whole intellectual climate in Sweden; Linnaeus was one of its many brilliant representatives. Domination by a mercantilist school of this particular orientation precluded the development of any Swedish equivalent to German cameralism. The Swedish mercantilists shared none of the cameralists' inclinations to subordinate the entire economy to the state and its financial interests. During the Age of Freedom the democratic constitution barred any such development, but in addition the country's political tradition probably exerted some influence in the same direction.

At the universities, mercantilist views gained a foothold primarily through the establishment in 1741 of a chair in economics at Uppsala, the fourth of its kind in Europe. The first occupant was Anders Berch who, in 1747, published a veritable textbook, Introduction to General Economy (*Inledning till allmänna hushålningen.*) True, the work does not bear any close resemblance to a modern textbook. It contained hardly any theory in the sense of a causal analysis of economic processes. Rather, it was a statement, in tempered language, of the correct attitudes to various economic problems, in complete accordance with the prevailing views of the authorities, which a professor at a state university was practically in duty bound to present and to defend. The book's weaknesses may seem flagrant to a modern reader, but it was nevertheless immensely superior to contemporaneous German works of the same kind, though this is not saying much. It was later translated into German, and remained the only Swedish textbook in the field for no less than eighty years, which is sufficient testimony to its impact on academic teaching in Sweden.

The other Swedish mercantilists were generally even less original than Berch, and none of their works deserve special presentation. Personally, however, some of them were colorful figures. One of the most remarkable, who has already been mentioned in passing, was Anders Bachmanson, better known by the name of Nordenkrantz which he adopted when made a noble. In his later days and under his new name he was to argue views almost completely opposed to the mercantilist position, but his early work, *Arcana oeconomiae et commercii* (1730), published under the name of Bachmanson, was one of the most exhaustive presentations of Swedish mercantilism, far more comprehensive and elaborate than Berch's work. He had previously been Swedish consul at Lisbon and took a special interest in shipping policy, but his book had a much wider span.

The manufactories found their most enthusiastic advocate in Eric Salander, one of the most indefatigable economic writers of the Age of Freedom. As Commissioner for the Manufactories he was vitally concerned with their prosperity and argued their case with extreme vehemence and intolerance.

Two more or less exclusively economic periodicals of thoroughly mercantilist coloring were published by Carl Carleson, the older brother of Edward Carleson, who has already been mentioned in his capacity as president of the Board of Trade, and who was also a contributor to his brother's periodicals as long as they appeared, that is, between 1730 and 1735. Some of the outstanding technologists of the time, like Christopher Polhem and Emanuel Swedenborg, also occasionally added their voices to the chorus, though rather hesitatingly, since they were primarily concerned with the iron industry which could never quite reconcile its interests with prevailing mercantilist views.

As for influences from the economic literature of other countries, German economics was then suffering an almost complete intellectual impoverishment and had little to contribute. The only important exception was a seventeenth-century writer, Johann Joachim Becher, a remarkably original but undisciplined thinker who dissipated his talents as a surgeon, chemist, and alchemist. His influence on Swedish economic writing in general, and especially on Salander's, was quite strong, and his treatment of the problems of monopoly and "polypoly" (free competition), which Salander adopted, is of definite interest.

Besides German, most educated Swedes of the time unfortunately read only French. The English literature, incomparably more extensive, independent, and original than the French in this field, was not read in the original, though it was nevertheless not unknown. A good many English works were available in French translations, so that lack of familiarity with the original meant little more than a delay, which tended to give some of the English economists of the previous century, especially Thomas Mun and Josiah Child, a greater prominence in this period than would otherwise have been probable. By the middle of the century, French contributions to economic thought became important; the so-called Reform Mercantilism in France in particular, which developed the ideas of several of the more independent seventeenth-century English economists, was in large measure responsible for the appearance of more liberal views in Sweden in the 1750's. By that time, however, the influence of some of the genuinely liberal English economists, like Hume, had reached Sweden.

There had been earlier isolated attacks on the mercantilist doctrine in Sweden. Lars Salvius' advocacy of the iron industry's opposition to the Swedish shipping policy has already been mentioned; it was expressed as early as 1738 in a weekly paper written exclusively by Salvius himself, entitled *Tanckar öfwer den swenska oeconomien* (Reflections on the Swedish Economy). In the following decade several voices were also raised in defense of agriculture, a branch of the economy the mercantilists had sorely neglected. This expression of pro-agricultural views was still far from a general rebellion; it engendered a lively dispute that came to be called "the controversy over industrial precedence." The many complications flowing from the reckless subsidization of manufactories also aroused a great many misgivings which precipitated a sharp attack on Salander in the late 1740's from the pen of Johan Fredrik Kryger, otherwise known as a good conservative and himself a Commissioner of the Manufactories.

In the fifties the structure of mercantilist thought came under more and more vigorous fire. Nordenkrantz and P. N. Christiernin, then Professor of Economics at Uppsala and endowed with a clear mind and a stinging pen, were the foremost monetary theorists; in other fields the Lord Counsellor Carl Fredrik Scheffer, Carl Leuhusen and two brothers, Edward Fredrik and Ephraim Otto Runeberg, made noteworthy contributions. Scheffer and Leuhusen especially were strongly influenced by French literature and were generally the most erudite of them all. Works by E. F. Runeberg, who was probably the most independent theorist, will be taken up shortly.

Unquestionably the most important of the Swedish economists was Anders Chydenius, a clergyman in Finland. In 1765, a torrent of extremely radical brochures from his pen suddenly burst forth in Stockholm where he was attending the *riksdag* as a member of the estate of the clergy. As a stylist he has few if any equals in the history of Swedish social science. It is no exaggeration to say that he is the most captivating writer within that field ever to appear in Sweden, and that his works even today still vibrate with life and excitement. His was not, however, an unusual theoretical talent; in fact, Chydenius' analytical powers were quite limited and distinctly inferior to those of many of his contemporaries.

It was above all the straightforward simplicity of his views that was most characteristic of Chydenius, and makes him so thoroughly representative of the Enlightenment and early liberalism. This urge to simplify actually made him into a quite exceptional radical. Any compromise was repugnant to him; he wanted to overthrow the entire social order of mercantilism. "Freedom" was his one and only lodestar. "I bespeak but this one blessed thing: freedom." "Fatherland without freedom is but a big word of no meaning." "Freedom with dry crumbs is sweeter to a man than rich food under another's rule." "Think not of freedom in one trade only, for then you could not go far without stumbling over hindrance and obstruction; undo in your thoughts all the ties that are trammeling the nation." [71] This was a frontal charge. He attacked the *produktplakat*, the subsidies to fisheries, the regulation of foreign trade, the Servants Act, agricultural legislation, and all the rest. Such uncompromising liberalism, eleven years before Adam Smith had published *The Wealth of Nations*, in a writer of virtually complete independence, suggests an extraordinary intellectual intensity. Though very much a product of his age, he was not notably influenced by any predecessors, particularly not by foreign authors from whom his ignorance of foreign languages isolated him.

Perhaps his most original trait was his social indignation, his firm conviction that the benefit of the masses, especially the rural proletariat, should be the ultimate objective of economic policy. This belief he couched in succinct phrases. "To toil for others' gain as long as he bears up, to be thrown into wretchedness in old age and die in beggary, such are the laurels which should prompt the working man to love his country." "Our vagrants seem to me like hunted deer; no sooner do they hear a noise than they arise and flee, crying *vestigia nos terrent* . . . If it was their fate to be born sons of cotters or paupers, or if they were unfortunate enough to be third, fourth, or fifth children of a peasant, then they were born to serfdom, as knights are born with noble blood in their veins." [72]

Chydenius' pamphlets attracted keen attention and provoked floods of counterattacks; he stirred the minds of his contemporaries to an extraordinary degree. But in the long run his influence was surprisingly small. He was soon forgotten, and the economists who succeeded him paid him little heed. It is only in the last few generations that his stature has been generally recognized.

The only really serious attempts during this period to formulate an economic theory were made in the 1760's when two publications by E. F. Runeberg appeared, the Discourse on the Values of Goods (*Tal om varors värden*, 1760), and the somewhat more extensive Reflections on the Value of Money (*Tankar om penningars värden*, 1762). While equally original, his writings are very different from those of Chydenius who was quick to submit his practical proposals even in pamphlets of a theoretical nature, especially in The National

Gain (*Den nationnale winsten,* 1765). Runeberg was an enthusiastic theorist and took great pride in being one, but on matters of economic policy his attitude was extremely cautious and restrained. Actually, his economics is not especially remarkable except as evidence of a theoretical frame of mind. He was ignorant of the already quite advanced development of economic thought in England and France, and his own intellect was not sufficiently sharp to permit a comprehensive analysis of the economic system. But his attempt, such as it is, provides yet another illustration of the vigor and enterprise of the intellectual climate of the time and of the undaunted courage with which any interesting problem was attacked.

The only Swedish physiocrat of significance was the Lord Counsellor C. F. Scheffer, tutor of Gustavus III during the king's minority. He was in contact with the French physiocrats who hailed him, as well as Gustavus himself, as one of their protectors. But Scheffer's study of physiocratic theory was fairly superficial and his opportunities for translating his theories into practice were limited. He claims our interest mainly because of his uniqueness on the Swedish scene.

The range of economic literature appearing after the Age of Freedom was much narrower, and contributors were far more isolated from one another than in the Age of Freedom when the publication of a pamphlet would often release a furious debate with dozens of counterattacks and rejoinders. Similar things did happen under Gustavus III, but quite infrequently, and the discussion generally moved on a lower plane. Nevertheless, two authors who were responsible for some of the major contributions of the period shall be noted briefly.

The first was an unsuccessful merchant by the name of Christian Ludvig Jöranson who, between 1792 and 1798, published an Essay on a System of Sweden's General Economy (*Försök til et systeme i Sveriges allmänna hushållning*). The other, today mainly remembered as a political theorist, was P. O. von Asp, a Swedish diplomat who in his youth had been Gustavus III's esteemed adviser on foreign policy. His Essay to Clarify and Collect the First Principles of Political Economy (*Försök att utreda och på ett ställe sammanföra de första allmänna grunderna i stats-hushållnings-ämnen,* 1800–01), was followed by *Om myntväsendets och allmänna hushålds-tillställningens värkan och återvärkan på hvarannan,* 1804. (The

Effects and Countereffects of the Currency System on the National Economy). But whatever hopes of a systematic treatment of economic problems such titles might have aroused were not realized; these books are uniformly vague in their rambling and incoherent treatment of a variety of problems. Their mode of presentation apart, the two authors were very different. Jöranson was an extraordinarily unbalanced and temperamental polemicist. Infuriated by his own bankruptcy he raged against "money jobbers and agio-hunters," "the serfs of egotism," who in his view had caused the many slumps of the period and strangled the credit market.[73] His own proposals amounted to nothing less than pure inflation, but the defense of his position was not without originality and in parts his book reads like a forerunner of the New Economics of our days of which Lord Keynes became the most prominent representative. Jöranson has some claim to a place among Keynes's "heretics," and not as one of the least. Von Asp was his opposite in most respects. He was moderate and restrained but lacked intellectual acumen; his mind was diffused rather than enriched by his extensive experience with "the teeming cities" in foreign lands.

It is particularly remarkable that the influence of Adam Smith was so negligible. Even today there is no complete Swedish translation of *The Wealth of Nations;* the only reasonably extensive translation appeared as late as 1909–1911. During the period presently under review brief excerpts were all that was published, and not the essential ones at that. In Denmark, for instance, the situation was strikingly different; a complete translation appeared only three to four years after the publication of the English edition. When, around and after the turn of the century, the Swedish public showed a fleeting interest in Adam Smith, his book strangely enough was translated from a drastically abridged German version rather than from the original. Probably it was ignorance of the English language which thus resulted in ignorance of English economic thought as well. Possibly also the original was considered too bulky to be readable in its entirety. If so, it confirms the impression that a certain superficiality and lack of ability to appreciate a systematic train of thought characterized the last part of this period.

Of the years between 1720 and 1815 it might be said that everything was tried and nothing achieved. The eighteenth century made few definite contributions to Sweden's economic and social growth. But it did establish the groundwork for much that was to come. Above all, by questioning all social institutions and categorically refusing to accept the sanction of tradition as sufficient *raison d'être* for the social framework, it created the spiritual climate in which the economic transformation of the nineteenth century could proceed.

# CHAPTER 6

# THE GREAT TRANSFORMATION (1815–1914)

THE RATE of development in the nineteenth century was so enormous that any attempt at a reasonably exhaustive presentation of the period is foredoomed to failure. In fact, it is impossible within the framework of this study to devote to the nineteenth century the attention it deserves in comparison with the preceding periods. To an even higher degree than in earlier chapters, I shall confine myself, therefore, to an outline of the main trends in this momentous development. The year 1914 marks the end of the period almost as clearly as, previously, the year 1720 separated the Age of Empire from the Age of Freedom. That should not mean, of course, that the First World War changed every single aspect of Swedish economic life, and in some cases I shall in this chapter pursue the development beyond 1914.

## BASIC CHARACTERISTICS

The first thing to be noted in a hasty survey of the basic characteristics of the development in this period, is the international orientation of the modern Swedish economy. Compared to western and central Europe, the country's economic development began late. It was then only to be expected that, during the great transformation, the stream of influences *to* Sweden considerably outweighed those *from* Sweden. Generally speaking, Sweden did not *cease* being on the receiving end until around 1910. Before 1870, England was the main source of influence, but thereafter Germany and the United States became increasingly important. As for Swedish activities abroad, they gradually tended to be diffused throughout the world.

Internationalism characterized the nineteenth century, but it was essentially economic internationalism. Political and, for that matter, ecclesiastical international relations were far closer in late Antiquity and in the Middle Ages than they were in more recent days. What was then conceived as the *orbis terrarum* possessed a unity of which our time has no counterpart. Economically, however, those early periods were marked by the very opposite of unity, and trading areas were then far smaller than modern national states. This contrast between economic and political developments is instructive. For one thing, it demonstrates that economic factors do not play the decisive role in social and political change that is sometimes accorded them.

Sweden had received strong international stimuli in the late Middle Ages as well as in the Age of Empire, but in both of these periods, and especially during the former, Swedish society was only superficially affected by the immigration through which those stimuli were transmitted. In the nineteenth century, however, ideas seemed to have legs of their own. Immigrants played a relatively insignificant part. Some of them were, it is true, pioneers of the modern forest industry — men like Dickson, Kempe, Röhss, Bünsow, and Astrup (one Scot, two Germans, two Norwegians) — but the only other field in which they were particularly influential was, perhaps not surprisingly, banking. In two of the three major Swedish banks Jewish immigrants played a decisive role; Theodor Mannheimer was the first manager of *Skandinaviska Banken,* and Louis Fraenckel reorganized the *Stockholms Handelsbank* (now *Svenska Handelsbanken*).

One of the most important factors in international economic relations during the nineteenth century was the international migration of capital. In the case of Sweden, the fifty years between 1860 and 1910 witnessed an import of foreign capital which in all probability was a vital prerequisite for the country's rapid economic upswing. Capital imports as such were of course nothing new; most notably, foreign importers of Swedish iron had often financed exporters in the Swedish seaports, enabling them in turn to extend credit to producers. But this was on a trifling scale compared to what took place in the nineteenth century. Above all, it was no longer a question merely of supplying short-term credit; much of the borrowing was done by relatively long-term bond issues, and the overwhelming part of the foreign borrowing was done by the government in connection with railroad construction. The result was an increase in the volume of credit at a lower interest rate than would otherwise have prevailed in Sweden; the fact that the inflow of foreign capital was used by the government did not detract from its significance for the economy as a whole. In turning to foreign countries to finance the most capital-absorbing operations of the time, the government released domestic savings for the use of private business which under other circumstances might have had to borrow abroad. Some private entrepreneurs actually did borrow abroad; foreign capital contributed to the financing of the mortgage banks in the 1850's, of the Grängesberg mining company, and of certain private railroads. But compared to the government's flotations, private borrowing remained completely insignificant.

Capital imports came to an end around 1910, that is, *before* the First World War. It is, of course, impossible to decide what would have happened if the war had not intervened. As it was, the fact that Sweden stayed out of the war whereas her major creditors were involved in it resulted in a change in Sweden's relative position. Capital formation in Sweden began to compare more favorably with that of foreign countries, and eventually the country was to become a net exporter of capital.

A second novel and important aspect of Sweden's international economic relations in the nineteenth century was the fact that business fluctuations in the rest of the world began to be transmitted to Sweden. There are, to be sure, earlier instances where Sweden might be said to have been affected by developments loosely resembling business cycles; we have already mentioned that the international stock market crisis of 1763 reached Sweden. But indisputably the more or less regular trade cycles occurring in the nineteenth century had a far stronger impact than the earlier fluctuations. The crisis which hit most countries after the end of the war in 1815 was also severely felt in Sweden, although in that case certain independent factors contributed to the difficulties. Beginning with the crisis of 1857, however, Sweden has regularly reflected the international business cycles. Even though sometimes the amplitudes of the fluctuations have been a great deal smaller than in other countries, Sweden has hardly ever remained unaffected by such developments abroad. In certain respects, the Swedish economy is particularly sensitive to foreign disturbances since most of her leading exports

— timber and wood products, iron and iron manufactures — are industrial materials, which are subject to more violent fluctuations than consumers' goods.

A third, not unrelated, development was the relative growth of Swedish foreign trade in general. New important export commodities appeared, and imports increased even faster than exports, owing to capital imports. It is extremely difficult to find a satisfactory measure for the importance of foreign trade in different countries and different periods, but a rough estimate shows that the Swedish volume of imports in 1914 was thirty times as high as in 1830, and the volume of exports twenty-six times as high.[1] This rate of growth considerably exceeds, for instance, that of British foreign trade. The difference is probably due principally to the late development of the Swedish economy. As to the per capita value of foreign trade, other things being equal, it will obviously be higher in a small country than in a large country, simply because the rest of the world, by comparison, will be so much larger. The per capita value of foreign trade in Sweden was indeed lower than in Norway, Switzerland, Denmark, and Holland, but it was somewhat higher than in Great Britain and, even more important, considerably greater than in Finland, although the population of the latter country is hardly more than half that of Sweden.[2]

Perhaps the most fundamental change of all was the tremendous increase in the international exchange of scientific and technological information. The growth of systematic industrial research and the appearance of an enormous body of technological literature, largely embodied in periodicals, has practically removed the veil of secrecy in which new techniques and processes used to be wrapped. This has been one of the main reasons why in modern times it is no longer necessary to import foreign industrialists and workmen in order to learn their methods. Although an innovation may still give the country in which it originates a lead, especially if supplemented by a steady flow of improvements, no country can expect to preserve a technical monopoly to the same extent as was once the case. Unintentionally, an inventor might now often find a foreign country reaping the greatest benefits of his labor.

The technological revolution in the nineteenth century had the most profound effect on the nature of economic development. First of all, the means of production acquired a new and added significance. There was a vast increase in mechanized equipment, but the most radical change was perhaps the introduction of systems of transmission for water, gas, and electrical power. The production of consumers' goods was reduced to a far smaller share of total output than before.

For Sweden, it was especially important that the change to more "capitalistic" methods of production created a tremendous demand for iron, one of the commodities Sweden was particularly fitted to produce. In spite of the drastic fall in the Swedish share of world output of iron, a momentous expansion in Swedish production and exports of iron took place. There was a similar but smaller increase in demand for Swedish forest resources. But the expansion resulting from the growing demand for timber for construction purposes was only a first stage. In the second stage the expansion of forest industries was more closely tied to the consumers' goods market; the swelling demand for wood pulp was above all the consequence of increasing literacy and the rise of the daily press.

Yet another basic feature of the century was the revolution in communications. Transport was actually one of the areas which benefited most from the technical upsurge. Relatively speaking, the change affected land transport more than water transport; it might therefore be said that Sweden profited more from this development than it would have done if its boundaries had not been changed by the Peace of Brömsebro (1645) and the Peace of Roskilde (1658). Advances in land transportation were also especially welcome because of the Swedish winter, which tended to obstruct water transport.

Thanks to this development, the relative isolation of the Swedish provinces from one another came to an end. Even in the late 1860's, Norrland was struck with near famine, at a time when crops in the southern provinces had been quite reasonable. The railway network had not yet been extended to the northern parts of the country; after its completion a local famine became unthinkable.

The industrialization of the country is also reflected in the population statistics. For a long time the non-agricultural industries had only just been able to keep pace with the agricultural population, though as a rule probably providing a somewhat higher *per capita* income. The agricultural population showed no relative decline before

1870 when its share still remained as high as 72.4 per cent; in absolute terms it did not decline until 1880.[3] The census of 1910 was the first to show an agricultural population of less than one-half of the total population (48.8 per cent), and not until 1936 did industry employ a larger share of the population than agriculture. At that date the percentage of agricultural population was exactly half what it had been in 1870.[4]

The motive power behind most social changes is a transformation in outlook and attitudes, and the industrial revolution is no exception. In the early days it was common to view the past as a golden age, an attitude which found expression in Horace's famous verse:

> *Aetas parentum, peior avis, tulit*
> *Nos nequiores, mox daturos*
> *Progenium vitiosiorem.**

The Enlightenment had already rejected that gloomy view, and the nineteenth century was stamped by the belief in progress — the belief that the golden age lay ahead, that the present could be surpassed only by the future, and that continual advance was the natural law of human development which, aided by a little good will and common sense, would always prevail. This overthrow of traditionalism had a momentous impact on all branches of the economy, notably on agriculture where conservatism had been most solidly rooted. The change in intellectual climate was accompanied by a virtually complete destruction of the system of industrial regulation that had been developed under mercantilism but in fact often stemmed from the Middle Ages. Compared to this even Chydenius' radicalism seemed feeble and dispirited.

The growth in population too must be related to the change in outlook. The increase stemmed not from a rise in the birth rate but from a reduction in mortality rates, especially infant mortality rates. In part, this reduction was probably caused by improvements in public health and medical care, although progress in those areas might not have affected the size of the population as much as its general state of health and thereby indirectly its productivity. However, the main cause of the reduction in mortality is easily shown to have been the rising standard of living, particularly

* "Our fathers have been worse than theirs/And we than ours;/Next age will see/A race more profligate than we."

A Walloon forge, with the characteristic two hearths. The hammer is seen on the left. Painting by Pehr Hilleström. *Krusenberg, Uppland.*

Anders Berch, the first occupant of the chair in Economics which was instituted at
University of Uppsala in 1741. Portrait by Frederik Brander. *University of Upps*

Lancashire smith. Coal drawing from the Korså works in Dalarna by Ferdinand Boberg.
e long white shirts, described by Linnaeus, were, and still are, worn for protection against the heat.

A Lancashire forge at the Häfla works in Östergötland.

Göransson's fixed furnace used at the first successful experiment with the Besse process which took place at Edsken on July 18, 1858. Water color by C. F. Cant Sandviken Jernverks, A.-B.

dietary improvement. But whatever the causes, once started the population growth had the strongest repercussions upon the whole social structure. The demographic change was possibly less dramatic in Sweden than in most other countries, for the rate of growth of the Swedish population seems to have been quite high already in the eighteenth century. Nevertheless, the change was substantial: in the second half of the eighteenth century the annual rate of increase had been .55 per cent; in the first half of the nineteenth century it rose to .81 per cent. In the second half it was .76 per cent; the decline was due to emigration rather than to a fall in population growth.[5] Certainly no other century ever witnessed such an enormous upsurge in population.

The growth of the cities in the nineteenth century depended on industrialization as well as upon the increase in population. As late as 1850, the urban population was only 10 per cent of the total;[6] in 1950 it had risen to 55 per cent,[7] and even the later figure under-estimates the numbers living under urbanized conditions. This is, for instance, indicated by the fact that in 1935 only 41 per cent of the population resided in communities where more than half of the population was employed in agriculture.[8]

The rise in levels of income and consumption was of course very considerable. Naturally, income of the industrial population in-creased more than that of the agricultural population. A stagnant or retrogressive sector of the economy will always find it difficult to retain the ambitious members of the community; it is incapable of offering wages which can compete with those in progressive indus-tries, and presents less opportunity for initiative and inventiveness. Yet for all groups of the population the improvement certainly ex-ceeded any that had previously been realized during any other hun-dred years of Swedish history. A prerequisite for such a develop-ment was the fact that the population, despite its rapid growth, did not increase as fast as production.

There can be no doubt that the developments of the nineteenth century amounted to a great transformation. Though the hand of the past never completely loses its grip, this time it was weakened more thoroughly and more rapidly than ever before. But neither in Sweden nor in most parts of the continent did the change amount to a revo-lution in the sense of an abrupt upheaval with severe dislocations in its train. Even in England, where the changes were more drastic than anywhere else except possibly in the United States, they were not as abrupt or as harmful as has sometimes been claimed. The fact that England took the lead and received the first blow undoubtedly facilitated the transition in other countries by enabling them to anticipate the strains and take appropriate measures to defend themselves. This was definitely true of Sweden.

In Sweden, the major changes occurred during the last forty years of the period, beginning around 1870, but the whole century was one of extraordinary dynamism compared to earlier periods. Whether the years 1815–1914 will seem as remarkable when another century has passed over the land is of course more difficult to say.

## THE IRON AND STEEL INDUSTRY

One of the more remarkable developments in the Swedish economy during the nineteenth century, though in the long run perhaps not the most important, was that of the iron industry.

The growth in industrial production along increasingly capitalistic lines all over the world, and especially in England, created a demand for capital goods and hence, for iron and steel. This evolution was largely made possible by the technological advances on which the large-scale production of cheap iron was founded. In the production of low-grade iron Sweden had no part, but the general economic expansion also stimulated the production of high-grade iron and steel. Thus, the introduction of cheap iron actually bolstered the demand for the old high-quality iron, even while this was being replaced by the new and cheaper product in many areas. The prospects for the Swedish iron industry were not so dark as might at first glance have appeared.

Nevertheless, the Swedish iron industry would certainly not have flourished as it did without the intense efforts of Swedish ironmasters, metallurgists, and ironworkers. Indeed, at this critical juncture they wrote one of the most glorious pages in Swedish economic history. Until then their task had been easy. Sweden had possessed ample resources for ironmaking while other countries had been suffering from an ever more serious fuel shortage. In fact, stringent measures had even been taken to limit the Swedish output. At this time, however, Britain had reached the same advantageous position as Sweden (and Russia). The English position was actually more favorable than the Swedish, since English coal and ore supplies were usually located in the same areas. In spite of this, Sweden managed to maintain and even to expand her iron industry. In doing so without access to mineral coal supplies, Sweden was practically unique in the world, which suggests the difficulty of the task as well as the greatness of the achievement.

To begin with, processes of ironmaking had to be developed which would make it possible to turn out high-quality iron at competitive prices without resort to mineral fuel. The first step was the adoption of the so-called Lancashire process, imported from England but adapted to Swedish conditions. It was already used sporadically in the 1820's and later became quite prevalent. To a layman, the new process did not seem very different from its predecessors. In his travel accounts, Linnaeus talks about "the shirted servants of Vulcan," referring to the fact that the hammermen in his days would wear only a long, coarse, white shirt to protect themselves against the heat from the hearth; the same sight is seen even today in the few forges still using the Lancashire process. For like its predecessors, the Lancashire process was based on hammering the pig iron at forges after it had been reduced to a doughy consistency. It resembled the old Walloon process in using different forges for the "fining" and for beating the iron into bars, but the quality of the product was superior and fuel consumption lower. The adoption of the Lancashire process was the most important and lasting development to come from the new position of the Swedish iron industry. Swedish output of Lancashire iron continued to grow until the early 1890's. Since then, however, it has fallen rapidly and now amounts to only a small fraction of one per cent of the total output of refined iron and steel.[9] Another innovation was the so-called Franche-Comté forge which was introduced around the middle of the century but never reached similar significance and disappeared long ago.

Technical advance, however, was not enough. The new situation required a far more radical adjustment, among other things a reform in commercial policy. Monopolistic practices were no longer feasible. In 1831, two of the leading ironmasters, Pehr Lagerhjelm and Emanuel Rothoff, criticizing the ancient regulations of the iron industry, stated: "That the price of iron in the world markets can be affected by a curtailment of our output is a belief which now lacks validity as well as adherents . . . A small and regular profit on a large trade is more honorable than a large profit on small trade." [10] The curtailment policy was not all that had to be abandoned. The maze of detailed and intricate prescriptions and injunctions contained in the old regulations of the iron industry which still remained on the statute books offered insuperable obstacles to industrial reorganization. The repeal of those statutes was a slow process, but by 1859 it was accomplished, perhaps the most extensive contribution to the clearing of the jungle of economic legislation inherited from the *ancien régime*.[11]

The result of those efforts was that the Swedish output and exports of bar iron not only remained at their old level but in the 1840's exceeded it and then continued to rise almost uninterruptedly, although output grew faster than exports.[12] It is true that market conditions were not as favorable as before, but nothing else was to be expected once the days of monopoly were over.

What had not been anticipated in Sweden and could not very well have been anticipated was that the revolution in iron was far from finished with the introduction of the puddling process in the late eighteenth century. There were no particularly radical developments during the first half of the nineteenth century, but the changes during the second half were momentous.

The introduction of processes whereby molten pig iron was converted into steel ingots almost as easily as pig iron was produced from ore had the most far-reaching consequences. Production of steel had previously been kept within narrow limits because it required an additional expensive process in which the carbon that had been removed in the making of bar iron was again added to the soft iron. Steel could therefore hardly be used in large quantities; the first steamers, for example, were made of iron, which made them extremely heavy. Where steel was indispensable, its use was kept down as far as possible; iron rails, for instance, were provided with a running surface of steel. The new technique for making ingot steel rendered all this superfluous; the carbon content of iron could be easily regulated. This advance in steelmaking marked the turning of a page in the development of industry and transportation.

The first of the new inventions was that of Sir Henry Bessemer, whose early experiments happened to be undertaken in Sweden where

Bessemer was assisted by a business acquaintance, G. F. Göransson, who later founded the Sandviken ironworks.[13] But Göransson went bankrupt, the invention had to be completed elsewhere, and it is consequently difficult to say how much, if any, of the credit for this pioneering step should go to Göransson. Be that as it may, the Bessemer process obviously suited Swedish requirements very well, since the iron was refined with the aid of an air blast, without the further use of fuel. The heat was supplied by the combustion of the carbon in the iron itself, so that the requirements of mineral fuel became quite insignificant. Though the process was developed before the end of the 1850's, it was not immediately adopted; in Sweden it was first used in 1866 and then only on a very small scale.[14]

The Bessemer process was followed, about ten years later, by the Siemens-Martin or open-hearth process. The Siemens-Martin process, however, consumed a great deal of fuel, and therefore seemed rather less fitted to Swedish conditions. But this obstacle was overcome through coal imports, and as early as 1868 the open-hearth process seems to have been taken up in Sweden. Since the 1890's it has actually been used more extensively than the Bessemer process.

The third main advance in steelmaking was the discovery in 1878 of a technique for the use of phosphoric ores. The Thomas-Gilchrist process, often simply called the basic process, solved the problem by lining the furnaces with basic material (limestone), which united chemically with phosphorus. The ground slag could then be used as a fertilizer, the so-called Thomas meal. The invention of the basic process, which could be applied to Bessemer converters as well as to open-hearth furnaces, seemed the final shattering blow to the Swedish iron industry. One of the foremost Swedish metallurgists of the time, Professor Richard Åkerman of the Royal Institute of Technology, declared that this event was "the last nail in the coffin of Swedish ironmaking." [15] In reality, however, basic open-hearth furnaces were introduced in Sweden around 1890, and all prophecies of a final surrender of the Swedish iron industry have so far been refuted by its ability to adjust to ever changing conditions.

The next important development was the introduction of electric power for heating both furnaces and steel forges, which took place during the first decade of the present century.[16] In view of the

Swedish fuel situation it was an important change. The production of pig iron was until that time fundamentally similar to what it had been since coke had been introduced in England at the beginning of the eighteenth century. In Sweden, where coal resources were almost entirely lacking, coke furnaces had been introduced only much later, and it took some time before they became predominant. At first, in the 1890's, a mixture of coke and charcoal was used; then some ten years later the use of coke alone was found more economic, since the vast expansion of the forest industries, especially the pulp industry, had made charcoal increasingly scarce and expensive. The introduction of electric power was therefore timely, but electric power had to be used in combination with charcoal or coke since the presence of carbon was required for reducing the ore into pig iron. Thus, it did not entirely supersede the old processes. Even at the present time less than one-fifth of the total Swedish output of pig iron comes from electric furnaces, most of which also use coke.

The introduction of electric forges was more important. On the one hand, it was a welcome boon to a country rich in hydroelectric power but poorly endowed with mineral fuel; on the other hand, the use of electricity was considered a serious menace to the traditional types of Swedish high-quality steel. In the end, the use of electric forges took root in Sweden; at present no less than 44.5 per cent of the total Swedish steel output is produced in electric forges.[17] Almost exactly the same amount is produced by the open-hearth process, while the Bessemer process has been left a poor third.

Metallurgical and technical details aside, the major trends of the Swedish iron industry may be summed up as follows. Most important, it has survived and even continued to grow in a country almost completely deficient in coal. Locationally, the industry has stuck by the ore, something which has happened in only a few countries. In 1951, the Swedish steel output was about 1,500,000 metric tons,[18] a small amount compared to the output of the great iron-producing countries, and yet at least thirty times as much as in the eighteenth century when Swedish iron knew hardly any serious competition anywhere in the world.

In pig iron production, the most striking change has probably been the increase in concentration, a tendency which has also characterized steelmaking, though to a lesser extent. The increase in size of blast furnaces has been remarkable, although less pronounced than in other countries, since the character of Swedish iron is not adapted to furnaces of the size that can be used for low-quality iron. The following figures tell part of the story:[19]

|                                              | *1861* | *1915* | *1935* | *1949* |
|----------------------------------------------|--------|--------|--------|--------|
| Days worked in the year                      | 122    | 297    | 277    | 279    |
| Annual output per furnace in metric tons     | 751    | 6,339  | 11,799 | 20,506 |
| Daily output per furnace in metric tons      | 6.15   | 21.34  | 42.57  | 73.70  |

Since 1861, the annual output per furnace has increased twenty-seven times, and the daily output almost twelve times. Even compared with 1915, the output per furnace, annual as well as daily, has almost doubled. And those averages for all furnaces are greatly exceeded by the furnaces using coke only, which, in 1949 had a daily output of 150 tons as against 40 tons for furnaces using charcoal only,[20] the latter of course yielding products of a superior quality.

Along with the increased capacity of the furnaces there has been an enormous scaling down in the number of furnaces. In 1861–65 there were 221 furnaces; in 1949, only 62.[21] When the largest Swedish ironworks were founded, toward the end of the 1870's, the new plant superseded no less than nineteen minor ironworks scattered throughout the province of Dalarna. As to the fuel consumed, charcoal, the historical fuel of both furnaces and forges, has tended to be displaced in Sweden as nearly everywhere else. At the present time more than half the Swedish output of pig iron is made with coke alone, and only a little more than one-fourth is made solely with charcoal. In this respect, as in most others, the Swedish iron industry is losing its distinctive traits.

In steel production, the most important change refers to the increasing use of scrap iron. The output of pig iron is now about 810,-000 tons;[22] steel output, as stated previously, is almost twice as high; while the consumption of scrap in the steel mills actually exceeds that of pig iron by about one-third. The adoption of the open-hearth process and the increasing use of scrap in that process are the factors that have made possible a change which, incidentally, has also reduced the relative fuel requirements.

Basic steel, whether from Bessemer converters or open-hearth furnaces, has come to dominate the steel output. At present, almost all the Bessemer steel is basic, as is two-thirds of the open-hearth steel.[23] The latter is especially noteworthy, since non-basic open-hearth steel of high quality has long been the special pride of the Swedish steel industry. Nevertheless a steady shift toward ordinary steel and away from quality steel has occurred. Ordinary steel now represents no less than three-fourths of the total output and dominates the Bessemer, the open-hearth, and the electrical processes.[24]

Few other developments are of comparable significance. That ordinary steel has come to supersede the high-quality product has almost inevitably brought about a redirection of the Swedish iron trade. The iron industry is now primarily oriented toward the home market. Accurate figures are difficult to find, but according to my own reasonably reliable estimates for 1871–75, 1911–15, and 1936–40, exports amounted to 82.7, 65.3, and 37.4 per cent of total output, respectively. The figures speak for themselves. While similar reorientation has also taken place in other industries, it is of special interest in the case of an industry which for so many centuries had been characteristically an export industry.

In her total iron trade, including pig iron as well as steel, Sweden has even turned into a net importer. However, the qualitative difference between imports and exports is great. The unit value of the outgoing iron is so much higher than that of the incoming iron that the exports and imports really may be said to represent entirely different commodities. The redirection of Swedish iron and steel to the home market still remains the fundamental change.

But the decrease in the exported share of steel output is largely the reflection of increased exports in the preceding as well as in the succeeding stages of production. The enormous expansion of ore exports since the 1880's followed upon the appearance of the basic process of steelmaking. Swedish ores are overwhelmingly phosphoric; before the advent of the basic process they were not only useless but even noxious. Steel made from those ores would break under the hammer, and for this reason the richest ore fields in central Sweden, the Grängesberg fields, were not allowed to be mined. The even more extensive ore deposits in the far north also contained too much phosphorus to be worked before the advent of the basic process. Nor could they be approached until a railway system connected them with export ports; however, the railways were a consequence rather than a cause of the sudden prominence of these deposits. The basic process gave Sweden her principal ore supplies.

At present about 14 million tons of iron ore are mined annually in Sweden;[25] approximately one-tenth of this tonnage remains within the country. The reserves are immense, compared to the needs of the Swedish iron industry. There was at one time considerable concern lest the country lose its natural advantage in this field by too rapid an exploitation of its ore supplies; hence the output is still limited by statute, but every survey reveals the existence of new reserves and they now seem well-nigh inexhaustible. There is ample reason for the strong foreign demand: no less than 86 per cent of the Swedish ores presently mined have an iron content as high as 60–70 per cent. Before and during the Second World War, those ores found their major outlet in the Ruhr district, which relied upon the Swedish phosphoric ores for the production of basic Bessemer steel.[26] This made Swedish ore exports a matter of high politics and influenced military operations on both sides. During the postwar period, the direction of Swedish ore exports has changed considerably, though increasing rather than diminishing their political significance. Britain has become the foremost customer, but Western Germany, the United States, and to a somewhat lesser extent Belgium, are all prominent receivers of Swedish ore.

More important yet has been the growth of the stage of production which follows the making of crude steel, in other words, the iron manufacturing industry. The contrast to eighteenth-century conditions is interesting in this context. At that time, iron manufactures were encouraged by the state in every conceivable way but the results were disappointing. In the latter part of the nineteenth century, on the other hand, state support was confined to moderate tariff protection, and the development was left to the unaided efforts of private individuals. The underlying cause of the upswing was of course the new demand for capital goods, especially machinery, from which Sweden came to benefit to an extraordinary degree. Natural resources and the tradition of the iron industry were certainly important prerequisites for this development, but it may perhaps be said that Swedes have shown particular aptitudes for the engineering industry. If this be so — and such things are hard to prove —

one might hazard a guess about the reasons. The old processes of ironmaking have already been described as being somewhat in the nature of a laboratory experiment, which conceivably may have fostered the diffusion of technical and mechanical abilities. Swedes cherish the belief that more than their share of major mechanical inventions have been made by Swedish civil engineers and that Swedish workmen have proved remarkably able to handle and improve machinery.

The last ninety years have seen the creation of many internationally known Swedish engineering and allied industries. The total value of their exports has greatly exceeded that of iron ore. It is difficult to draw a line doing justice and no more than justice to this variegated and steadily expanding group; we might estimate that it represents something like 25–30 per cent of total Swedish exports. At any rate these exports are clearly second only to forest products. To this category belong products such as telephone equipment, ball bearings, electrical machinery, lighthouse equipment, railway material, ships, possibly also matches, and the like. Swedish concerns which have established themselves in many foreign countries usually belong to this motley crowd, for example, SKF (ball bearings), L. M. Ericsson (telephone equipment), AGA (lighthouse equipment), the many-sided Electrolux, Swedish Match, and so forth. The prominence of those particular concerns has frequently been exaggerated, especially during the short and factitious ascendancy of Ivar Kreuger. Actually, the corporations controlled by him never occupied a central position in Swedish economic life. But that they have been and still remain important cannot be denied, although they have frequently found it necessary to transfer part of their productive capacity abroad in order to overcome foreign tariff barriers.

## THE FOREST INDUSTRIES

The Swedish forest was the base on which, during the nineteenth century, one of the major branches of Swedish industry was built. First came the expansion of the lumber industry, beginning almost exactly at the middle of the century but preceded, during the 1840's, by a rapid growth in output of unsawed timber. This development acquired special significance from the iron industry's failure to keep pace with the rapidly growing population; yet the really remarkable thing is perhaps not that the expansion occurred at that precise moment but rather that a country more than half covered with forest had to wait so long for the appearance of a major forest industry.

When we look more closely, the causes of the delay are easily apparent. First of all, Norway was far better located with regard to the important markets in the West. Foreigners saw no reason to go into the Baltic for timber when it was to be had on the shores of the North Sea. Apart from their geographic advantage, the Norwegians also possessed a technological superiority which was a further bar to the growth of Swedish timber exports. Legislation was another obstacle; sawmills were regarded as somewhat disreputable competitors for the wood demanded by the iron industry. Actually, the iron industry of those days might well be described as a forest industry, since charcoal was by far the most important product of the forest. Finally, the English protectionist policy during the Napoleonic wars set a premium on Canadian timber and discriminated almost prohibitively against timber from other countries; but this, of course, hit the Norwegians as much as the Swedes.

The rise of the Swedish timber industry was dependent on a reversal of most of these conditions. The Norwegian forest reserves, especially those along the coastline, had been heavily depleted, so that the country was completely incapable of satisfying the enormous demand for timber. This demand, in turn, was related to the industrialization and particularly to the mushrooming of the English cities. It was naturally of the greatest advantage to Sweden that timber and iron were at first complementary rather than competitive commodities. Equally important was the reversal of English commercial policy — her adoption of free trade, and the abolition of colonial preference, which was completed with the famous repeal of the Navigation Act in 1849.[27] The tariff on timber was also reduced in 1842 and 1851.

These developments in commercial policy coincided with the introduction of steam saws in Sweden. The use of steam made it possible to set up saws along the coastline where they were easily reached by timber floating down the rivers as well as by timberships. Previously, the saws had been bound to those spots on the rivers where a water wheel could be placed. The steam saw was in fact one of the major contributions of the industrial revolution in Sweden. Simultaneously, a major improvement occurred in timber transportation when the rivers were cleared for flotage. Finally, the timber industry attracted the most capable as well as the most ruthless Swedish entrepreneurs of the nineteenth century; their methods often roused understandable resentment but as a result this basic branch of the economy became solidly entrenched.

Especially during the two booms in the 1850's and the 1870's, the timber industry grew at a truly American pace. It was a gold-rush-like experience to which there was no counterpart in earlier Swedish economic history. Unlike the iron industry, the timber industry had to attract laborers from other parts of the country and house them in jerry-built communities of the most primitive kind, thus further accentuating the American character of the development. At this time the southern parts of the country were displaced as leading timber producers by the central and northern parts of Sweden where the new sawmills were founded. The labor force gathered by the new industry, rooted neither in its occupation nor in its environment, was inevitably very different from that of the iron industry, with its traditional attachment to the craft and to the mining regions. It was far from a coincidence that the first serious industrial conflict in Sweden was the strike of 1879 in the sawmills at Sundsvall.

The growth of the forest industries was obviously limited by the available forest reserves. For centuries much of the forest had been regarded mainly as a grazing and hunting ground, although its use for construction and fuel was probably of far greater economic significance. In iron-producing districts some measures of forest conservation had been introduced long ago. (See page 97.) In the country at large, however, the abundance of wood had been such that no serious thought was given to its consumption until the forest had already been severely depleted.

Most notably in the north but also elsewhere, a great deal of the forest remained in the possession of the state. The wisdom of this arrangement was now questioned. Impressed with the superiority of private enterprise, the *riksdag* of 1823 decided to transfer state forests to private hands. The measure was bitterly opposed by C. A. Agardh,[28] a versatile scientist who was to end his days as a bishop, and who, at a much later time, restated his views on forest policy in a Statistical Essay on the Political Economy of Sweden (*Försök till en statsekonomisk statistik öfver Sverige*). In some respects, events were to prove him eminently correct.

In the northern parts of the country, special conditions prevailed. There the holdings of the government were not yet clearly separated from the peasant forest. The first step was therefore to clarify property rights. In the same spirit that had sponsored the sale of state forest in the south, the lion's share was given to the peasants in order to wipe out, as far as possible, the holdings of the crown. Enormous properties were thus transferred to the peasants of Norrland. Allotments per peasant in some communities rose to 11,000–16,000 acres of woodland on the average. To this were added the so-called "impediments," which actually also contained a great deal of timber. Many peasants received domains as large as a small German principality. At the time, however, these allotments were considered fairly useless since the value of the forest was negligible before the rise of the timber industry. In reality it was a gift of far-reaching consequences. The speculators who initially tended to dominate the timber industry would purchase or lease the forest for a trifle.[29] The peasants indeed sold their birthright for a mess of pottage.

It is hard to say what alternative course the government could have followed. Large-scale forestry is certainly not a peasant industry, and to operate a sawmill without control of the timber supply is extremely difficult. It was almost inevitable that the sawmill operators would strive to acquire their own forest in order to meet the violent market fluctuations. If they had failed in this, the well-consolidated firms which succeeded the first robber barons might never have arisen. The accumulation of capital in those companies made it possible to preserve and develop Swedish forest resources in a period when the forests of many other countries were ruthlessly exploited and annihilated.

Nevertheless, it seems quite possible that a more cautious way could have been taken. The government might have transferred the forest to the companies step by step, at a price more faithfully corresponding to its value to the buyers. The peasants' share might have been the same or only slightly higher, yet if they had never been allotted those princely domains in the first place and had not afterwards been cheated out of their riches, their resentment would not have been so bitter. The social strains which came to plague the north of Sweden might then have been avoided. The only question is whether such a course would have been feasible without obstructing the growth of the industry; if so, it would certainly have been more in line with the Swedish tradition of orderly industrial development, and the problems of chaotic settlements and rebellious labor movements would never have arisen.

By the turn of the century the expansion of the timber industry had spent itself. The primitive forest had been practically exhausted, and there was a growing shortage of timber. While there has been no real decline since then, the stagnation was unmistakable and the immediate consequence was a slight setback. The expansion had lasted almost exactly half a century, a trifling span of time in comparison with the century-long growth of the iron industry. Yet Knut Wicksell, Sweden's greatest economist, actually referred to this factor as one of the impelling motives to limit the population of Sweden; he saw no possibility of maintaining the standard of living as long as the forest was being depleted. Although the future turned out rather differently from what he expected, the population problem was undoubtedly graver at that time than fifty years earlier when the timber industry arose to offset the slackening growth of the iron industry.

But his apprehension proved to be largely groundless, and the Swedish economy showed an impressible vitality up to the outbreak of the First World War. Once more a favorable turn of events came to the rescue. This time it was the rise of the pulp industry which grew at a phenomenal rate, greatly exceeding that of the timber industry. The statistics for sawn timber are admittedly very unsatisfactory, but production may be estimated to have increased fourfold in the forty years between 1856 and 1896. Pulp production, the record of which is much better known, increased tenfold in half that time (1894–1914).[30] Just before the First World War, Sweden became the leading pulp exporter of the world, a fact of far-reaching consequences during and after that war. On the one hand, the strong foreign demand for pulp contributed to the inflation of the Swedish price level during the war, but on the other hand it facilitated considerably the subsequent return to the gold standard.

The tremendous expansion of the pulp industry, however, made a much weaker impression on the public mind than the rise of the timber industry. The reason was that the concomitant social disturbances were slight. The pulp industry had smaller requirements of manpower in relation to the value of output than most of the major industries in Sweden; moreover, it was generally located in the same areas as the timber industry. Thus there was no need for a migration of labor. If anything, the danger was that the pulp industry would not be able to support the population already settled in the north, a problem which eventually arose. Another reason why the rise of this new industry attracted less attention was simply that Swedish capitalism had overcome its growing pains. It no longer indulged in the excesses which had characterized the rise of the timber industry, but had embarked upon a process of quiet and steady though less spectacular growth.

The demand and the supply situation combined to make the pulp industry expand with lightning speed. On the demand side there was the prodigious growth of the daily press; and on the supply side, the invention of chemical wood pulp, which was an adequate substitute for the scarce and expensive linen rags in paper making.

The early pulp industry was quite primitive. The wood was ground into fibers, and the lignin which causes the disintegration of the product was not removed. The paper made from mechanical pulp was quite poor, so that sometimes other fibers had to be admixed. Mechanical pulp had already appeared around the middle of the nineteenth century, but its growth was at first quite sluggish and even though it accelerated later it never reached the same position as chemical pulp.[31]

The crucial step was the introduction of chemical processes for dissolving the lignin from the wood, leaving a pure cellulose from which strong and durable paper could be made. A Swede, Carl Daniel Ekman, was one of the two inventors who simultaneously arrived at a solution to the problem, although the calcium bisulphite used by his competitor turned out to be more suitable than the magnesium bisulphite used by Ekman. In 1872, the first chemical pulp factory in the world was founded at Bergvik in the North of Sweden;[32] the real growth of the sulphite pulp industry, however, did not set in until the 1890's. By then a process based on sodium sulphate had appeared, but the paper made from sulphate pulp is of the coarse *Kraft* quality, mainly used for wrapping paper. The relation between the two branches of the chemical pulp industry is therefore not exclusively competitive, and both have shown considerable strength. They have also been supplemented by a paper industry of growing importance.

The advent of a pulp industry had strong repercussions on forest economics. The sawmills had been primarily interested in fir, which commonly occurred together with spruce. As the fir was cut the mixed forests were transformed into pure spruce and the price of spruce was depressed. But the sulphite industry, when it came, used spruce exclusively, which for some time tended to make spruce scarcer than fir. The sulphate industry, finally, by using both spruce and fir rather indiscriminately imparted an unanticipated but essential balance to Swedish forestry.

Economically, it was also significant that the period of production in the pulp industry was shorter than in the timber industry. Accordingly, the former did not require as much capital to be tied in forests as the latter. The pulp industry was not dependent on the large trunks needed for boards and planks or on the very big spar and mast timber. The old way of growing and cutting trees of the same age together was abolished. Instead, forests of mixed age were grown from which the trees were picked at the proper age, younger trees for pulp wood, older trunks for the sawmills. Thus, the turnover of the forest could be stepped up, and Wicksell's concern about the consequence of the disappearance of the primitive forest turned out to be at least premature.

Part of the country's capital resources was therefore freed for use elsewhere, and it is rather striking that the termination of the Swedish capital imports in 1910 almost coincided with the end of the first phase of expansion in the pulp industry. There was at that time considerable interest in the question of the proper rate of turnover of the forest. In many quarters there was strong opposition to a shortening of the turnover period to a point where the forest could yield an adequate return on invested capital, but the further growth of the pulp industry at the expense of the timber industry soon solved the problem.

In other respects, the development was not so painless. It has already been briefly mentioned that the new competition for cheap wood served to raise the price for charcoal. The sawmills had consumed trunks bigger than those usually burned for charcoal, but the shift of emphasis to the pulp industry immediately raised a problem for the part of the iron industry that continued to use charcoal. In addition, large timber soon became extremely scarce, and many saw mills were starved to death in the weeding-out process that set in during the First World War. Lately, a certain scarcity of cheap wood has also been felt, and the pulp industry has pushed hard against the limit set by availability of raw materials. Only a very slight growth is to be expected in the future. Wicksell's forecast finally seems to have become relevant.

In the present situation, four possible roads seem open for future expansion. The first is an improvement in silviculture, accelerating the growth of the forest without impairment of quality. The prospects in this respect are promising. Secondly, processing of the wood can be carried further and more pulp converted into paper than before. However, the world trade situation and the tariff policies of many countries make this a dangerous course. In the third place, there appear to be innumerable possibilities for extracting wood substances which now run to waste in the wood pulp factories. One step in this direction has already been taken with the distillation of sulphite alcohol. Long suppressed by legislation, it now contributes about six-sevenths of the Swedish output of alcohol. Wood contains many other valuable products, and a great deal of research is currently going on in order to make their extraction possible. Though the results so far have been slight, there is still hope of some success in this area. Finally, a number of diversified industries have arisen, based on waste wood from the large timber-consuming industries. The individual firms in this group are usually small, often of peasant origin; but in total labor force and aggregate value of output they compare favorably with the sawmill industry. Their products include veneer, plywood, wallboard, casks, doors and windows, pre-fabricated houses, furniture, and similar carpentry products.

As an export industry, timber never attained the predominance held by iron in its heyday. At the beginning of the Age of Freedom, iron had accounted for no less than 75 per cent of total exports; timber never accounted for more than 40–45 per cent of Swedish exports.[33] Still, this was more than sufficient to make the timber industry indisputably Sweden's leading export industry in the late nineteenth century. When timber exports stagnated, the pulp industry appeared, and the combined exports of wood and wood products have since then constituted between 45 and 50 per cent of total exports and have remained at that relative level even after the Second World War.[34]

## OTHER INDUSTRIES

Among the other industries the textile industry is of special interest. The stagnation, and in some cases retrogression, of this industry in the eighteenth century, which occurred despite heavy subsidization, later gave way to a sharp rise. Its growth was undoubtedly promoted by the tariff protection the industry enjoyed in the nineteenth century, but government support during this period did not even faintly resemble that accorded the manufactories of the eighteenth century. We have already pointed out that the manufactories actually did not provide the foundation or even the starting point for the modern textile industry; its most vigorously expanding branch, in Sweden as in England and elsewhere in the world, has been the cotton industry, which was quite insignificant in the eighteenth century. Cotton weaving must, however, have played an increasing part in domestic industry; to the extent that the modern textile industry had any roots at all in the eighteenth century, this is where we find them. The same was the case in most other countries, and particularly so in England, where the cotton industry was also based on domestic industry, albeit of a rather different sort from the Swedish. In England, domestic industry was almost completely organized as a merchant-employer or putting-out system in which the employees seem to have been in the nature of industrial workers, though scattered over the countryside. In Sweden, the putting-out system in pure form was less prevalent and most of the domestic production took place in farming households where it was not the only source of income.

The ties to the old household industry were especially strong in the so-called Seven Hundreds (*Sjuhäradsbygden*), seven of the hundreds of Alvsborg County, where the modern cotton industry found its main seat. The position as a textile center which this region established while peddlers were its only marketing outlet is impressive evidence of the dynamic economic function that for centuries was performed by the barely tolerated rural trade. Technically, its position rested on the traditional skill of the population in the area. A similar situation existed with regard to shoemaking in the Örebro area where the modern Swedish shoe industry developed.

A general remark must be made here about the importance of local skills in industrial history. In many cases this has been very considerable, even in an economically young country like the United States, and the reason is simply that, next to land, labor is probably the least mobile of all the factors of production, however strange that may sound. A thoroughly skilled labor force is quite likely to attract factors of production which might otherwise have tended to favor another location of the industry — provided, of course, that the old skills are not made entirely obsolete by new technology. The clearest Swedish example is the iron industry, which has remained unshakably rooted in the middle of Sweden rather than in the north, close to charcoal, or on the coast, near imported coal. In other countries, the ore has usually moved to the fuel. In Sweden it has been the other way around; coal and electricity have moved to the ore. But they were attracted not so much by the ore itself — for in that case the iron industry would also have tended to move north — as by the traditional craftsmanship of the ironworkers in Bergslagen.

## THE LABOR MOVEMENT

It is well known that the Swedish labor movement has become one of the strongest in Europe. Its most proximate source of inspiration was Denmark, then, less directly, Germany. The first political and ideological prophet of the Swedish labor movement, a tailor by the name of August Palm, had spent long years both in Denmark and north Germany. Upon his return to Sweden, Palm began in 1881 his long campaign for the spread of socialist ideas. Internationally speaking, this was late, the main reason for the delay being probably the very special situation in the iron industry. Swedish ironworks were generally located in isolated rural communities which served to reduce contacts between workers of different plants. The establishment of trade unions and the ability to conduct a successful strike were almost inevitably dependent on such contacts and on coöperation and financial support of a large number of workers. The rural location also tended to make the ironworkers dependent on their employer. They were supplied by his stores; they lived in his houses and could be evicted in the event of a strike; moreover, to leave and seek a new job in the same or another trade was not easy. A guild-like organization and the pride of workmanship were further stabilizing factors; and, finally, a traditional bond existed between employer and employee that was conspicuously absent in the manufacturing industries.

Certainly, the ironworkers had their grievances; we have already observed that the iron industry's prosperity under inflation in the eighteenth century partly rested upon a reduction of real wages. But the fact remains that, in their patriarchal spirit, the ironmasters provided for their workmen in a way which had no equivalent in other industries. As the companies' books reveal, an old worker always enjoyed some pension; and when the workers had incurred unmanageable debts, cancellation was so common that it could be regarded as a regular cost-of-production item. In addition, the Statute of Hammermen of 1766 had provided for certain health and unemployment contributions from the employers, partly administered in coöperation with the guild-like organization of the workers.[35] On the other hand, the system tied the workers to the firm, since the large majority of them were indebted to their employer and could not move unless another employer was willing to take on their debt. These restrictions upon their freedom as well as the benefits conferred upon them obviously obstructed the organization of the ironworkers.

It has been noted that the first major strike in Sweden occurred in the sawmills at Sundsvall in 1879. In their independence of traditional ties with regard to their occupation and residence, the workers in the timber industry resembled industrial populations abroad far more than the ironworkers. But the strikers at Sundsvall were not organized; in fact, they were partly under the sway of a nonconformist religious sentiment, in sharp contrast to the ideology which was to characterize the Swedish labor movement. Trade unions proper did not make their appearance until the 1880's. Very soon local unions were organized into nationwide unions. From that point on the movement grew rapidly in strength, even though considerable obstacles had still to be overcome in rural areas, and particularly within the forest industry.

In 1898, *Landsorganisationen*,[36] the national labor organization, was established, after only two decades of trade-union activity. In fact, at that time the labor side was a great deal better organized than the employers, who in many industries faced the unions completely on their own. However, only four years later, the employers created the Swedish Employers Association (*Svenska Arbetsgivarförening-en*),[37] thereby completing the pattern of organization of the Swedish labor market. Although the general strike of 1909 led to a blistering defeat for labor,[38] it recovered with remarkable ease, and today the Swedish labor force is more completely organized than those of most other countries. In consequence, free competition has practically disappeared from the labor market; but, unexpectedly enough, the balance between the two strong organizations on the labor market has resulted in an abatement of social conflict. This reorganization of the labor market probably was the most remarkable change overtaking Swedish society in the nineteenth century. Government policy and legislation remained conspicuously absent in this development. Not until the 1930's did government policy promote the growth of trade unionism, and then only indirectly. In the fight against the depression, the government placed the unemployed in public works where they did not threaten the wage rates attained by collective bargaining. But by that time, the organization of labor was already so complete that no credit for its growth really falls to this policy.

On the other hand, legislation in Sweden, unlike that of many other countries, never impeded the growth of the unions, except insofar as the old statutes against vagrants and "sturdy beggars"[39] were applied against the workers in the very first period of union organization. Far more obstructive than any legislation, however, was the opposition on the part of the authorities, especially the police, and the pressure of conservative public opinion in the press where the trade unions were represented as agents of revolution and subversion. But even this opposition melted away more painlessly than elsewhere, and on the whole the rise of the Swedish labor movement was extraordinarily free from social conflict.

## ECONOMIC LIBERALISM AND ITS REVERSAL

The liberalization of commercial policy in Sweden in the eighteenth century followed approximately the same course as that taken in other European countries. It expressed the liberal intellectual climate of the time, and the elimination of congeries of economic legislation which had accumulated for centuries was of considerable significance. In Sweden, as already indicated, the repeal of the statutes for the iron industry was perhaps the main achievement along that line. Otherwise, the importance of the liberalization should probably not be exaggerated, in view of the inadequate enforcement which usually seems to have characterized the earlier regulations.

The guild system in Sweden did not extend to the small towns until the middle of the eighteenth century, and was destined to survive for only a hundred years. By 1846, most guild regulations were wiped out by statute, except that the proficiency test for a master's certificate was retained in those crafts where the guilds had their deepest roots. In 1864, even the last remnants of the guild system were removed from the statute books, although it probably survived to some slight degree in the form of friendly societies.[40] Not even the oldest Swedish trade unions, however, appear to have originated from *compagnonnages* or other similar associations of the guild period. Thus the guilds disappeared leaving hardly any trace, in spite of their long history, at least in certain crafts and in certain parts of the country, and without ever having played a major part in Swedish economic development.

Liberal legislation aroused a great deal more attention in the field of foreign trade. In all probability the legislative swing to liberal trade policies had some real impact on the country's development, although that impact too has undoubtedly often been overrated.

Not only tariff protection but prohibition of imports was the mark of Swedish trade policies in the early nineteenth century. Actually, this did not completely bar the imports of prohibited goods, but the smuggling costs served as a tariff barrier. It is well known, for instance, that merchants' houses in Ystad, on the southern coast of Sweden, at the time a respectable trade center, concealed huge caves for contraband, their entrances hidden behind mirrors in the wall in a veritable cloak-and-dagger fashion; and there is no reason to assume that similar conditions did not prevail in other commercial cities. Thus, the transition from prohibition to protection was probably not such a major step as the statutes might suggest. Trade no doubt received a certain stimulus, but to a large extent the change amounted to a legalization of already prevailing practices.

The first relaxation of the old commercial policies was the disintegration of the Swedish Navigation Act, the *produktplakat,* which occurred through navigation treaties concluded with various countries who were thereby exempted from the restrictions imposed on foreign ships in Swedish ports. The original statute was retained on the books and has not yet been repealed, although it has gradually been suspended with respect to one country after another.

In regard to commodity trade, however, it was not until the middle of the century that there was any major change in policy. At that time, the Cabinet was joined by Johan August Gripenstedt, a vigorous champion of the liberal ideas that were sweeping country after country. In Sweden, French economic thought and practice were a leading source of inspiration. Gripenstedt himself was strongly influenced by French thinking, notably by Frederic Bastiat, who enjoyed considerable fame as a popularizer of liberal economic principles. It is quite possible that Gripenstedt regarded himself as a Swedish Napoleon III, destined to introduce economic liberalism for the benefit of the people, unhampered by petty concessions to the opinion of the representatives of the people itself. In the course of the 1850's and 1860's he managed to do away with all prohibitions against imports or exports, to abolish all export duties, to reduce the import tariffs for manufactured goods and to establish free trade in agricultural products. The international price rise touched off by the California gold discoveries promoted his efforts considerably; the boom facilitated the adjustments, and the price burden of the tariffs seemed more unfair and unfavorable than usual.

Gripenstedt was vigorously criticized for the eloquent economic optimism of some of his main speeches in 1857. Immediately after his speeches the crisis of 1858, brief but sharp, set in, seemingly refuting his confident interpretation of the situation. But very soon the crisis had passed, and Gripenstedt's liberal faith remained unshaken. Although the attitude of the *riksdag* by and large was hostile, a new opportunity for liberal reform was offered with the spreading of the French treaty system which had been founded on the Cobden-Chevalier treaty of 1860. Through Sweden's entry into that system, Gripenstedt confirmed his earlier tariff reductions and achieved several new ones, without the necessity of consulting the *riksdag* at the early stage of the negotiations. The very same tactics were used by Napoleon III. In the session of 1865–66 — the year of the reform bill introducing bicameralism in Sweden — the French treaty was submitted to the *riksdag* for ratification, and the respect which the Swedish parliament generally accorded to international agreements made it fairly easy for Gripenstedt to achieve its approval. This was about as far as free trade would ever get in Sweden.

There is no reliable study of the impact of free trade on Swedish economic development. The many liberalizing reforms of domestic economic policies which occurred at the same time blur the picture and make such an assessment a difficult task. That the tremendous expansion of timber exports was facilitated by *laissez faire* is fairly obvious, for such policies will almost always promote foreign trade in general. For the same reason, the liberal trade policies must also have stimulated the rise of engineering industries early in the 1870's. Consequently, they may be said to have promoted the industrialization of the country.

No major changes in the tariff policy occurred until the competition of American grain gave rise, in Sweden as in other countries, to a new tide of protectionism. Agricultural tariffs, which will be discussed in connection with the general agricultural development, were followed in 1892 by an increase in tariffs on industrial goods. During the first decade of the twentieth century, Sweden was drawn into the German protectionist treaty system which produced further increases in industrial tariffs.[41] This step was taken initially for bargaining purposes in negotiations with Germany, but the new tariffs were later retained. At the time of the First World War, Swedish industry was thus protected by a certain tariff barrier, although it seems very moderate in comparison with the tariffs of more recent days. The general inflation during the war served to reduce the tariff level; and, in contrast with the many countries resorting to vehemently restrictive policies after the war, Sweden appeared as a country of relatively free trade.

The impact of this policy is not easy to assess, but a few points are quite evident. Since the beginning of the 1890's the intention was to realize a "solidarity" policy of the German type, that is, to achieve the task — almost absurd by definition — of favoring *all* branches of the economy at the same time. The effect must have been in the direction of increased autarky; protection could yield no support to the export industries, which instead had to contribute to the rest of the economy; retardation of the export industries served to restrict imports. It is also reasonably clear that the differentiation of industry was encouraged. If those features of the Swedish economy which have proved of great value in periods of war and blockade have been the result of Swedish protectionism, it must immediately be added that there was no deliberate and planned effort in this direction. Had that been the case, the tariff schedules would have looked very different.

To proceed beyond such general observations would lead us into more controversial areas, although it is probably justified to say that in peacetime protection was a somewhat retarding factor in the general growth of the Swedish economy because it imposed burdens on profitable branches of industry in favor of the unprofitable ones. On the other hand, the price rise prevailing throughout the major part of the protectionist period provided a stimulus which served to conceal this aspect of the tariff policy. The main conclusion, nevertheless, is that, apart from the agricultural sector, the Swedish economy was probably not vitally affected in one direction or another. More frequently than either protectionists or free traders are usually inclined to admit, the consequences of foreign trade policies have probably been rather negligible.

One field where all the evidence suggests that protection is a vital factor is industrial organization. The effect of protection is to insulate the domestic market from foreign competition, thereby facilitating the formation of cartels and encouraging the use of monopolistic pricing in order to maintain the highest price level possible under the shelter of the tariff. This effect was certainly present in Sweden too. The most conspicuous case was that of the sugar trust, which was created in 1907 after the failure of several attempts at cartelization of the industry.[42] It was the strongest and most profitable of the industrial combinations in pre-1914 Sweden. Weaker combinations of the same kind occurred in the milling and oleomargarine industries. The significance of the tariff policies is fairly clear in those cases, but there was surely also a general tendency, independent of any protection, toward industrial combination. The growth of cartels was characteristic of the last few years before 1914 in Sweden as elsewhere, and it was to gain momentum after the war, in the transition from a basically competitive to a largely monopolistic economy.

### COMMUNICATIONS

There is little doubt that the revolution in transport was far more important than foreign trade policies. Especially in land transport an enormous task had to be solved. The lack of a developed highway system was acutely embarrassing in a country as extensive and as sparsely populated as Sweden.

The problem was most serious in Bergslagen, seat of Sweden's heavy industry. The methods of heavy transportation, which to a modern eye appear so extremely primitive, give an indication of the gravity of the problem. While the snow lasted, the winter roads were still available, permitting reasonably convenient traffic across land and water without any reloading. But summer was another story, and the growing need for speedy deliveries made it increasingly difficult to confine all heavy building to the winter months. The solution was an intricate combination of land and water transport with incessant reloading. The highways were followed only to the next port or loading place, where the cargo was then shipped across lakes or along rivers; not infrequently the same cargo was reloaded up to a dozen times. Steam railroads were introduced quite slowly; for a few decades railways with horse-drawn wagons were used. After several insignificant efforts in the beginning of the century, the first horse railroad of this type was built in 1849 in the province of Värmland; it was still in operation as late as the 1870's. Those early railroads took the same course as the previous traffic and were designed to serve as links between the waterways.

Following this traditional pattern, the first Swedish railroad project was of a most peculiar nature. Adolf Eugene von Rosen, the earliest Swedish champion and builder of railroads, was, in spite of his studies abroad, particularly in England, to an almost inexplicable degree influenced by the old Swedish transport system. His first and only chartered line, never to be completed, was to run between the two lake ports of Köping and Hult, its sole purpose being to connect the two lakes. How completely unrealistic this design was may be demonstrated by the fact that the loading place at Hult, the planned terminal of the line, even today has no railroad connection.

The actual creator of the Swedish network was a man of another sort. Nils Ericson, a brother of John Ericsson* of *Monitor* fame, was a born leader who at an early stage had evolved a design for a complete Swedish railroad network and who worked with immense force and unwavering purpose to realize his plan. Needless to say, it was a plan in which there was little room either for Rosen or for his ideas. Ericson wanted the state to control the main inter-regional trunks of the railroad network. The private lines linked to the state system would have no choice but to accept the policies dictated by the government. In Ericson's mind a map of the primary railway system was laid out in minute detail, and he was able to enforce the realization of his plans with hardly any change. It seems doubtful, however, whether he would have attained the approval of the government and especially of the *riksdag*, had it not been for the support of Gripenstedt who threw himself into the battle on Ericson's side. The parliamentary struggles about the directions of projected railroads were unusually bitter. In a few cases, Ericson's proposals were rejected, but the changes were too small to affect the major outlines of his grand design.

Nils Ericson's approach to the planning of the railroad system was criticized for his "horror of waterways and cities." The mainspring of his thinking was that the railroads were to stimulate economic development in those parts of the country which, through the absence of communications, had been left behind. As a consequence many of the old cities, especially in the interior, were retarded rather than favored by the early railroads. In this regard, Sweden differed from most of the European countries. On the other hand, the railroad stations became the nuclei of a great many new communities which sprang up along the railroads. Ericson's intentions were aided by the curious reluctance of certain old towns to become railroad centers.

* *Translator's note:* Nils, who remained in Sweden, changed his name from Ericsson to Ericson when he was titled for his public services.

In a few cases, the result was that areas without any potentialities for development were equipped with railroads exclusively designed to carry through traffic, a function which might have been better served by avoiding the area in question altogether.

Ericson's original plan broke down in one significant respect. Initially, the private railroads grew at a slower rate than the state lines, and for some time it seemed as if the state system would retain its lead. But even the construction of state railways proceeded very slowly; the first short stretches were not opened until late in 1856. The international boom in the 1870's, which everywhere and particularly in the United States was characterized by railroadization, imparted a tremendous stimulus to private railroad building in Sweden. During the 1870's alone the private network increased its mileage 6.5 times whereas the state lines grew only 3.5 times in the same period.[43] At the end of the century, private mileage was more than twice that of the state system. Even more important was the fact that two of the new private lines were in the nature of main trunk lines, fairly independent of the state network. Both of them served the heavy industry of Bergslagen, and the reason for their emergence was certainly in part that Ericson had neglected this area, in which the need for heavy transport made itself very sharply felt.

The growth of private mileage, however, easily suggests a degree of private independence that was not really attained. All the railroads except the merely local lines were intimately affected by their coördination with the government railroads; and the rates for joint use of state and private lines were set by the government, which thereby exercised considerable influence over the entire rate structure. Secondly, although the private lines were longer than the state lines, their capital equipment was inferior and so was their volume of traffic. Hence there is little doubt that the original intention to establish substantial state control was realized.

Despite the many inconveniences that almost inevitably characterized this mixed system, it was long considered satisfactory, combining as it did private and local initiative with national unity of administration and control. But in recent times the situation has changed. Many smaller railways found it more and more difficult to compete with the highways, and the government, by advancing substantial loans to private railroads, acquired an interest in their operation. At the same time, faith in state ownership and management increased. The result has been a gradual nationalization of most of the private railways so that by now the state network covers practically the whole country.[44]

The early state railways were primarily financed by foreign borrowing, but for some lines, especially those not expected to pay for themselves, current tax revenues were deployed in considerable amounts.[45] In consequence, the state network was always able to service its foreign loans, even when the return over total capital fell below the rate of interest at which the foreign borrowing had been undertaken. Undoubtedly, the Swedish government's position on the foreign capital market was strengthened by this policy.

The private railroads were financed in a more complex fashion. Several bond issues were floated at home and a few abroad; a great deal was borrowed from the state, local authorities and various credit institutions; and some capital was raised by stock issue. In many cases contributions were engineered by local interests expecting no actual dividends but staking their hopes on the general economic development in the area.

After the initial resistance to the railroads the public fell into a somewhat uncritical enthusiasm, so much so that the railroads were often expected, as if by magic, to bring throbbing prosperity even to regions without any prerequisites for economic development. However, since the freight rates adopted by most Swedish railroads were set on a cost basis, average rates were lower for long than for short hauls. Accordingly, it frequently happened that activities hitherto carried on in an area moved out as a railroad was built through it.

Various studies of the railways' impact on regional distribution of the population conclusively demonstrate that their main effects were felt before their completion, through the migration of the labor force and through the expectations roused by the construction programs. Once in operation, the railroads attracted the population to the railway stations and especially to the junctions, but between the main stops the population tended to decrease. On the other hand, the general effect on the country's economic development was enormous. As suggested in the beginning of the chapter, it was extremely important, in a country of Sweden's extent, that the various regions be connected. The impact of the railroads was for that reason probably strongest in the remote regions of Norrland, although the network there was and remains relatively sparse. As late as the 1860's a famine had occurred in the north, and only in 1873 did a railroad reach Krylbo, no more than one hundred miles from Stockholm.[46]

The appearance of the motor car and the growth of road transportation has put an end to the expansion of the Swedish railroad system. Its growth, long insignificant, has now come to a complete stop; in fact, in recent years the mileage has even been somewhat reduced.

In water transport, the changes during the nineteenth century were far less revolutionary than in land transport. The technological development in this field reached Sweden at a very late date. Although the steamship did appear in Sweden in 1818, as the result of Samuel Owen's immigration from England, a long time elapsed before sailing vessels gave way to steamers.[47] Owen's early experiment had few successors, and even if the steam tonnage is tripled to make conventional allowance for greater speed, it did not match the sailing tonnage until the 1880's.[48] Considering that Robert Fulton operated his famous steamer on the Hudson in 1807, some twenty years before the appearance of the railroads, this delay was almost inexplicably long, despite the fact that the adoption of steamers ran into serious obstacles in most countries. But beginning with the 1890's, Swedish shipping progressed rapidly; sailing vessels were displaced by steamships and motor ships, and the size of the shipping companies increased considerably. Since the beginning of the century there has been transoceanic shipping under the Swedish flag.

THE MERCHANTS

One of the few branches of the economy which tended to recede in the course of the nineteenth century was wholesale trade. The decline of the large merchant houses was one of the phenomena most indicative of the transition from the basically old-fashioned economy of the early nineteenth century to the modern system which replaced it. Until approximately the middle of the century the large merchants held on to their dominating position in the economy. Since the end of the eighteenth century, Tottie & Arfvedson in Stockholm had exercised a considerable influence on the economy in general. For one thing, they handled far and away the largest share of the vital iron exports from Stockholm. Next in importance was the house of Michaelson & Benedicks, also in Stockholm, one of the relatively few large Jewish firms in Sweden. It acquired a certain repute because of its participation in the sale by Charles XIV (Marshall Bernadotte) of some Swedish men-of-war to the insurgent Latin American colonies.

Göteborg experienced a short but feverish boom throughout the duration of the Continental System. It became a European center for the transfer of colonial wares and manufactures from Great Britain to the Continent in violation of the Napoleonic blockade. When the Continental System came to an end, the inevitable result was a deep and prolonged setback that lasted well into the 1820's. Yet, in general, the role of wholesale trade in Göteborg was even more prominent than in Stockholm, but the trading houses were more numerous and none of them occupied a position of undisputed leadership.

A good illustration of the position of the merchants at that time is the fact that an enterprise of such magnitude as the rebuilding of the Trollhätte Canal in 1838–1844 was entirely financed by the house of Schön & Co. in Stockholm. It is inconceivable that any merchant today would be capable of a similar operation. It is also illuminating to find that the banks, when they appeared, were likely to seek assistance from the major trading houses in situations where the reverse would occur nowadays. The development in Sweden differed from that of other countries only in that the Swedish trading houses, in spite of their positions at home, were far inferior to the leading houses in the principal trading countries abroad. Possibly it was more difficult in Sweden than elsewhere to maintain mercantile traditions and to keep the trading houses alive from generation to generation. Furthermore, the fact that Sweden's main port faced east rather than west or south, thus establishing a certain remoteness from the mainstream of European commerce, was presumably not without significance.

The reasons for the profound transformation during the second half of the century are fairly evident. The curtailment of the risks of trade — brought about in part by the arrival of the telegraph and telephone with their facilities for immediate communication with almost any spot on the globe — also scaled down the profit margins. Moreover, the merchants could now hand over the task of transportation to independent and well-organized carriers, while previously they or their factors had staked lives and fortunes on the delivery of goods "across sand and sea," as the saying ran. Similarly, the banking function which had formed a large part of the merchants' business was taken over by separate, equally well-organized banks. Finally, the wholesale distribution of manufactured goods was in some measure taken over by the producers themselves. In the late 1860's, the second head of the Sandviken steel mills, Henrik Göransson, began to travel abroad himself in quest of foreign outlets for his products.[49] He is supposed to have been the first Swedish ironmaster to break with the tradition that all iron exports were handled by trading companies. Göransson's initiative is also held to have been one of the chief causes of his company's enormous upswing, and by and by most Swedish export industries created their own export organizations, many of them establishing special sales offices abroad.

Thus the functions of the trading houses either disappeared or were taken over by others. This was partly the effect of a process of integration of the economy by which producers and consumers were brought into closer contact, by-passing the intermediate level. Even more important was the displacement of the individual as an economic agent by large organized units.

## Capital Supply and the Credit System

As industrial production tended to be more capital-intensive, provision of capital came to be regarded as one of the central problems of entrepreneurship. In a branch like the iron industry even in premodern times the question of how to find a merchant willing to extend credit (under the *Verlag* system) had been extremely bothersome to ironmasters and manufacturers. It is difficult to say how generally the merchant-creditor was displaced during the first half of the century, but eventually the modern capital market emerged, with the creation of independent and solvent banks and with the introduction of bond and stock issues in order to raise long-term capital from the public.

As in other countries, this development was hampered by the inadequacies of joint-stock company legislation. For a long time it was

Old type electric furnace. Water color by Ragnhild Nordsten. *Stora Kopparbergs Bergslags, A.-B.*

The sawmill at Skutskär in the 1860's. Drawing by Robert Haglund.

village tailor at work in a farm house. His assistant is pressing clothes;
the farmer's wife is seated at the loom. Aquatint by J. F. Martin.

On the frozen Dalälven the lumber logs await the spring floating season.

Scene outside an emigration agency, 1888.

Emigrants on their way to the United States, 1892.

far from clear whether companies of limited liability could be founded without specific permission in each case. After the first experiences with joint-stock companies in other countries, the institution had fallen into some disrepute and was not accepted in Sweden until a very late date. Legally, its position was settled by the Joint-Stock Company Act of 1895. Since then, however, the corporate type of organization has become unusually popular in Sweden; in fact, it is used by a great many small firms which in other countries would probably have chosen a less elaborate form of organization.

Where did the industrial capital come from? There seems to be little doubt that the financing of the industrial expansion in countries like Sweden followed the same pattern as that of the much earlier Industrial Revolution in England. Profits, sometimes swelled by semi-monopolistic positions, were the principal source of capital. Recent studies of Swedish development demonstrate how the early captains of industry maintained a modest living standard in order to provide the capital required to expand their enterprises.

In what measure foreign capital contributed to the financing is less clear. Obviously, capital imported for railroad construction and for the establishment of mortgage banks contributed indirectly to the financing of private industry by releasing domestic capital for other uses; the question is to what extent foreign capital was used directly by industrial concerns. It is quite difficult to point to any such private capital imports, which means that they probably did not play any major part. That the big Swedish merchant houses contributed to the financing of the industrial expansion, however, is quite evident, and there were also other domestic sources. But by and large, there was no such thing as a capital market; hence the distribution of capital among various industries as well as individual firms was more fitful and haphazard than was really necessary. Around the middle of the century, the influence of the banks began to make itself felt, particularly in the timber industry, the most rapidly expanding of them all. That the industrialists were not governed by any marked "liquidity preference" is certain; they usually invested the last penny at their disposal and consequently were often in trouble.

Whether directly or indirectly, the influx of foreign capital was one of the main prerequisites for the expansion of the Swedish economy throughout practically the whole period ending with the outbreak of the First World War. Swedish bonds held abroad, which were obviously only a part of the total foreign indebtedness, were estimated at 75 million *kronor* in 1858, at 240 million in 1870, and at close to one billion in the year 1908.[50]

Although Great Britain was always a major outlet for Swedish exports, British influence on the Swedish economy was smaller than might have been expected. To be sure, English engineers were frequently hired by Swedish companies, and many ideas were transmitted in other ways. As already mentioned, Samuel Owen, builder of the first Swedish steamship, was an Englishman; A. E. von Rosen was subject to English influence and imported a few English railroad engineers; some private railroads were financed by English capital; several futile attempts to exploit the ore deposits in the north were made by Anglo-Swedish companies. Those were some of the most outstanding instances of British influence. But in view of the fact that Britain for centuries had been Sweden's principal customer and was the leading industrial country, a good deal more might have been expected. Language difficulties probably played their part.

Since the English capital market was of little importance, at least directly, it was Hamburg that became Sweden's principal foreign creditor, after Amsterdam fell from its position as the foremost European trade center. It retained that position until French lending assumed major proportions. In the half-century between 1860 and 1910, France was undoubtedly the main market for the Swedish government's bond issues, although they were also floated on a great many different exchanges and often were made redeemable in different currencies.

The fact that foreign borrowing was undertaken mainly by the government tended to prevent foreign financial interests from wielding any considerable influence upon the Swedish economy. The government was far more capable of dealing with foreign financiers on an independent basis than individual businessmen would have been. On the other hand, the financial experience and skill represented in *Riksgäldskontoret* (The Bureau of the National Debt), the government agency entrusted with the management of the debt, was far inferior to that of private business circles. Consequently, foreign lending undoubtedly took place on terms that were not as favorable as they might have been. At a later date the government's foreign borrowing was entrusted to Swedish banks, which was undeniably an improvement in that regard.

But insofar as foreign capital was used directly in Swedish industry, this too was accompanied by a remarkable degree of independence of foreign financial groups. The explanation was largely that such financing generally took the form of borrowing; only in exceptional cases was stock sold to foreigners. The latter did occur, especially in certain mining companies and railroads, but on a very trifling scale. It is of course possible that this situation was not entirely advantageous; it may have deprived the country of foreign entrepreneurial talent, thereby retarding its economic development.

The banks were eventually to become the principal source of working capital, though not until quite late. The banking system in Sweden had a long history which was essentially that of the *Riksbank*. But the *Riksbank's* contribution to commercial credit was highly limited. Its rate structure was fixed by the parliament and could not be altered between sessions; the volume of credit was limited by fixed ceilings. Thus, there was no such thing as a free credit market. Repeated attempts were made to affiliate commercial credit institutions of various sorts to the *Riksbank;* in the beginning of the nineteenth century there were the so-called *diskonter,* and later the *filialbanker.* The former collapsed in the crisis succeeding the Napoleonic war, and the latter never showed much vitality. Before the reorganization of the *Riksbank* (1897), private credit was infinitely more important.

In 1831, however, a tentative organization of the credit market took shape with the emergence of a system of private banks, the first of which was *Skånska Privatbanken* (later *Skånes Enskilda Bank,* then finally absorbed by *Skandinaviska Banken*).[51] All those private banks were based on note issue, which enabled them to extend a volume of working credit far beyond the capacity of the *Riksbank.* On the other hand, their interest in note issue generally went along with a neglect of the deposit side, and for a long time those banks were probably less instrumental in the procurement of capital than the merchant houses and other private lenders.

A more extensive banking system was created with the appearance of the joint-stock company banks (*aktiebanker* or *kreditaktiebolag*), basing their operations on their own capital and the public's deposits rather than on note issue. The first of those banks, *Skandinaviska Kreditaktiebolaget* (now *Skandinaviska Banken*) was founded in 1863. As the name suggests, it was originally intended as an all-Scandinavian institution, a plan supported by C. F. Tietgen, the leading Danish financier and industrialist of the time. This project collapsed, however, and the bank became an exclusively Swedish enterprise, at first even limited to Göteborg.

Though in due time the joint-stock company banks were to displace the note-issuing banks, it so happened that a private bank of the earlier type assumed the leadership in the development of modern banking in Sweden. This was *Stockholms Enskilda Bank,* founded in 1856 by A. C. Wallenberg, which at an early stage played a leading part in financing the timber industry. Almost immediately, it proved able to pull through the crisis of 1857 without any trouble. The crisis of 1878–79 caused greater strains; they were withstood but their aftermath continued to plague the bank for many years. When the government's foreign borrowing was put in the hands of the private banks, *Stockholms Enskilda Bank* became the government's principal agent, although for a long time it competed in this function with *Stockholms Handelsbank* (now *Svenska Handelsbanken*) which had been founded in 1871 and soon after came under the management of the German-born Louis Fraenckel.

But the completion of a modern banking system in Sweden also required a reorganization of the *Riksbank* as well as the establishment of a clear distinction between the functions of the central bank and the commercial banks. During the last decades of the nineteenth century there was a considerable improvement in the management of the *Riksbank* under J. W. Arnberg, perhaps the most competent man ever to guide its affairs; his work was crowned by the act of 1897, giving the *Riksbank* exclusive rights of note issue. The private issue banks were thus forced into borrowing from the public. The *Riksbank* also adopted the English policy of flexible discount rates and developed into a real central bank, while the commercial banks grew to unexpected power.

At the conclusion of this period the two major power groups of the Swedish economy were the industrial leaders and the large banks.

They wielded the strongest influence in most branches of the economy, and nothing new was likely to succeed without their support.

## RETAIL TRADE AND CONSUMER'S COÖPERATIVES

At least one important branch of the economy, however, rested in other hands. Retail trade developed along lines very different from those followed by wholesale trade. While the latter declined, retail trade tended to grow in importance, primarily because of the rising living standard which enlarged the freedom of choice in consumption and included an increasing number of luxuries. Almost inevitably, this enhanced the importance of selling, since customers needed more persuasion than was required when dealing in necessaries. Yet while the retailing function was becoming more vital, manufacturers showed no inclination to venture into retail trade as they had into wholesale trade. Retail trade remained independent and was not absorbed by any other branch of the economy. On the other hand, the retailers did not wield much influence; the individual firms were small, generally weak, and incapable of attracting entrepreneurial talent. Those conditions were changed somewhat by the introduction of department stores, but the chief innovation in Swedish retailing had entirely different roots.

It was engineered by what we now call the coöperative movement, which was based on the principle of economic activity in the *direct* interest of the consumers, through enterprises owned by the consumers themselves.[52] Within such an organization, the interests of producers and distributors could not clash with those of the consumers. Certainly, ordinary profit-oriented economic activity may be said to be guided by the consumers' interest under the stimulus of competition. But in a monopolistic situation, business interests might be radically at variance with the interests of the consumers.

Neither the theory nor the practice of consumers' coöperation originated in Sweden. The idea was taken over without any major change from the English consumers' coöperatives; but in scope and extent the Swedish coöperative movement eventually overtook and even outgrew its English preceptor. Although it caught hold around the turn of the century, as a semi-utopian organization, no spectacular upswing occurred until the First World War. Since then it has developed into an organization dominated by increasingly sober and pragmatic ideas. The consumers' coöperatives spread throughout the country; in communities of industrial workers the coöperative stores dominated the entire retail market. Thanks to their efficient and skillful management, moreover, the coöperatives succeeded in penetrating into other groups of buyers as well, so that their activities were simultaneously extended far beyond mere retail trade. The national organization, *Kooperativa Förbundet,* developed into the country's largest wholesaler, and the volume of its turnover made for considerable economies of scale.

The next step was to enter into production. The primary motive was a desire to manufacture consumers' staples like flour and shoes, in coöperative factories, but a secondary motive, of greater significance to the economy as a whole, was the desire to break the power of various industrial monopolies. Such intentions were the natural consequence of the ideology of the movement. In fact, the coöperative movement was the only power which managed to cope with the monopolies successfully. *Kooperativa Förbundet* bought or built its own factories in industries where monopolistic abuses were especially prevalent. Nonetheless, the coöperative movement never attained any position in Swedish industrial production comparable to that which it has come to occupy in distribution. The Swedish manufacturing industry is dominated by the production of industrial materials and semi-finished goods, and it is quite obvious that activities in those branches of industry lie too far afield from the basic interests of consumers' organizations. But within the limits set by its nature, the coöperative movement became a prime factor in the Swedish economy and one radically different from the other main power groups.

## THE MONETARY SYSTEM

The unparalleled expansion of most European economies between 1815 and 1914 was certainly in part dependent on the fact that the monetary system in this period achieved an unprecedented degree of organization and stability.

As previously mentioned, Swedish currency at the beginning of the period was an irredeemable paper money of highly erratic value. A currency reform was generally held to be in order, but the decision was not taken until 1830. It took four more years before Sweden actually returned to a silver standard and generally stable exchange rates.[53] The silver currency remained in force until 1873, when it was replaced by the gold standard.[54] Foreign economic relations were not particularly affected by the change from silver to gold; moreover, the transition was far more painless than in many other countries, since Sweden was able to complete the switch just before the sudden drop in the price of silver and could therefore dispose of its silver supply without losses. The transition was all the easier because in Sweden, unlike most other countries at that time, the circulation of metallic currency was insignificant and bank notes were the normal medium of exchange. Yet it is quite remarkable that this system of redeemable paper money could be maintained for so long, particularly in view of the fact that the rules covering the note issue were not designed to inspire too much confidence, and that the variety of note-issuing private banks caused a certain confusion in note circulation. During crises, a few runs occurred on individual banks, but the banks generally managed to get the situation under control. The ties with foreign credit markets were usually strong, which undoubtedly contributed to monetary stability. There were no major disturbances in international financial relations; Sweden became a member of an international system which under the leadership of Britain attained a higher degree of stability than had ever been seen before.

The adoption of the gold standard coincided with the creation of a Scandinavian currency union, at first comprising only Sweden and Denmark, but in 1875 extended to include Norway.[55] On the whole, the union functioned successfully until 1914, though its scope was limited, since bank notes, the standard form of currency, were not made common tender. Occasional negotiations were sufficient, however, to prevent any divergencies in the rates of the three countries' paper money.

Naturally, such peaceful monetary conditions must have been of the utmost significance for the growth of Swedish credit institutions and the economy at large. Paradoxically, one might perhaps even say that the situation was too peaceful; the public tended to lose the caution by which former generations had protected themselves against the frequent monetary crises. When the First World War brought down the monetary structure, the confusion was enormous, severely upsetting all contractual relations as well as any deliberate planning of economic activities.

Throughout the stable period Swedish price developments were intimately bound to the international price level. In the long run, the price trend was rising as in many other countries. Nevertheless, the years from approximately 1830 to the middle of the century were characterized by price stagnation, and there was a trough of low prices beginning in the early 1870's that lasted for some twenty years. In these and other ways, Sweden was affected by the international trade cycle although the impact of the crises was not especially disturbing. Those of 1815, 1857, and 1878–79 have already been mentioned briefly in various contexts; graver than those — or at any rate than the last two — was the shallow but prolonged depression of the 1880's. In the 1850's and the 1870's, on the other hand, there were pronounced booms; both of them were related to speculation in the timber industry, and the 1870 boom was also helped by the excessive growth of the railroads. None of those developments was peculiar to Sweden; Swedish fluctuations were usually comparatively faint reflections of the general European cycles.

## POPULATION

Few developments during the century preceding the First World War were more dramatic than the population growth. It was a development which completely revolutionized the conditions of human life. As late as 1816–40, the average life expectancy of a newly born Swedish infant was hardly more than 41.5 years; in 1941–45 it was 68.3 years, a rise of 27 years.[56] Apparently, then, human life has been prolonged by almost two-thirds. Obviously, this fabulous change created certain problems.

Thus, in spite of the industrial expansion after 1850, industry was far from capable of absorbing the enormously increasing population. Before the 1870's there was a slight decline in birth rates, from 3.3 to 3.0 per cent, but the fall in death rates — from 2.3 to 1.8 per cent — was sharper. Hence, the net rate of increase was not only high but rising, until in the 1870's it reached the very high level of 1.2 per cent a year.[57]

[ As in the eighteenth century, the agricultural sector had to support the growing population. Occupational data are most inadequate before 1870 and conclusions on their basis can be drawn only gingerly, but there appears to be no reason to assume that the agricultural population suffered any relative decline before 1870. For that year the first reliable data are available; as previously mentioned, they indicate that 72.4 per cent of the population was supported in agriculture. Therefore the pressure of population upon agriculture was high. The 1820's stand out especially as a decade of unparalleled growth.[58] The high birth rate which prevailed in those years was presumably a reflection of a comparably high birth rate in the 1790's, just a generation earlier; and it was also in the twenties that the secular downward trend in mortality rates set in. Most probably it was this factor which in the following decades kept the population increase at a level lower indeed than in the twenties but still a good deal higher than in the eighteenth century.

Since most of the population increase appeared in rural areas, the threat of pauperization in agriculture became serious. The ranks of the agricultural proletariat, the landless farm workers, were swelled. The cottagers, the least unprosperous of this landless army, declined in numbers while the crofters increased; on the large estates a new type of landless laborer appeared, the *statare,* who received his wages in kind. The Swedish economy proved unable to absorb the surfeit. The solution was emigration to the United States.

Emigration occurred on a minor scale in connection with the bad harvest failures in the late 1860's, but not until 1880 did it become a more or less permanent phenomenon.[59] It remained on a very high level for about a decade, then revived briefly at the beginning of the twentieth century. The reasons for the exodus were plain, and the grieved astonishment it aroused in patriotic circles was hardly justified. At the root of the matter lay simply the great discrepancy between living standards in the Old and the New World. The drastic retort to the indignation about the defection of "Swedish flesh and blood" was, "What do you prefer, Swedish flesh and blood in America or Swedish skin and bones in Sweden?" It took some time, of course, before the population became aware of this difference in levels of consumption and was able to overcome the natural inertia. But letters from America and the information spread by the shipping lines did their work; and once the emigration had started, it was not un-usual for many who had remained to feel closer ties to their friends and relatives in the United States than to their neighbors in Sweden. [The emigration changed the population picture not only in the areas where the exodus was concentrated but in the whole country.] The official emigration figures are somewhat too low, but the situation is illustrated by a comparison of gross rates of growth (excess of birth over death rates) and net rates of growth (corrected for emigration) in the period of the heaviest outflow.[60]

|                       | *1881–85* | *1886–90* | *1891–95* |
|-----------------------|-----------|-----------|-----------|
| Gross rates of growth | 1.18%     | 1.24%     | 1.08%     |
| Net rates of growth   | .51       | .43       | .56       |

Less than one-half of the natural increase in population — which happened to be remarkably large — remained in the country.

Next to the decline in the rate of growth, the most important economic aspect of the emigration was the fact that it was the agricultural population which left the country. Certainly the first move was often to the city, but when conditions there were no more satisfactory than in the countryside emigration was the next step. Moreover, it was primarily the landless agricultural classes who chose to leave, and thus in the short run their departure saved the country from agrarian pauperism. In the long run a somewhat different view may be taken. Had the emigration not occurred when it did, it is highly questionable whether it would ever have reached such proportions. Later on, rapid industrialization and the declining birth rates, even in the absence of emigration, probably would have eliminated a good deal of the margin between the Swedish and the American standards of living. The landless agrarian masses would have been absorbed by the growth of industry. The land flight in Sweden had primarily signified the absorption, first by the United States and later by the Swedish cities, of the *increase* in the agricultural population. But the agricultural population began to show a slight decline as early as the 1880's. Over the fifty years between 1880 and 1930 this amounted to roughly 22 per cent. When, at the time of the First World War, emigration came to an end, the decline in agricultural population did not cease but continued unabated.

## AGRICULTURE

The appearance of American grain on the European markets in the late 1870's imparted a heavy blow to the agricultural population. In the discussion of this momentous change it is easy to overlook its prime significance, to wit, provision of cheaper grain for Europe. The underlying cause of the sudden competition was the expansion of transportation facilities. In the United States, the railroads connected the wheat-growing Midwest with the Atlantic coast, and the development of trans-Atlantic shipping brought about a tremendous drop in freight rates. Naturally the cheap fares for ocean passage also stimulated emigration. Basically, of course, the revolution in transport in turn depended on the progress in iron- and steel-making.

Yet although the appearance of trans-Atlantic wheat in the last analysis conferred a benefit upon European consumers, it nevertheless created a completely unexpected and very serious crisis in European farming. The response to this situation varied from country to country. In England practically no action of any sort was taken, and consequently agricultural production declined steeply. Danish agriculture changed from grain production to animal farming, which radically improved its position, and found a secure market in England, at least as long as trans-oceanic competition in animal produce was prevented by the lack of shipping equipped with refrigerating plants. But in most European countries agriculture was supported by protection as far as possible. Agrarian protectionism had not previously found many advocates; even List, the champion of modern protectionism, had opposed it and recommended only industrial tariffs. However, following the example of Austria and Germany, country after country resorted to agricultural protection. In Sweden, agrarian tariffs were imposed in 1888, though only after an exceptionally vehement political struggle. They have remained in force ever since.

A comparison with the Danish case suggests that the abandonment of free trade undoubtedly served to maintain a larger cereal production than would otherwise have survived. Yet the farmers as a group probably lost rather than gained. Actually, a great number of Swedish farmers bought their grain; moreover, four years later, agricultural tariffs were supplemented by industrial tariffs. Nevertheless, the tendency to switch from cereal production to animal farming was too strong to be checked by the relatively moderate tariffs. Protection did not prevent a structural change in Swedish agriculture similar to but less marked than that which took place in Denmark.

The agricultural crisis did not lead to a permanent deterioration in the standard of living of the agricultural population, although this might have occurred in the absence of emigration. In the years around 1880, money wages of farm laborers took a plunge, absolutely as well as in comparison with industrial wages, and for a few years there was also a sharp drop in their real wages. On the other hand, the situation improved considerably long before the turn of the century — possibly because of the preceding emigration.

⌈ That the Swedish farmers were so severely affected by the low prices prevailing throughout the 1880's and the early 1890's was essentially the result of heavy indebtedness. The farmers' money income was reduced while the burden of their mortgages remained fixed. This increase in the real burden of mortgages was quite independent of what happened to the terms of trade between agriculture and industry. The farmer still would have suffered even if agricultural prices had not fallen more than industrial prices. If it had not been for the mortgages, there would never have been any direct pressure to leave the farms; the worst that could have happened would have been a reduction of real income for those farmers who sold their grain, with a corresponding improvement for those who bought. Hence, the difficulties of the farmers could have been alleviated by reducing amortization payments or by scaling down mortgage values. But such measures were entirely alien to the mood of the time and would, moreover, have caused other serious repercussions. ⌉

Trans-Atlantic competition in grains by no means put a stop to the growth of Swedish agricultural production. Between 1866–70 and 1936–40 the output of cereal crops more than doubled;[61] per capita of total population, the increase was less, amounting to only 39 per cent. Earlier in the nineteenth century and especially around the middle of the century, agricultural production even tended to grow faster than the population, thus creating a considerable export surplus, which in the case of oats persisted throughout the free trade period.[62]

Despite the tariff, however, by the outbreak of the First World War the imports of wheat had risen to roughly the same level as domestic production, and no less than 29 per cent of total grain consumption was met by imports.[63] This was the main cause of the acute grain shortage during that war. After the war, the situation changed completely, partly owing to government support on an unprecedented scale and partly as the result of the application of agricultural research. Ever since the sixteenth century, rye had been the leading Swedish bread grain, but the scientific breeding of new mutations gave an enormous stimulus to other crops, particularly to wheat.[64] Consequently, Sweden attained virtual self-sufficiency with regard to bread grains just on the eve of the Second World War, although some imports of artificial fertilizers were still required.

The reform of agricultural techniques began long before the First World War. Use of artificial fertilizers was combined with scientific soil analysis. The practice of drainage was generally adopted. In the rotation, the fallow gave way to root crops; sugar beets and turnips widened the fodder basis of animal husbandry and at the same time impressed upon the farmers the benefits of deeper plowing and more careful weeding. Finally, production of milk and milk products changed enormously with the introduction of scientific dairy techniques.

Directly or indirectly, the government played a large part in this transformation by granting various subsidies and especially by employing a growing staff of agricultural research workers. In addition, there were the government-sponsored agricultural societies, normally one for each county, which maintained their own staffs of experts. To some extent, the contributions made by research workers tended to be primarily technological and to neglect economic considerations, although some arrangements were also made to teach accounting techniques and agricultural economics.

## NATIONAL INCOME AND STANDARD OF LIVING

The development of national income and the changes in levels of consumption in Sweden have been made the subject of a series of studies at the University of Stockholm which, however, cover only the period after 1860. National income in real terms apparently increased some 4.4 times between 1861 and 1914, while the corresponding per capita increase was some 3.1 times.[65] The per capita income of industrial workers increased approximately 2.7 times in the same period;[66] it might be estimated that it increased about four times between the middle of the nineteenth century and the Second World War. Though the data for farm labor are less reliable, the income of farm laborers seems to have increased some 2.3 times between 1861 and 1914.[67] It is indeed striking that not even the industrial workers' real income kept pace with the average income of the population as a whole. True, the greater part of savings were probably created in other social groups, but one must still assume that between 1861 and 1914 the workers' level of consumption lagged behind that of the rest of the population. That farm laborers did not do as well as industrial workers is less surprising, since agriculture was a relatively stagnant branch of the economy. On the other hand, it is evident that the agricultural population too had a considerable share in the general improvement of living standards which almost certainly exceeded that of any other similar period except the sixteenth century.

Incomes of industrial laborers tended to grow far more rapidly in the interwar period than ever before; the 1920's were marked by an especially rapid growth in hourly wages.[68] Perhaps it is not unduly emotional to say that Swedish workers had at last come into full possession of their rights as Swedish citizens.

## ECONOMIC THOUGHT

Something must be said about the economic literature produced in this period. Quantitatively, it was far below that of the eighteenth century, and the general change in economic climate affected both the tone and the character of economic writings in the nineteenth century. In the earlier period there had been almost universal agreement on basic economic philosophy, apart from the brief anti-mercantilist rebellion in the 1750's and 1760's. Larger issues were usually not introduced into the discussion; rather it was the specific, practical questions which had roused the contentious spirits and produced the vehement pamphleteering contests. In the nineteenth century, the opposite was true. The economics of the *ancien régime* lingered for some time, but eventually retreated before the advance of liberal economic philosophy which then, in turn, was attacked by new forces. Thus, the very foundations of political economy were at issue and in our survey we can pass lightly over the more ephemeral arguments on special problems.

We have already mentioned in the previous chapter that Swedish economics remained under mercantilist influence for a very long time. In part this must undoubtedly be explained by a reorientation in Sweden's general intellectual affiliations with foreign countries. In the eighteenth century, France had been a principal source of inspiration; in the beginning of the nineteenth century, English economic literature arrived in garbled translations, but soon Swedish intellectual life fell under the sway of Germany. In Germany, mercantilist views held their ground far longer than in most other Western countries, and this put a heavy stamp on Swedish economics.

In 1747, Berch had published the first Swedish textbook in political economy. The second, which did not appear until 1829, was written by Lars Gabriel Rabenius. Rabenius taught economics at the University of Uppsala for no less than forty-five years and occupied the only chair in the subject for thirty years, so that he should have had ample opportunity to impress his views upon many generations of students. His textbook was certainly more modern than Berch's, but his basic views were essentially those of his predecessor. Though he was not entirely ignorant of the progress of liberal economic theory, he had no inclination to accept its conclusions; instead he continued to teach a somewhat modernized version of mercantilism.

The same was true of other Swedish social scientists in the early nineteenth century. Hans Järta, for example, who was possibly the country's foremost political thinker in those days, complained bitterly of "mechanistic and atomistic" conceptions of the state which overlooked its organic nature. In consequence, he took a harsh view of individualistic liberal economics, although he remained a stern critic of a good deal of the antiquated economic legislation inherited from past centuries. Another Uppsala man, Erik Gustaf Geijer, historian and poet and certainly Järta's intellectual superior, took a similar stand. Some of Geijer's most explicit attacks upon economic liberalism were made after his conversion to political liberalism. He expressed himself emphatically concerning the corrosive effects on the community of a pursuit of wealth in which men reduced their neighbors to mere tools. Toward the end of his life, however, Geijer developed an increasing respect for English economic thought which he seems to have studied in some detail.

Whereas Järta and Geijer did not devote themselves to specific economic problems, the University of Lund produced another dilettante economist, still a mercantilist, who applied himself far more assiduously to concrete issues. He was Carl Adolf Agardh, scientist, bishop, and politician. The ties between natural science and economics — an old Swedish tradition — were still strong, and Agardh began his studies of economics when already a professor of botany. His views are reflected in a whole array of publications but most clearly in his last work, *Statistical Essay on the Political Economy of Sweden* (*Försök till en statsekonomisk statistik öfver Sverige*), the first volume of which appeared in 1852. It is a highly independent study of Swedish society at large, with ambitious attempts at historical analysis. Agardh insisted that the basic subject matter of economics is not the wealth of the nation but its power to preserve its independence. Yet he did not attempt to demonstrate how this principle would affect economic analysis, as he had tried to do twenty years earlier, in a far less interesting little pamphlet. His *chef d'oeuvre* nevertheless remains a remarkable performance which strongly fortified the traditional economic position.

The conservative outlook shared by all those writers and many more had a variety of roots, the strongest perhaps in mercantilism, but others in German *Naturphilosophie* and early nineteenth-century German philosophy in general. Agardh is probably the most outstanding exponent of this influence. But there was also a steady flow of publications of more or less liberal tendencies. These were not original Swedish publications but translations, more often than not translations from imitative German sources, greatly inferior to the English originals upon which they drew. We have already mentioned the case of Adam Smith; a provisionally appointed law professor at Uppsala by the name of Holmbergsson had by the turn of the century translated Sartorius' bowdlerized version of *The Wealth of Nations*. Apparently the original version was supposed to be beyond the grasp and interest of the students. For a long time, German and some Danish followers of Adam Smith were translated into Swedish.

Around the middle of the century, however, a sudden turn toward liberalism occurred. But as a source of inspiration Germany had now given way to France; with very few exceptions it was the French variant of economic liberalism that was adopted in Sweden. It was still principally a question of translation. Long before, in the first decades of the century, a few popular works by J. B. Say had been published in Swedish, and had even occasionally influenced parliamentary debate. Now the time had come for the translation of Bastiat, the famed popularizer of liberalism, who was perhaps more overrated in Sweden than anywhere else. Bastiat, for instance, provided a good deal of the reasoning in Gripenstedt's political speeches; and apart from him a great many other French writers were introduced, such as Garnier, Rossi, Courcelle-Seneuil, Chevalier, Coquelin, and Ambroise Clement. At the same time Swedish writers of the same cloth made their appearance. Suffice it to mention two — Hans Forssell, the brilliant essayist, historian, and statesman, and J. W. Arnberg, who was to become the driving force at the *Riksbank*. In 1877, the foundation of the Economic Society (*Nationalekonomiska föreningen*) created a forum for the liberal elite, consisting primarily of higher civil servants and businessmen.

In the early 1880's the first opposition to liberal economics was voiced, a reflection of German *Kathedersozialismus* and, to some extent, of the new German protectionism. A number of Swedish works of this nature were published, and quite a few studies of actual economic conditions were inspired by the tariff issue. Nevertheless, few original contributions were made, for as a rule German protectionist ideology was accepted without much modification.

Beside the debate of principles, there were of course many discussions of economic problems of a more limited scope. As in the eighteenth century, monetary questions provoked the liveliest controversy, especially during the years prior to 1834, since the monetary system remained relatively chaotic until that time. The writings on money sometimes reveal a greater familiarity with English economic discussion than the ideological literature does. But it would be hardly worth while to present a catalogue of the many writers in this category.

One of the major participants in the controversy was the Rev. F. B. von Schwerin, a leading exponent of economic conservatism in Sweden in his day and a permanent parliamentary figure in the decades after the *coup* of 1809. Another contributor was C. A. Agardh, who for many years remained preoccupied with the monetary issue. Among the writers of more or less liberal tendencies appearing around the middle of the century was C. D. Skogman, the influential State Secretary, President of the Board of Trade and author of the first history of the *Riksbank*. Considerably later, liberal views found a prominent advocate in G. K. Hamilton, a professor at the University of Lund.

But until the very last decades of the nineteenth century, Swedish economic literature was essentially devoid of originality, even when it went beyond the mere reproduction of German or French books. Two closely related traits remained characteristic. First, English economic thought was neither directly nor indirectly communicated to Swedish readers. Hans Forssell is a case in point; while generally oriented toward Germany and England, nevertheless in economic matters he was principally influenced by French ideas. He seems to have remained entirely ignorant of English economic theory, although its superiority over the French was quite evident to any reasonably serious student of the field. Secondly, there were hardly any Swedish attempts to attack the basic problems of economic theory. The same lack of interest in rigorous theory also characterized the selection of translations.

However, a change was in the offing, and during the last few decades of the century a series of theoretical writings of high quality appeared. For the first time economic theory in the strict sense of the word received serious attention in Sweden. In the course of the following years and especially after the First World War, Swedish economists have been able to make a not unimportant contribution to international economic thought. The foundation for this development was laid by David Davidson (1854–1942) and Knut Wicksell (1851–1926), both of whom had published their major works before the turn of the century. Somewhat later, Gustav Cassel (1866–1945) was added to this group. Yet the three men in no sense constituted a common school.

Davidson always remained remarkably free from influence of any school. Of an extremely critical and analytical bent, he never produced any comprehensive "principles," but he contributed approximately two-hundred papers to *Ekonomisk Tidskrift*, the Swedish economic journal which he founded in 1899 and continued to edit until 1939. His own contributions as well as the very existence of the journal greatly furthered the interest in a variety of economic fields, primarily perhaps in monetary matters but also in pure economic theory. Time and again, he sought and found his way back to Ricardo and developed into a great authority on the Old Master. Davidson was a *Zu-Ende-Denker,* pursuing the implications of whatever premises were chosen to a length matched by few economists, in Sweden or elsewhere. The contrast between this approach and the looseness of most early economic thought in Sweden serves to emphasize the extent of the change that had occurred.

Although Wicksell and Davidson generally tended to agree on the theory as well as the practice of political economy, Wicksell was an entirely different type of scholar. His interest was in the synthesis of economic theory, and he very definitely belonged to the Austrian marginal utility school. Actually, he reached far beyond the Austrians, especially in his study of interest and prices, probably his most original contribution. He presented the principles of economic theory in his *Lectures* (1901, 1906) which summarized most of his work. This, I believe, was the first Swedish textbook to be published after that of L. G. Rabenius in 1829. From the turn of the century on, Wicksell participated vigorously in the public debate on theoretical and political economic issues; outside the professional brotherhood he attained early fame as one of the first and most enthusiastic proponents of neo-Malthusianism. The combination of a fiercely radical spirit with an extraordinary talent for ruthless and pointed formulation of unpopular opinions involved him in a series of predicaments. An intensely controversial figure, he might in many another country have been refused the chair for which his intellectual qualifications made him the obvious choice. As it turned out, he held the chair in economics at Lund for fifteen years. His influence on the subsequent generation of Swedish economists was probably unparalleled, and he received a great deal of international recognition, although mostly after his death when he came to be regarded as one of the forerunners of so-called dynamic economics.

Cassel, at an early stage in his economic career, was exposed to English liberal thought and remained, by and large, a liberal economist throughout his life. He presented the body of his economic theory in the *Theory of Social Economics,* completed immediately before the First World War but published in its first, German, edition in 1918. The book shows the strong, though unacknowledged, influence of Léon Walras. Brilliance of presentation and a comprehensive conception of the interdependence of economic phenomena probably constitute its main virtues. For some time it was highly influential in Germany where neglect of economic theory had been particularly serious. In the interwar period, especially, Cassel also attained unusual international recognition as an economic expert, notably on the reparations problem and on international currency questions. In addition, he was a regular contributor to the economic columns of the daily press, from the first years of the century to the end of his life.

Cassel's economic journalism contributed significantly to the economic education of Swedish public opinion. Previously, Swedish economic debate had undeniably been quite superficial in comparison with, for instance, the English, but things took a turn for the better, especially when, following Cassel's example, a great number of other economists began to contribute regularly to the daily press. This, on the other hand, tended to discourage non-economists from participating in the debate, thereby depriving it of a range of practical experience which could not be expected from pure theorists.

These fragmentary notes on the development of Swedish economics must suffice; a more complete treatment of that subject would lead us outside the boundaries of economic history. Insofar as it has concerned current problems of policy rather than economic theory, recent Swedish debate has been in line with Swedish traditions, and has actually shown numerous parallels with that of the eighteenth as well as that of the nineteenth century. This has hardly been the result of any lingering influence of older writings; indeed, any such influence has been conspicuous by its absence. In contrast to a great many other countries, Sweden has suffered from a notable lack of continuity in the field of economic thought and ideology. Because of the sporadic nature of her economic thinking, it has not infrequently happened that findings which were advanced long ago have fallen into oblivion only to be independently rediscovered.

# THE DISINTEGRATION OF
# NINETEENTH-CENTURY SOCIETY

by

Gunnar Heckscher

# THE DISINTEGRATION OF NINETEENTH
## CENTURY SOCIETY

THE NINETEENTH CENTURY had developed a well-functioning inter-
nationalist economy. Two world wars left little of that complex but
remarkably efficient economic mechanism. Total war — itself made
possible by the economic upsurge of the preceding century — enlisted
the entire populations of the warring nations and erected imposing
autarkic structures. Economic nationalism tended to displace the
sympathies for international exchange which had emerged during
the nineteenth century. The necessity for self-sufficiency in war entailed autarky in peace. The elimination of foreign competition stimulated the growth of monopoly. Above all, the powers of the state
were immensely strengthened both by technological change and the
trend to bigness and by the exigencies of war. And the rise of a well-
organized and loyal civil service gave the new Leviathan what the
old had wanted: an efficient tool to translate decree into reality.

Under the impact of technological change, a social structure
emerged which in some respects was more rigid than that of the
"atomistic" society. Incessant innovation, on the other hand, called
for further far-reaching changes of the whole social fabric. From this
conflict stemmed much of the insecurity of twentieth-century society.

In some measure, the new economic system was the product of
tendencies inherent in nineteenth-century conditions. To this extent,
no definite date can be set for its emergence. The outbreak of the
First World War in 1914 marks the most convenient dividing point.
Yet it cannot without qualification be considered the beginning of
a new era. At the end of the war and the depression which followed
in its wake, there arose an almost unanimous desire to return to
pre-war conditions and to rebuild along the old lines what had been
destroyed. But the image of the past proved elusive. The new gold
standard rested on more precarious foundations than the old; important obstructions to foreign trade permanently survived the war;

unemployment was higher than before 1914; and restrictions on international migration and capital movements served to maintain and emphasize differences in economic conditions.

Nevertheless, the 1920's saw the last attempt to restore the liberal economic system which had met with such remarkable success in the previous century. But the Great Depression which set in at the end of the decade delivered the death blow to the old system. It is not quite clear why this depression but not the previous one, following the First World War, had such an effect. It was probably quite important that the United States — which had come to be considered the outstanding example of successful capitalism, and which, unlike most European countries, had pulled through the postwar crisis relatively painlessly — this time was affected at least as strongly as Europe; thus the strongest testimony in favor of a laissez-faire economy was shattered. Possibly the first crisis was regarded as a natural consequence of the war, while the second seemed to reveal fundamental flaws in the structure of the postwar economy. Unemployment had already been high throughout the twenties and was enormously increased in the depression. To the Keynes of the *General Theory* — a book which perhaps influenced public opinion more than any other treatise of economics since Adam Smith — unemployment was the overriding concern. Thus the liberal creed was widely shaken in theory and virtually abandoned in practice.

Sweden remained neutral in both World Wars; but with respect to the development which has been outlined here the differences between her and the belligerent nations are remarkably small. As to the "New Economics," it might perhaps even be said to have made its appearance in Sweden earlier than in the Anglo-Saxon world.

## THE FIRST WORLD WAR

Sweden, like all other countries except possibly Germany, was unprepared for a war such as the First World War turned out to be. Agricultural and industrial protection, the former since 1888, the latter at least since 1892, might have been expected to make the country somewhat more self-sufficient than before. To some extent it probably was, though little thought had been given to that aspect. Nothing had been done specifically with a view of providing for the exigencies of a blockade. No stocks had been laid up; no emergency

legislation had been prepared, let alone passed; no economic programs had been drawn up.

By far the most serious shortage created by the allied blockade
was that in foodstuffs. In the last few years before the war, something like one quarter of all food cereals consumed was imported;
certain feeds like corn, oil cake, and bran came exclusively from
overseas, and so did fertilizers. The total nutritional deficiency
produced by the blockade, according to the report by a Royal Com-
mission on War Preparedness, was 22.5 per cent of total food consumption (in terms of calories) during the last years before the
war.

The Swedish Government had adopted a policy of strict neutrality
as circumscribed by traditional international law. This led to dis-
agreements with the Allies, especially with Britain, which in turn
resulted in restrictions upon Swedish imports and Swedish trade in
general, in principle designed to prevent supplies from reaching
the Germans. The considerable difference between the treatment
of Sweden and that of Denmark is a measure of the cost incurred
in championing international law. Still it should be added that
the consistency of Sweden's policy wrung reluctant recognition
from the British which stood her in good stead after the war. It is
hard to say whether the food shortage inflicted lasting harm. The
heavy influenza epidemic in the fall of 1918 has been ascribed to it,
but against that interpretation speaks the incidence of the disease
which was virtually the same in the countryside as in the towns,
although the food shortage was far less acute in the country.

The food situation was hardly improved by the trade with Germany, for the proximity of Germany and the German control of
the Baltic enforced exports which Sweden could ill afford. Especially,
exports of animal produce and cattle rose to many times their pre-
war volume.

The blockade remained in force until an agreement was reached
with the Allies that took effect only just before the armistice. Poor
harvests — partly caused by lack of fertilizers — further aggravated
the food situation. In addition, a perverse food policy had the effect
of reducing the nutritive value of the food resources that were available. Prices of vegetables and cereals were kept down, whereas meat
and dairy prices could not — so it was alleged — be controlled

equally well. In relation to pre-war levels, prices of bread, flour, and grits had risen two-and-a-half times; Those of dairy products, eggs, and margarine, four times; and those of meat and pork, five times. Consequently, an increasing acreage was shifted to animal production, which is, of course, far less efficient in terms of calories per man and acre. In 1917, the worst year of the war, output of cereals and vegetables was only 44.5 per cent of the average annual output during the last five-year period before the war. Because it illustrates the considerable increase in food consumption during the previous century, it may be recalled that in 1810, the severest year of the Napoleonic wars, the curtailment of food supplies in England by a mere 12–16 per cent was felt as a very heavy strain indeed.

In Sweden, the war itself caused no fundamental change in economic ideology. War economy was indeed characterized by universal state intervention, but this was generally regarded as a necessary evil. As soon as possible after the end of the war, wartime regulations were swept away. It is important to note that the rescinding measures were not opposed by the increasingly powerful labor groups; while socialist in name, they actually tended to support liberal policies.

### THE INTERWAR PERIOD

In the fall of 1920, the crisis, which in the course of the year had spread throughout the world, reached Sweden and developed into an unusually deep depression. But not even that experience resulted in a repudiation of traditional economic principles. Rather, it was regarded as a lingering consequence of the war economy, a painful but unavoidable adjustment to peacetime conditions. Of all Western countries, the United States and Sweden seem to have most consistently adhered to this opinion. The return to pre-war conditions was pursued vigorously in spite of the considerable strains it engendered.

During the war, Swedish currency had been appreciated over and above its gold value. But during the first postwar years, Swedish prices rose and an overvaluation of the crown developed. The return to the gold standard at the old level after the war added a further deflationary strain to the postwar depression, a complication not present in countries which, like the United States, had maintained the gold standard throughout the war. On the other hand, the solution of the problem was simplified by the strong demand for Swedish exports, above all for pulp. In addition, different political pressure groups for varying reasons advocated policies which tended to accelerate the adjustment. Above all, it was important that the unemployment, which by Swedish standards was exceptionally large, was met by measures designed to bring the unemployed back to employment in private enterprise rather than public works; and that all attempts to exclude foreign competition by means of increased tariff barriers were rebuffed. The unemployment policy was the result of an alliance between all non-Socialist groups, the free trade policy was supported by a coalition of Socialists and Liberals. Owing to this harsh but effective cure, Sweden was able, as the first among all European countries, to return to the gold standard. The pre-war par value was already reëstablished in practice at the end of 1922 and legally early in 1924.

Throughout the 1920's, developments in Sweden largely paralleled those in the United States. While the rest of Europe struggled with considerable hardships, Sweden experienced a real boom, although the abrupt conversion to peacetime conditions also resulted in persistently higher unemployment than before the war. For labor as a whole, however, this was more than offset by rising real wages.

The Great Depression reached Sweden relatively late, in the second half of 1930. In agriculture, however, troubles had already been felt for a few years, and that was the first area in which, as early as 1930, a major departure from *laissez faire* was made. In 1931, Great Britain abandoned the gold standard, and Sweden followed suit immediately. The unemployment policy of the 1920's, which had once been called "the Swedish system," was abolished in 1933 and replaced by the principle that the unemployed should be offered work at normal wage rates instead of at rates below those of the market. Foreign trade was restricted, first by the new agricultural policies and later by other measures, largely occasioned by similar developments elsewhere. So-called economic planning was accorded functions unprecedented in Swedish experience. To some extent, economic policy aimed not merely at the assistance of those who were suffering from the crisis but at the depression itself, primarily by the inflation of general purchasing power.

The effectiveness of that policy is still a controversial question. Presumably, it was not very considerable. The improvement in economic climate, which began even before 1933, seems to be explicable by changes in political and economic conditions outside Sweden and, on the whole, Swedish economic development was paralleled in countries with very different economic policies. But there are many who firmly adhere to a different view and assert that Sweden was saved by contra-cyclical policy.

The framework for economic policy that had been created during the depression was essentially maintained throughout the thirties, even after the depression gave way to a minor boom. International rearmament created a vigorous demand for such Swedish export products as iron ore, steel, pulp, and machinery. At the same time, the working classes managed, partly by strengthening the trade unions, partly by use of political power, to acquire an increasing share in the national product, which stimulated consumers' goods industries. But the new policies were applied with great gentleness and caused a minimum of social struggle. Trade unions, employers' associations, producers' and consumers' coöperatives — all these participated increasingly in their formulation and execution.

## THE SECOND WORLD WAR

During the Second World War, and especially after the invasion of Norway and Denmark in April 1940, Sweden was cut off from the outside world to an extent unknown in the previous war. However, in spite of prolonged and virtually complete isolation, the Swedish people suffered no deprivations similar to those of the First World War. Although the food situation at times looked serious, there was nothing like the hunger years of 1917–18. It can hardly be denied that this was at least in part due to the pre-war policies with their autarkic tendencies. The artificial stimulation of agricultural production had left the country with a considerable stockpiled surplus by the time the war broke out; the level of output was so high that not even a succession of bad crops and a shortage of fertilizers managed to depress it below domestic requirements. Modest supplies were even available for export to neighboring countries. The experiences of the First World War made it possible to introduce rationing and other regulations at an early stage and thus to husband the available resources from the outset. Finally, but perhaps most importantly, the public was aware of the necessity for wartime regulations and willing to abide by them, and economic interest groups were already organized and accustomed to mature coöperation with the government and each other. Indeed, this factor probably contributed more than any other to the maintenance of stability and relative prosperity.

In view of all this, it is natural that at the end of the war there was no such desire for abrupt changes in policy as after the First World War. The war economy as such had by no means compromised the principle of "economic planning" — on the contrary it could be argued that planning was precisely what had made all the difference between the Second and the First World War. In Sweden as elsewhere, there was also a widespread anticipation of postwar depression, and economic policies were deliberately framed with this in mind.

## The Population Problem

For all the importance of external and political factors in determining Swedish economic development since 1914, there were fundamental changes which were by no means caused by political events. Some were even actively resisted by political action, and of these far and away the most important one was the stagnation in population growth. The fall in birth rates in Sweden was actually greater than anywhere else, though Norway and Britain were not far behind.

For the pre 1914 period, Gustaf Sundbärg, a prominent Swedish statistician, estimated that fertility within marriage had remained about constant in Sweden until the late 1880's; thereafter a decline set in and the previous level was never again attained. But what happened before the First World War was nothing compared to what was to follow. In the first five-year period of the century, the crude birth rate was 26.12 (per thousand), which was the lowest figure so far. In 1931–35, it reached the minimum of 14.10, hardly more than half the figure of thirty years before. Such a change had no earlier counterpart. Later, the birth rate recovered somewhat, and in 1941–45 it was 18.70. The improvement was attributable to several factors — a relative increase of fertile age groups, earlier marriages, and possibly the policy of financial inducement and exhortation which was initiated in the thirties. Since 1945, however, a new and rapid decline has set in. Interestingly enough, the birth rate has recently been considerably higher in urban than in rural areas, mainly because of the desertion of the countryside by the young.

Mortality rates have continued to fall and have so far kept ahead of the birth rate so that total population has never quite ceased to increase. But the fluctuations in birth rate have, of course, affected the age composition. To begin with, the fall in the rate raised the proportion of productive age groups in relation to pre-productive and post-productive age brackets. This in turn raised the productivity per capita of total population, but also created a certain employment problem. Later, falling mortality and a rising birth rate combined to increase the relative size of the non-productive age groups, contributing to an increase in demand and a scarcity of manpower.

AGRICULTURE

The retardation in the growth of population was a primary cause of the crisis in agriculture, but the rise in the standard of living and the increase in agricultural productivity also were contributing factors. Rising living standards eventually result in a stationary per capita demand for foodstuffs — indeed, the demand for basic foodstuffs declines. In the case of Swedish bread consumption this process began even before 1939. As the growth of the population was outstripped by the increase in agricultural productivity, an agricultural surplus became inevitable. Substitution of domestic for imported foodstuffs was only possible to a limited degree; Sweden rapidly became self-sufficient in grains, and of animal produce, especially butter, there was a traditional export surplus. An increase in agricultural exports was impossible in the 1930's since the agricultural crisis was nearly universal and had caused most countries to erect high barriers against agricultural imports. Immediately after the Second World War, there was a strong demand for food imports in various European countries, but its duration was short and the problem of the agricultural surplus still remains to be solved.

The agricultural policies initiated in 1930 included elimination of foreign competition, guaranteed minimum prices and export subsidies. In the war and postwar years, the problem was to keep food prices below the world market level, but in 1950 the system resumed its previous character. Prices have been withdrawn almost entirely from the influence of the world market, and agriculture has been made wholly dependent on government policy. This, needless to say, goes far beyond anything in the way of agricultural protectionism before 1914.

The support of agriculture could not prevent a continual decline in the agricultural population which was not only relative but also absolute. Between 1890 and 1930, the agricultural population decreased by about 550,000, or 18.7 per cent; in 1945, it had declined by another 400,000 and was 31.9 per cent below the figure for 1890. In 1890, agriculture accounted for 62.1 per cent of the total population; in 1945 for 30.1 per cent. Since 1940, the agricultural population has been smaller than the industrial. The latter, in 1945, was 40.6 per cent of the total population.

## INDUSTRIAL DEVELOPMENT

In 1920, working hours were limited by law to forty-eight hours a week. To be sure, the forty-eight-hour week had already been adopted in a great many industries, but in others the law precipitated far-reaching changes. Wage rates were actually raised to compensate the workers, and during the rest of the 1920's real wages continued to rise, partly owing to falling prices. The ratio of wages to prices of industrial products actually increased by no less than 41 per cent from 1913 to 1924; and from 1913 to 1929 the rise was 71 per cent. Failing to achieve tariff protection, Swedish industry was forced into rapid modernization. In the course of the rationalization movement, there was a general increase in mechanization, and especially in the use of electric power. The consequent advance in productivity resulted in considerable increases in total industrial output. In 1921, at the bottom of the postwar depression, it was estimated at 75 per cent of the 1913 level. In 1924, in spite of the forty-eight-hour week, it was higher than before the war, and in 1929–30, immediately before the depression, it was 50 per cent higher than in 1913. In 1938, it was 135 per cent higher than in 1913. After a slight decline after the beginning of the Second World War, the rise was resumed, and by the end of the 1940's, industrial output was almost 50 per cent higher than in 1939, or between three and four times as high as in 1913.

Since the increase was partly the result of increased production per man-hour, employment in industry naturally did not grow at the same rate. But an increasing segment of the population found its way into industry, and between 1890 and 1920 the share of industrial to total population rose from 21.7 to 35.0 per cent. By 1945, it had increased to 40.6 per cent which implied a much lower rate of growth. Relatively speaking, the expansion of the industrial population had thus almost come to an end after the First World War. The same process was simultaneously observed in most countries with much longer industrial tradition. In this sense, Sweden had overtaken countries where the Industrial Revolution had occurred at least fifty years earlier.

## COMMERCE AND TRANSPORTATION

After 1914, the relative importance of distribution and transportation increased considerably. Statistics do not fully reveal the extent of that change because a good deal of the increase in commercial activities proceeded within industry itself and appears therefore as industrial expansion. To some extent, this is reflected in the growing importance of administrative industrial personnel. The ratio of administrative to manual labor increased from 6.3 per cent in 1913 to 14.4 per cent in 1939, and to 29.7 per cent in 1945.

As to the part of the total population employed in commerce and transportation outside industry, it grew from 5.2 per cent in 1870 to 18.2 per cent in 1930 and 20.5 per cent in 1945. Trucking and motoring has of course increasingly taken the place of shipping by rail or boat. The small vehicle and the need for gasoline and service stations proved more labor-absorbing than the traditional facilities. In addition, motoring has undoubtedly affected the economy as a whole by providing a new and much more flexible pattern of transportation. It must have been one of the causes of the growth of small enterprise since 1914, which was contrary to the tendencies of the preceding period. Another factor, incidentally, of similar effect was the growing use of electricity available to small and large plants on the same terms.

## FOREIGN TRADE AND CAPITAL MOVEMENTS

The neutrality, which had spared Sweden the ravages of the First World War and the disorganization of the postwar years, was a major reason for the change in Sweden's capital position. Sweden became a rich country compared to most others. During the war the major part of Swedish foreign-held bonds were repatriated. Wartime scarcities, however, made it undesirable to maintan an export surplus, and the capital exports of those years were certainly not the result of deliberate policy. After the war, on the other hand, a conscious effort was made in that direction.

Swedish capital exports did not exclusively or even primarily take the form of lending. For the most part, Swedish companies were formed abroad with Swedish capital and under Swedish management. To a large extent, this direct investment was the consequence of tariff barriers abroad. In this manner, a number of Swedish corporations took on a more or less international character. Obviously the transfer of production facilities abroad served to limit employment opportunities at home except insofar as the foreign markets otherwise would have been inaccessible to the output of the relevant industries which often seems to have been the case; in addition, capital exports *ceteris paribus* tend to raise the rate of interest and thereby to depress the wage level. Nevertheless, it is not unlikely that in Swedish conditions of the period capital exports on balance benefited the economy of the country.

A curious episode in this connection was the Kreuger story, which deserves some mention. The Swedish match industry, which always had enjoyed a dominant position in the world market, was made into a monopoly by Ivar Kreuger, who then extended his activities into the international field. By arranging loans for various governments he received in return concessions for match monopolies, whereupon he transferred match production from Sweden to the respective countries. On that basis, he erected an enormous corporate structure, partly extending to other types of industry as well. The internal relationships between the components of the Kreuger empire were skilfully hidden from the public eye; this, however, only raised their attractiveness as objects of international speculation. Some of the companies were wholly fictitious; others were created primarily to channel profits into countries with low corporate taxes. Swedish participation in this venture was actually rather limited, most of the capital being American, and Kreuger's suicide in the spring of 1932 and the consequent collapse of the entire edifice did not in the long run severely affect the Swedish economy. But coming, as it did, in the depths of the depression, the crash was nevertheless felt to be a serious setback.

The activities of Swedish companies abroad were largely interrupted by the Second World War, and after the war it was often difficult to resume previous relations. Swedish exports too found it difficult to regain their markets. The two major export commodities, pulp and steel, had not even in 1950 managed to recover their prewar levels. A prime reason lay in the disruption of Sweden's former relationship with her two principal trading partners, Britain and Germany. Before the war, a sizable Swedish export surplus to Britain was used to pay for an import surplus from the United States; trade with Germany tended on the whole to be in balance. The temporary disappearance of Germany from the world economy and the suspension of sterling convertibility created serious difficulties.

## STANDARD OF LIVING 1913 —

Of the increase in national income since the early twenties, labor has received a considerable share. From 1913 to 1929, annual real wages in industry increased by 52 per cent, in spite of the reduction in working hours. In terms of hourly earnings, real wages rose by no less than 88 per cent. The difference is due to the reduction in working hours, but presumably also to the increase in unemployment. Even considering that unemployment was higher, there is no doubt that, in the aggregrate, the workers received higher wages for less work. From 1939 to 1949, there was an increase of 25.5 per cent in annual real wages, and of 27 per cent in hourly earnings in real terms. There was no important reduction in working hours and practically no unemployment; thus annual and hourly earnings followed the same course.

This is not a bad record. The rise in real wages was probably faster than anywhere else in Europe. In addition, unemployment disappeared almost completely. It should also be remembered that the increase in social security and welfare services has principally benefited the workers, raising their total income over and above that represented by the wage level. Finally, owing to the decline in the size of the average family, income per capita rose faster than income per head of family. The increase in standards of living was especially noticeable in housing, which was as natural as desirable, since at the beginning of the century this had been a badly neglected field as compared with other countries.

No other group in the population seems to have enjoyed a similar rise in income. The real income of clerical and administrative personnel in private employment increased by only about 11 per cent from 1913 to 1939. Between 1939 and 1949, however, real income of women office workers increased by approximately 25 per cent, or, by as much as the annual income of industrial workers; but the increase for male white-collar workers was only about 16 per cent. Moreover, this group probably did not profit as much as manual workers from the increases in welfare benefits.

Farm labor had originally been excluded from the limitation of working hours. In 1936 and 1937, however, legislation on this point was extended to include agricultural as well as industrial workers. As in industry, the reduction coincided with an increase in real wages. Earlier, the growth of real income for farm labor had been modest, of the order of 11–13 per cent between 1913 and 1939. After 1939, on the other hand, the relative increase has been much higher than that for industrial labor, and for the period from 1939 to 1949 it might possibly be estimated at 50 per cent. This development is, of course, entirely dependent upon government measures to protect the profitability of farming.

## THE NEW ATMOSPHERE

Undoubtedly a great deal of institutional change in the world economy since 1914 has served to create a more static rather than a more flexible society. So far this has not simply meant a return to a pre-industrial type of stationary state. Indeed, advance in technology and industrial organization in many spheres has been unrelenting or even accelerated, and social change has been incessant. But it is impossible to overlook the existence of powerful forces which work in the opposite direction.

The outcome of the conflict between the impulse to change, which is inherent in technology, and the attempt to resist it by state control cannot be foreseen. Economic history hardly knows of any case in which it proved possible to stifle progress and improvement in individual welfare permanently. On the other hand, the revolutions in bureaucratic technique have increased the power of the state immensely. Governments adhering to other political principles and resorting to other instruments of power than those current in Sweden may be capable of acquiring virtually complete control over the economy; such nations may extend their power to increasing areas of the world. About those matters, it seems impossible to make any predictions before the resolution of the present great conflict.

So far we have been discussing tendencies appearing all over the world. But the Scandinavian countries, and especially Sweden, are frequently regarded as the exponents of tendencies different from those manifested elsewhere.

We have earlier emphasized the similarities between Swedish economic development and that of the United States in the interwar period. Both countries profited more than the major European nations from new economic possibilities. But passing from economic conditions in a narrow sense to general characteristics of society, we must note fundamental differences between the United States and Sweden. American society is characterized by a mobility — geographic, occupational, even social — which is almost entirely absent in Sweden. Swedish society is probably even more static in this respect than other European countries. Unlike many other European countries, Sweden has been spared the impact of war and revolution, and unlike the United States, her population has never been increased by any sizable immigration. Thus, despite her rapid industrialization, Sweden still displays some of the basic traits of pre-industrial society.

Certainly, the relationships between the various social groups have not remained unchanged. On the contrary, a distinctive feature of Swedish society in mid-century is economic leveling. But productivity increases have made it possible to attain a large measure of egalitarianism at a fairly high level of output without drastically infringing upon the incomes of the "upper classes."

One instrument of egalitarianism has been the development of welfare policies. More than in most countries, social security has become an accepted institution. Society is held responsible for providing a decent minimum standard to its members. At times, the principle might have been carried to the extreme, in neglect of man's responsibility for himself and for society, but on the whole this does not seem to have been a very serious danger.

In view of what has been said, it is not surprising that Swedish society is far from competitive in character. The individual is more inclined to better himself by improving the position of the group to which he belongs than by moving into another. By the same token, Swedish society is far from being torn by dissension and conflict. Compromise and coöperation rather than competition have been the vehicles of social change. Trade unions, employers' associations, and similar organizations have attained virtually complete control over such social groups as they represent, but they have been able to coöperate with one another and with the holders of political power rather than act as "pressure groups." This fact has, of course, further emphasized the static nature of the Swedish social structure. It is indeed difficult to envisage a situation in which an organized interest group — let alone an unorganized one — would be permitted to improve its position in Sweden without compensation to the others.

It is at the present time particularly difficult to predict Sweden's economic development even in the near future. Assuming that Sweden will survive as an independent nation, its economic future is largely dependent on circumstances outside its own control. In the past, a friendly fate provided us with unexpected advantages — the demand for lumber and pulp, and the processes for utilizing Swedish iron ore were some of them. Such advantages may of course be withdrawn, either by high-handed action on the part of other nations or by technological change. On the other hand, it seems possible to say without unwarranted pride that the Swedish people have shown a capacity for turning events to their advantage by perseverance and work, realism and hopefulness, and by a genius for compromise. There is reason to believe that those traits in Swedish character will survive even if unfortunate events should deprive the nation of many of the material gains reaped in the past and force it back upon those resources that moth and rust do not corrupt.

# APPENDIX A

*Chronology of Main Events in Swedish History*

| | |
|---|---|
| 800–1050 | Expeditions of the Vikings. |
| 1164 | Archbishopric in Uppsala. |
| 1279 | Introduction of secular *frälse*. |
| About 1350 | Codification of national laws for town and country. |
| 1389 | Margaret, Queen of Denmark and Norway, conquers Sweden. |
| 1397 | Eric of Pomerania, Margaret's nephew, elected King of Sweden, Norway, and Denmark. "The Scandinavian Union" is established at Kalmar and continues an intermittent existence for most of the fifteenth century. |
| 1435 | Meeting at Arboga, traditionally considered as first Swedish Parliament. |
| 1477 | The University of Uppsala founded. First in Scandinavia. |
| 1521 | Gustavus Vasa Lord Protector. |
| 1523 | Gustavus Vasa king (Gustavus I). |
| 1527 | Church reform and secularization of church property. |
| 1534–1536 | Revocation of Lübeck's privileges. |
| 1544 | Sweden made hereditary kingdom. |
| 1563–1570 | War against Denmark and Lübeck (Northern Seven Years War). |
| 1592 | John III dies. His son, Sigismund of Poland, becomes king of Sweden. |
| 1595 | Sweden's participation in the long Livonian War (1557–1582) formally concluded by the Peace of Teusima, by which Estonia, including the city of Narva, is acquired. |
| 1597 | Duke Charles, son of Gustavus I, rises against Sigismund who returns to Poland. |
| 1610 | Swedish intervention in the Russian civil war. Moscow captured. |
| 1611 | Danish attack. King Charles dies. His son, Gustavus Adolphus, becomes king (Gustavus II Adolphus). |
| 1613 | Peace with Denmark at Knäred, providing for the redemption of the fortress of Älvsborg. |
| 1617 | Peace with Russia in Stolbova. The whole territory in the inner part of the Finnish Gulf goes to Sweden. Consolidation of Parliament as consisting of four Estates (Nobility and Gentry, Clergy, Burgesses, Peasantry). |

| | |
|---|---|
| 1621 | Livonia with Riga captured. |
| 1626 | Creation of the House of Lords (representing nobility and the patented gentry). |
| 1630 | Gustavus Adolphus joins the Thirty Years' War. |
| 1632 | Gustavus Adolphus, killed in the battle of Lützen, is succeeded by his daughter Christina, a minor. |
| 1643–1645 | War with Denmark, ended by the Peace of Brömsebro. Gotland, Ösel, Jämtland, Härjedalen go to Sweden. Halland to remain under Swedish occupation for thirty years as a guarantee for Danish concessions regarding Sound toll exemptions. |
| 1648 | Peace of Westphalia. Parts of Pomerania, the city of Wismar and Bremen-Verden acquired by Sweden. |
| 1654 | Queen Christine, converted to Roman Catholicism, abdicates Charles X Gustavus becomes king. |
| 1655 | Reversion of one-fourth of all alienated and all "inalienable" lands. Attack upon Poland. |
| 1657 | War with Denmark. Charles Gustavus crosses Danish Sounds on ice and dictates peace in Roskilde. Skåne, Bornholm, Bohuslän and the province of Trondhjem go to Sweden. |
| 1658–1660 | New war with Denmark. Charles Gustavus dies in 1660, and in the peace Denmark reacquires Bornholm and the province of Trondhjem. Peace with Poland. Charles Gustavus succeeded by his minor son, Charles XI. |
| 1668 | University of Lund established. |
| 1675 | A Swedish army, participating in Louis XIV's war, is defeated at Fehrbellin in Brandenburg. |
| 1676 | Danish attack upon Skåne where peasants rise in revolt against Sweden. |
| 1679 | Peace with Denmark. |
| 1680 | Restoration of absolute monarchy. Far-reaching reversion of alienated lands. |
| 1686 | New church law, foreshadowing general collection of vital statistics. |
| 1697 | Charles XI dies. His son Charles XII becomes king. |
| 1700 | War with Russia, Denmark-Norway, and Poland-Saxony. Denmark forced to make peace. A Russian army defeated at the battle of Narva. |
| 1701 | Charles XII invades Poland. Poland forced into alliance with Sweden. |
| 1706 | Saxony forced to make peace. |
| 1707 | Charles XII invades Russia. |
| 1709 | The Swedish army surrenders in Russia after the battle of Poltava. Danish attack upon Skåne. |
| 1710 | The Danish army defeated in the battle of Hälsingborg. |
| 1712 | Hanover occupies Verden. |

| | |
|---|---|
| 1714 | Prussia enters into an alliance with Russia. |
| 1718 | Charles XII killed during invasion of Norway. His sister Ulrica Eleanor elected queen. |
| 1719 | New constitution limiting royal power, ending Carolingian absolutism. Peace with England-Hanover (loss of Bremen-Verden). |
| 1720 | Frederic of Hessen, husband of Ulrica Eleanor, elected king (Frederic I). Peace with Prussia. Loss of parts of Pomerania. Peace with Denmark. |
| 1721 | Peace with Russia. Loss of Transbaltic provinces and parts of southeastern Finland. |
| 1734 | Issuance of a new code replacing the old laws for the countryside and the towns. Party of *Hats* is formed in Parliament. |
| 1738 | The *Hats* acquire parliamentary majority. |
| 1741–1743 | War against Russia leading to loss of another part of southeastern Finland. |
| 1751 | Frederic I dies. Succession of Adolphus Frederic. |
| 1756 | An abortive royalist coup d'état. |
| 1757–1762 | War against Prussia. |
| 1765 | The *Caps* acquire majority in Parliament. |
| 1771 | Adolphus Frederic dies. His son Gustavus III becomes king. |
| 1772 | Coup d'état by the king. New constitution with enlarged royal powers. |
| 1788 | War against Russia. Denmark commences war against Sweden. |
| 1789 | Further extension of royal power. |
| 1790 | Peace with Russia recognizing the status quo in Värälä. |
| 1792 | Gustavus III murdered, is succeeded by his minor son Gustavus IV Adolphus. |
| 1800 | League of armed neutrality between Sweden, Russia, and Denmark. |
| 1805 | War against Napoleon. |
| 1807 | Loss of Danish navy to England. Denmark joins Napoleon. |
| 1808 | Russia invades Finland. |
| 1809 | The king deposed by revolt. His uncle, Charles XIII, accedes to the throne. New constitution to end Gustavian absolutism. Peace with Russia in Frederikshamn depriving Sweden of Finland and the Åland Islands. |
| 1810 | French Marshal Jean-Baptiste Bernadotte elected successor to the throne as Charles XIV John. |
| 1812 | Treaty of alliance with Russia. |
| 1814 | Attack upon Denmark. Peace at Kiel. Norway ceded to Sweden by Denmark. Norwegian revolt against Sweden quelled. Union between Norway and Sweden. |
| 1846 | Abolition of craft guilds. |

| | |
|---|---|
| 1853–1854 | State Railroad Act passed. |
| 1856 | First railroads. |
| 1859 | Oscar I dies. His son becomes king as Charles XV. |
| 1865 | Constitutional reform. Parliament divided into two chambers. |
| 1872 | Charles XV dies and is succeeded by his brother Oscar II. |
| 1889 | Social-Democratic Party formed. |
| 1898 | Trade Union Federation (L.O.) formed. |
| 1899 | Creation of the Consumers' Coöperative Association. |
| 1901 | New army organization based upon conscription. |
| 1902 | Employers' association formed. |
| 1905 | Union with Norway dissolved. |
| 1907 | Oscar II dies. His son Gustavus V accedes to the throne. |
| 1909 | Universal male suffrage introduced. |

# APPENDIX B

*Kings and Regents of Sweden from 1250 to date*

## The Folkunga Dynasty

Birger Jarl, Regent 1250–1266
Valdemar 1250–1275
Magnus Ladulås 1275–1290
Torgils Knutsson, Regent 1290–1298
Birger Magnusson 1290–1318
Magnus Ericson, Regent 1319–1332, King 1332–1365
Eric 1357–1359 and Håkan 1362–1371
Albrecht of Mecklenburg 1363–1389

## The Scandinavian Union

Margaret 1389–1412
Eric of Pomerania 1396–1439
Engelbrecht, Regent 1435–1436
Charles Knutsson, Regent 1436–1440
Christopher of Bavaria 1440–1448
Charles Knutsson, King 1448–1457
Christian I of Denmark 1457–1464
Charles Knutsson, King 1464–1470
Sten Sture the Elder, Regent 1501–1503
Svante Sture, Regent 1504–1520
Sten Sture the Younger, Regent 1512–1520
Christian II of Denmark 1520–1521

## The Vasa Dynasty

Gustavus Vasa, Regent 1521–1523
Gustavus Vasa (Gustavus I), King 1523–1560
Eric XIV 1560–1568
John III 1568–1592
Sigismund of Poland 1592–1599
Charles IX, Regent 1595–1604, King 1604–1611
Gustavus II Adolphus 1611–1632
Christine 1632–1654 (Regency under Chancellor Axel Oxenstierna 1632–1644)

*The Palatinate Dynasty*

Charles X Gustavus 1654–1660
Charles XI 1660–1697 (Regency 1660–1672)
Charles XII 1697–1718
Ulrica Eleanor 1718–1720
Frederic of *Hessen* (Frederic I) 1720–1751

*The Holstein-Gottorp Dynasty*

Adolphus Frederic 1751–1771
Gustavus III 1771–1792
Gustavus IV Adolphus 1792–1809 (Regency 1792–1796 under Duke
Charles, later Charles XIII)
Charles XIII 1809–1810

*The Bernadotte Dynasty*

Charles XIV John 1810–1844
Oscar I 1844–1859
Charles XV 1859–1872
Oscar II 1872–1907
Gustavus V 1907–1950
Gustavus VI Adolphus 1950–

# NOTES

*Abbreviations*

SEH                Eli F. Heckscher, *Sveriges ekonomiska historia från Gustav Vasa*

Konung Gustaf    *Konung Gustaf den förstes registratur*

SOS               *Sveriges officiella statistik*

SOU               *Statens offentliga utredningar*

*(There are no notes for Chapter 1.)*

## Chapter 2. The Middle Ages

1. The Provincial and National Codes were published in their original Old Swedish between 1827 and 1877 by C. J. Schlyter (and H. S. Collin) under the double title of *Corpus iuris Sueo-gotorum antiqui*, or *Samling af Sweriges Gamla Lagar*, 13 vols., including a general glossary. This publication of the texts is considered almost faultless. A translation of the Provincial Codes into modern Swedish, with commentaries, has been made by Å. Holmbäck and E. Wessén under the title *Svenska landskapslagar tolkade och förklarade för nutidens svenskar*, 5 vols. (Uppsala, 1933–1946). *Svenskt Diplomatarium* or *Diplomatarium Suecanum* was started in 1829 but remains unfinished although the work continues; it has of course had many different editors. There are different series, each with their supplements. The principal one has now reached 1355; then there is a gap, and the next series so far covers the period 1401–1420; a third series containing *acta cameralia* from Vatican archives has been completed until 1370.

2. *Stockholms stads tänkeböcker* have been published for the years 1474–1591 (Stockholm, 1917–1948), and the publication of those and

other records of the capital continues under the auspices of the City Archives. Corresponding material for other towns is being prepared for publication.

3. *Rikshufvudboken för 1573 jämte sammandrag af rikshufvudboken för 1582*, in *Historiska handlingar*, XII:I (Stockholm, 1883), 77, 79 f., 88.

4. B. Boëthius, "Dalfolkets herrarbete," *Rig*, 16:1 (1933).

5. *Konung Gustaf den förstes registratur*, 29 vols. (Stockholm, 1861–1916), XV, 400.

6. *Konung Gustaf*, XXVIII, 597.

7. *Ibid.*, XXV, 262.

8. Hans Forssell, *Anteckningar om Sveriges jordbruksnäring i sextonde seklet* (Stockholm, 1884), p. 110.

9. Å. Holmbäck and E. Wessén, *Svenska landskapslagar*, I, 159.

10. *Lärda tidningar*, 1755, p. 54.

11. Eli F. Heckscher, *Sveriges ekonomiska historia från Gustav Vasa*, I:1–2, II:1–2 (Stockholm, 1935–1949), I:1, Appendix IV. Hans Forssell, *Sveriges inre historia från Gustav den förste*, 2 vols. (Stockholm, 1869, 1875), Appendix I, Table C5. J. A. Almquist, *Den civila lokalförvaltningen i Sverige 1523–1630 med särskild hänsyn till den kamerala indelningen*, 4 vols. (Stockholm, 1917–1923), I, 84 ff.

12. See note 9.

13. *Konung Gustaf*, XVIII, 310.

14. Eli F. Heckscher, "Un grand chapitre de l'histoire du fer: le monopole suédois," *Annales d'histoire économique et sociale*, 4:135 ff. (1932).

15. W. Koppe, *Lübeck-Stockholmer Handelsgeschichte im 14. Jahrhundert* (Neumünster-Holstein, 1933), pp. 18 ff.

16. *SEH*, I:1, 149.

17. F. R. Tegengren *et al.*, *Sveriges ädlare malmer och bergverk*, in *Sveriges geologiska undersökning*, Series Ca 17 (Stockholm, 1924), Table 2.

18. *Ibid.*, Table 1.

19. *Konung Gustaf*, IV, 405; XXI, 118, 167; XXII, 105, 235; XXIII, 121, 201 f., 229, 131; XXIV, 241. *Privilegier, resolutioner och förordningar för Sveriges städer*, 2 vols. (Stockholm, 1927, 1933), I, Number 205 and *passim*.

20. G. Berg, "Boskapsskötsel och jordbruk i det gamla Stockholm," *Samfundet S:t Eriks Årsbok* (Stockholm, 1932), p. 189.

21. *SEH*, II:1, 112.

22. Henrik Schück, *Stockholm vid 1400-talets slut*, in *Kunglig Vitterhets Historie och Antikvitets Akademiens Handlingar*, XLVIII (Stockholm, 1940), 59.

23. See note 2.

24. A. Johansson, "Penningväsendet under Gustav Vasas regering," *Historisk tidskrift*, 1926, pp. 215 ff. Also, Eli F. Heckscher's survey article in the same volume, "Gustav Vasas myntpolitik," pp. 370–375.

*Chapter 3. The Maturity of the Medieval Economy (1520–1600)*

1. *SEH*, I:1, 228 ff.
2. *Konung Gustaf*, XV, 400.
3. Heckscher, "Un grand chapitre de l'histoire du fer," pp. 135 ff.; Tegengren *et al.*, Tables 1 and 2.
4. Documents in Kammararkivet, "Varuhus och handling." See also *Konung Gustaf, passim.*
5. *Konung Gustaf*, XV, 256.
6. *Samling af Sweriges gamla lagar*, ed. C. J. Schlyter, XI (Lund, 1865), 13.
7. A. A. von Stiernman, *Samling Utaf Kongl. Bref, Stadgar och Förordningar &c. Angående Sweriges Rikes Commerce, Politie och Oeconomi Uti Gemen*, 6 vols. (Stockholm, 1747–1775), I, 433 ff.
8. *SEH*, II:1, 248.
9. Johansson, "Penningväsendet under Gustav Vasas regering," and Heckscher, "Gustav Vasas myntpolitik" (above, n. 24, Chapter 2).
10. Ehd, "Några bidrag till belysning af den sista myntförsämringen under Johan III:s tid," *Historisk tidskrift*, 1910, pp. 287, 277.

*Chapter 4. Foreign Influences and Economic Change (1600–1720)*

1. Eli F. Heckscher, "Ett svenskt krigsskadestånd för 300 år sedan," *Ekonomisk tidskrift*, 1933, p. 3.
2. *Rikskanslern Axel Oxenstiernas skrifter och brevväxling* (Stockholm, 1888–ﾠ), Second Series, I, 734.
3. Assessment lists *(mantalslängder)* available in Kammararkivet.
4. G. Wittrock, *Karl XI:s förmyndares finanspolitik från blå boken till franska förbundet 1668–1672* (Uppsala, 1917), p. 287, n. 3.
5. The information on Swedish mining essentially derives from documents in Kammararkivet and in Bergskollegii arkiv.
6. G. Wittrock, *Svenska handelskompaniet och kopparhandeln under Gustav II Adolf* (Uppsala, 1919), pp. 16 f., 19 ff., 29 ff., and *passim.*
7. "Afledne Bergmästaren, sedermera Assessoren Erich Odelstiernas Relation till K.M.," a document in Kungliga Biblioteket, Rålambska samlingen, Folio Vol. 21, Bergskollegii arkiv. See especially pp. 160 ff.
8. Tegengren *et al., Sveriges ädlare malmer*, Table 2.
9. *SEH*, II:2, 443 ff.
10. *Ibid.*, I:2, 453.
11. *Ibid.*, 602.
12. *Ibid.*, 603.

13. *Jacob Bircherods Reise til Stockholm 1720*, ed. G. Christensen (København, 1924), p. 60 f.

14. *SEH*, II:2, 602.

15. Eli F. Heckscher, "The Bank of Sweden in Its Connection with the Bank of Amsterdam," in *History of the Principal Public Banks* (The Hague, 1934), p. 161 f.

16. Carl Sahlin, *Valsverk inom den svenska metallurgiska industrien intill början av 1870-talet* (Stockholm, 1934), pp. 98, 103 ff.

17. *SEH*, I:1, Appendix V, Table II.

18. *Ibid.*

19. *Ibid.*, I:2, 472.

20. H. Scrivenor, *A Comprehensive History of the Iron Trade* (London, 1841), pp. 325 ff.

21. *SEH*, I:2, 472.

22. E. Lipson, *The Economic History of England*, Vol. II: *The Age of Mercantilism* (London, 1931), pp. 155 ff., 189, and *passim*.

23. *Lettres, instructions et mémoires de Colbert* (Paris, 1861–1873), III, 6 f., 85, 182 f., 245. Also *SEH*, I:2, 470.

24. E. W. Dahlgren, *Järnvräkeri och järnstämpling* (Stockholm, 1930), pp. 378 ff.

25. Eli F. Heckscher, "Den gamla svenska brukslagstiftningens betydelse," *Ekonomi och historia* (Stockholm, 1922), pp. 153 ff.

26. *SEH*, I:2, 468 f.

27. S. Rinman, *Bergwerkslexicon*, 2 vols. (Stockholm, 1788–1789), pp. 1056 ff. *SEH*, I:2, 463 ff.

28. *Ibid.*, 468.

29. "Forge-tax ledgers" (*hammarskattelängder*) available in Bergskollegii arkiv, Riksarkivet.

30. Kammararkivet, "Depositioner i Riksarkivet 1893–94."

31. I. Lind, *Göteborgs handel och sjöfart* (Göteborg, 1923), p. 56.

32. *SEH*, I:2, 482.

33. "Bergskollegii relation 1697," in *Handlingar till kon. Carl XI:tes historia*, ed. S. Loenbom, 15 vols. (Stockholm, 1763–1774), XII, 180 f., 189; XII, 18, 22.

34. *SEH*, I:1, 24; I:2, 478, 534, 568 f., 581 f., 688 f.

35. H. Munktell, *Bergsmans- och bruksförlag intill 1748 års förlagsordning* (Uppsala, 1934).

36. For a full account see Carl Sahlin, *Svenskt stål före de stora götstålsprocessernas införande* (Stockholm, 1931).

37. C. Heijkenskjöld, "Svensk styckegjutning och lodstöpning av järn under perioden 1540–1840," *Artilleri-Tidskrift*, 1935, pp. 17 f.

38. *Christopher Polhems minnesskrift* (Stockholm, 1911), esp. pp. 30 ff.

39. *SEH*, I:1, Appendix V, Table II.

40. C. Fyhrvall, *Bidrag till svenska handelslagstiftningens historia*, Vol. I: *Tjärhandelskompanierna* (Stockholm, 1880), pp. 43, 54, 66.

41. W. Carlgren, *De norrländska skogsindustrierna intill 1800-talets slut* (Uppsala and Stockholm, 1926), p. 26.

42. E. W. Dahlgren, *Louis De Geer 1587–1652* (Uppsala, 1923), *passim.*

43. *Svenska riksrådets protokoll* (Stockholm, 1878–1929), VI, 64.

44. *Louis De Geers brev och affärshandlingar,* in *Historiska handlingar,* XXIX (Stockholm, 1934), *passim.*

45. P. Sondén, "Bröderna Momma-Reenstierna," *Historisk tidskrift,* 1911, pp. 143 ff.

46. For a detailed account, see J. A. Almquist, *Uddeholmsverken* (Stockholm, 1899).

47. *Christopher Polhems minnesskrift,* p. 3.

48. Heckscher, "Ett svenskt krigsskadestånd" (above, n. 1); and *SEH,* I:2, 360 ff.

49. E. Wendt, *Det svenska licentväsendet i Preussen 1627–1635* (Uppsala, 1933). See also Eli F. Heckscher, *Mercantilism,* 2 vols. (London, 1935), I, 67; and *SEH,* I:2, 371.

50. H. Almquist, *Göteborgs historia,* 2 vols. (Göteborg, 1929, 1935), I, 69, 81 ff.

51. See *Lettres, instructions et mémoires de Colbert.*

52. H. Almquist, *passim.*

53. *SEH,* I:2, 366.

54. *Sveriges ridderskaps och adels riksdags protokoll,* 2nd ed., 3 vols. (Stockholm, 1904–1906), III, 295.

55. Eli F. Heckscher, "Den ekonomiska innebörden av 1500- och 1600-talens svenska stadsgrundningar," *Historisk tidskrift,* 1923, p. 317.

56. *Ibid.,* 322.

57. *Ibid.,* 324 ff.

58. B. Steckzén, *Umeå stads historia 1588–1888* (Umeå, 1922), p. 54.

59. Nils Ahnlund, *Sundsvalls historia,* I (Sundsvall, 1921), 118.

60. *SEH,* I:2, 533.

61. *Handlingar rörande Skandinaviens historia,* 40 vols. (Stockholm, 1816–1860), XXXVII, 178 f.

62. *Svenska riksrådets protokoll,* VI, 406.

63. *SEH,* I:2, 533.

64. *Ibid.,* 386.

65. *Ibid.,* 390. See also notes 50 and 55.

66. Heckscher, "Den ekonomiska innebörden," p. 317.

67. Heckscher, *Mercantilism, passim.*

68. A. Johnson, *The Swedish Settlements on the Delaware,* 2 vols. (New York, 1911), pp. 164 ff., and *passim.*

69. *SEH,* I:2, 592, 601.

70. *Ibid.,* 179, 590 f., 597.

71. B. Fahlborg, *Ett blad ur den svenska handelsflottans historia 1660–1675* (Göteborg, 1933), pp. 28 f.

72. *SEH*, I:2, 562.
73. Stiernman, *Samling Utaf Kongl. Bref*, I, 714 ff., 685 ff.; II, 400 ff.
74. Ellen Fries, "Johan Classon Risingh," *Historisk tidskrift*, 1896, pp. 31 ff. See *SEH*, I:2, 692 ff.
75. *SEH*, I:2, 426.
76. P. Nordmann, *Finnarna i mellersta Sverige* (Helsingfors, 1888), pp. 1 ff., 40 ff., 156, and *passim*.
77. *SEH*, I:1, Appendix III, Table 6B.
78. *Ibid.*, I:2, 383.
79. *Ibid.*, 381.
80. *Ibid.*, 382.
81. *Statistisk årsbok för Sverige*, 1951, Table 40.
82. *SEH*, I:1, Appendix IV.
83. *Ibid.*, I:2, 317.
84. *Handlingar rörande Skandinaviens historia*, XXI, 172 ff.
85. Sam Clason, *Till reduktionens förhistoria* (Stockholm, 1895), Appendix IX.
86. *Svenska riksrådets protokoll*, XIV, 343.
87. *SEH*, I:2, 300 ff.
88. V. E. Svedelius, *Om reductionen af krono- och adeliga gods under k. Carl X Gustafs och k. Karl XI:s regering* (Uppsala, 1849–1851), *passim*.
89. *SEH*, I:1, Appendix IV, Tables 2 and 3; I:2, 339 ff.
90. F. F. Carlson, *Sveriges historia under konungarne af Pfalziska huset*, 8 vols. (Stockholm, 1855–1910), IV, 215, n. 1.
91. S. Hedar, *Enskilda arkiv under karolinska enväldet* (Stockholm, 1935), pp. 8 ff.
92. F. F. Carlson, *Sveriges historia*, V, 142, n. 1.
93. *Svenskt biografiskt lexikon*, 13 vols. (Stockholm, 1918–1950), V, 720. S. Hedar, *Enskilda arkiv*, pp. 158 ff.
94. E. Tegnér, *Svenska bilder från 1600-talet* (Stockholm, 1896), p. 298.
95. *Ibid.*, 287. Also *Svenska slott och herresäten*, 9 vols. (Stockholm, 1918–1923), *Skåne*, p. 371 and *passim*.
96. *Svenskt biografiskt lexikon*, X, 729.
97. *Sveriges ridderskaps och adels riksdags protokoll*, 17 vols. (Stockholm, 1855–1902), XV, 322 ff.
98. J. A. Almquist, *Frälsegodsen i Sverige under Storhetstiden*, I:2 (Stockholm, 1931), 771.
99. *SEH*, I:2, 290 ff.
100. *Ibid.*, 358.

Chapter 5. The Foundation of Modern Sweden (*1720–1815*)

1. *Statistisk årsbok,* 1952, Table 8.
2. *Ibid.,* Table 39.
3. *Ibid.,* Table 40.
4. A. Hjelt, "De första officiella relationerna om Svenska Tabellverket," *Fennia,* 16:73 (Helsingfors, 1899).
5. *Statistisk årsbok,* 1952, Table 40.
6. A. Hjelt, p. 34.
7. E. Arosenius, *Bidrag till svenska tabellverkets historia* (Stockholm, 1928), pp. 37 f., 51, Appendices 9 and 10.
8. *Statistisk årsbok för Stockholms stad,* 1905, Tables 10, 11, 16–18.
9. *SEH,* II:1, 87.
10. *Ibid.,* 116.
11. Carl von Linné, "Iter ad exteros," *Ungdomsresor,* II (Stockholm, 1929), 206.
12. *SEH,* II:1, 123.
13. *Ibid.,* 91.
14. *Ibid.*
15. *Ibid.,* II:2, Table 5.
16. *Ibid.,* II:1, 210 f.
17. *Ibid.,* 183 ff.
18. G. Utterström, "Potatisodlingen i Sverige under Frihetstiden," *Historisk tidskrift,* 1943, pp. 145–185.
19. *Ibid.,* 173 ff.
20. *SEH,* II:1, 205.
21. *Ibid.,* 212 ff.
22. *Ibid.,* 183 ff.
23. *Ibid.,* 190.
24. B. Hanssen, "Jacob Faggots memorial 1755," *Ekonomisk tidskrift,* 1946, pp. 275 ff.
25. *SEH,* II:1, 251 ff.
26. *Ibid.,* 257 f.
27. N. Holmberg, *Enskiftet i Malmöhus län* (Lund, 1939), Chapter 4.
28. C. C. Halling, *Minnen,* in *Samlingar utg. för de skånska landskapens historiska och arkeologiska förening,* VII (Lund, 1877), 29 f., 33.
29. *Svenska lantmäteriet,* Sällskapet för utgivande av lantmäteriets historia, 3 vols. (Stockholm, 1928), I, 83.
30. *SEH,* II:1, 137, 277 ff.
31. *Ibid.,* 263.
32. *Ibid.,* 262.
33. *Ibid.,* 264 f.

34. Nils Wohlin, *Den svenska jordstyckningspolitiken i de 18:de och 19:de århundradena* (Stockholm, 1922), p. 124.

35. *SEH*, II:1, 265.

36. Eli F. Heckscher, "Ett kapitel ur den svenska jordbesittningens historia. Skatteköpen under 1700-talet," *Ekonomisk tidskrift*, 1944, pp. 111 f.

37. *Ibid.*, 113.

38. *Ibid.*, 106, 115.

39. A. Montgomery, "Tjänstehjonsstadgan och äldre svensk arbetarpolitik," *Historisk tidskrift*, 1933, p. 245.

40. *SEH*, I:2, 552; II:1, 149.

41. *SEH*, II:1, 363.

42. Eli F. Heckscher, "Den svenska kopparhanteringen under 1700-talet," *Scandia*, 1940, pp. 26 f.

43. *SEH*, II:2, Appendix, Table 13.

44. *Bergshantering* (*SOS*), 1950, Table 4.

45. *SEH*, II:2, 398.

46. Eli F. Heckscher, "Betydelsen av vår historiska brukspolitik," *Ekonomi och historia* (Stockholm, 1922), pp. 155 ff.

47. *SEH*, II:2, Appendix, Table 12.

48. B. Boëthius and A. Kromnow, *Jernkontorets historia*, I (Stockholm, 1947), 192 ff.

49. "Bergskollegii berättelse om bergverkens tillstånd den 29 april 1773," in Bergskollegii arkiv.

50. "Acta privatorum," Vol. I, in Kommerskollegii arkiv.

51. *Blad för bergshanteringens vänner*, XV.

52. *SEH*, II:1, 421.

53. *Ibid.*, 450 ff.

54. *Ibid.*, separate vol. of diagrams, Chart XXV.

55. *Ibid.*, Charts XXIV and XXV.

56. *SEH*, II:1, 106.

57. G. H. Stråle, *Alingsås manufakturverk* (Stockholm, 1884), pp. 183 f.

58. *SEH*, II:2, 559 ff.

59. *Ibid.*, II:1, 526.

60. *Ibid.*, 534.

61. *Ibid.*

62. *Ibid.*, 523.

63. E. Söderlund, *Stockholms hantverkarklass 1720–1772* (Stockholm, 1943), p. 204.

64. *SEH*, II:1, 328 ff.

65. *Ibid.*, II:2, Table 29.

66. Eli F. Heckscher, "Produktplakatet," *Ekonomi och historia*, pp. 164 ff.

67. For a detailed account see Eli F. Heckscher, "Sveriges fram-

gångsrikaste handelsföretag. Ostindiska kompaniet," *Historieuppfattning, materialistisk och annan* (Stockholm, 1944).

68. Eli F. Heckscher, "Det svenska penningväsendets öden," *Historieuppfattning*, p. 281 ff.

69. L. Stavenow, "Ur Gustav III:s och statssekreterare Ruuths brevväxling," *Uppsala universitets årsskrift* (Uppsala, 1921–1928), II, 8.

70. *SEH*, II:2, 819.

71. A. Chydenius, *Tankar om husbondes och tienstehions naturliga rätt* (Stockholm, 1778), Paragraph 12, p. 360.

72. *Svar på den af Kgl. Wetenskaps academien förestälta frågan: Hwad kan wara orsaken, at sådan myckenhet swenskt folk årligen flyttar utur landet? och genom hwad författningar det kan bäst förekommas?* (Stockholm, 1765), Paragraph 18, p. 25; Paragraph 28, pp. 37 f.

73. Eli F. Heckscher, "Moderna inslag i svensk ekonomisk diskussion mot 1700-talets slut," *Ekonomisk tidskrift*, 1942, p. 125.

## Chapter 6. The Great Transformation (*1815–1914*)

1. A. Montgomery, *The Rise of Modern Industry in Sweden* (London, 1939), p. 119. A. Montgomery, *Industrialismens genombrott i Sverige* (Stockholm, 1947), pp. 170, 212. *Statistisk årsbok*, 1951, Table 117.

2. *Ibid.*, Table 367.

3. Dorothy Swaine Thomas, *Social and Economic Aspects of Swedish Population Movements* (New York, 1941), Table 7.

4. *Folkräkningen den 31 december 1910 (SOS)*, p. 17, Table C.

5. *Statistisk årsbok*, 1950, Table 40.

6. Thomas, *Social and Economic Aspects*, p. 20.

7. *Statistisk årsbok*, 1952, Table 9.

8. *Särskilda folkräkningen 1935–36 (SOS)*, VIII, 21–24.

9. *Bergshantering (SOS)*, 1950, Table 4.

10. Eli F. Heckscher, "Den gamla svenska brukslagstiftningens betydelse," in *En bergsbok. Några studier över svensk bergshantering tillägnade Carl Sahlin* (Stockholm, 1921), p. 185.

11. Montgomery, *Industrialismens genombrott*, p. 85.

12. Sven K. Stockman, *Den svenska järnhanteringens utveckling med särskild hänsyn till åren 1890–1913 (SOU 1922:52)*, p. 21.

13. Eli F. Heckscher, "Sandvikens historia," *Historieuppfattning*, pp. 167 ff.

14. *Statistisk årsbok*, 1926, Table 91.

15. Carl Sahlin, "Basiska Martinprocessens införande i Sverige," *Jernkontorets annaler*, 1940, p. 538.

16. Montgomery, *Modern Industry*, p. 170.

17. *Bergshantering*, 1950, p. 46, Table 4.

18. *Statistisk årsbok*, 1952, Table 106.

19. *Bidrag till Sveriges Officiela Statistik: Bergshandtering 1861. Commerce Collegii underdåniga berättelse för år 1861*, p. 12. Also *Bergshantering*, 1916, p. 21; 1936, p. 15; 1950, p. 17.

20. *Bergshantering*, 1950, p. 17.

21. *Ibid.*, 1913, p. 21; 1950, p. 16.

22. *Statistisk årsbok*, 1952, Table 106.

23. *Bergshantering*, 1950, Table 4.

24. *Ibid.*

25. *Ibid.*, p. 10.

26. See e.g. *Handel (SOS)*, 1937, Table 5:V; 1940, Table 5:V.

27. Montgomery, *Modern Industry*, p. 88.

28. Eli F. Heckscher and Ernst Söderlund, "Svensk industry i historiskt perspektiv," *Sveriges industri*, Sveriges Industriförbund (Stockholm, 1948), pp. 56 f.

29. See note 27.

30. Heckscher and Söderlund, p. 59. Also "Statistisk översikt över det svenska näringslivets utveckling åren 1870–1915 med särskild hänsyn till industri, handel och sjöfart," *Statistiska meddelanden*, Series A, III (1919).

31. "Statistisk översikt," Tables 198, 199.

32. *Sveriges industri*, p. 395.

33. Montgomery, *Modern Industry*, p. 161, Table XII.

34. *Statistisk årsbok, passim.*

35. *Bergsordningar*, Paragraphs 8, 14–16, 18, 19, 23, 24. See also *SEH*, II:2, p. XXXVII.

36. S. Hansson, *Den svenska fackföreningsrörelsen* (Stockholm, 1930), p. 39.

37. C. Hallendorf, *Svenska arbetsgifvareföreningen 1902–1907. Minnesskrift* (Stockholm, 1927), pp. 28 ff.

38. Montgomery, *Modern Industry*, p. 207.

39. A. Montgomery, *Svensk socialpolitik under 1800-talet*, 2nd ed. (Stockholm, 1951), p. 164.

40. Montgomery, *Modern Industry*, p. 112.

41. A. Montgomery, *Svensk traktatpolitik 1816–1914*, in *Tull- och traktatkommitténs utredningar och betänkanden*, VI (Stockholm, 1921), 196 f.

42. *SOU* 1924:37, p. 263.

43. Montgomery, *Industrialismens genombrott*, p. 205.

44. *Statistisk årsbok*, 1951, Table 142.

45. Montgomery, *Modern Industry*, p. 104.

46. Montgomery, *Industrialismens genombrott*, p. 206.

47. Montgomery, *Modern Industry*, p. 111.

48. *Statistisk årsbok*, 1951, Table 129.

49. Heckscher, "Sandvikens historia," *Historieuppfattning*, pp. 167 ff.

50. I. Flodström, *Sveriges nationalförmögenhet omkring 1908*, in

*Finansstatistiska utredningar utgivna genom finansdepartementet,* V (Stockholm, 1912), 219 ff.

51. Montgomery, *Modern Industry,* pp. 96 ff.

52. M. Bonow, "The Consumer Cooperative Movement in Sweden," *Annals of the American Academy of Political and Social Science,* May 1938.

53. Montgomery, *Modern Industry,* pp. 96 ff.

54. *Ibid.,* 135.

55. *Ibid.*

56. *Statistisk årsbok,* 1951, Table 59.

57. *Ibid.,* Table 40

58. *Ibid.*

59. *Montgomery,* Industrialismens genombrott, pp. 180 ff.

60. *Statistisk årsbok,* 1951, Table 40.

61. *Ibid.,* Table 78.

62. *Ibid.,* 1916, Table 71.

63. *Ibid.,* Tables 3, 71, 107.

64. *Ibid.,* 1950, Table 78.

65. The staff of the Institute for Social Sciences, University of Stockholm, *Wages, Cost of Living and National Income in Sweden 1860–1930* (London, 1933–1937), III:1, 234, 248.

66. *Ibid.,* II:1, 62.

67. *Ibid.,* II:2, 114 f.

68. *Ibid.,* II:1, 255.

# INDEX

Åkerman, Richard, 219
*Ägoblandning,* 25
Älvsborg: redemption of, 79, 85, 105
Agardh, Carl Adolf, 226, 262, 264
Age of Empire, 16, 79, 128
Age of Freedom, 130–131
Agriculture: medieval, 22–24; in towns, 50–51; 1600–1720, 115–117; 1720–1815, 150–155; 1815–1914, 213–214, 256–259; interwar period, 276–277. *See also* Enclosures, Land ownership
Alienation, 117–120
Alströmer, Jonas, 186, 196
Arnberg, J. W., 250
Assessment lists, 80–81
Autarky: of households, 18–19; regional, 74–75; national, 18–19, 75, 172

Baltic trade, 45–47
Banks: first bank, 91; rise of, 249–251. *See also* Riksbank, Credit
Bay of Bourgneuf, 48
Basic process, 219, 221–222
Bastiat, Frederic, 263
Becher, Johann Joachim, 203
Beer, 21, 69
Berch, Anders, 39, 201, 261
Bergslagen, 42, 98
Berlin, 145
Bessemer, Sir Henry, 218–219
Bessemer process, 219, 221–222
Birger Jarl, 51
Birka, 49, 51
Birth rate: stability of, 135; and harvest fluctuations, 137–139; decline in, 275–276
Bothnian trading restriction, 73, 144
Blast furnace: introduced, 43–44
Brahe, Nils, 123
Brahe, Per, 81, 118, 123

Brass, 92
*Brukspatroner:* see Ironmasters
Business cycles: transmitted to Sweden, 211, 254; the Great Depression (1930), 273. *See also* Economic fluctuations
*Bytvång,* 25, 27, 155
Byzantium, 48

Capital: exports, 278–280; imports, 210–211, 243, 247–249; sources of, 246–247. *See also* Credit, Banks
Caps, 138, 187, 197–198
Carleson, Carl, 202
Carleson, Edward, 180, 202
Cassel, Gustav, 264, 266
Charles IX, 61, 71–75, 109
Charles XI, 73–74, 81, 98; and reversion, 120–123, 128
Charles XII, 84, 91, 125
Charles XIV (Marshal Bernadotte), 245
Child, Josiah, 203
Christiernin, P. N., 204
Christine: alienations under, 119
Church: landholdings of, 30, 67
Chydenius, Anders, 170, 195, 204–206
Cities: *see* Towns
Coal production, 175
Cobden-Chevalier treaty, 238
Coinage: medieval, 33, 37, 55–59; 1520–1600, 75–77; 1600–1720, 88–91. *See also* Money
Colbert, 65, 95, 108
Coleridge, Samuel Taylor, 95
Colonization: external, 111; internal, 153–154
Communications: medieval, 37–38; railroad, 240–244; interwar, 278. *See also* Railroads, Winter roads, Shipping
Cooperatives, consumers', 251–252